AN AMERICAN EPIC

Famine in Forty-Five Nations

Organization Behind the Front

1914–1923

VOLUME II

HERBERT HOOVER

An American Epic

Famine in Forty-Five Nations

Organization Behind the Front

1914–1923

VOLUME II

HENRY REGNERY COMPANY

CHICAGO: 1960

LIBRARY OF CONGRESS CARD CATALOG NUMBER: 59:13696

MANUFACTURED IN THE UNITED STATES OF AMERICA

This volume
is dedicated by the author to
**THE HOOVER INSTITUTION ON
WAR, REVOLUTION, AND PEACE**
from whose archives much
of this material has derived

CONTENTS

SECTION I

Providing Food for the Allies and Neutrals
During the War

SECTION II

The American Voluntary Charitable Agencies

SECTION III

Organization Behind the Front to Meet the Famine In Forty-Five Nations

SECTION IV

The United States Government Agencies Behind the Famine Front

SECTION V

Special Joint Actions Behind the Front

INTRODUCTION

ORGANIZATION BEHIND THE FRONT

This is the second volume of *An American Epic.* The Introduction to Volume I of these memoirs states the basic purpose of the first volume and three volumes to follow. In brief, my statement was that the purpose of these volumes is to record the sacrifice of the American people in providing, throughout forty-five years, the margins of food, medicine, and clothing which saved the lives of 1,400,000,000 people who otherwise would have perished; that the American people provided this service without any consequential monetary repayment; and that, in fact, we are yet paying its cost through interest on the considerable portion of our national debt which arose from this action.

The return to our people has come through the demonstration to the world of the ideals and power of a free people. And we have satisfied our own conscience that we have not neglected our duty as our "brother's keeper."

* * *

The first volume of *An American Epic,* already published, records "The Relief of Belgium and Northern France" during five years of the First World War and its aftermath. That enterprise of compassion was directed by American volunteers and the voluntary staff of the Belgians. It was financed by private charity and subsidies from the British, French, and American governments.

This second volume of *An American Epic* has presented some

difficulties in arrangement. To attempt a chronological history of our complex activities, with its myriad of ramifications into every corner of the economic and political world, would utterly confuse the reader. For the sake of clarity, I have therefore divided this narrative into five sections, even though they overlap a few months in time.

Two apt expressions are used by military authorities to define two different types of organization; the two terms are: "organization behind the front" and "the front line." These expressions, which were incorporated into our daily work in describing aids to civilians, are used in these memoirs.

Section I of this volume records the provision of supplies to 170,000,000 people in the Allied and Neutral nations by the United States Government—from the American entry into the War in April, 1917, to the defeat of Germany, Austria, Hungary, Bulgaria, and Turkey, marked by the Armistice on November 11, 1918.

Section II records the support by the American charitable organizations up to the end of the war, as marked by the Armistice on November 11, 1918.[1]

Section III records the world situation in food at the Armistice; American food shipments prior to the Armistice; the negotiations with the Allies concerning the "behind the front" organization of food, medicine, clothing, and reconstruction to meet the famine in forty-five nations; and the withdrawal of the blockade of Europe.

Section IV records the organization of the United States governmental agencies behind the famine front.

Section V records some of the great co-ordinated activities of the United States with the Allies "behind the front."

* * *

[1] Because of the vital shift in the world scenes with the signing of the Armistice, it is necessary to separate in this text the descriptions of activities before and after that shift. I have therefore made a division between "before the Armistice" and "after the Armistice." The date of November 11, 1918, is not always applicable as the precise date of this division. Some agencies record their policies, accounts, and reports on a monthly basis, and their "before" and "after" can be marked as October 31. Some of them kept their records in calendar years. Thus the "before and after" date becomes December 31. Consequently, in this text, "before and after the Armistice" is anywhere from October 31 to December 31, 1918.

This volume of *An American Epic* cannot be convincingly presented for the shelves of history without much documentation and detail of administrative action and statistics.

To present to the reader the dimensions of these enterprises in compassion, as far as possible I give the quantities of supplies furnished. I also give the dollar value of supplies. These can be accurately stated in respect to United States Government activities. However, the accounts of American charitable agencies do not give summaries of quantities and I have been compelled to use dollar values alone for illustration of the measure of their activities. Either quantities or dollars are a poor index to the measure of service in aid to the suffering and the saving of lives.

The Introduction of Volume I outlines the immensity of documentation—more than 3,500,000 items, the examination of which was imperative in preparation of these volumes. The task would have been impossible but for the aid of many of my old colleagues and my staff, who reduced the number of those items pertinent to this volume to dimensions which I could personally examine.

In presentation of these documents, I have condensed them as much as possible, and the parts omitted are indicated. And for brevity, I have omitted diplomatic and other polite phrases. The full texts of these documents can be found in the Hoover Institution on War, Revolution, and Peace at Stanford University—or, when they were derived from other sources, references are given.

* * *

It is my duty to pay tribute to Arthur Kemp, Bernice Miller, Thomas Thalken, Loretta Camp, James Atkinson, and Diana Hirsh, who at different times over the years engaged in research for this volume. Theirs has been a devoted service.

SECTION I

PROVIDING FOOD FOR THE ALLIES AND NEUTRALS DURING THE WAR

INTRODUCTION

The provision of the necessary margins of food, medicine, and clothing for the 170,000,000 people in the Allied and Neutral nations in Europe during the period of American participation in the First World War has been the subject of some fragmental and partial publications. But the whole story of this great American undertaking has not yet been told.

It is a story of increased hours of labor on our farms—even of their operation by the wives and children of the men at the fighting front.

It is a story of patriotic self-denial in every cottage and every public eating place.

It is a story of the voluntary, efficient, and patriotic co-operation by the vast majority of the men who administered the processing and distribution of our food products.

And this record of service of the American people has other importance to history. The conduct of these activities illuminates the background of a great battle to maintain overseas transport against the destruction of the unlimited German submarine war. It also illuminates the background of military strategy. It demonstrates the powerful effect of food policies on military strategy and on speeding the surrender of the enemy. It gives many sidelights on leading personalities of the period.

Beyond this, here is the record of the revolutionary shift of American economic life imposed by war.

And there is value in preserving the methods by which problems were solved and the results of their application, for the organization and conduct of food supplies not only affected every phase of American and Allied life, but also that of the enemy.

It is a story which reaches even further.

That our slogan, "Food Will Win the War," was no mere billboard sign was amply confirmed by British Prime Minister Lloyd George:

> The food . . . [supply] decided the issue of this war. It was directly responsible for the downfall of Russia, finally was the element that led to the collapse of Austria and Germany. Indirectly it was responsible for bringing America into the War, since Germany's indiscriminate submarine warfare was her answer to our blockade.[1]

Lloyd George could have added even more. The Allies would have collapsed from deprivation of food by the German submarine war had it not been for the increased production and sacrifices of the American people.

He could have added further that but for the stimulation in American production, a score of nations in Europe would have been destroyed by the flames of anarchy or Communism.

The weight of this load of relief on the United States was certain to increase as the war went on because of the continued decline of production in the major Allied countries. Such decline was the inescapable result of increased manpower drafted to military service, the decline in agricultural-machinery production because of the demand for munitions-making, and the decrease in fertilizer output caused by the demands for explosives. And added to this was the continued destruction of food cargoes at sea by German submarines.

One single statistic is proof of how successfully America carried this gigantic burden. The three-year prewar average of exports of American-produced food was about 8,180,000 tons. Our exports for the year 1918, despite drought and the deterioration of our animal herds, were about 18,400,000 tons (including West Indian sugar crops, which we purchased).

[1] *War Memoirs of David Lloyd George* (Boston, Little, Brown and Company, 1934), Vol. III (1916–1917), pp. 199–200.

Elsewhere,[2] I have discussed at length the prelude to America's entry into the war.

I was one of the few Americans, aside from the diplomatic corps, who were allowed to move freely across enemy lines. I traveled frequently from London to The Hague; to Brussels; to the German Army's various headquarters and into its Army zones in the North of France; to Berlin; to Switzerland; to Paris; and to the headquarters of the Allied armies in France. Because of the obligation into which we had entered with the belligerent governments in our Belgian Relief agreements, I took no part in military information, but my appraisals of the state of mind in the combatant countries were sought by the President's representative, Colonel Edward M. House, and our Ambassadors.

I have dated the beginning of this section, which is devoted to "Providing Food for the Allies and Neutrals During the War," as February 13, 1917. On that date began a series of incidents which led to the creation of the Food Administration and my appointment to its leadership.

At that moment I was in the United States because of Belgian Relief difficulties arising from the Germans' unlimited submarine war, which began on February 1. At Colonel House's request, I furnished him a memorandum outlining the problems, including the problem of food, and the nature of organization necessary should we become involved in the war. Although this memorandum has already been published in part, it has such a bearing on subsequent events that I reprint its most important paragraphs here:

13th February 1917

DEAR COLONEL HOUSE:

Apropos of my conversation with you this morning, my own views as to immediate steps to be taken in case we go to war with Germany are as follows:

1. I trust that the United States will enter into no political alliance

[2] *The Memoirs of Herbert Hoover: Years of Adventure, 1874–1920* (New York, The Macmillan Company, 1957), pp. 213–16; *An American Epic* (Chicago, Henry Regnery Company, 1959—), Vol. I, pp. 271–72, 286–91; *The Ordeal of Woodrow Wilson* (New York, McGraw-Hill Book Company, Inc., 1958), pp. 4–9.

with the Allied Governments, but will confine itself to naval and military *cooperation.*

2. The first step for such cooperation would be to bring to bear the whole weight of our naval, shipping, and other resources to supply England, France, and Italy with food-stuffs and munitions.

3. It will probably be necessary for us to open to them all the facilities of which we are capable, to enable finance of such purchases in the United States.

4. Although, as you know, I have had no sympathy with the food blockade of Germany, this measure has proceeded to such a length that from a military point of view it is necessary that it should be now continued to the end and we would therefore need address ourselves to the reinforcement of it at every point. You are also aware that the Allied Governments have found themselves embarrassed by the necessity of bending to the demands of this country in connection with trade with the northern neutral governments. As a consequence, a considerable leakage of their native food supplies filters into Germany from these quarters, but by cooperation with the Allied Governments in the restriction of permits for the shipment of food-stuffs from this country to these neutral Powers, we could no doubt further restrict the native supplies now going into Germany.

5. It would probably be necessary for this government to direct as much American shipping to the assistance of the Allies as possible, but we can go one [step] further if we join with the Allies by pressure upon neutral shipping to serve the Allies. For instance, if we cooperate with the Allies in refusing bunker coal to shipping except on terms that they serve the Allies beyond their regulated self-needs, we can force a great deal of neutral shipping into the service of the Allied Governments. . . .

In Paragraph 6, I explored the possibility of allowing the French Army to recruit more American men and the need for mosquito vessels to protect shipping.

7. It appears to me that the political situation which will eventuate out of this war makes it absolutely necessary that this country should not only be protected by a large defensive force, but that we should have a force in being when peace approaches. As our terms of peace will probably run counter to most of the European proposals, our weight in the accomplishment of our ideals will be greatly in proportion to the strength which we can throw into the scale.

8. It appears that the world will be faced with a food shortage before the next harvest and that some measures will be necessary for the control of food consumption in this country if we are adequately to supply the Western Allies. Such measures do not need to take the form of rationing the people, or any drastic measures of that character, but there are many indirect methods of repressing food consumption, such as the suppression of the consumption of grain and sugar for brewing and distilling purposes and a long list of other measures with which we are well familiar.

HERBERT HOOVER

In a meeting with President Wilson a few days later, he expressed his approval of this memorandum and suggested that when I returned to Europe, it might prove helpful if I would study the organizational setup of the Allies for the economic conduct of the war.

While I was in Washington on this occasion, Secretary of the Interior Franklin K. Lane, a member of the Council of National Defense, told me that if we did enter the war, I would be needed in Washington in connection with our food problems.

Since all North Atlantic passenger service had been suspended because of the submarine war, I was unable to book passage to Europe until March 13, when I finally sailed, on an antiquated Spanish ship, for Cadiz. I reached London, via Madrid and Paris, on March 25—a twelve-day journey.[3]

When the United States declared war, I was not surprised at a notification from the American Embassy in London that Mr. Wilson wanted me to return to Washington to take the food post. I accepted—on condition that I continue to conduct the Belgian Relief at the same time. I also asked to delay my departure for a few weeks because of the necessity to organize the Belgian Relief for war and to complete the mission which the President had suggested.

I arrived in Washington on May 6. I saw Mr. Wilson on the eighth and tenth. On May 19, I was appointed United States Food Administrator, directly responsible to the President.

[3] I have given an account of some interesting experiences during this journey in Volume I of *An American Epic*, pp. 314–16.

CHAPTER 1

A MISSION FROM PRESIDENT WILSON

Upon my return to Europe in April, 1917, I at once began work on the President's request that I make a special study of the Allies' economic experience and organization in the war. In this work I had the assistance of our experienced Belgian Relief staff, which we had, upon the United States' declaration of war, withdrawn from Belgium and for which we had substituted Dutch and Spanish representatives; but we continued to deliver supplies to the Belgian frontier.

In the first two years of the war, Allied economic organization had not been a complete success, but it had resulted in much negative enlightenment. The primary difficulty arose from the fact that for the first time the world was to learn that legislative bodies in representative governments at war are slow to delegate new and strange economic powers required to meet the emergency. The Allied parliaments were not only fearful of delegating these powers, but they were even more fearful of anything that looked like centralization of such powers.

The result of this attitude was a multitude of boards, commissions, and committees among which power was to be divided. And in this departure from centuries of experience in the administration of private enterprise, there was no single individual in administrative command. The history of a few of these boards, committees, and commissions not only revealed the faultiness of such a setup but also contained lessons for war organization in the United States.

The British Royal Commission on Sugar was appointed on August 20, 1914. The organization was changed by royal proclamation on October 26, 1914, its powers were enlarged in 1916, and it remained independent of other food agencies until June, 1917.

The Royal Commission on Wheat, including all cereals, was established on October 10, 1916. On November 29, 1916, its powers were expanded and co-ordinated with those of the other Allies into the "Wheat Executive," which was another board. The control of British overseas imports of meats and fats began in the War Office in 1914 but was partially under the Board of Trade. The French and Italians delegated their purchases to the British Board of Trade. This setup proved so ineffective that on August 29, 1917, the Inter-Allied Meats and Fats Executive—another board—was created and given enlarged powers, but the Board of Trade continued to exercise control over part of the operations.

These food agencies were operated independently until the military crises which arose from the Battle of the Somme and the defeat of Rumania two and one-half years after the war began. These disasters determined the Allies to consolidate all food powers in ministries of food under a single minister in each country. Italy set up such a ministry on January 16, 1917. The British established a ministry of food on December 26, 1916, but with deficient powers, which were finally remedied in June, 1917. The French established an overall food ministry in September, 1917. Thus the unification of food agencies required two and one-half years in Italy and three years in France.

Until these consolidated ministries were set up, all agricultural policies and controls were conducted by long-established departments of agriculture, and these had guaranteed some prices to induce production. In the creation of these new ministries, however, the essential agricultural regulations were brought under the ministries' control.

The Commission for Relief in Belgium, organized in 1914, was unique from the start because its Chairman was responsible for all the food problems outside and inside Belgium. Aside from being the pioneers of a food administration in the world, the Commission had to deal with all the British, French, and German food and shipping agencies. Nor was I ignorant of Allied methods, for I was often called upon for advice on their problems and to listen to their griefs over lack of authority to do their jobs properly in the public interest.

THE ALLIED PURCHASING AGENCIES—AND AMERICA

There was one phase in the operations of these Allied purchasing agencies which particularly affected American interests. They controlled practically all of the purchases of food for the Allies (which included the minor Allies), and they were planning to control purchases in the United States by some of the Northern European Neutrals.

Although these agencies were absolutely needed to preserve order in world markets, they were not charitable institutions run for the benefit of the farmers in producing countries. As an indication of our need to control their activities within the United States, I asked the "Wheat Executive" what price they believed they should pay for American wheat. They suggested about $1.50 per bushel at our ports as an equitable price. Such a price would have been below the American farmers' costs and would have stifled our production.

In the meantime, panicked by the unlimited submarine war, the Neutral nations, bidding against the Allies for American supplies, had raised the price of wheat to more than $3.00 per bushel in Chicago and the wholesale price of sugar to 8.45 cents per pound in New York. Furthermore, their activities in handling feed grains had stifled the yield of our animal products.

OTHER ALLIED WAR ORGANIZATIONS

My colleagues and I also studied the other Allied economic organizations for war. Their munitions manufacture and procurement, with constant shifting of organizations in the first two years of the war, had been the subject of many disagreeable exposures and bitter criticism in the press. However, at the time of our inquiry, they had pulled themselves together with centralized ministries or other forms of one-man leadership in these fields.

Shipping, vital as it was, had no adequate inter-Allied organization. An Allied shipping committee had been set up in January, 1917, but it soon proved entirely ineffective because it was without adequate authority and because private interests and national jealousies dominated the committee. Later in this text there will appear evidence of confusions and failures before shipping control was properly organized.

THE FOOD NEEDS OF THE EUROPEAN ALLIES, THE BELGIANS, AND THE NEUTRALS

One of the major purposes in our investigation was to determine the Allied food needs. My colleagues from the Belgian Relief staff collected a mass of statistics concerning prewar production, consumption, imports, sources, and needs for the crop year ahead, that of 1917–1918.

For our appraisal we had to study the war devastation of production in each Allied country. For instance, as of the spring of 1917, the number of French cattle had decreased from a prewar 14,000,000 head to 12,000,000; their sheep from 16,000,000 to 9,000,000; their hogs from 7,000,000 to about 3,000,000. They informed us that with the shortage of feed, their milk production had decreased from 2,200 pounds per annum per cow to 1,540 pounds; this, combined with the loss in dairy cattle, had decreased their dairy products about 1,400,000 tons. The British animal count had not decreased substantially, but a shortage of feed had reduced their animal products by about 12 per cent.

Formerly, the British had relied mostly on beet sugar from the Continent, but from the beginning of the war they were wholly dependent upon imports from other sources. The prewar combined French and Italian beet-sugar production had been about 1,190,000 tons per annum and was sufficient for their own needs, but now it was reduced to only 300,000 tons. The decrease was in both countries due largely to the shortage of labor and fertilizers and to the urge to plant bread grains, which called for much less labor.

The combined Allied prewar production of feed for animals, barley, corn, and oats had decreased from about 690,000,000 bushels to about 440,000,000 bushels.

The only bright spot—and even it was somewhat dimmed—was the Allies' wheat and vegetable production. Through the replacement of other crops by wheat and the diligence of their women and children, they had fewer decreases in these two crops than in others. Every back yard and every roadside were planted with potatoes.

I will not encumber the text at this point with the calculations we made as to their needed overseas supplies. They varied from a maximum of what would restore prewar supplies to a minimum of what would be needed under the grim rations which we had to impose on the Belgians. However, as a contribution to economic history, I give statistical calculations of Allied needs in those chapters of this memoir which are devoted to the separate major food commodities.

When we emerged from this wilderness of statistics, our conclusion was that the Allied supplies depended on unpredictable factors, such as how much shipping could be saved by making the short journey to North America as compared to journeys, twice the length, to the Southern Hemisphere and the Far East. Our only firm conclusion was that the survival of the Western European nations would require every atom of food that could be produced and transported from overseas.

CONCLUSIONS CONCERNING AMERICAN FOOD POLICIES

From our experience in Belgium and our observations of German, British, and French food controls, it was clear that certain lessons had to be applied in setting up our own American food organization:

First, in order not to dissipate our energies in production and conservation, we had to concentrate our efforts on eight major commodities—cereals, fats, meats, sugar, beans, peas, dried fruit, and canned goods.

Second, if the Allies were to survive, we had to stimulate production and decrease our own consumption of these staples.

Third, to stimulate production, the American farmer had to be assured a price at which he could sell his products; otherwise he could not be expected to take the risks of war.

Fourth, in order to save shipping, we had to supply animal products instead of feed.

Fifth, the Belgian and German rationing methods for reducing consumption by the use of individual cards and coupons had proved to require a great bureaucracy, with committees of issuance in every community. These were all accompanied by inspectors, involving arrests, court trials, and great expense. There was widespread evasion through black markets. Moreover, 40 per cent of our American population could obtain supplies over and above any ration we might impose because they lived on farms or near farmers. Therefore, card rationing would not produce the best results in our case.

Sixth, we decided that we could secure better results through the great sense of voluntary action and self-sacrifice in war from the American people. Appeals to housewives would include the farmer's wife. Appeals to public eating establishments could be strengthened by asking their customers to co-operate. The trades would require certain regulation to eliminate waste and decrease consumption.

Seventh, the inevitable scarcity in the United States, already created by Allied and Neutral buying, would be increased because of the supplies we would have to send overseas. The law of supply and demand would be obsolete. We had to control prices and prevent hoarding and profiteering.

Eighth, to protect the consumer and regulate the flow of supplies to the Allies, our Government had to buy the major commodities as near to the farm-market level as possible and resell them to the

Allies and to our domestic processors and distributors under regulations covering markups, profits, and conservation measures.

Ninth, our food organization had to control all exports of food in order to prevent excessive exports, which would endanger our own supplies, and to secure just distribution to serve the needs of foreign countries.

Tenth, the outstanding lesson from European food-control organization was that the American food organization had to be an independent agency directly under the President, with ample power, and had to assume all functions relating to food, including the policies which influenced production.

I fully realized that many of these ideas would be a shock to the Congress, the farmers, the distributors, and the consumers, but we were in a life-and-death struggle. The record will show that I advocated these principles immediately upon my return to Washington.

CHAPTER 2

THE PROBLEM OF OVERSEAS SHIPPING

Before describing further the development of the U.S. Food Administration, I must amplify the background situation in overseas shipping.

Throughout the war and the famine which followed, our food operations were dominated by the amount of shipping available. The damage done by the Germans' unlimited submarine war and by normal attrition not only affected our food policies, but it also had important effects on military strategy. At no time while the United States was in the war did we have enough ships, and our transport life was one crisis after another.

In the previous chapter I have referred to the totally inadequate organization and co-ordination of all Allied shipping. As early as April 21, 1917, while I was still in London, I made the following report to Ambassador Walter Hines Page, who transmitted it at once to Washington:

Shipping position is so critical that it is urgently necessary to create at once a committee that will undertake all chartering both for neutral and Allied tonnage for account commercial and governmental purposes, forbidding absolutely any . . . chartering except through such committee. This charter committee to cooperate with Allied charter committee existing here. During past ten days rates on neutral shipping have risen nearly 100 per cent due to frantic bidding of . . . shippers for neutral tonnage to be used to a considerable degree for purposes other than transport of food and materials into war zone. Of equal importance is to create simultaneously bunker committee which will license purchase of bunker coal with a rigorous prohibition established upon sale of any American coal whether at home or abroad directly or indirectly to any ship unless it have such a license. This committee by cooperating with existing Allied bunker committee here will control practically all bunker coal in the world and neutrals must accept service in carrying food and materials at the peril of being without bunkers. As an example of present situation Spanish ships formerly carried almost entire Spanish iron to English furnaces. Since unlimited submarine warfare has been declared Spain refuses to allow her ships to continue in this trade and in order to keep English furnaces and consequently English munitions going it has been necessary to divert English shipping to carry this iron ore. Further than this, Spanish Government now compels these English ships to transport coal to Spain in exchange for iron ore; beyond this again Spain requires them to devote 20 per cent of their iron ore space to carrying oranges to England where they are not wanted; further than this, Spanish shipping is now being chartered at high market rates to American shippers and others for mercantile trade to neutral countries and to neutrals for inter-neutral trade. The net result of Spanish action has been to greatly diminish available shipping and imperil food and munition supply and could at once be corrected if bunker coal were placed in entire control so that Spain should be compelled to carry her iron ore to England in exchange for coal. This matter is of most critical importance and requires immediate action.

HERBERT HOOVER

The Allies were painfully slow in co-ordination. On November 17, 1917, five months after my warning, the American Shipping Board, having been continuously frustrated, sent an urgent message to London demanding immediate action. Two weeks later, on November 30, a meeting was convened in London, presided over by Lord Robert Cecil, Under Secretary for Foreign Affairs. He presented an admirable proposal for organization and pressed for quick action. The British and French shipping representatives balked; each nation wanted to control its own ships. The only result of the conference was to create the "Allied Maritime Transport Council," but its powers were limited to the control of charters of Neutral vessels. It was not until three years after the outbreak of the war in Europe, when the situation became absolutely desperate after the German attack on the Western Front in March, 1918, that full unified control was expanded to cover all Allied and American shipping, as well as the Neutral charters.

There were wide differences between the American and British naval authorities on how to deal with the submarine attack. In late April, 1917, before I left London for Washington, my good friend Admiral William S. Sims, who represented the U.S. Navy, came to see me. He told me that submarine sinkings of merchant vessels had taken toll of far more tonnage than the public knew of, that the Germans were sinking 800,000 tons a month, and that at this rate Allied merchant shipping would be so depleted as to cause loss of the war. He gave me two urgent messages to deliver to President Wilson. First, he wanted more destroyers and light craft sent over and many more built to combat the submarine menace. Second, he wanted the President to demand that the Allies adopt a convoy system across the Atlantic. They had hitherto refused to do so, on the ground that it would restrict all ships to the speed of the slowest one. So deep was the Admiral's conviction that he asserted that the British, by not adopting convoys, had probably lost, unnecessarily, two million tons of shipping. The Admiral was endowed by nature with strong "sailor language," and in this instance he embellished it with emotional extras. I softened the saltier parts of the Admiral's message in delivering it to the President.

It was not until five months later, in September, 1917, that convoys were fully organized. The subsequent savings in ships, as shown in the statistical tables I give below, were proof of the Admiral's contention.

For the Allies, shipping was limited to the tonnage available among the Allied nations, the United States, and the Neutral nations of Europe. Enemy shipping had been driven into refuge, either in enemy ports or in those of Neutral nations, and was available only after the Armistice. The Japanese, Chinese, Latin-American, and other nations, including the European Neutrals, required a considerable part of their merchant fleets for their own supplies. The constant degeneration of shipping is shown by the following table:

THE POSSIBLE SHIPPING AVAILABLE
TO THE ALLIES, PREWAR (1914)

Allies	Tons
United States	2,216,000
Great Britain	18,197,000
France	1,602,000
Italy	1,310,000
Belgium	210,000
	23,535,000
European Neutrals	
Norway	1,978,000
Sweden	1,022,000
Denmark	804,000
Holland	1,492,000
Spain	886,000
	6,182,000
Grand Total	29,717,000

THE MERCHANT-SHIPPING SITUATION ON FEBRUARY 1, 1917

Prior to Germany's launching its unlimited submarine war on February 1, 1917, there had been some ship construction, but there had also been great losses from normal wreckage and German attacks. The net decrease in the above holdings at that time was about 7,300,000 tons, leaving about 22,500,000 tons.

THE MERCHANT-SHIPPING SITUATION AT THE BEGINNING OF THE FOOD ADMINISTRATION

The Food Administration did not receive its authority from the Congress until August 10, 1917. By this time the submarine war and normal sea losses had decreased the available merchant shipping by the following amounts:

1917	Tons
February	536,500
March	590,500
April	866,600
May	574,300
June	665,400
July	549,400
	3,782,700

Thus the total Allied, American, and European Neutral overseas shipping was at this time about 18,704,000 tons, or nearly 40 per cent less than prewar.

THE MERCHANT-SHIPPING SITUATION AT THE ARMISTICE, NOVEMBER 11, 1918

To indicate the havoc in shipping during the war, I give the further net losses of Allied, American, and Neutral shipping prior to the Armistice in November, 1918:

1917	Tons	1918	Tons
August	488,700	January	303,600
September	342,100	February	305,500
October	429,500	March	320,700
November	284,500	April	275,000
December	385,800	May	263,400
		June	241,400
		July	237,900
		August	276,500
		September	166,600
		October	113,100
			4,434,300

Thus at the Armistice the available tonnage was about 14,270,000 tons, or less than 50 per cent of prewar.

From a food-transport point of view, many deductions had to be made from the totals given above. The merchant fleets consisted of passenger ships, tankers, and cargo ships. The passenger tonnage necessarily had to be devoted to the transport of troops and the maintenance of a few world-wide liners for important passengers and mail. These ships had some cargo-carrying capacity, but because of their speed they were largely used by the military. In addition, the military used many cargo ships for carrying munitions and other supplies to the troops. Some tonnage was always out of action for repairs, and the tanker tonnage was not available for food cargoes.

The European Neutrals required about 1,600,000 tons of merchant ships for their own needs. In any event, except for the Norwegians, whose fleet had escaped from Norway, they were loath to serve in dangerous waters and were under constant threats from the Germans not to charter their ships to the Allies. Under these threats, many of their ships went into refuge in their own or neutral ports. Moreover, there were huge profits to be made by the use of Neutral ships for trade in the Pacific, Indian, and South Atlantic oceans, and in areas where there was little danger from attack.

After all these deductions, a rough estimate of the overseas dry cargo tonnage available for civilian needs in food and raw materials was a scant 8,000,000 tons at the time the Food Control Law was enacted by the Congress. And this volume, as shown above, decreased every month during the war.

The most efficient use of available tonnage was the short voyage between Europe and North America. While food and other supplies were available in the Southern Hemisphere and the Far East, these voyages were twice as long. These markets were gradually cut off until, by March, 1918, they were abandoned.

AMERICAN SHIPBUILDING

A major shipbuilding program was undertaken by the United States when we entered the war in April, 1917. However, the program was very slow in starting because of inadequate organization, bickering in our Shipping Board, and lack of a single head at the top. Not until four months after we entered the war, when, on July 24, 1917, Edward N. Hurley was appointed Chairman, with full powers to direct matters, did things improve. But despite Mr. Hurley's efforts, the total net gain of the American fleet during the war was only about 1,337,000 tons, and the total net tonnage available to the Allies had decreased steadily every month of the war.

Many of the war-built American ships were slow, small, and extravagant in coal consumption and for a long time after the war were not even salable as junk. The Food Administration could not use these smaller ships for overseas food during the war, but after the Armistice we used some of them for transport between European ports.

It was all a sad story.

From all of these causes, we were met with a shipping crisis at our every step during the war.

CHAPTER 3

THE IMPACT OF MILITARY STRATEGY ON FOOD

The overseas movement of food and raw materials, both to ourselves and to the Allies, shifted with the military tides and strategy, mainly because these determinations controlled the amount of available shipping for civilian purposes. For an understanding of the impact of military strategy on food, it is necessary to begin the narration with a reference to the period prior to the United States' entry into the war.

In the summer of 1916, the Allied armies had been stalled in their great Somme attack upon the enemy. In the fall of 1916, their Rumanian ally had been invaded by the Central Empires. Because of these losses, the war on the Western Front had settled down to the attrition of trench warfare.

The Allied navies had driven enemy surface craft from the seas except for occasional raiders. Their blockade had cut off all overseas supplies to the Central Empires, and had further reduced enemy supplies by blockade pressure on border Neutrals.

I knew from my own observations on the spot of the steady degeneration in progress in food and other supplies in the Central Empires. They, like the Allies, had diverted agricultural manpower to their armies, fertilizers to explosives, and agricultural-machinery manufacture to munitions-making. Their armies and munitions workers had to be given prewar normal food, and their farmers naturally secreted approximately a normal supply from their products.

Therefore, the impact of the food shortage fell mostly on the noncombatant urban populations, which were suffering greatly.

From all these events and pressures, the strategy of the European Allies at the time we came into the war, and for the following year, was to "wear down" the enemy by holding the trenches and the blockade. The United States was to furnish naval strength; sustain the blockade; fight German submarines; send air forces and other technical services to Europe; provide food, raw materials, and ammunition; build ships; and supply token ground troops in Europe for morale purposes, with General Pershing in command.

That "wear them down" was the strategy can be demonstrated by a few quotations. Colonel House wrote to President Wilson on March 19, 1917, two weeks before we declared war:

DEAR GOVERNOR:

. . . It has seemed to me that we should constitute ourselves a huge reservoir to supply the Allies with the things they most need. No one looks with favor upon our raising a large army at the moment, believing it would be better if we would permit volunteers to enlist in the Allied armies.[1]

General James G. Harbord, General Pershing's Chief of Staff, says of this period:

In those April days of 1917, when French and British Missions descended upon Washington, our Government heard much of the desirability of sending to Europe thousands of laborers, railroad and otherwise, carpenters, miners, chauffeurs, foresters, nurses and doctors, and little about fighting troops. The military chief of the British Mission deprecated the prospect of an American army in France as making one more weakening joint in the Allied line. The French General Staff, as quoted from France, were "not particularly interested in having American troops in France." Marshal Joffre's principal staff officer thought it would be better if we gave money instead of men. The two Missions were a unit in believing we "could not raise, train, and transport an army of sufficient size to have any effect in the European theater of war." Marshal Joffre, how-

[1] Charles Seymour, *The Intimate Papers of Colonel House* (New York, Houghton Mifflin Company, 1928), Vol. III, p. 6.

ever, asked for the immediate dispatch of one division to show the flag, and added, "It will cheer our people if you will send over some of your troops." [2]

General Harbord also noted:

When General Pershing went to France not even the Allies believed that we should ever land and support an army of sufficient strength to be a factor in determining the war.

Concerning the token forces sent to France, General Tasker H. Bliss, then Chief of Staff, wrote in 1917:

". . . General Pershing's expedition is being sent abroad on the urgent insistence of Marshal Joffre and the French Mission that a force, however small, be sent to produce a *moral effect.* We have yielded to this view and a force is being sent *solely to produce a moral effect.* . . . Our General Staff had made no plan . . . for prompt dispatch of reënforcements to General Pershing, nor the prompt dispatch of considerable forces to France. . . ." [3]

Again speaking of this time, General Bliss said:

There was no definite plan in any mission. Some individuals urged that what was wanted from the United States was not men, not an army, but money, food, munitions, supplies of all kinds; others said, send men, trained or untrained, and send them quickly; still others, send one small division to France to show the flag and inspire the hope that others will follow quickly, but then take a year, if need be, to train those others.[4]

The major dissenting voice to this "wear them down" strategy was that of General Pershing, who demanded large American armies as fast as they could be prepared. While these policies prevented

[2] James G. Harbord, *America in the World War* (New York, Houghton Mifflin Company, 1933), pp. 25–26.

[3] John J. Pershing, *My Experiences in the World War* (New York, Frederick A. Stokes Company, 1931), Vol. I, p. 78.

[4] Tasker H. Bliss, "The Evolution of the Unified Command," *Foreign Affairs,* Vol. I, No. 2 (December 15, 1922), pp. 3–4.

sending him the armies he wanted, his influence greatly stimulated their preparation at home in case of need.

On July 6, 1917, General Pershing cabled, asking for an additional one million men and urging that transportation be arranged with the Allies. He later wrote:

> The question, in its finality, was, therefore, one of sea transportation, but so far all efforts to get the Allies, especially the British, to consider giving help to bring over men and supplies had been futile. . . . They seemed to regard the transportation of an American army overseas as entirely our affair. This apparent indifference also gave further color to the suspicion that perhaps an American army as such was not wanted. . . .[5]

Pershing also recalled the mood in London on a visit there during this period:

> Underneath the surface of the seeming cheerfulness there was more than a suggestion of serious apprehension. . . . it was easy to conclude that if the destruction of British shipping continued at that rate there would soon be none left either to help transport an American army to Europe or to supply it after arrival.
>
> Under the circumstances, the apparent unconcern of the British as to our need of shipping is not difficult to understand. They were seriously alarmed regarding their own food situation. . . .[6]

Pershing wrote further, with reference to American assistance:

> . . . I gave [to the London Conference of Allied Military Leaders, July 26, 1917] in detail the situation. . . . A cablegram had just been received in response to mine of July 6th. . . . This message, indicating that the War Department foresaw small chance of securing the necessary tonnage, was read to the conference. . . .
>
> About this time further disturbing reports were submitted to me . . . by Admiral Sims. They were based upon tonnage losses for May, June and July, and seemed to confirm the conclusions of a month previous that there would soon be insufficient Allied shipping left to bring over an American army of the strength required, and that the Allies would find

[5] Pershing, *op. cit.*, Vol. I, p. 95.
[6] *Ibid.*, pp. 54–55.

it difficult to keep up their supply of food from overseas and provide matériel necessary to carry on the war. . . .[7]

General Pershing added that in the latter part of September, 1917:

> . . . in conference . . . with Lord Derby, the British Minister of War, I was told that his Government could not be counted on to furnish us ships as transports.[8]

On October 11, as a probable consequence of Pershing's urgings, British Foreign Secretary Balfour cabled Colonel House:

> England now considers it important to clearly state that she sees no possibility of carrying on her military and naval part in the war, transporting civilian and military supplies in British bottoms and continuing to furnish her [European] Allies with as many ships as in the past.[9]

The situation drifted on, with British reluctance to furnish transport for the ground armies demanded by General Pershing. At the end of January, 1918, nine months after we entered the war, by the use of American ships, there were only about 150,000 American combat troops in France and about 65,000 service troops.

These "wear them down" Allied attitudes were confirmed to me in many talks I had with the President, although I find no memoranda on these conversations. However, I do find in my files the following notes, in my own handwriting, on conversations with top officials concerning the strategy then in use.

July 15, 1917 [Discussion with Balfour, British High Commissioner]
Pershing asking for million man army in France. French Generals here favor it but British say no ships. They don't seem to think it necessary anyway.

July 30, 1917
Saw Col. House last week. He says: Pershing wants a million men in France; French Generals agree with him but French civilian and British

[7] *Ibid.*, pp. 118, 120.
[8] *Ibid.*, p. 171.
[9] Seymour, *op. cit.*, Vol. III, p. 191.

Military and *Civilian* officials say it cannot be transported overseas, in view submarine losses, etc. I said French have lost no consequential tonnage; that only way such an army can be transported is by the British; if they say it can't be done they ought to know.

AUG 5

Bliss said to me he did not think Pershing's estimate of million men in France is feasible. Certainly unless British will do major job transport. And that British think it unnecessary anyway.

AUG 10

Secty Baker tells me President puts no faith in large Army to France, that British advise against it. Want food, munitions.

I understand Army here all against the idea with any shipping now assured.

In the midst of all this, on July 30, 1917, my office received the following message from Colonel House. The office record stated:

Telephone message from Colonel House asking what the present arguments were against sending a large army to France. Said he needed them to impress some of our foreign friends that they must supply the shipping and guarantee to carry them through.

I sent the Colonel a memorandum, basing the arguments I cited therein upon the opinion already expressed by our own and Allied leaders.[10]

[10] During the Second World War, I protested that men were being drawn from the farms faster than they could be trained or transported abroad, thus needlessly endangering our food production. The War Department reacted by having Senator Theodore F. Green of Rhode Island make a smear speech, saying that I had opposed sending an army to Europe in 1917. His text was founded upon some of the sentences in my memorandum to House, taken out of their context and only partially representing several discussions with Colonel House. The discussions concerned the dangers of sending large armies to Europe—unless the convoy system were adopted, the British and French stopped using their ships for commercial trade, reliance were placed on the short haul from North America instead of the long voyages from the East Indies and the Southern Hemisphere, and the British agreed to furnish the ships.

It appeared that Yale University had furnished War Department officials with a copy of my memorandum for House from the *House Papers* in their keeping. Professor Ralph H. Lutz of the Stanford War Library made a spirited reply based on the actual records. He issued a booklet entitled *A Typical New Deal Smear and Distortion* (17 April 1943).

I demanded and received an apology from Secretary of War Stimson.

With the failure of the "wear them down" strategy, all military plans shifted overnight. This reversal of Allied policies was later described by General Peyton C. March, who was Chief of Staff at this time, as follows:

> The debacle of Russia in 1917, followed by the signing of a separate treaty of peace with Germany by the Bolsheviks on March 3, 1918, by Finland on March 4, 1918, and a preliminary treaty of peace by Rumania on March 5th, had released many German divisions from duty on the Eastern Front for service on the Western, so that Hindenburg was able to strike with a clear numerical superiority at that point. The Allies at once turned to America, the only source of man power left, to make up the deficiency. They were bled white and could put no more men on the firing line.
>
> The Premiers of Britain and France, therefore, united in a cablegram to President Wilson [April 1, 1918] emphasizing the crisis which had arisen, and asking him to send to France, if possible, 120,000 men a month for four months. . . .
>
> . . . Every request which we had hitherto made of the British Government for additional ships had been met with statements that all her ships were imperatively needed to bring food and supplies of all kinds not only for her armies in France, including Canadians, Australians, and others, but for the civilian population at home; that they had rationed their people and had given us every available spare ship they had. Their losses from German submarines were set forth, and the impossibility of doing anything further in the way of furnishing us ships had been asserted and reasserted.[11]

The result of this change in military strategy was to have a profound effect upon our food operations, as I relate in Chapter 18. Fortunately, President Wilson, with General Pershing's advice, had insisted upon our being prepared for any eventuality by the assembling, training, and equipping of huge American armies.

[11] General Peyton C. March, *The Nation at War* (Garden City, Doubleday, Doran & Company, Inc., 1932), pp. 79, 82.

THE PRESIDENT STATES THAT WE ARE NOT AN ALLY BUT AN ASSOCIATED POWER

It is well to note in full the letter which I received from the President stating his attitude toward the notion of any formal political union with the Allies:

10 December 1917

My dear Mr. Hoover:

I have noticed on one or two of the posters of the Food Administration the words, "Our Allies." I would be very much obliged if you would issue instructions that "Our Associates in the War" is to be substituted. I have been very careful about this myself because we have no allies and I think I am right in believing that the people of the country are very jealous of any intimation that there are formal alliances.

You will understand, of course, that I am implying no criticism. I am only thinking it important that we should all use the same language.

Woodrow Wilson

THE COLLAPSE OF THE "WEAR THEM DOWN" STRATEGY

As stated by General March, eleven months after the United States entered the war, the whole "wear them down" strategy crashed. And our food policies were thrown into complete chaos from the use of all available shipping to transport and supply the American armies.

CHAPTER 4

SETTING UP THE FOOD ADMINISTRATION

With the background of the previous three chapters, it is possible to present more briefly and more clearly the complicated organization, problems, and policies of the Food Administration.

In my first talk with the President after my return to Washington from Europe the first week of May, 1917, he formally asked me to join his administration and be in charge of food matters. He proposed a food commission, of which I would be chairman. This commission was to embrace representatives of agriculture, labor, and business. The President, like the Allied leaders in the early stages of the war, had to meet the reluctance of the Congress to delegate the wide and strange powers needed for the emergency. For this reason, or perhaps his own predilection, he had already set up several boards, commissions, or committees to handle other problems. With this idea, however, he was headed for the old rock of divided responsibility, which had caused many of the Allied administrative wrecks during their earlier years in the war. The attitude of the Congress was not improved by the press, which, recognizing the recent centralization of food-control powers in Europe, at once greeted my arrival with headlines of "Food Dictator" and "Food Czar."

I informed the President of the failures of European administrative boards and commissions, with their inescapable frictions, indecisions, and delays. I suggested that the whole genius of American business—and even of our governmental organization—prescribed a single responsible executive, with boards only in an advisory, legislative, or judicial capacity. I proposed that there would have to be a single head to oversee the whole food problem and that his authority would have to cover stimulation of production, conservation, exports, imports, purchases and sales of some commodities by the government, and every phase of food from production to consumption. I suggested that an individual could induce a wealth of voluntary action which no impersonal board could command and that in such action lay our safeguard against "Prussianizing" the country.

I also found that the President was fearful that my desire to have a hand in the stimulation of production would stir up conflict with the Department of Agriculture. I already knew Secretary of Agriculture David F. Houston's view that the function of his department was to encourage production by giving guidance to the farmers. He felt that his department was a great scientific research, experimental, and statistical institution, and he was anxious not to be entangled in economic problems, except for advice. He feared that the farmers' certain antagonism toward controls would injure the Department. He expressed his support of my views to the President.

Finally, Mr. Wilson was convinced that the board idea, as applied to food, would be impracticable. Possibly his mind was won over by my proposal of a new term: "administrator," as the head of an administration. I suggested that the term itself would connote, not dictatorship, but both co-ordination and executive leadership. I believe this was the first time this title was used for a public function.

As the war went on, one after another of the President's boards and commissions fell into squabbles and other difficulties. Before the war was over, he had given every one of them a dominant head, either by granting complete authority to their chairmen or by organizing them into single-headed agencies.

THE DESPERATE FOOD SITUATION IN THE UNITED STATES

I have referred to our shortage of food for export at this time in Volume I on the Belgian Relief. But more details are appropriate here.

The day after I arrived in Washington, Secretary Houston gave me an inventory of food resources and his forecast for the coming year. The Secretary's presentation of the outlook was terrifying, but even his estimates proved overoptimistic. Because of drought, the prospects for the crop year from July 1, 1917, to July 1, 1918, indicated that the grain harvest would cover no more than our normal domestic consumption, the necessary seed, and the pipeline carry-over to the next year. Statistically, there would be no consequential surplus of grain for supplies to needy nations. Houston also reviewed the actions of the Allies and Neutrals, who, from a desire to accumulate supplies against the hazards of the submarine war and to use the shortest shipping route, had been recklessly buying not only grain but also grain futures on the Chicago Board of Trade. I discuss our actions in this situation later on, but I may say here that their buying methods had so greatly increased the prices of grain products to the American consumer that penalties of more than $600,000,000 a year above prewar prices were imposed on them. Secretary Houston also presented to me an appalling picture of the supply of meats and fats to the Allies. He stated that Allied and Neutral panic-buying methods in feed grains had so distorted the ratio price of corn to hogs that the farmer could more profitably sell corn than feed hogs. He predicted that the slaughter of hogs during the year 1917 would be about 57,000,000, as compared to 70,000,000 during 1916. He added that the number of breed hogs on the farms at this time was about 5,000,000 less than at the same time the year before, which meant, at best, 15,000,000 fewer hogs for the autumn and winter markets. He also stated that with the exorbitant price of feed, the dairy farmers were reducing their products.

Our difficulties were not limited to grains, meat, and fat products. The Allies and some of the Neutrals, being forced into Western Hemisphere markets for sugar, had, with their buying methods, so increased the price as to impose penalties on our consumers of more than $400,000,000 a year over prewar. Also, the alarming reports of Allied shortages and Congressional discussion of prospective legislation for food controls had caused a rush of hoarding and speculation by American individuals, processors, and distributors. Along with all of these difficulties, we were faced with finding unprecedented supplies if the Allies were to survive.

To aid in setting up the food organization, I had brought with me to Washington some of our most experienced men from the Commission for Relief in Belgium. They were Edgar Rickard, Prentiss Gray, John Beaver White, Captain J. F. Lucey, Ben S. Allen, Professor Alonzo E. Taylor, and Dr. Vernon L. Kellogg. Within a few days, we quickly added to this list Ray Lyman Wilbur, President of Stanford University, Mark L. Requa, Duncan McDuffie, Harry A. Garfield, President of Williams College, and others.

It was obvious from Congressional attitudes that there would be long delays in the legislation which would enable us to deal properly with the gigantic emergency. In the meantime, the American people were consuming food at their normal rate. It was imperative that we should not await legislation to establish, as far as we could, an organization to save waste and reduce consumption. I presented the situation to the President, suggesting that we begin work in this field at once. I stated that we could explain that our activities were limited to voluntary conservation pending legislation and that it should cause no friction with the Congress. I also asked for a modest appropriation from the President's emergency fund.

On May 19, the President, in announcing my appointment, included an outline of powers needed from the Congress. As will be shown later on, I was compelled to present to them, at an executive session of the House Agricultural Committee, the whole story, which would be made public because leaks had occurred. I drafted the announcement, and Mr. Wilson approved it:

It is very desirable, in order to prevent misunderstandings or alarms and to assure co-operation in a vital matter, that the country should understand exactly the scope and purpose of the very great powers which I have thought it necessary in the circumstances to ask the Congress to put in my hands with regard to our food supplies. Those powers are very great, indeed, but they are no greater than it has proved necessary to lodge in the other Governments which are conducting this momentous war, and their object is stimulation and conservation, not arbitrary restraint or injurious interference with the normal processes of production. They are intended to benefit and assist the farmer and all those who play a legitimate part in the preparation, distribution, and marketing of foodstuffs.

It is proposed to draw a sharp line of distinction between the normal activities of the Government represented in the Department of Agriculture . . . [and] the regulation of food distribution and consumption on the other. . . .

I have asked Mr. Herbert Hoover to undertake this all-important task of food administration. He has expressed his willingness to do so on condition that he is to receive no payment for his services and that the whole of the force under him, exclusive of clerical assistance, shall be employed, so far as possible, upon the same volunteer basis. . . .

Although it is absolutely necessary that unquestionable powers shall be placed in my hands in order to insure the success of this administration of the food supplies of the country, I am confident that the exercise of those powers will be necessary only in the few cases where some small and selfish minority proves unwilling to put the Nation's interests above personal advantage, and that the whole country will heartily support Mr. Hoover's efforts by supplying the necessary volunteer agencies throughout the country. . . .

The proposed food administration is intended, of course, only to meet a manifest emergency and to continue only while the war lasts. Since it will be composed, for the most part, of volunteers, there need be no fear of the possibility of a permanent bureaucracy arising out of it. All control of consumption will disappear when the emergency has passed. . . .

The last thing that any American could contemplate with equanimity would be the introduction of anything resembling Prussian autocracy into the food control in this country.

It is of vital interest and importance to every man who produces food and to every man who takes part in its distribution that these policies thus liberally administered should succeed and succeed altogether. It is only in that way that we can prove it to be absolutely unnecessary to resort to the rigorous and drastic measures which have proved to be necessary in some of the European countries.

WOODROW WILSON

The same day, I issued an amplifying statement:

In accepting President Wilson's request that I should become head of the new food administration, it is entirely upon the assumption that Congress will grant broad powers to the President on which a competent administration can be set up.

I hold strongly to the view that while large powers are necessary for minority cases . . . [there] will probably . . . [be little need for their application to] the vast majority of the producing and distributing elements in the country. [They] are only too willing and anxious to serve our national necessities. I have represented to the President five cardinal principles of food administration.

First. That the food problem is one of wise administration and not expressed by the words "dictator" or "controller" but "food administrator."

Second. That this administration can be largely carried out through the coordination and regulation of the existing legitimate distributive agencies of the producers, distributors, and consumers.

Third. The organization of the community for voluntary conservation of foodstuffs.

Fourth. That all important positions, so far as may be, shall be filled with volunteers.

Fifth. The independent responsibility of the food administration directly under the President, with the cooperation of the great and admirable organization of the Department of Agriculture, the Department of Commerce, the Federal Trade Commission, and the railway executives.

I conceive that the essence of all war administration falls into two phases:

First. Centralized and single responsibility.

Second. Delegation of this responsibility to decentralized administrative organization.

I then reviewed the food problem at home and abroad, elaborated the method of organizing the Food Administration in order to make the above-mentioned points effective, and concluded:

> Probably more seriously than anyone else in the country, I recognize the difficulties and possibility of failure in this work and I appeal to the patriotism of my countrymen for their support. I have no instinct to be a food dictator. My ambition is to see my own people solve their own problem. Those men and women who can not serve in the trenches . . . can show their patriotism in no way so fully as in this service, and I feel that we have as much right to call upon them to serve in this administration as we have a right to call upon . . . [their sons] to serve in the trenches.

ORGANIZING THE SAVING OF FOOD

We immediately set up an organization for reduction of food consumption and elimination of waste under the direction of Dr. Wilbur, who quickly recruited an effective staff. He at once separated the problems of the home from those of public eating places, putting the former under the direction of leading women and the latter under experienced restaurant managers. We then set about organizing the other necessary divisions of our work in preparation for the passage of the Food Control Bill, which did not come until four months after we had entered the war. In the meantime, however, we had determined most of our policies and had recruited most of the necessary staff on a volunteer basis.

Our organization was based upon intense decentralization under state and county food administrators for purposes of conservation and enforcement of some sections of the law and upon equally intense decentralization, commodity by commodity, of our activities for production, processing, and distribution. At one of our preliminary staff meetings, an energetic soul presented his view of our future organization with charts showing squares, circles, and connecting lines for our future guidance. I suggested that a short-lived emergency organization could be best established by finding a particular person for a particular job, giving him a room, desk, pencils, paper, and a wastepaper basket, and telling him to recruit his own staff from people of experience and to forget charts, since they only created rigidities and problems of protocol.[1]

Washington, at our declaration of war, had no surplus office space. We first set up shop in a few rooms at the Willard Hotel. We then moved for a few weeks to the Interior Building and thence, as we expanded, to a dilapidated old hotel. In August, 1917, we decided to put up temporary wallboard buildings costing $400,000. John Reed Kilpatrick (later Major General), who managed the construction for the contractor, did such an efficient job that we moved into these quarters within sixty days. He opined that they might last for three years.[2]

[1] The quality of our volunteer staff is indicated by their subsequent positions in public life. Two became Cabinet officers—Ray Lyman Wilbur and William N. Doak. Four became Governors of states—Edwin F. Ladd, Huntley N. Spaulding, John M. Parker, and Alfred M. Coates. Four became United States Senators—Robert A. Taft, H. Alexander Smith, Frederic Walcott, and Frederick Sackett. One became Assistant Secretary of State—Joseph P. Cotton—and one a long-time efficient public servant —Sidney A. Mitchell. Two became editors of great publications—Charles Merz and Gertrude B. Lane. And many achieved prominent professional and business positions.

Among those to rise to great eminence was Lewis L. Strauss. He had applied for military service but had been rejected as not physically strong enough. Still determined to volunteer for service, he applied to us but was told by our personnel director that we had openings only for people of experience in food. To emphasize this, the director told him that the only vacancy was for an office boy. Lewis promptly accepted the job. A little later, my secretary being needed for a special job, I made Lewis my secretary. He served during the entire war and the Armistice. Later he became an important banker, and in the Second World War, attached to the financial staff of the Navy, he rose to the rank of Admiral. Still later he became Chairman of the Atomic Energy Commission and has performed many other great public services.

[2] So good was the construction that one building was used for Government offices until 1956—nearly forty years. When it was torn down, Admiral Strauss had the insignia over the door removed and sent it to me as a reminder of many mutually strenuous days.

CHAPTER 5

FOOD-CONTROL LEGISLATION

Although the country was at war, the Allies were dependent on our supplies, and our own markets and production were demoralized, the Congress, fearful of giving the powers for which we asked, delayed action almost four months. The whole concept of government control of the elementary necessities of life was repugnant to most Americans, including members of the Congress, and their education was necessarily slow.

The House Committee on Agriculture, under Chairman Asbury F. Lever, began consideration of a food-control bill on April 21, 1917, or about two weeks before I could return from Europe and explain the authority we needed. The draft of Lever's bill had been prepared by Department of Agriculture officials, who had no understanding of the problems involved.

On May 7, the day after I arrived in Washington, presumably at President Wilson's suggestion to Chairman Lever, I was requested to appear before the Committee. From an advance chat with the friendly Chairman, it was evident that part of the inquiry was to probe my capacity to be Food Administrator. He also indicated that some members of the Committee entertained fantastic ideas of food control and that some of them wanted no controls whatsoever.

This was my first appearance before a Congressional committee, and I was to learn that while most members of such bodies were able and quite helpful, others, mostly from lack of understanding, were somewhat less than accommodating. At this session the Chairman stated that because it related to war measures, the session would be "off the record."

They closely interrogated me on my experiences with Belgian Relief and the Allies; the situations in Germany, Russia, and the Allied countries; and the shipping problem. I soon discovered that the only positive authority in the minds of most of the Committee was to control prices and profiteering by fixing legal minimum and maximum prices of food commodities, but with exemptions to farmers. They leaned toward placing any food control under the Secretary of Agriculture. One of the views expressed was that since we were short of wheat, the Allies should be furnished corn instead. Another was that wheat for our domestic use should be milled to somewhere between 90 and 100 per cent. I explained why these ideas would not work.

It was with a great deal of trepidation that I presented some of my own ideas on what was necessary for effective food control. They were, in general, the conclusions we had reached from the study of Allied experience (see Chapter 1). I was able to dissolve some of the shock over such intrusion in American life and such demands for delegation of power.

Chairman Lever consulted with the President and agreed that my proposals should be adopted. He formulated them into an amendment to his first draft, and the amended bill was reported to the House on June 11 and passed on June 23. It embraced most of the principles for which we had contended.

But Chairman Albert Gore of the Senate Committee on Agriculture was wholly unco-operative. He introduced a food bill of his own which totally emasculated the Lever Bill. The majority of the Committee, however, were sensible. At the suggestion of Senator Kenyon, a member of the Committee, I sent the following note to President Wilson on June 15, 1917:

DEAR MR. PRESIDENT:

Senator Kenyon informs me that he believes great expedition could be accomplished with the Food Bill in the Senate by the introduction of the

Lever Bill at once. . . . I understand from him that the Committee, owing to its internal divisions, would only be likely to do this "by request" and that the request would need come from yourself. If it were done it would place the Food Bill in front of the discussion on the Revenue Bill and would probably save a month or two in time.

HERBERT HOOVER

The President made the request on June 18.

On July 15, Senator James A. Reed, Democrat from Missouri, a bitter opponent of the President, delivered a stinging personal attack upon me on the Senate floor. I discovered later that Reed's law firm had received retainers from certain processors who objected to the prospect of regulated profits during the war. One of his charges was that I was a tool of the British; another was that I and others had grafted money from the Belgian Relief. I did not reply, but John White, who had been one of the Directors of the Belgian Relief and was now on our staff in Washington, without consulting me, smashed out a reply in the press. He quoted from the minutes of the Commission which anticipated that some "swine" would accuse us of graft and that we had, at the very outset of the Commission, appointed an independent firm of auditors to check the money and the accounts. White implied that the swine had now appeared. The Senator turned his hose of slime onto poor John. Among other things, he alleged that White was an Englishman. White assembled his ancestral heritage over seven generations and proved that he had deeper roots in America than the Senator. Senator James Phelan of California delivered an eloquent and powerful oration in answer to Reed. But Senator Reed never relaxed on food matters.

On June 19, at its request, I appeared before the Senate Agricultural Committee. I had prepared an opening statement which reviewed the Lever Bill and the reasons for it. Some parts of this statement have interest as illustrating the Allied and our own food difficulties at this time:

The first question that arises is whether national necessity has reached the point which demands immediate legislative action. It seems scarcely necessary to prove that there has been a shortage in the world's food supply this last year. The terrific drain on our surplus and the extraordinary prices paid to us for food are ample evidences of this. The real question is whether this shortage will continue next year; whether the necessities of our allies require special effort on our part to increase our export to them, and what our own internal situation has become and is likely to develop into under this shortage.

I then detailed the European and other world supplies and continued:

The deficiency . . . [in Allied supplies] must be made up of self-denial on their part and rigid economy and saving of waste on our part. I am confident that with sufficient endeavor . . . we can increase our surplus to meet . . . [their] demands. It in any event means privation to them, but such effort on our part . . . [will assure] their constancy in the war, for without adequate food supply no European population will continue to fight and we shall find ourselves alone as the enemy of Germany.

We already have one bitter experience of identical character. The revolution in Russia . . . [started from a food shortage]. We see unfolding before our eyes at least the temporary paralysis of an ally. If through any failure of ours, we should bring about this situation among our western allies or among our own people, there will rest upon us the responsibility for a failure of civilization. . . .

We are just finishing a year of preliminary experience with unchecked suction from the food vacuum of Europe, and, as the food supply of the world will be even less next year than last . . . we already find ourselves with unprecedented prices and with our distributing trades rampant with speculation. This speculation is not wholly deliberate, but arises from the endeavor of every link in the distributing chain to protect itself from the uncertainties of the future. . . . [For instance] we have such a situation in the canning trade, where the entire output of the American canners for 1917 has been sold to the jobbers before the vegetables, fruit or fish to be packed have . . . [been picked or caught].

We are confronted daily and hourly with . . . a large amount of rank speculation . . . by persons not engaged in actual commerce or distribution. Thousands of men in this country who never owned a commodity in their lives have bought canned goods, flour, wheat, and every food commodity to speculate . . . [on] the rise of prices.

We now have a . . . cost of living . . . [transcending] the abilities of certain sections of the population to . . . secure proper nourishment. Unless we can ameliorate this condition and unless we can prevent further advances in price, we must confront an entire rearrangement of the wage level, with all the hardships and social disturbances which necessarily follow.

The character of the legislation . . . [should endow] us with the tools. . . .

The legislation proposed does not confer food dictatorship, nor does the administration . . . contemplate anything of that nature. The food administrations of Europe and the powers that they possess are [necessarily] of the nature of dictatorship. . . . Our concept of the problem in the United States is that we should assemble the voluntary effort of the people and the men who represent the great trades; that we should, in effect, undertake with their cooperation the regulation of the distributing machinery of the country. . . . And at the same time we propose to mobilize the spirit of self-denial and self-sacrifice . . . in order that we may reduce our national waste.

If democracy is worth anything, we can do these things by cooperation, by stimulation, by self-sacrifice, by the patriotic mobilization of the brains of this country. . . .

Food administration, as we see it, falls into four great branches: The *first,* the control of our exports; *second,* the instrumentalities which we set up . . . to regulate trade to the exclusion of both legitimate and illegitimate speculation; *third,* the mobilization of the women and men of the country . . . as actual members of the food administration to carry out . . . the advice and directions which we give to them . . . *fourth,* the erection in every State in the Union . . . [of the same] form of food administration and . . . decentralization of our functions. . . .

We must . . . put such restrictions upon the export of foodstuffs as will leave us a proper supply for our own people, lest with the great pull of this tremendous vacuum, we be left next spring with insufficient . . . [food].

. . . [With regard to] the elimination of speculation and evil practices —If we assume that the farmer . . . himself last year received an average of . . . $1.60 per bushel for his wheat, then, with the addition of the normal manufacturing cost, righteous profits of distribution, the wholesale price of flour should not . . . in the larger consuming centers have exceeded $9 per barrel, and yet the price of flour at a great many centers

. . . has been as high as $15 per barrel. . . . Some one is taking . . . [this toll per] barrel on 10,000,000 barrels per month. . . .

I did not convince Senator Gore.

On July 21, after a long delay, most of which was caused by the Senator, a bill was finally passed by the Senate—with a mass of amendments and impossible provisions. On July 25, it was sent to joint conference with the House. A large majority of the conferees favored the Lever Bill, and with one serious deletion, that version emerged. It was passed by the House by unanimous vote. Its foes in the Senate argued for a few more days, but the Senate finally passed the conference report on August 8, with sixty-six votes for and only seven against. It was signed by the President on August 10, 1917—my forty-third birthday.

SUMMARY OF THE FOOD CONTROL ACT

The Food Control Act comprised more than 7,500 words. The following is a summary of its provisions:

Section 1 authorized the President to make such regulations and issue such orders as were essential to carry out the provisions of the Act.

Section 2 authorized the President to enter into any voluntary arrangements or agreements, to create and use any agency or agencies, to accept the services of any person without compensation, to cooperate with any agency or person, to utilize any Government department or agency, and to coordinate their activities so as to avoid any preventable loss or duplication of effort or funds.

Section 3 provided that no person acting either as a voluntary or paid employee, or member of advisory committees having a personal interest, should use his position to influence contracts or employment, with the further provision that such a person should declare his interest and not participate in awarding such a contract.

Section 4 made it unlawful to wilfully destroy or waste supplies of necessities, to impede or limit facilities for harvesting, transportation, manufacture, storage or distribution, to exact excessive prices, or to aid or abet such acts.

Section 5 authorized the President to require licenses for importation, manufacture, and storage or distribution of necessities, to prescribe regulations for conduct thereunder, and upon proof of violation of these regulations to revoke the license of the offender. Exemption was granted to farmers and to retailers whose gross sales were less than $100,000 per annum. The licensing provision was not to be used to impose taxes on imports or movement of articles in interstate commerce.

Section 6 prohibited wilful hoarding of necessities, holding them beyond a reasonable time, or contracting or conspiring with any other person to do so. Farmers and certain produce exchange operations were exempted.

Section 7 provided for legal proceedings against hoarders and the disposition of the commodity hoarded.

Section 8 provided penalties for any person who wilfully destroyed necessities or restricted their supply.

Section 9 provided penalties for conspiracies or agreements to violate any provisions of the Act.

Section 10 authorized the President to requisition necessities and storage facilities for support of the Army and Navy at just compensation (with right to court review), reasonable trade needs being exempted.

Section 11 authorized the President "from time to time to purchase, to store, to provide storage facilities for, and to sell for cash at reasonable prices, wheat, flour, meal, beans, and potatoes. . . ." The price paid was not to be less than determined minimum prices, and moneys received from sales could be used as a revolving fund and balances recovered into the Treasury.

Section 12 authorized the President, for public use connected with the common defense, to requisition any factory, packing house, or other plant in which necessities might be processed, and to make regulations for operation of such facilities. Compensation and moneys received from such operation could be used as a revolving fund or paid into the Treasury.

Section 13 authorized the President to prevent undue depression, fluctuation of prices, injurious speculation or unjust market manipulation, and misleading market quotations, and to prescribe regulations governing or prohibiting transactions on any exchange or Board of Trade.

Section 14 provided that the President, in order to stimulate production of wheat, could guarantee a reasonable price of wheat based on

No. 1 Northern Spring or its equivalent in the principal markets, and provided that the guaranteed price for the 1918 harvest be no less than $2 per bushel.

This section also authorized the President to fix import duties which would bring the price of imports up to the guarantee levels, to buy and sell wheat in order to support the guarantees, and to use the proceeds from sales as revolving funds.

Section 15 prohibited the making or import of distilled spirits and authorized the President to fix alcoholic content and regulate the use of fruit, food or feed for vinous or malt liquors.

Section 16 authorized the President to commandeer distilled spirits at just prices and redistribute them in public interest.

Section 17 provided penalties for persons who wilfully assaulted, resisted or impeded any employee or agent of the United States in the execution of his duties.

Section 18 authorized an appropriation of $2,500,000 for administrative expenditures to June 30, 1918.

Section 19 authorized an appropriation for $150,000,000 working capital and provided for regular reports to the President and the Congress.

Section 20 provided that employees under the Act were not exempt from military service.

Sections 21, 22 and 23 required from the Food Administration accounts, annual reports and other routine formalities.

Section 24 terminated the Act at peace except for the fulfillment of outstanding obligations.

Penalties for violation varied from fines of $5 to $10,000 to one to two years in jail, or both.

A separate act authorized the President and the Secretary of Agriculture to make food surveys and conduct agricultural research.

The major weakness of the legislation was the deletion of authority to buy and sell animal products and sugar. In the course of this narrative, I will show that in these commodities there arose crises which brought great dangers to our farmers and which, at one time, endangered our whole economic stability.

CHAPTER 6

ORGANIZATION OF OTHER WAR-SUPPLY AGENCIES

The methods by which other war-supply agencies were organized materially affected the Food Administration because we needed coordination with and among all of them.

I have noted that in the early stages of the war the President had a penchant for setting up war agencies in the form of commissions, boards, or committees in order to avoid Congressional obstacles in delegations of authority. Most of these early creations were considered incomplete without a resurrected colonel of the Spanish-American War. Also, many civilians in these agencies were given Army or Navy commissions. In full session, with all their papers in front of them, these boards were truly impressive. The Food Administration stood alone as the only war agency unencumbered with costume jewelry.

These were good men who worked in these other agencies. I spent much time listening to moans and frustrations concerning their organizations. Democracy has to learn many of its lessons with tears—or laughter.

These boards and commissions soon began to fall apart because of conflicts, quarrels, and several scandals. In July, some of their leading men urged the President to appoint a single directive head, and I joined in this recommendation, citing the Allied experience in the first year of the war. The President was himself a good administrator, with a strong instinct for delegating work, and in the end, he did ensconce a single administrative head for each war agency. Such was the slow evolution in the Railway Board, which was abolished in December, 1917; Secretary of the Treasury William G. McAdoo was appointed Railway Administrator. Edward N. Hurley was appointed Chairman of the Shipping Board and given full administrative powers. Likewise, Vance McCormick, Chairman of the War Trade Board, was given complete authority in October, 1917. In March, 1918, full powers of administration over the War Industries Board were given to Bernard Baruch. All were most able men.

CREATING THE FUEL ADMINISTRATION

In August, 1917, President Wilson asked if I would include in my organization coal, oil, and fuel control generally. He stated that the existing setup had proved very unsatisfactory and that fuel control had been provided for in the Food Control Act. He added that he understood that Congressman Lever had discussed the coal provisions with me while the bill was in committee and that I knew the coal business and had no connection with the coal industries. I proposed to him that fuel control be set up as an independent agency with a single administrator directly under himself, as it could then deal on an equal footing with all the other war agencies. I told him that there were three men in my own organization who were performing tasks less exacting than they were qualified to do and who might be used. I recommended that President Harry Garfield of Williams College be appointed Fuel Administrator, and he appointed as his assistants two men from the Food Administration—Mark L. Requa, a highly qualified petroleum engineer, and, as legal adviser, Walter Hope, an able lawyer.

I subsequently found Dr. Garfield an able head for his coal division—Henry Taylor. These men organized the agency in the same manner as the Food Administration was set up and did a successful job.

THE AMERICAN WAR COUNCIL

The members of all the war agencies spent endless time getting inter-agency problems settled. The Government broke out with a rash of co-ordinating committees of co-ordinators. We ran the words "co-ordination" and "co-operation" ragged. Some examples of the problems involved were: whether American ships were to be used for food or for the Army; whether railway facilities were to give priority to transport coal or food; and whether farm boys were to be drafted away from food production.

The prewar Government departments, except War, Navy, Agriculture, and Interior, were politically dominated agencies panting for publicity. Daily, one saw one of these departments grab a piece of war work and run to the press with the glad tidings. But after news of the prize had faded from the front page, some upstart war organization usually had to take it over in order either to kill it or to make it function.

Finally Dr. Garfield, Vance McCormick, and I joined in a recommendation to Mr. Wilson that he call periodic meetings of the war-agency heads where all sides of an inter-agency question could be thrashed out in his presence and his decision made on the spot.

On March 20, 1918, the President called the first weekly meeting of what became known as the American War Council, consisting of the Secretaries of War, Navy, and Treasury, together with the heads of the Munitions, Food, Fuel, Shipping, Railway, and War Trade agencies.

The Council dealt not only with such questions as co-ordination of land and sea transport and distribution of manpower and priorities, but also with economic strategy. The President came more and more to rely upon this group for advice on matters affecting the war.

Hurley graphically described one Council sitting in his book, *The Bridge to France,* saying, "In the thirty years of my business career, I never had been associated with a group who worked together so harmoniously and effectively." McCormick described it as "a clearing-house of facts and policy."

THE EXCESS-PROFITS TAX

Early in July, 1918, I urged upon the President the necessity for broad tax action by the Congress in order to prevent excessive profits by low-cost processors of food and other war supplies, a problem which arose from Government price-fixing. We had to set prices which would spur high-cost producers to action, and thus low-cost producers were making inordinate profits out of the war. Mr. Wilson asked Senator F. M. Simmons to go into the question with me. The Senator warmed to the idea and requested that I spell it out in a memorandum. I did so on July 8. The memorandum set forth the problem and recommended a graduated tax on profits in cases where prices were fixed by the Government. My memorandum is too long for quotation here, but Senator Simmons presented it to the Senate Committee on Finance, and the memorandum appears in its records. On the Senator's recommendation to the Congress, the proposal was enacted into law, terminable with the coming of peace.

CHAPTER 7

MISCELLANEOUS PROBLEMS IN THE ORGANIZATION OF THE FOOD ADMINISTRATION

Our concept of food administration was that it should be based upon the co-operation of the food trades and reinforced by public opinion. We set up committees, under strong executive chairmen, representing the producers, processors, and distributors of the various food commodities. We entered into contracts with them covering the measures necessary for them to aid in our work. We found among the trades a fine desire by the great majority for national service, as befitted men whose sons were in the fighting forces. However, we had to deal with a small minority of dissenters.

THE ANTI-TRUST LAWS

Many problems arose in consequence of this method. At once our trade committees raised the question of whether these activities violated the Anti-Trust Laws. Judge Curtis H. Lindley, the head of our Legal Division, had assured me that contracts entered into with these committees by an authorized Government official to control prices, profits, and distribution would not be a violation of these laws. But the trades wanted, and rightly, more assurance than a legal opinion from us. Therefore, on August 22, 1917, I addressed the President and the Attorney General on the subject:

DEAR MR. PRESIDENT:

We are squarely up against the determination of a matter of policy that I feel is of so much intrinsic importance that I have no right to act without your approval. I attach hereto an application to the Attorney General for an opinion which needs your approval.

In . . . bold terms, it is . . . the creation by the Food Administration, representing yourself, of a combination in restraint of trade. . . .

I then cited several instances where such contracts would protect both the farmer and the consumer.

The President approved as follows:

23 August 1917

MY DEAR MR. HOOVER:

Personally I entirely approve of a "combination" such as the one here proposed, for it is *not* in restraint of trade.

I have taken pleasure in approving your request for an opinion from the Attorney General.

WOODROW WILSON

My letter to Attorney General Thomas W. Gregory was as follows:

August 22, 1917

DEAR SIR:

An important question has arisen in connection with functions and powers of the U.S. Food Administrator, an office created by Executive Order pursuant to the provisions of the Act of Congress generally known as the Food Control Act, approved August 10, 1917.

Your official opinion is respectfully requested on the following inquiry:

Section 2 of the Food Control Act gives the President, acting through a delegated agency, power "to enter into any voluntary arrangements or agreements."

It has become apparent that to accomplish what is contemplated by the Act, as set forth in Section 1, "to establish and maintain governmental control of necessaries," it is necessary to enter into certain contracts or agreements with the different trades, which in normal times, if entered into between private parties, would be declared void under the provisions of the anti-trust laws of the United States.

For example,—in order to control and stabilize the price of sugar it would be necessary to obtain an agreement between the Food Administrator and the sugar beet manufacturers in the United States whereby they would bind themselves to sell their output for a price not greater than that determined by the Food Administrator,—to be a fair and just one. It would also be necessary for these beet sugar producers to pool their product and provide for its distribution through the means of a selling agency,—under such regulations as may be provided by the Food Administrator.

Has the President, acting through the U.S. Food Administrator, the power to enter into this class of contracts with parties engaged in the various trades,—or to accomplish the same results by regulations made by the Food Administrator and accepted by the parties, which contracts would be in violation of the law if entered into between private individuals acting without intervention of a governmental agency? . . .

HERBERT HOOVER

Attorney General Gregory's opinion of August 23 fully sustained Judge Curtis Lindley's opinion, and with his approval, we made it public. There were no legal proceedings against the co-operating trades either during or after the war.

CONTROL OF IMPORTS AND EXPORTS

One of the most important instruments of the Food Administration was the control of exports and imports of food and collateral commodities. Control of the outward flow was necessary to prevent any excessive flow or manipulation of our markets by foreign purchasing agencies, and equally important was the need to direct the flow to those nations where supplies were needed to win the war.

The delay by the Congress in the Export and Import Control Act for two and one-half months after the President requested it resulted in great losses, both to our own people and to the Allies. When the law was finally enacted, on June 22, 1917, the President issued an executive order establishing an "Export and Import Commission," under the chairmanship of the Secretary of Commerce, of which I was a member.

At the recommendation of this Commission, the embargoes were tightened by the President on July 15, 17, and 22. On August 27, further restrictions were imposed to prevent Neutrals from trading with the enemy. The Trading with the Enemy Act of October 6 vested in the President still wider powers over these matters.

The management of export and import licenses was carried out initially by the Department of Commerce, but its work was slow and very unsatisfactory. Moreover, negotiations with foreign governments were taking up too much of the Commissioners' time.

At the Commission's recommendation, the President, by executive order on October 12, created the War Trade Board. Chairman Vance McCormick was given the necessary authority for leadership. The members of the Board were selected, in co-operation with Mr. McCormick, by the Departments of State, Treasury, and Commerce, the Shipping Board, the War Industries Board, and the Food Administration. John Beaver White and Dr. Alonzo E. Taylor represented us on the Board, and the Board made all licenses for food exports and imports subject to the approval of the Food Administrator.

CONSOLIDATION OF FOOD PURCHASING AGENCIES

The Army, Navy, and Marine Corps, the Allied purchasing agencies, Neutrals, and the Red Cross were each independently purchasing their own supplies. Their competition with each other and the consuming public raised havoc in the food markets and increased prices unnecessarily. They muddied the channels of distribution, and in consequence there was much profiteering. Immediately upon the passage of the Food Control Law in August, 1917, we required that all export purchases of grain and cereal products by the Allies and Neutrals be made through the Food Administration's Grain Corporation as a condition for granting them export licenses.

A committee was set up in the War Industries Board to co-ordinate Allied purchases of all other kinds of food. This did not work satisfactorily because the War Industries personnel were not food men, and on September 24, 1917, I addressed the President concerning this category of purchasers as follows:

DEAR MR. PRESIDENT:

In accordance with our conversation, it seems to me desirable that some direction should be given by yourself as to the conduct of Allied Government food purchases in this country. The control of these purchases rests under the Treasury Agreement of August 24th, in a committee of Judge Lovett, Mr. Baruch, and Mr. Brookings.

The Allied requirements in certain commodities are so large as to require . . . daily, and even hourly, cooperation in coordinating them to the ebb and flow of our domestic . . . supplies. . . . It is, therefore, hopeless to try to work the Food Administration without our having the immediate direction of their purchases. . . .

. . . I believe it is highly desirable for you to give . . . [this committee] direction that their responsibilities should be delegated to us. . . .

Some direction of this kind is . . . necessary . . . in order that we should have authority to direct Allied [food] purchasing agents to look to us for direction, and to furnish us with data as to their requirements.

HERBERT HOOVER

Bernard Baruch, Chairman of the War Industries Board, supported my proposal in a letter to the President on September 26. The next day, Mr. Wilson directed the transfer of these functions to the Food Administration.

CONSOLIDATING ALL OFFICIAL FOOD BUYING

After lengthy negotiations with the military agencies and at the President's urging, these agencies agreed to do their purchasing of food and collateral supplies under our general direction. On October 24, 1917, we set up a Division of Coordination of Purchase in the Food Administration and announced its purposes through the press:

. . . to coordinate the purchases of the Allies and the Food Administration of such important staple food supplies as those mentioned in the

President's Proclamation of October 8, 1917, and to cooperate with the Army, Navy, and other governmental departments in an endeavor to coordinate so far as practicable their purchases of such food supplies.

To facilitate the military purchases, we set up, in co-operation with the Secretaries of War and Navy, the Food Purchase Board, comprised of the head of our Division of Coordination of Purchase, Herbert Gutterson, as Chairman; the Quartermaster General of the Army, General R. E. Wood; the representative of the Navy, Admiral Samuel McGowan; and Dr. F. W. Taussig, representing the Federal Trade Commission. The Food Purchase Board had offices in our building, and its work was conducted by our staff.

One of our problems in this field was that the military departments required large offerings of commodities produced by small processors which no one processor could fulfill. The resulting effect was that brokers and commission houses were buying competitively to secure large enough quantities to make a bid. This was particularly the case in canned vegetables, for there were many thousands of small canneries. We therefore sent the following memorandum to the military agencies, proposing an allocation of orders rather than bids:

The Food Administration . . . considers that it is vital to the general welfare that these large purchases in certain commodities shall be made by plans of allocation among manufacturers at "fair and just" prices, the efforts of the Federal Trade Commission to be directed to see that costs are not inflated.

In every case where plans of allocation are determined, none of the buying agencies above mentioned shall go into the market independently without the approval of the Division of Coordination of Purchase of the Food Administration.

The detailed procedure in carrying out allocations shall be in accordance with the plan of procedure issued from time to time by the Division of Coordination of Purchase for the individual commodities.

It required about six months to bring the large domestic and all foreign governmental food purchases under Food Administration control. Because of the enormous quantities involved, this control, as will be seen later, became a major instrument of the Food Administration in regulating prices in order to stimulate production by the farmers and to protect the consumers. The money payments for purchases were made directly by the various departments concerned.

The total of all purchases made under the Division of Coordination of Purchase during the First World War amounted to more than $2,300,000,000. This did not include the purchases controlled by the Grain Corporation and the Sugar Equalization Board, which are described later.

QUALITY OF FOOD

Since food purchases passed through the Food Administration, we had a responsibility for the quality of the food. We determined that the Food Administration would not be involved in the "embalmed beef" or other food scandals which had disgraced the Spanish-American War. The Department of Agriculture conducted its usual inspection of certain products under the Pure Food and Packing House regulations. But to be doubly sure that everything was covered, we created an inspection service of our own to include every purchase by the Division of Coordination of Purchase. We never had a complaint from the Allies, and the American soldiers and sailors were the best-fed fighting men in the world.

THE FOOD CONTROL ACT WAS TOO DRASTIC

Under the Food Control Act, we had a multitude of possible infractions of the law to look after. The Congress, in providing penalties for infractions, had no constitutional difficulties concerning interstate commerce because that would come under federal-court jurisdiction. But the Congressional committees were posed with the problem of enforcement in case of intrastate violations. They could not constitutionally impose the duty of enforcement on local authorities or courts. To avoid this difficulty, they devised a licensing system whereby the licensee was to do business under stated regulations. Without powers of enforcement in local courts, the only penalty for violation of the licensing regulations which the committees could devise was to cancel the violator's license and thus close up his business. In practice, this was far too drastic a penalty, for it meant that the transgressor, whether willful or otherwise, was deprived of the opportunity to earn a livelihood for himself and his family and was often ruined in business.

About 95 per cent of patriotic processors and distributors were controlled by the co-operating committees of the trades and by the regulations contracted with them. But it developed that there were about 5 per cent who refused to join in our trade-committee agreements and sought to gain special advantages for themselves. In time, we were compelled to license several entire trades in order to circumvent these poachers. Reluctantly, we had to undertake the huge burden of issuing more than 250,000 licenses. During the period in which the licenses were in force, our Enforcement Division had about 8,000 cases of violations. Most of them were not willful, and our officials simply reminded the offenders of the law and gave them a reprimand.

In some cases of more gravity, we settled for a modest contribution to the Red Cross. In one case, a meat packer willfully violated his license three times for huge profits. Our representative suggested the contribution of a very large sum to the Red Cross, which the packer paid rather than lose his business. Others contributed as much as $10,000, but most of these cases brought small sums. We actually canceled only about 200 licenses out of 250,000, and those for willful or repeated violations. The number of transactions in the business world under our voluntary agreements and licenses probably amounted to hundreds of millions every day, and hundreds of millions of dollars changed hands. The meager percentage of transgressors was a great tribute to the high level of integrity and patriotism of the American people.

CHAPTER 8

REDUCTION OF FOOD CONSUMPTION AND WASTE IN HOMES AND PUBLIC EATING PLACES

Our program of conservation was directed mainly to the staples we needed for support of the Allies—wheat, meat, fats, dairy products, and sugar. In previous chapters I have described the Allied food needs and the desperate situation in our United States supplies, which, because of drought, the orgy of foreign buying prior to the Food Control Act, and other dislocations, amounted to a statistical vacuum of supplies for the Allies. I have stated that we were convinced that the intelligence and sense of service of the American people would be more effective than card-coupon rationing enforced by law. The housewives of America controlled at their own tables about 80 per cent of the nation's food consumption, and public eating places controlled the remainder. It was up to us to mobilize them for the practical tasks they could perform.

We began our organizing with a statement from President Wilson on June 12, 1917:

My dear Mr. Hoover:

It seems to me that the inauguration of that portion of the plan for food administration which contemplates a national mobilization of the great voluntary forces of the country which are ready to work toward saving food and eliminating waste admits of no further delay.

The approaching harvesting, the immediate necessity for wise use and saving, not only in food but in all other expenditures, the many undirected and overlapping efforts being made toward this end, all press for national direction and inspiration. While it would in many ways be desirable to wait [for] complete legislation establishing the food administration, it appears to me that so far as voluntary effort can be assembled, we should not wait any longer, and therefore I would be very glad if you would proceed in those directions at once.

The women of the Nation are already earnestly seeking to do their part in this our greatest struggle for the maintenance of our national ideals, and in no direction can they so greatly assist as by enlisting in the service of the Food Administration and cheerfully accepting its direction and advice. . . .

I trust, therefore, that the women of the country will not only respond to your appeal and accept the pledge to the Food Administration which you are proposing, but that all men also who are engaged in the personal distribution of foods will co-operate with the same earnestness and in the same spirit. I give you full authority to undertake any steps necessary for the proper organization and stimulation of their efforts.

WOODROW WILSON

Under Dr. Wilbur's Conservation Division, we made a preliminary test in July, 1917, of the feasibility of taking housewives of the country into the Food Administration itself. This test, made by our state food administrators in about one million households in twenty states, proved so successful that after the passage of the Food Control Law we expanded this method into a nation-wide campaign beginning in September, 1917.

Those who wished to join with us were furnished, by our local food administrators, a placard for their front windows or doors proclaiming that they were members of the Food Administration. They were also furnished a card describing methods of saving food and the commodities which we vitally needed for the Allies and our armed forces. Any changes in our programs were communicated through the local food administrators and the press. In response to the campaign, between 13,000,000 and 14,000,000 housewives out of 20,000,000 signed up.

John McE. Bowman, a leading hotel man, undertook under Dr. Wilbur the task of the Public Eating Division, with subdivisions for hotels, restaurants, dining cars, and ships. The proposals concerning the items to be conserved were the same as those made to the housewives, although the rules differed in every trade. All eating places were asked to pledge themselves to our purpose and to become members of the Food Administration. Upon acceptance, they were authorized to display our insignia. Their co-operation was magnificent.

Since the co-operation of the press was vital to us, we sent an appeal to 2,500 newspapers and magazines. It said:

> The world as a whole is faced with a definite and growing food shortage. . . . we must enlarge our food service to the world, not only as a war measure, but as a measure of humanity itself. If we can secure the emplacement of this idea in the minds of the people, the sequent suggestions of constructive order which we may make will fall not only on a receptive mind but upon a convinced intelligence. . . . We believe that we must first prove the case. . . .
>
> . . . we are wholly and absolutely dependent upon the press of the country. If we do not receive this support, the problem is hopeless. If we do have it, it can be solved.

The press response was immediate and heartwarming.

Through our Education Division, we secured an amazing amount of free billboard, streetcar, newspaper, magazine, and retail store window advertising space, contributed to us without charge, proclaiming that "Food Will Win the War."

We won the co-operation of practically all nation-wide civic associations, as well as that of the churches. We organized a bureau of volunteer speakers, primarily for inspirational purposes, but also for the instruction of our state, county, city, and village food administrators.

We set up programs of food conservation directed toward children. On August 23, Mr. Wilson directed this special appeal to school officials for their co-operation:

> The war is bringing to the minds of our people a new appreciation of the problems of national life and a deeper understanding of the meaning and aims of democracy. Matters which heretofore have seemed commonplace and trivial are seen in a truer light. The urgent demand

for the production and proper distribution of food and other national resources has made us aware of the close dependence of individual on individual and nation on nation. The effort to keep up social and industrial organizations in spite of the withdrawal of men for the Army has revealed the extent to which modern life has become complex and specialized. . . .

In order that there may be definite material at hand with which the schools may at once expand their teaching I have asked Mr. Hoover and Commissioner [of Education] Claxton to organize the proper agencies for the preparation and distribution of suitable lessons for the elementary grades and for the high school classes. Lessons thus suggested will serve the double purpose of illustrating in a concrete way what can be undertaken in the schools and of stimulating teachers in all parts of the country to formulate new and appropriate materials drawn directly from the communities in which they live.

By January, 1918, we were confronted with our most difficult food crisis in obtaining sufficient supplies for the Allies. To launch further restrictions, we secured a strong proclamation from the President on January 18, 1918, establishing "wheatless" days. It said:

Many causes have contributed to create the necessity for a more intensive effort on the part of our people to save food in order that we may supply our associates in the war with the sustenance vitally necessary to them in these days of privation and stress. The reduced productivity of Europe because of the large diversion of man power to the war, the partial failure of the harvests, and the elimination of the more distant markets for foodstuffs through the destruction of shipping places the burden of their subsistence very largely on our shoulders.

The Food Administration has formulated suggestions which, if followed, will enable us to meet this great responsibility, without any real inconvenience on our part.

. . . Consumers should reduce their purchases of wheat products for home preparation to at most 70 per cent of those of last year, or when buying bread should purchase mixed cereal breads from the bakers.

To provide sufficient cereal food, homes, public eating places, dealers, and manufacturers should substitute potatoes, vegetables, corn, barley, oats, and rice products, and the mixed cereal bread and other products of the bakers which contain an admixture of other cereals.

In order that consumption may be restricted to this extent, Mondays and Wednesdays should be observed as WHEATLESS DAYS each week, and one meal each day should be observed as a WHEATLESS MEAL.

In both homes and public eating places, in order to reduce the consumption of beef, pork, and sheep products, Tuesday should be observed as meatless days in each week, one meatless meal should be observed in each day; while, in addition, Saturday in each week should further be observed as a day upon which there should be no consumption of pork products.

. . . I am confident that the great body of our women, who have labored so loyally in cooperation with the Food Administration for the success of food conservation, will strengthen their efforts and will take it as a part of their burden in this period of national service to see that the above suggestions are observed throughout the land.

WOODROW WILSON

The omitted paragraphs in this quotation referred to processing and trade regulations, which I take up later.

The Food Administration added the following to the President's rules:

The Food Administrator in each State will announce the meal to be observed as a wheatless meal in his State. If no meal is designated, the . . . Food Administration prefers that the evening meal be wheatless.

It is further desired, in order that meat and pork products be conserved, that one meatless day (Tuesday) in every week, and one meatless meal in every day be observed, and, in addition, two porkless days (Tuesday and Saturday) in every week be strictly kept. By "meatless" is meant without hog, cattle, or sheep products. On other days use mutton and lamb in preference to beef or pork. By "porkless" is meant without pork, bacon, ham, lard or pork products, fresh or preserved. Use fish, poultry, and eggs.

For . . . situations where exceptions are necessary application should be made to the State Food Administrators.

And we added this advice:

Loyalty in little things is the foundation of the national strength. Disloyalty in little things gives aid to the enemy. Do not limit the food of growing children. Eat sufficient food to maintain health; the Nation needs strong people.

Cooperate with your local and Federal food administrators. Take their advice.

Preach and practice the "gospel of the clean plate."

Housekeepers should help the stores to cut down deliveries.

Use local supplies; this saves railroad transportation.

The housewives and the public eating places did such a job of saving fats and our farmers such a job in sending fatter hogs to market that in the shipping crisis of mid-February, 1918, our storage became overcrowded and we had to retreat on the pork-products front and order a mild relaxation of our rules. On May 2, we abandoned meatless days, and on June 12, we suggested the following substitute method to conserve beef:

The demand for beef for our army, the armies of the Allies and their civil population . . . [is] beyond our present supplies. On the other hand we have . . . [an] increased supply of pork [products]. . . . It will therefore be a direct service to our armies and the Allies if our people will in some degree substitute fresh pork, bacon, ham and sausage for beef products.

We request all hotels and restaurants not to place on their menus or serve . . . beef more than two meals weekly, beef steak more than one meal weekly, and roast beef more than one meal weekly. We ask householders not under any circumstances to buy more than 1¼ lbs. of clear beef weekly . . . per person in the household.

The housewives and eating places responded so quickly that we were able to increase shipments of beef products, and our temporary surplus of pork products decreased—for a while.

We received a multitude of amusing and expressive letters from children. I became convinced that mothers and fathers were using my name to replace their own responsibilities and to restore the disciplines of their own earlier years.

CHAPTER 9

MY PREACHMENTS ON FOOD PROBLEMS

Lest anyone believe that I personally was not vocal on the need for saving food and the reasons therefor, I may mention that between May, 1917, and the Armistice in November, 1918, I made twelve public addresses, issued sixteen press releases in my own name, and wrote twelve magazine articles. I give a condensation of some of them because they illuminate the problems with which we were dealing:

Brown University, May 20, 1917:

. . . I wish to present but one theme to your minds. Our whole food problem revolves around one single factor—the diminishing productivity of Europe and the disruption of commerce by armed barriers.

Since the wonderful world harvest of 1915 the food supplies of the world have been steadily lessening. This year we are faced with a world shortage, and next year this shortage will be greater. Seventy million men in Europe have been called out of productive labor and devoted to fighting and the production of implements of war. The women have been unable to in full renew the harvests, and there has been a great diversion of animals and transport to war. The land is no longer receiving the fertilizer of old. In order to decrease the production of fodder grains and increase the production of bread grains . . . Europe is eating into her capital of animals. . . . foodstuffs are beyond this daily being destroyed at sea in shiploads. Our own allies are separated [by the war] from their normal markets of Russia, Bulgaria, Roumania. . . . [The long journey to the Argentine and Australia limits this source of supplies.]

. . . The impact of this shortage . . . has knocked at every door in the United States. . . . the reverberation of Europe's shortage would have thundered . . . menacingly even had we never entered the war. . . .

I then briefly described our price problems and continued:

These problems are not insoluble if taken in time. In their solution lies a prime test of democracy; the question is, can our form of government put forward the organization, the devotion, the self-denial, the efficiency, the preparation in advance of [the] storm? Must we wait until disaster is upon us and then reap the whirlwind in a lament of "too late"? Can it not only do this in time but can it also do so without resort to measures of Prussianism? I believe it can. I believe our faith is right. . . .

HARVARD UNIVERSITY, JUNE 21, 1917:

This is a civilian's war also. At one time the world summoned to war a small portion of the community, and . . . [the armies] required in their support another small section, and the great . . . [mass] of the nation went its normal courses. To-day autocracy has limited the call of its manhood to the fighting line only by the . . . [need] of the men and women . . . to supply . . . food and munitions. . . .

. . . The food problem is much in our minds to-day because the world's shortage has knocked at every door in this land with the imperious clamor of rising prices. . . . our [will] power alone . . . [can] keep the wolf from the door of the world. . . .

The challenge of Germany is not that men of this democracy will not fight. The challenge is that democracy can not mobilize its civilians to war.

The following is a condensation of a statement published in a prominent women's magazine in August, 1917:

Never before has the American woman faced the opportunity and the responsibility that are before her today. . . . The final success of the war . . . depends upon our ability to produce more food, and upon our thrift and self-sacrifice in conserving food. . . .

Great world decisions may follow upon a multiplicity of comparatively minor acts of large groups of our people. The American woman and the American home can, by voluntary act and by thrift, by good will and by patriotic devotion, bring to a successful end the greatest national task that has ever been accepted by the American people.

We were receiving complaints from a minority of the business community about our control measures. Some of them objected to price fixing, others to priorities in supply of coal and manufactured goods; others objected generally to interference with the law of supply and demand. I therefore concluded that an address to the United States Chamber of Commerce might be useful in clarifying some of the facts of life in war. Some parts of this address of September 19, 1917, were as follows:

> Food has gradually, since the war began, assumed a larger place in the economics, the statesmanship, and the strategy of the war until it is my belief that food will win this war—starvation or sufficiency will in the end mark the victor. . . .

I then stated that we were constantly being told that if we would free the law of supply and demand, then rising prices would be the best restraint on consumption. And I added:

> We have . . . listened to the specious arguments of the siren of high prices. . . . It is true high prices reduce consumption, but . . . the burden is thrown on to the class of the most limited means. . . . There is no national conservation in robbing our . . . [workers] of the ability to buy food . . .
>
> . . . If we are to have ascending prices, we must have ascending wages . . . [and that] is the door leading to strikes, disorder . . . [inflation] and defeat. . . . The verdict of the whole of the world's [war] experience is in favor of price control as the lesser evil. . . .
>
> We shall find as we go on with the war and its increasing economic disruption that first one commodity after another will need to be taken into control. We will, however, profit by experience if . . . we deal with every situation on its merits. So long as demand and supply have free play in a commodity, we had best leave it alone. Our . . . [action] in other commodities must be designed to repair the break, not with a view to setting up new economic systems or theories. . . .
>
> . . . let no one be under the illusion that selfishness or greed has dis-

appeared from this great Republic . . . [although it represents only a small minority of a devoted people. But let there be no mistake, we will stop it with all the power of Government.]

The Food Administration has appealed to the commercial community to march with it . . . to our defense.

. . . beyond this they will have proved that democracy is a faith worthy of defense.

The Food Administration was also plagued by complaints and criticisms from professional economists who lived in the world of prewar economics. I determined to answer them in a speech at Pittsburgh on April 18, 1918. The following is a condensation of this address:

The necessity for the creation of food administrations in all the countries at war with Germany arises solely from the situation in overseas shipping. Over one-third of the world's carrying capacity has been diverted directly and indirectly to military purposes, and of the remainder there has been an unceasing loss during the war. There is an abundance of food accessible to the seas, but there are not the ships to carry it from distant points and to still conduct the war.

. . . Every steamer we can save from these long journeys means the possibility of an additional shipload of soldiers and munitions to France. . . .

. . . Nor will the burden grow less in the near future, for every ship we build will be needed to replace losses and to increase our army at the front. This is conservation of ships as well as of food. . . .

In the daily toil of all these Food Administrations there have grown up new . . . terms strange to the lips of all but scientists three years ago. . . . These strange terms [calories, carbohydrates, fats, and vitamins] are . . . silhouetted against this background of world tragedy. . . .

Europe to-day is eating to live, and to live it matters little, for instance, whether fats are drawn from creamery butter, from margarin, from lard, or from vegetable oil or cheese. What does matter to Food Administrators is how much fats can be secured and can be delivered to the needy points with the least use of ships. . . . at one time Europe produced most of her own fats . . . [by import of] a large tonnage of forage for their animals. It requires three times the tonnage to transport fodder than it does the fats. . . .

Aside from the prime necessity of protecting our independence and our institutions, there is but one possible benefit from the war, and that is the stimulation of self-sacrifice in the people, the lifting of its ideals. . . .

There is another side of all this to those of us who have lived behind the German lines. No hour goes by but our . . . [minds] are haunted by the scenes of long lines of emaciated women and children who to-day and for three years have gathered in Belgium for their daily bread from America. That pittance . . . represents scarcely the wastes from American tables. This winter these lines have, for the first time during the war, gathered in the poorer sections of England, France, and Italy. Not only should this pull at our hearts, but beyond this, it is a menace to our very safety. In the presence of a common enemy we sit at a common table with all people. . . . Is the daily call of the Food Administration for less waste, for simpler living, to eat only for strength, not a call to conscience? Is it not a vital call of defense? . . .

The reduction of food supplies below normal . . . caused new currents in our economic life, and the Food Administration has, by force of necessity, had to pioneer untraveled paths in the economic jungle of war. . . .

. . . the European Governments have been compelled to undertake . . . the single-handed purchase of their supplies both for civil and military purposes. There has thus grown up an enormous consolidation of buying of 120,000,000 European people, a phenomenon never before witnessed in the economic history of the world. . . .

Furthermore, we have . . . [called something over 4,000,000 men to arms.] . . . The buying for these men is necessarily concentrated in one agency instead of [retail outlets]. . . .

In order that these . . . buying agencies should not get in each other's way, it has been necessary to place them under control. . . . Therefore, not through any theory, but through an actual physical fact, the price made by this gigantic buying dominates the market.

This is price fixing in a light never contemplated in economic history or theory, and it is time that economic thinkers denude themselves of their procrustean formulas of supply and demand and take cognizance of the facts of life. . . .

. . . Again, [inland] transportation . . . is subject to every vicissitude of war. Temporary stoppages in transport can produce every . . . [variety of] disaster unless some stability is given to markets. Therefore both sides, consumer and producer, must be safe-guarded by wise controls. . . .

But right at this point arises to me a fundamental principle in national war economics. I do not believe that any person in this United States has a right to make 1 cent more profit . . . than he would have made under prewar conditions. I do not care whether this refers to the farmer, to the laborer, to the manufacturer, to the middleman, or to the retailer; to me, every cent taken beyond this standard is money abstracted from the blood and sacrifice of the American people.

I do not believe that extortionate profits are necessary to secure the maximum effort on the part of the American people in this war. If we are going to adopt that theory, we have admitted everything that has been charged against us of being the most materialistic, the most avaricious, and the most venal of people of this world. . . .

. . . a rough calculation indicates that already we have diverted from eight to ten million men from their normal occupations . . . [into arms and the supplies they require]. That is from one-quarter to one-third of our normal productive units. It is possible that we can increase the exertion of the remainder of our productive population. . . . We cannot, however, compass the whole, and the deficiency can only be overcome by the reduction in the consumption of commodities [among civilians].

This does not apply to food alone; it applies to every commodity of which we consume more than is necessary for our health. . . .

. . . The American ideal in executive work is efficiency, but efficiency does not alone mean the best appliances and the greatest numbers made for the least cost. In war it involves a new factor . . . and that is speed. . . .

In this light measures taken, results attained, cannot be judged by the microscopic inspection of the threads of the tapestry. . . . [We do not have] years of careful development. It will be of no avail to us if we lose a war, even though it may cost less per unit than any war in history.

. . . if we are to win the war it will be only because every man, woman, and child charges himself daily and hourly with the test: Does this or that contribute to win the war?

Nor is this the gospel of gloom; it is the gospel of the full health, spirits, and strength of our people. . . .

The foundation of our civilization lies in the stimulation and freedom of self-initiative—the fullest development of the individual. It is the philosophy of peace. . . .

We are in a life-and-death struggle to stamp out a system, to right a [gigantic] wrong, to preserve our institutions, our freedom, to [assure a lasting] peace. . . . We may become the last hope of 350,000,000 over-run, liberty-loving men, [and] women. We must . . . [succeed], or we are no longer free people.

While at Pittsburgh, I explained to the press representatives that the official life of a European food administrator was at most nine months and that having now survived through twelve months, I was hopeful. In any event, as the war persisted and the people better understood our problems, the complaints became fewer and fewer until, with approaching victory, they disappeared.

CHAPTER 10

PROVISION OF SUBSIDIARY FOOD COMMODITIES AND COLLATERAL NON-FOOD COMMODITIES

At this point in the narrative I begin a description of the activities of the Food Administration on a commodity-by-commodity basis. Wherever available, I give the exports each year to the Allies and Neutrals. As far as statistics can show, these figures represent the extra hours of labor and self-denial of the American people.

In total war the entire economy goes awry. Upsets of the law of supply and demand in major commodities disrupt the supply of many collateral commodities. We were extremely loath to expand our controls, but one by one, we were forced to take action on ten secondary food commodities and six collateral non-food articles. The ten secondary foods were:

Rice	Canned Fish
Beans	Canned Corn, Tomatoes, and Peas
Coffee	Dried Fruits
Dairy Products	Cottonseed and Cottonseed Products
Canned Meat	Fresh Fish

The six non-food commodities were:

Ammonia	Binder Twine
Ice	Tin Plate
Arsenic	Jute Bags

RICE

Our Rice Division was originally headed by J. R. Leguenec; upon his joining the Army, he was succeeded by Dana T. Ackerly.

Rice was of importance as a domestic substitute for the wheat needs of the Allies. The Japanese found profitable business in increased exports of Asiatic rice to the United States. Prior to passage of the Food Control Act, the price had risen 50 per cent, and speculation was rife.

In early September, 1917, a month after the Food Control Act was passed, we called in Washington a meeting of a committee of the rice millers and distributors chosen by the trades. We made the usual agreement with them to establish standards of quality, restrict hoarding, and limit profits. The committee recommended that we extend this regulation to all processors and distributors by licensing them all, since some of them would not otherwise co-operate with the committee. The rules were made effective on a trade-wide basis on November 1, 1917.

It was necessary to stimulate production by assuring a price at which the rice farmer could sell his 1918 harvest profitably; also, we had to set a limitation on price to protect the consumer. After many conferences with the rice committee, the Food Administration entered into agreements with it concerning the prices to be paid for the 1918 crop and for imports. The prices for the different grades varied from $6.75 per barrel to $7.50. The markups or profits to be added by millers and distributors were also fixed; these arrangements reduced prices for consumers. We were able to assure the farmers' price through purchases from the rice millers by the Division of Coordination of Purchase and by the Grain Corporation.

These controls were maintained for twenty-one months, until June 21, 1919, by which time the 1918 crop had been marketed. The result of our policies is shown by the following table (in pounds):

Year	Production	Imports	Consumption
Prewar average	681,166,000	209,814,000	874,765,000
1917–1918	964,972,000	298,980,000	1,056,364,000
1918–1919	1,072,389,000	558,048,000	1,462,499,000

The increased production and imports of rice meant a savings in other grains needed more by the Allies. Our shipments of rice to the Allies were (in tons):

Prewar average	16,000
1917	104,000
1918	84,000
1919	188,000

BEANS

We placed the organization of beans under the Grain Corporation, in order to have the advantage of that Corporation's authority to purchase and sell. Because beans are so highly concentrated a food, have such good keeping qualities, and are so easy to prepare, the demand from the military forces greatly increased as the war went on. Prices had increased from about three cents a pound prewar to about twelve cents before the Food Control Act became effective.

We were not able fully to control the 1917 crop because it had been harvested and partly marketed before the Food Control Act went into operation. However, we called a meeting of representatives of the growers and the different levels of distributors on August 21, 1917, ten days after passage of the Act. As a result of this meeting and the organization of a representative committee, we, at their recommendation, licensed all of the trade to prevent further price rises and speculation in the distribution of the remainder of the 1917 crop.

For the 1918 crop, the Food Control Act gave us the authority to buy and sell beans, and we guaranteed a price at which we would purchase the crop from the farmers, varying with the varieties of beans, which we continued with some adjustments, including the 1919 crop. The effect of these policies was (in bushels):

Year	Production	Imports	Consumption
Prewar average	11,166,000	1,492,000	12,319,000
1917–1918	16,045,000	4,343,000	18,545,000
1918–1919	17,397,000	4,210,000	19,507,000

Our exports of beans to the Allies were as follows (in tons):

Prewar average	10,000
1917	56,000
1918	72,000
1919	168,000

COFFEE

During December, 1917, and January, 1918, great speculation in coffee started in the New York Coffee and Sugar Exchange on the theory that the price of everything would go up. There was no scarcity of coffee, and the speculation was all the more unwarranted because the United States was practically the only large market open to Latin-American growers. To meet the situation, we created the Coffee Division under George W. Lawrence and, on January 30, 1918, brought all dealers in coffee under license with regulations which stopped speculation and limited the markups or profits at the various levels of processing and distribution.

Late in June, 1918, São Paulo, the largest coffee-producing state of Brazil, was visited by the heaviest frost in thirty years. Reports indicated that damage to the trees varied from 40 to 80 per cent. The Brazilians hiked their prices, and in October, 1918, with the prospect of peace, the Brazilian market went wild. However, for the ten months of the Food Administration's control of coffee, from January, 1918, to the Armistice in November, 1918, the price to the consumer was held at our restrained level.

The imports and retail prices of coffee during the period of Food Administration control were (in pounds):

Year	Imports	Consumer Price *
Prewar average	907,899,000	.298
1917	1,286,524,000	.302
1918 (until the Armistice)	1,052,202,000	.305

* Green São Paulo—per pound.

The relative index of prices was:

Prewar	100
1917	101
1918 (until the Armistice)	102

After controls were lost at the Armistice, the index was as follows:

1919	145
1920	158

DAIRY PRODUCTS

Our dairy-products operations were placed in our Perishable Foods Division, with William E. Lamb in charge of fresh milk and George E. Haskell in charge of dairy products in general.

Dairy products proved very troublesome. There was no way of determining costs, and consequently prices, because much of the production of dairy products was a sideline for millions of farmers, and the costs to exclusively dairy farmers varied all over the country. Moreover, with the many different end-products, no cost could be assigned to a single item, such as ice cream, cheese, butter, or canned (condensed) milk.

We were plagued by the chronic disputes among dairy farmers, distributors, and consumers of milk in the large cities. Chiefly through our state food administrators, who appointed commissions to negotiate these disputes, a degree of peace was achieved and the milk kept moving.

Because of the decrease of dairy production in Europe, the requirements of the Allies for condensed milk, combined with those of the Belgian Relief, were practically unlimited in amount. They were originally much beyond the capacity of our processors, but condensing milk was an easy addition to milk-processing plants, and under our urging, the capacity was hugely increased. From a prewar average annual export of 15,665,105 pounds, the United States increased the total export in the crop year 1918–1919 to 852,865,414 pounds.

Manufacturers and large distributors of canned milk, butter, and cheese were held under licensing control from November 1, 1917, until two months after the Armistice—January 10, 1919. Under the licenses, the usual regulations were made with regard to profits, markups, and the elimination of waste. Through purchases of our Division of Coordination of Purchase, we were able to assure reasonable prices to the producers and protection to the consumers of these products. Our exports of dairy products to the Allies were as follows (in tons):

Prewar average	13,000
1917	290,000
1918	560,000
1919	751,000

OTHER CANNED GOODS

We set up a Canned Goods Division under Charles H. Bentley and created the usual industry committees (which included the producers of condensed milk, mentioned above). Canned goods were not only a civilian necessity; the war had created an enormous demand from both the American and the Allied military forces.

In Chapter 7, I have described our method of allocation of orders to the many small producers. The great majority of canners cooperated fully under voluntary agreements, but a minority would not go along. We were thus compelled, on October 8, 1917, to license all canners with a capacity of more than five thousand cases annually and to prescribe under the law the rules to which the majority had agreed through their committees. Even this measure proved inadequate; on November 1, to stop bootlegging, we extended the licenses to cover canners of five hundred cases annually.

In preparation for the 1918 season pack, we asked the Federal Trade Commission to make a report on costs in the various branches of the canning industry, upon which basis we fixed fair prices. The canned-food control problems varied with each different commodity placed in cans, and their complexities can only be made clear by some examples.

CANNED MEAT

Practically all canned meat was produced by the larger meat-packing firms; price controls, etc., were conducted under our regulations of the packing industry.

CANNED FISH

In the salmon industry, which was concentrated on the Pacific Coast, the 1917 pack was largely sold to distributors before the Food Control Act went into effect, and we could do little about it. For the 1918 pack, we appointed a committee of our Pacific Coast state food administrators, together with a representative of the Food Administration's Canned Goods Division, to investigate and recommend reasonable prices. The canners accepted the prices, and the Food Administration allotted governmental orders among them.

Sardines were canned in Maine, Canada, and California. In 1917, through an agreement with the Maine packers, a price of $5.60 per case was set. For the 1918 pack, the Maine Food Administrator called a meeting of the fishermen in April, 1918, at which a price of $25 per ton for raw fish was agreed upon. Through the Canadian Food Administrator, an arrangement of the same price was also made with Canadian fishermen. Having established the basic price with the fishermen, the Maine Food Administrator arranged for a committee of the sardine-canning industry to go to Washington, where, on June 5, our Canned Goods Division arranged the price at which the final product would be sold. The same method used in Maine was agreed upon by California fishermen and canners.

A similar procedure was followed in the case of canned tuna.

CANNED CORN, TOMATOES, AND PEAS

These vegetables were produced by hundreds of thousands of growers all over the country and were canned by thousands of processors whose costs varied greatly. From a report of the Federal Trade Commission, we were able, under licenses, to fix maximum margins of profit for canners and markups for distributors. The industry and prices were stabilized through the purchases of our Division of Coordination of Purchase.

ANNUAL SHIPMENTS OF ALL CANNED GOODS TO THE ALLIES (CALENDAR YEAR)

Unfortunately, the Government statistics on canned goods revealed that some of them were kept in tons and some in dollars. However, the results in supplies to the Allies were as designated below (in tons):[1]

Commodity	Prewar Average	1917	1918
Condensed milk	7,833	214,288	275,570
Beef	5,839	32,735	70,729
Pork	2,382	2,689	2,634
Sausage	1,278	3,365	3,175
Salmon	23,729	58,982	55,030
Total	41,061	312,059	407,138

[1] The Food Administration's Statistical Division was dissolved during 1919, and the largest exports were for that year.

Those designated in dollars were:

Commodity	Prewar Average	1917	1918
Other canned fish	$1,233,019	$ 4,789,641	$10,029,197
Other meat products	1,130,998	5,420,841	8,819,996
Fruit	3,570,735	6,859,498	7,302,764
Vegetables	2,158,042	5,450,340	12,419,464
Total	$8,092,794	$22,520,320	$38,571,421

An estimate of the tons in the dollar value of canned goods indicated a total of 333,000 tons for 1917 and 438,000 tons for 1918.

In 1919, the military services' demands were diminished by the Armistice, and their 1919 shipments decreased. We estimated that our needs for the rehabilitation of children, however, amounted to about 300,000 tons of condensed milk alone in 1919.

DRIED FRUITS

The 1917 pack and distribution of dried peaches, raisins, and apples were so far along by the time the Food Control Act was passed that we were able to do little except manage the purchases for the military forces and the Allies.

Most of the dried fruit came from California. Because the 1918 crop presaged a short pack, it was necessary for us to intervene to prevent exorbitant prices. Ralph P. Merritt, California Food Administrator, convened conferences of the growers and the packers at which prices to be paid by the packers to the growers were agreed upon. Provisions were made in the licenses of packers and distributors for markups or profits, and rules expediting delivery and eliminating waste were set. The subsequent increase in supplies of dried fruit to the Allies and Neutrals is indicated by the following figures (in tons):

Prewar average	71,000
1917	59,000
1918	44,000
1919	115,000

COTTONSEED AND COTTONSEED PRODUCTS

We set up a Cottonseed Division under Dr. George H. Denny, President of the University of Alabama. Cottonseed was of importance during the war because it was our major domestic source of vegetable oil for margarine manufacture; the linters and hulls went into the manufacture of explosives; and the cottonseed meal was a major cattle feed. The volume of business amounted annually to about $500,000,000.

Prior to the Food Control Act, there was great instability in this commodity as a result of the large number of steps in the passage of cottonseed products from the farmer to the consumer. This involved the cotton grower, the ginner, the seed brokers, the oil refiners, the lard and butter-substitute manufacturers, and the dealers in end-products. Previous to regulation, all these transactions during the marketing season were a gamble on the price of the end-products the following spring.

We called the usual conferences with representatives of the different elements in the cottonseed business. On their recommendation, made on October 5, 1917, we placed all stages under license in order to work out the problem. It soon became evident that the base of action had to be a stabilized price for the seed. This was accomplished through agreements between representatives of the farmers and the different trades and the Food Administration.

The stabilization program worked with extraordinary success throughout the crop year 1917–1918. By these agreements, prices were greatly reduced from those which prevailed in this otherwise speculative business. When we came to the 1918–1919 crop, the producers of seed at first demanded an increased price over 1917. However, at the meeting of the farmers, ginners, crushers, refiners, and lard and butter-substitute manufacturers, there was unanimous agreement on a plan to hold prices at the level of the 1917 crop. In order to effect this agreement, the Food Administration guaranteed to the cottonseed producer the price for the crops of 1918 and 1919.

Cottonseed oil was the largest of our vegetable-oil products. Our vegetable-oil exports to the Allies and Neutrals were (in tons):

Prewar average	165,000
1917	70,000
1918	150,000
1919	120,000

FRESH FISH

Fresh fish interested the Food Administration chiefly as a meat substitute. On August 11, 1917, the day after the passage of the Food Control Act, we set up a Fish Division under Kenneth Fowler; the major purpose was to encourage consumption of fresh fish and to stimulate the supply. One of the Division's accomplishments was to secure Navy co-operation in reducing its requisitions of fishing boats and trawlers. The Division was also able to secure provision of nets and gear not otherwise available. We placed the industry under license, primarily for the purpose of suspending state laws which restricted fishing. The licenses also provided for control of storage and transportation and elimination of waste.

COLLATERAL NON-FOOD COMMODITIES

War necessities and disturbances to production and distribution forced us to extend our activities to items even further afield than the miscellaneous food commodities. Ammonia, ice, arsenic, binder twine, tin plate, and jute bags all became involved in our food problems. To handle them, we created the Division of Collateral Commodities in November, 1917, by merging various scattered activities of our organization under the direction of Charles W. Merrill, an eminent engineer.

AMMONIA

A problem in ammonia arose because of the enormous wartime requirements for explosives. These requirements were greater than the entire domestic production before the war. The shortage would unavoidably have caused exorbitant prices and endangered the supply of ammonia for fertilizers, artificial ice, refrigeration, and other domestic products. The War Industries Board and the War Department insisted that the Food Administration deal with the matter.

We called a meeting of the ammonia manufacturers and concluded a voluntary agreement with them that their production should be allocated by the Food Administration. We created an interdepartmental ammonia committee made up of representatives from the Departments of War, Navy, Agriculture, and Interior, the Food Administration, and the War Industries Board. Through this committee, relative needs were considered and allotments determined.

Another agreement with the ammonia manufacturers stopped the upward flight of prices by providing for a price of 8.25 cents per pound for aqua ammonia and 30 cents a pound for anhydrous ammonia in carload lots. A campaign was carried on among the manufacturers to conserve ammonia and increase its production. To combat hoarding, plants were forbidden to carry more than a sixty-day operating supply.

As a result of these various measures, including control of artificial ice, we passed successfully through a season in which at the outset we had been faced with an expected shortage of sixty million pounds of ammonia without curtailing any essential use or inflicting any hardships.

ICE

The shortage of ammonia created difficulties in the artificial-ice industry. Conferences were therefore called with the ice producers and dealers, and in early 1918, agreements were reached with the industry to close the ammonia-consuming artificial-ice production during the winter. As a substitute, we put on a campaign, through the state food administrators, to increase the harvesting of natural ice, which resulted in the largest stock in history. By agreement with the natural-ice producers, the artificial producers secured supplies for their customers over the next summer. All parties co-operated, and there was not only a saving in ammonia, but also an ample supply of ice, with no increase in price.

ARSENIC

A shortage of arsenic threatened as a result of the increased demand for war uses. In the autumn of 1917, the prevailing high prices were limiting its use as an insecticide on food crops and in cattle dips. The entire industry, including both producers and distributors, was put under license by the Food Administration on November 15, 1917. The license regulations contained the usual rules regarding reports, unreasonable profits, resales, and non-essential uses. Permits to sell arsenic were required and issued by the Food Administration. Producers were assured of fair prices and urged to increase their output. They responded handsomely.

Another problem in arsenic arose in August, 1918. The Chemical Warfare Division demanded 6,400 tons of arsenic for the manufacture of poison gas, and the British demanded 2,000 tons. An inventory of American and Canadian sources showed that more restrictions would have to be placed on the other uses of arsenic. However, the War Department was slow in the manufacture of poison gas, and the Armistice finally saved the situation, for there would not have been enough arsenic to go around.

I greatly disliked the idea of the Food Administration's having anything to do with poison-gas activities, and I was relieved when General Pershing decided not to use this lethal weapon.

BINDER TWINE

American harvesting machinery at this time required a special twine to bind the sheaves. The major source was sisal hemp from the state of Yucatán in Mexico. The minor sources had been shut off by the shipping shortage. In 1918, we were faced with an enormous crop of grain and consequent increased needs for twine.

The sisal growers in Yucatán organized a state-enforced monopoly. They steadily increased the price to American twine manufacturers from a prewar 4.5 cents a pound to a demand of 19 cents a pound for the 1918 crop. The heightened cost to the American farmer would thus have been about $50,000,000 for the harvest. The price asked was extortionate, and both farmers and manufacturers demanded that we do something about it.

We combined our manufacturers in an agreement with the Food Administration not to compete for sisal and opened negotiations with the Yucatán monopoly. We reached the agreement that a joint commission be appointed to determine the costs of sisal production and a fair price. The Food Administration guaranteed to purchase an amount of the crop to cover American needs. When the price set by the joint commission was below that demanded by the Yucatán growers, they repudiated the agreement and held out for their nineteen cents a pound. We had to stand it—but most unwillingly.

TIN PLATE

The shipping shortage restricted our supplies of tin and palm oil for use in making tin plate. Moreover, our military forces and the Allies were demanding more goods in tin cans. Practically all tin was under British control. At the Food Administration's request, the British diverted the small amount of shipping needed and we made the purchases of tin metal at an agreed fair price. We joined the War Industries Board in the creation of a tin-plate conservation committee representing the manufacturers and the canners. Methods of substituting containers and eliminating wastes were drawn up and made effective by Food Administration licenses on October 1, 1918. A month later, we were saved by the Armistice from the further threat of calamities from this quarter.

JUTE BAGS

Since most of our grain bags were made from Indian jute, the shipping shortage plunged the Food Administration into still another difficulty. There was an ample supply of jute in India, but in anticipation of our abundant 1918 grain crop, speculation in that country was skyrocketing prices. To deal with this situation, on February 26, 1918, we entered into voluntary agreements with our bag manufacturers by which they pledged to sell all standard new Calcutta or domestic wheat bags on hand at a price no higher than twenty-five cents per bag. The Grain Corporation fixed relative prices for wheat in bags to wheat in bulk, which decreased the demand for bags.

But in May, 1918, the Indian jute producers formed a monopoly and demanded still more exorbitant prices. In the meantime, we had stimulated the manufacture of other types of containers made from strong paper and cotton. This, added to our shifts from bags to bulk shipments, decreased the need for jute imports. With this background we secured an agreement among our manufacturers to reduce their purchases of jute for the crop of 1918 to four million bags. After lengthy negotiation and the use of the above weapons, the Indian producers agreed to a lower price. It was still exorbitant, but through our reduced consumption the Indians learned a lesson on how not to cut their own throats. Thus they had a great surplus of jute left after the war.

The stimulation of production, the control of prices, and the support of the Allies in most of the commodities other than food were vested in the War Industries Board under Bernard Baruch. It became a most efficient agency under his direction and contributed greatly to the support of the Allies. As will be shown later, there was no real financial return to the American people for their supplies.

CHAPTER 11

PROVISION OF SUGAR FOR THE ALLIES

If comparison of war upsets in production and distribution can be made, the sugar supply was the most disrupted. Sugar is not needed to maintain public health as much as it is to maintain personal equanimity. On the road of progress from an occasional snack of honey, the discovery of how to make sugar in bulk developed a host of new tastes and habits. The shortage of sugar inspired more immoral practices to get it than any other food shortage and therefore made conservation more difficult.

Beet-sugar production in France and Italy became a victim of war because of its intensive need for labor and fertilizers. The beet sugar from other parts of Europe was mostly shut off by the Central Powers. Thus Britain, France, and Italy were forced to go to the West Indies for supplies. All this required sugar rationing or suppression of less essential uses in some form to the Allied and American people.

Before our Food Control Act was passed, Allied buying in the Western Hemisphere, in competition with the United States, forced a huge rise in the price of raw sugar. Our retail price rose from 5.5 cents per pound to 12.5 cents—"eight pounds for a dollar." Speculation and profiteering were rampant.

In the face of world shortage, there was no effective way to stimulate production, control distribution, set prices, and co-operate with our Allies. We asked for authority to buy the sugar crops of the

Western Hemisphere and resell them to the Allies and our American refineries. On June 19, 1917, I appeared before the Senate Agricultural Committee, which was then considering the Food Bill, and urged this method, saying in part:

> At the present moment our sugar refiners are competing with the . . . [Allies] for the purchase of Cuban sugar. It must be patent that if we [could] create a sugar commission . . . [to] cooperate . . . with the Allies and the Cuban producers to . . . buy the Cuban crop at . . . [an agreed] price . . . we can effect a considerable saving on the present inflated price of raw sugar . . . we can stabilize the price of sugar throughout the whole of next year. . . . [Thus] there would . . . be no incentive to speculation, and the savings to the public on its sugar should reasonably amount to 20 to 25 percent [less than at present].
>
> There can be no loss in such an operation, because one half of the American sugar supply would be in the hands of the Sugar Commission, and . . . [this] Commission should be able to make a price to cover the whole of its outlay. . . .
>
> In order to carry out such operation as this we must have the operation of section 3 in the bill for voluntary agreements; we must have section 5, by which we can impose a license on refiners and . . . [distributors] in such a manner that they play their part in this teamwork; we must have the use of section 9, giving the power to buy and sell, and section 19, to finance the trade.

Congress refused us this authority.

During the four months' delay in the passage of the Food Control Law, however, we set up our Sugar Division and its staff under George M. Rolph in preparation to use such powers as we could obtain. Mr. Rolph was the manager of a great cane-sugar refinery in California, conducted as a co-operative by the Hawaiian sugar producers. He had no personal interests in sugar and was accepted by the whole industry as an independent, most able, and experienced man.

Statistics illustrating the situations in sugar in various countries are inexact because the figures on production are kept on the basis of crop years, while figures on imports and exports are kept in calendar years. Nevertheless, the figures are revealing. The situations were (in tons):

GREAT BRITAIN

Calendar Year *	Imports	Consumption
1909–1913 Average	1,853,605	1,821,002
1917	1,206,705	1,205,470
1918	1,008,377	1,007,475
1919	1,715,481	1,714,071

* The British had no domestic production.

FRANCE

Crop Year	Production	Cal. Year	Imports	Consumption
1909–1910/1913–1914 Av.	759,426	1909–1913	186,197	738,726
1916–1917	204,405	1917	595,552	704,728
1917–1918	225,752	1918	187,752	345,168
1918–1919	121,374	1919	627,131	661,588

ITALY

Crop Year	Production	Cal. Year	Imports	Consumption
1909–1910/1913–1914 Av.	208,675	1909–1913	9,249	217,924
1916–1917	159,690	1917	61,982	221,672
1917–1918	102,100	1918	40,819	142,919
1918–1919	119,524	1919	87,612	207,136

THE UNITED STATES

Crop Year	Production	Cal. Year	Imports	Consumption
1909–1910/1913–1914 Av.	920,457	1909–1913	2,122,517	3,003,290
1916–1917	1,131,557	1917	2,472,044	3,098,203
1917–1918	1,011,047	1918	2,585,488	3,395,387
1918–1919	1,045,350	1919	3,511,810	3,819,456

With the Congressional denial of the powers we needed, we were compelled during the first year of the Food Administration to stimulate production and control prices. We used circuitous devices and tedious, inadequate controls under agreements with the trades, the anti-hoarding law, and other measures.

In co-operation with the sugar producers, we set up strong committees representing nine separate regions—Cuba, Hawaii, the Philippines, Puerto Rico, Louisiana, Florida, and the beet growers of California, the Rocky Mountains region, and the Middle West. Each section produced its sugar at different costs. We entered into separate agreements with each producers committee concerning prices and distribution and set up committees representing the refiners and beet-sugar factories. To reinforce these agreements, we secured a Presidential embargo on all sugar exports except those approved by the Food Administration. In addition, we obtained from the Cuban Government a similar embargo, and to thwart speculation, we suspended all dealings in sugar futures on the exchanges.

OUR AGREEMENTS WITH PRODUCERS

On August 26, 1917, the beet producers committees agreed to reduce their prices at that time by 1.5 cents per pound, saving more than $25,000,000 to consumers. Our agreement with the cane-sugar refiners provided that they were to pay not more than a certain price for raw cane sugar and also provided for markups and profit margins. On October 1, we entered into an agreement with the refiners that all imported sugar should be allocated by a committee appointed by the Food Administration. By these measures we were able to bring more order into the chaos of rising prices and growing speculation—but with many difficulties. All producing sections co-operated except the Louisiana cane producers. They refused to the end to co-operate and sold their sugar on the black market.

On October 12, to stimulate production, we issued this statement to our beet-sugar producers:

> One of the most vital problems confronting the nation is that of procuring sufficient sugar to meet the requirement of our people and of the Allied Nations fighting our common battle. The production of cane sugar in this hemisphere can and will be increased to a limited degree. But we must rely upon the farmers in sugar-beet producing sections of the country for a part of the needed supply. I, therefore, earnestly appeal to every farmer, so situated, to come to his country's aid in this hour of need.

Without the cooperation of the American beet growers our task will be very difficult. . . .

It developed that beet farmers in the West were refusing to sign the customary contracts for acreage with the beet-sugar factories because the prices they were offered made competing crops more profitable. We thereupon appointed local commissions in the principal beet-growing states to investigate costs of production. We assured the factories that upon the decisions of these commissions, the Government, in turn, would undertake, insofar as it was able, to increase prices to the factories. The factories co-operated and thus prevented any reduction in production.

Aside from all this complexity of agreements with two dozen different groups of producers, refiners, distributors, and the Allies, there was an underlying weakness. The basic price to producers varied, and there was no way to establish positive prices for the consumers. Without going into the difficulties of distributing these different-priced sugars, I may say that the result was to reduce the amount of sugar to the consumer from about twelve and one-half pounds for a dollar to about eight pounds.

SUGAR AGREEMENTS WITH THE ALLIES

On June 17, 1917, about two months before the Food Law was enacted, we proposed to the British Food Minister that we consolidate all Allied and American activities in sugar and thus avoid further speculation and rising prices. Lord Rhondda approved.

Immediately after passage of the Food Law, we set up with the Allies the International Sugar Committee—with two members appointed by the Allied Sugar Purchasing Committee and two by the American cane-sugar refiners. The fifth member (and Chairman) was George Rolph, the head of our Sugar Division. We agreed that the functions of this committee would be:

1. To determine the most economical sources of sugar supply from the standpoint of overseas transport.

2. To arrange for transport of sugar at uniform rates.
3. To allocate and distribute sugar between the United States and the Allies.
4. To agree on a price for Cuban sugar.

On December 27, 1917, with the help of our cane-sugar refiners committee, we joined in an agreement with the International Sugar Committee and the committee representing the Cuban producers to fix the price of Cuban sugar substantially lower than the prevailing price. We also agreed with the Allied Purchasing Commission on the division of West Indian and Latin-American sugar between us. These arrangements worked efficiently.

THE SUGAR EQUALIZATION BOARD

These complicated agreements with a dozen committees presented enormous administrative difficulties and had little assurance of continuity. We had to depend on our Treasury to lend money to the Allies for the purchase of Latin-American sugar and then collect the money for them to pay the American refiners. We constantly had to rearrange all of these payments, with adjustments for changing transportation and overhead costs. Worse still, our refiners and wholesalers were buying their supplies at various prices from the producers under our agreements, and we were plagued with uncertainty about the retail price in different areas.

In late May, 1918, I proposed to our staff a complete revolution in our method of handling sugar. The method was, in effect, the same as our original proposal, which had been spurned by the Congress a year before. This time it was based on the war powers of the President and not on the Food Control Act. We proposed the plan to the President on June 15, 1918. In summary, it was that we should form a government-owned corporation through which we could buy all sugar crops in the Western Hemisphere and then sell at equalized prices to our refiners, distributors, and the Allies. We proposed to Mr. Wilson that he subscribe five million dollars from his emergency fund to stock in the corporation; we told him that we would finance the operation (probably one billion dollars annually) through the refiners, the banks, and the Allied governments.

I presented a detailed memorandum to the President setting out the background and our proposal. It showed that the saving to the American people would amount to about $40,000,000 per annum.

The interview at which this memorandum was taken up with President Wilson was illustrative of his economic understanding and his ability to dispatch public business rapidly. When he finished reading the memorandum, without a word, he took his pen and wrote "Approved W.W." and handed it back to me. The whole matter had required less than ten minutes.

There being no federal incorporation law at that time, we incorporated the Sugar Equalization Board in Delaware on July 11, 1918, and elected the following board of directors:

HERBERT HOOVER, *Chairman of the Board of Directors*
GEORGE M. ROLPH, *President*
THEODORE F. WHITMARSH, *Treasurer*
ROBERT A. TAFT, *Secretary*

We appointed as Directors George A. Zabriskie from our Wholesale Division; Professor Frank W. Taussig, the head of the Federal Trade Commission; and Clarence Woolley of the War Trade Board. Later, Rolph found it necessary to return to his private business and Zabriskie became President.

The Board drew upon the Wholesale and Retail Distribution and the Statistics divisions of the Food Administration for its detailed work and made use of our nine producers committees in settling purchase contracts; it adopted the work of our refiners committee and the distributors committees.

The Cuban contracts were made with the Cuban Government, which required the formal approval of our Government. I submitted them to the President on August 29, 1918, and he approved them.

THE EFFECT OF OUR CONTROLS ON SUGAR PRICES TO THE CONSUMER

Bearing in mind that the retail price of sugar was about 12.5 cents per pound at the time the Food Control Act was passed, the results of our various activities were as follows:

The complicated agreements with a dozen committees representing producers, refiners, and distributors had reduced the average price to the consumer to about 9.8 cents per pound, varying somewhat in different parts of the country. With the establishment of the Sugar Equalization Board we reduced the price to 9.2 cents per pound over the whole country, and we held it at that level for about twelve months prior to the signing of the Peace and for six months thereafter.

The Allies bought their sugar at the same prices as we, but their average prices per pound to consumers during the war period were:

	Cents per Pound
Great Britain	12.5
France	15.15
Italy	19.7

STIMULATION OF PRODUCTION

While our price system held up our domestic sugar production, the intensive labor requirements of beet production limited any substantial increase in acreage. On the other hand, our agreements and pricing produced important results in the West Indies. Its production was (in tons):

Year	Production
Prewar average	2,931,783
1916–1917	3,890,000
1917–1918	4,655,728
1918–1919	4,170,030
1919–1920	4,685,000

SUGAR PRICES

At the time sugar controls were set up in September, 1917, the retail price of sugar in the United States was, generally, 12.5 cents per pound.

The exports of American domestic sugar and West Indian sugar to the Allies and Neutrals were (in tons):

Prewar average	2,243,000
1917	3,880,000
1918	3,950,000
1919	3,040,000

CHAPTER 12

PROVISION OF MEATS AND FATS FOR THE ALLIES

I have described in Chapter 1 the great decrease in the herds in Allied countries and, consequently, the decreased production. With the submarine war and shortage of shipping, it was impractical to ship the amount of feed grains needed for even their depleted herds. The only solution was to increase greatly the production of meats and fats in the United States.

The three-year prewar average of our combined exports of beef, pork and dairy products, and vegetable oils was about 750,000 tons. But the exports which the Allies urgently needed were at the rate of about 2,000,000 tons yearly.

There was little hope of stimulating our production of meat or dairy products by an increase in our cattle because it would take three years to expand the herds substantially. Sheep were not a large element in our animal products and had decreased in number from forty-three million prewar to thirty-five million at the time we entered the war. The only hope of adequate meat and fat supplies for the Allies lay in a strenuous reduction in our consumption, the elimination of waste, and increased production of the American hog, which could reproduce quickly. In order for the reader to understand our activities with the animal, it is necessary to describe again our hog situation at the time we entered the war.

After the start of unlimited submarine warfare on February 1, 1917, and up to the passage of the Food Control Law on August 10,

1917, the Allies and Neutrals had indulged in an orgy of uncontrolled buying of feed grains that raised the price of our corn to a level at which it was more profitable for our farmers to sell the corn than to feed it to hogs.

The generally accepted formula of the farmers required twelve bushels of corn to raise one hundred pounds of hog, and the price relationship during this period was such that the farmer could not afford to feed hogs more than the following amounts:

May 1917	11.0 bushels of corn
June 1917	10.0 bushels of corn
July 1917	9.7 bushels of corn
August 1917	8.0 bushels of corn

As I have stated, in May, 1917, the Secretary of Agriculture warned me that the number of breeding hogs had decreased to about five million, and the probability was that the number sent to slaughter in the next twelve months would be only about fifty-seven million—compared to seventy million the year before. From all this it was evident that the price of corn would have to fall, or the price of hogs rise, if meat and fat production were to be increased and the Allies supplied.

Our hands were tied prior to the passage of the Food Control Law. However, we did prepare in advance to meet the crisis by setting up our Meats and Fats Division. I appointed Joseph P. Cotton, a distinguished lawyer, to head this division. I chose Cotton not only because of his outstanding abilities but also because I wanted someone who was completely disassociated from the meat industry. We furnished him with expert advisers.

Since the distorted corn-hog ratio seemed to be the root of the problem, I wrote President Wilson on September 4, 1917, suggesting a plan which would both stimulate production and stabilize prices. In addition to a description of the critical situation in these products at home and among the Allies, the essential parts of my letter were as follows:

> . . . we should consider a definite plan of stimulating the production of hogs. The world's demands for meats and fats will increase steadily dur-

ing the war due to the degenerating animal situation among the Allies, and after peace the additional demands from the inevitable famine in the Central Powers will be enormous and long-continued.

Hogs in the United States are, in the last analysis, a corn product. The cost of production and price are interdependent. . . .

Owing to the violent fluctuations in demand for corn and hogs, there have been five periods since the war began in which it was more profitable to sell corn than feed it to hogs. . . . these fluctuations . . . are, I believe, the fundamental reason why our hog production has not increased. . . .

Although complicated and filled with difficulties, it is not, I believe, impossible [to set up an arrangement with the packers to stabilize the situation]. . . .

The weakness in this chain lies in that someone must assure the packer a market for the products at the agreed ratio to the price [at which] he buys hogs. This, I believe, could be solved by a contract with the Allies to take the whole production in excess of domestic demands at the price above arrived at. . . .

There are thus three parties to be organized and consulted:

(a) The producers.
(b) The packers.
(c) The Allied Governments.

Before, however, I open negotiations as to the acceptance of the principle with these elements, I wish to secure your approval. . . .

HERBERT HOOVER

The President was not enthusiastic about the plan, and after he consulted Secretary of Agriculture Houston, I found him actually opposed to it. Houston later confirmed his own adverse views in a letter which I shall cite shortly.

I was unable to secure from the Secretary any constructive alternative, except that his department would urge the farmers to do better. This was not likely to happen as long as it was more profitable to sell corn at the current market price than feed it to hogs.

Failing to get any helpful support from Houston, we turned to the livestock men for help. We called a meeting of representatives of the National Livestock Association in Washington. This group advised that in order to increase production, the assurance of a fair price based on a proper corn-hog ratio would have to be given to the farmer immediately. Their recommendations were supported by the National Swine Growers Association. Both associations advocated immediate action. We also called an exploratory conference with the representatives of the packers and found them to be co-operative.

On October 16, still considering it highly desirable to get his co-operation, I wrote the Secretary of Agriculture:

DEAR SECRETARY HOUSTON:

I have been having some negotiations with the packers over the question of pork, and there has been some discussion about fixing the ratio between corn and hogs. . . . I could simplify this whole matter considerably . . . if the Department of Agriculture will state to us officially the cost of producing pork in terms of bushels of corn. . . . I have some reason to believe I might get the packers to guarantee this . . . minimum price of hogs for the next 12 or 18 months. I do not assume that it amounts to more than 11½ or 12 bushels per 100 pounds of pork products.

This is not a case of fixing the price of hogs or corn, but a question of giving a minimum guarantee, and a guarantee based only on actual cost. It would, of course, not be operative until new corn was freely in the market.

I should, indeed, be glad if you would . . . have me supplied with a statement of the Department's views as to this ratio.

HERBERT HOOVER

The Secretary strongly urged me not to attempt the plan, and on October 26, he confirmed his objections in writing:

DEAR MR. HOOVER:

I have been carefully canvassing with the officers of the Department your idea of getting the packers to guarantee a minimum price for hogs for the next 12 or 18 months. You state that you have been having some negotiations with them over the question of pork and some discussion about fixing the ratio between corn and hogs. . . .

The opinion of the officers of this Department dealing with matters of this kind is that it would be unwise to take this action. . . .

He summarized his reasons thus:

1. It would be exceptionally difficult to arrive at any figure for the relation between corn and hogs—that is, the cost of producing pork in terms of corn—which would have any special validity or significance. . . .

2. It is pointed out that, while in some sections hogs are grown principally on corn, in other sections, such as the Northwest, the Southwest and the South, hogs are grown principally on other feeds. . . .

3. The close interdependence which exists between hogs, beef cattle, sheep, and other animals as factors in the meat supply and market conditions still further complicates the problem and would seem to make it impracticable to attempt to regulate hog prices, directly or indirectly, independently of prices for other sorts of animals.

4. Any intervention of the packers in an effort to fix prices to producers would probably be misinterpreted and be deeply resented. The livestock producers very generally believe that the packers have been the most adverse influence in the livestock world and have developed conditions resulting in injustice to livestock producers. . . .

5. The matter is further complicated by the fact that one of the largest of the packers is also the largest grain handler in the world. This fact is generally known and would merely emphasize the suspicion that the whole matter was handled in the interest of the packers.

For the present the only steps which seem feasible to the people in this Department are:

1. The continuation of the efforts now under way in this Department to increase the production of all meat animals particularly hogs. . . .

2. Such effective control of the packing plants, especially at the three central points—Chicago, Kansas City, and Omaha, which create the market conditions largely—as will remedy any of the more serious evils in the purchase and handling of livestock. . . .

3. The extension of the publication of current livestock market information now being undertaken by the Bureau of Markets. . . .

The Secretary then repeated some statistics which he considered a favorable augury for increased production. The Secretary was a good professor of economics, and at that time the Department of Agriculture was a statistical and research institution, staffed wholly by men who were inexperienced in the practical problem we faced. That problem involved the supply to the Allies of a commodity without which they could not maintain public health and morale.

Despite Secretary Houston's hopeful statistics, the currents were running entirely adverse to his forecasts. At the date of his letter, the amount of corn a farmer could afford to feed to produce a hundred pounds of hog was 11.2 bushels, and thus at the pricing of corn he would get back only 60 per cent of his money. A month later, the ratio became worse, dropping to 10.7 bushels. As a result, the farmer was selling his corn and marketing his pigs far underweight, with no incentive to raise more.

We were heading into the worst world famine in fats known to modern history. In an interview concerning the matter, the President indicated to me that he was impressed with Houston's advice—but said, "The responsibility is yours." Therefore, I determined to act.

On October 19, I appointed a special committee composed of representatives from the leading agricultural colleges and the hog growers. This committee insisted that if we wanted real stimulation of production, we had to establish prices for hogs based on the price of fourteen bushels of corn—with a guaranteed minimum of sixteen dollars per one hundred pounds of live hog at Chicago.

Our problem was how to assure the packers a fair price for products if they undertook to purchase hogs on this basis. We believed that this could be done with our plan of combined buying for the Army, Navy, Allies, and Neutrals because this total would amount to about 40 per cent of the inspected slaughter.

On October 25, I called a meeting of the packers' representatives, of whom Thomas E. Wilson was Chairman. They agreed to the plan and expressed the belief that purchasing 40 per cent of the inspected production could hold the price. They confirmed their agreement in writing. This arrangement was approved by the special livestock committee in a resolution the same day.

I was prevented from issuing the guarantees by delays in obtaining the consent of all departments for the unification of all official buying, but we finally completed that arrangement early in November. I authorized Cotton, on November 3, to issue the following statement establishing a minimum price and the ratio of corn to hogs. His statement was:

The main purposes of the Food Administration as to hogs are four: To see that the producer at all times can count on a fair price for his hogs so that it will be profitable to him; to see that the farmer increases the number of hogs bred; to limit the profits of the packer and the middleman; and to eliminate speculation.

All these purposes are necessary because we must have more hogs . . . [and that the Allies and our consumers] shall at all times get an adequate supply of . . . [pork products] at the lowest feasible price.

We shall establish rigid control of the packer. Fair prices to the farmer for his hogs, we believe, will be brought about by the full control which the Food Administration has over the buying of the Allies, our Army and Navy, the Red Cross, the Belgian Relief, and the neutrals, which together constitute a considerable factor in the market.

The first step is to stop the sudden break in prices paid for hogs at the central markets. The prices must become stable so that the farmer knows where he stands, and will feel justified in increasing hogs for next winter. The prices so far as we can affect them will not go below a minimum of about $15.50 per hundred-weight for the average of the packers' droves on the Chicago market until further notice.

We have had, and shall have, the advice of a board composed of practical hog growers and experts. That board advises that the best yardstick to measure the cost of production of the hog is the cost of corn. The board further advises that the ratio of corn price to hog price on the average over a series of years has been about 12 to 1 (or a little less). In the past, when the ratio has gone lower than 12 to 1, the stock of hogs in the country has decreased. When it was higher than 12, the hogs have increased. That board has given its judgment that to bring the stock of hogs back to normal under present conditions the ratio should be about 13. Therefore, as to the hogs farrowed next spring, we will try to stabilize the price so that the farmer can count on getting, for each 100 pounds of hog ready for market, 13 times the average cost per bushel of the corn fed into the hogs.

Let there be no misunderstanding of this statement. It is not a guaranty backed by money. It is not a promise by the packers. It is a statement of the intention and policy of the Food Administration which means to do justice to the farmer.

The minimum price of $15.50 for the average of packers' droves as announced was roughly equivalent to the price of $16 per hundredweight for good grades.

CONTROL OF PACKERS' PROFITS AND PRICES

To protect the consumer, we established an equitable margin of profits for the packers and distributors. On November 24, 1917, I issued the following statement announcing packing regulations:

There are in this country hundreds of packing concerns, many of them small, which slaughter live stock and sell meat, but are not large enough or strong enough to carry great stocks, nor do they carry their manufacturing processes in connection with live stock products to great refinements.

There are, however, given concerns relatively much larger, which have many establishments, storage plants, branch houses, cars, and facilities for nation-wide distribution. These large packers do carry out, to great refinements, manufacturing processes in live stock products and allied products. Not only is their business more diversified and more stable than the small packers, but they carry, at all times, large stocks.

It is essential that the smaller packer shall continue his operations to the fullest extent, and his earnings, in view of his risk, must be liberal. The system of regulation which restricts his earnings must be simple and easy to apply. After investigation and consideration, it has been determined to permit the packers (except the five large packers) to earn an annual profit equal to 2.5% of their total annual sales. This profit is to be net after expenses are paid; interest on borrowed money will be treated as an expense, but not federal taxes, which the packer must pay himself out of his profits.

For the five large packers, in addition to the restriction of profits to 2.5 per cent on sales, we made the further restriction that profits should not exceed 9 per cent on the average capital required in that part of their business concerned with livestock slaughtering.

We set up the supervision of packers' accounts by the Federal Trade Commission. Subsequently, an investigation of the packers' books by the Federal Trade Commission revealed that for the period from November 1, 1917, to November 1, 1918, their profits amounted to $40,594,935. The total investment of the five packers for this period was given by the Federal Trade Commission as $714,187,204, thus making their actual rate of profit on investment only 5.6 per cent.

This was certainly no large margin, considering the risks of carrying huge stocks of perishable products—with no federal money available to meet losses which might occur in a shifting war.

The packers protested that the restrictions were entirely too severe. After meeting with them, on Cotton's advice, we agreed to a minor modification concerning capital outlays in a letter dated December 1, 1917. The packers agreed to this compromise. The whole arrangement imposed great risks on the packers—both large and small. As will be shown later, they came to the very edge of complete ruin because of the shift from war at the Armistice. However, they stood firm and performed a patriotic service of which American business may well be proud—and they made a great contribution to food for the Allies.

Two of our men—Gifford Pinchot and E. C. Lasater—became impatient with our progress and methods in handling the animal problems and food generally. They started a public campaign against the Food Administration. On November 19, 1917, lest the President be disturbed by Pinchot's utterances, I wrote him the following note:

DEAR MR. PRESIDENT:

I have unfortunately had a tea-pot storm in my department. Mr. Houston and I appointed a joint committee to undertake propaganda for the stimulation of animal production. I selected, amongst others, Mr. E. C. Lasater, a Texas cattle-man, and Mr. Gifford Pinchot for the committee. Mr. Pinchot, whose views are followed by Mr. Lasater, instead of confining himself to stimulation of production in a patriotic way, and devising methods for a better distribution of our young cattle and other portions of the program, took upon himself to advise me with regard to financial measures to be undertaken and more especially that we should take over the packing plants in the country and operate them for the Government, and other radical measures. These measures were practically all outside the powers of the Government aside from their visionary character. After some time he resigned and his resignation was followed by that of Mr. Lasater on the ground that we were not conducting the Food Administration for the public welfare. I have declined to answer any of their newspaper propaganda.

The fault is of course mine for having even placed them on a . . . committee, although my one justification was that their personalities could be turned to good account in this emergency.

I merely wished to inform you of this as I do not propose to take any action whatever in the matter.

HERBERT HOOVER

The President's reply was:

20 November, 1917

MY DEAR MR. HOOVER:

Thank you for your memorandum about Mr. Gifford Pinchot. The same thing happens wherever he is involved.

WOODROW WILSON

OUR HOG PLAN SUCCEEDS

By the end of 1917, we began to see results from our stabilization of prices and stimulation of hog production. Even Secretary Houston became reconciled to the plan. Four months after we put it into effect, he reported to me that the number of hogs—great and small—was rapidly increasing and that the weight of the animals sent to slaughter was also increasing.

The Secretary, however, had been right when he predicted that I would get into trouble. While we were thus stimulating production, our Conservation Division was carrying on, simultaneously, a vigorous campaign for a reduction in meats and fats consumption among housewives and restaurants. Also, Cotton had set up successful conservation measures with the packers and meat dealers by which they cut off the unnecessary fat from the meat before it was marketed. This arrangement saved much fat that otherwise would have gone down the sewer because housewives and public eating places could not use it all.

I have mentioned that in February, 1918, a combination of forces presented us with a major headache because of a shortage in shipping. The packers' warehouses were filled to the rafters with more than a billion pounds of meat and fat products—and more hogs were coming. All of our price guarantees threatened to collapse because our storage facilities could take no more. Yet every ounce of this supply would be needed by hungry people. I sought to relieve the situation by asking the Allies to increase their imports and store them for later use, when our supplies would be diminished. On March 1, 1918, I cabled Lord Rhondda, the British Food Controller, as follows:

> We cannot allow the result of this glut to break the price to lower levels than at present or we will discourage our farmers and demoralize the whole of next year's production. To solve this situation we are confronted with several alternatives.
>
> The first is to remove all of our restrictions on the consumption of meats for at least two or three months. This will greatly destroy the whole sentiment toward food conservation and will mean that our population will be eating excessive quantities of meat which will in fact be interpreted into decreased exports to the Allies at a later date.
>
> The second alternative is for the Allies to undertake a blanket order for all excess production of pork products until the end of April and to either ship them to the Allied countries for storage against the period of shortage, or, alternatively, to make such financial arrangements as will allow the extension of storage in this country. This will mean that the Allies will have to be prepared to take up to 1,000,000,000 pounds of pork products in March and April.

I also wrote Lord Reading, the British High Commissioner, who headed all British economic agencies in the United States. After describing this temporary situation in the same terms, I added:

> . . . as you are aware, we are entirely short of breadstuffs in the United States and I do not see how we can go on exporting [them] at the present rate per month. It appears to me that, in this situation, food is food and that the natural thing would be that the Allies should take the whole of our excess production where we have an excess and not drain our shortages deeper in other directions. If the consumption of pork products in Europe could be materially increased, it would certainly reduce the demands for butter, cheese and breadstuffs.
>
> HERBERT HOOVER

However, this warehouse relief plan failed with the Allied need to use every ship in defense against the German drive on the Western Front in March, 1918.

We were compelled to retreat on conservation measures, but we weathered this crisis without a break in our assurances to the farmers.

THE AGRICULTURAL ADVISORY COMMITTEE

Feeling that we needed a closer tie with the farmers themselves, early in March, 1918, I mentioned to Secretary Houston the desirability of creating a new committee. The Secretary and I agreed on the following members of the "Agricultural Advisory Committee."

Former Governor Henry C. Stuart of Virginia was appointed Chairman, and Wilder H. Haines of the Food Administration was made Secretary. The first meeting of the Advisory Committee took place on March 26, 1918, with the following membership:

C. J. Barrett, Union City, Ga., President of the Farmers Educational and Cooperative Union

E. S. Brigham, St. Albans, Vt., Vermont Commissioner of Agriculture

W. L. Brown, Kingman, Kans., Member, Kansas State Board of Agriculture

Milo D. Campbell, Coldwater, Mich., President, National Milk Producers Federation

D. R. Coker, Hartsville, S.C., Chairman, State Council of Defense and its agricultural divisions

W. R. Dodson, Baton Rouge, La., Dean, Louisiana College of Agriculture

Eugene E. Funk, Bloomington, Ill., President, National Grain Association

N. H. Gentry, Sedalia, Mo., President, American Berkshire Association

W. G. Gordon, Humboldt, Tenn., Cotton Grower

John Grattan, Broomfield, Colo., Editor, Agricultural Journal

J. N. Hagan, Bismarck, N.D., Chairman, State Commissioner of Agriculture

F. J. Hagenbarth, Spencer, Idaho, President, American National Wool Growers Association

W. W. Harrah, Pendleton, Ore., Member, Farmers Union and Farmers Cooperative Association

C. W. Hunt, Logan, Iowa, Livestock Farmer

H. W. Jeffers, Plainsboro, N.J., Member, State Board of Agriculture
Isaac Lincoln, Aberdeen, S.D., Grower of Seed Grains
D. O. Mahoney, Viroqua, Wis., President, American Tobacco Growers Society
D. M. Massie, Chillicothe, Ohio, Farm Management Specialist
W. F. Pratt, Batavia, N.Y., Trustee, Cornell University
G. C. Roeding, Fresno, Cal., President, California State Agricultural Society
Martin Samson, Fort Worth, Texas, Livestock Grower and Member, Board Federal Reserve Bank, Dallas
C. J. Tyson, Floradale, Pa., President, Pennsylvania State Horticultural Association
Oliver Wilson, Peoria, Ill., Farmer

All of the committee members actively operated their own farms, orchards, or ranches. The group performed a great service on many critical occasions.

STILL ANOTHER HOG CRISIS

In the autumn of 1918, prior to the Armistice, we had to meet another hog crisis. In October, things had gone well for the Allies on the Western Front, and the end of the war was in sight. There was in the Argentine a large backlog of corn resulting from a lack of ships for transport. Our farmers began to calculate what might happen if this corn came into the market. In fright that we would thereupon lower our guarantee with decreasing prices of corn, they began rushing their hogs to market. The slaughter under federal inspection increased in September to 36 per cent over the year before. The price of corn dropped forty cents per bushel.

In this situation I called for a meeting of our Agricultural Advisory Committee under Governor Stuart on October 15. Urgings to farmers from the Committee and a pledge that we would adhere to the minimum price checked the flood of marketing. We got by this crisis.

I received this heartening letter from Governor Stuart at the approach of the Armistice:

DEAR MR. HOOVER:

In behalf of the . . . Agricultural Advisory Board and the swine producers associated therewith, I wish to express in so far as I may as chairman the full confidence of the entire committee in the valuable work you have already done both for the producers and for the whole people, and to be-speak your further valuable support . . . of the rights of the great army of agricultural producers of the country.

H. C. STUART

But we were by no means over our meats and fats troubles because our guarantees to the farmers extended beyond the Armistice to the end of March, 1919, and our most heartbreaking crisis in meats and fats was yet to come—in January, 1919. That is the subject of a special chapter on the Armistice period.

RESULTS

Since the regulations of the Food Administration's prices and profits favorably affected cattle and sheep, I include them in our statistical results.

The animal population as given by the Department of Agriculture was:

	(Estimated) July 1, 1917	January 1, 1919
Hogs	53,000,000	64,000,000
Sheep	38,000,000	41,575,000
Cattle and Calves	70,000,000	72,094,000

From combined stimulation of production and reduction of consumption, our exports to the Allies and Neutrals were (in tons):

	Prewar Average	1917	1918	1919
Pork products	498,000	820,000	1,535,000	1,310,000
Beef products	73,000	320,000	390,000	560,000
Dairy products	13,000	290,000	560,000	751,000

CHAPTER 13

PROVISION OF GRAIN FOR THE ALLIES

I have already referred to the drought which struck our 1917 grain crops. The actual result of the harvest as compared with the prewar average was (in bushels):

	Prewar Average	1917 Harvest
Wheat	876,568,000	636,655,000
Corn	2,744,831,000	3,065,233,000
Barley	202,056,000	211,759,000
Oats	1,314,309,000	1,592,740,000
Rye	48,570,000	62,933,000

Although these statistics indicate some surplus for supplies to the Allies, there was not only no surplus at all, but a statistical vacuum for our domestic needs. The European buying orgy prior to the Food Control Act had diminished the supplies in our pipeline from the farmer to the consumer to almost nothing. A considerable part of the wheat was off grade and had to be fed to animals. We had to reserve seed for the largest planting in our history if the Allies were to be supplied during the next year. In addition, since the prewar-average statistics were compiled, our population had increased by almost three million.

While statistically the number of bushels of corn was larger than the year before, the crop proved to be very "soft." The nutritional value was probably 300,000,000 bushels less than the crop statistics indicated. Our need to increase the production of meats and fats theoretically called for the entire crop. Moreover, soft corn ferments in storage and we were thus forced to erect new drying facilities for overseas shipments, since the country had little of that equipment.

In the five months before the enactment of the Food Law, the panic buying by the Allies and Neutrals had raised the price of No. 2 red winter wheat from about $1.80 per bushel to about $3.45. The price of flour had risen from about $8.60 to $17.25. As a result, our consumers were paying at the rate of $600,000,000 per annum in increased prices. The farmers were not receiving the benefit of this price rise because they had already marketed most of their previous crop before this buying orgy began. The Allies had bought a huge amount of futures in the Chicago Board of Trade—thus cornering the market. At my suggestion, the Chicago Board of Trade suspended all dealings in futures and required a compromise settlement of "future" contracts made by the Allies.

ALLIED NEEDS

Over and above all this was the huge problem of the Allied peoples' morale. Their diet of wheat and cereals was more than half their food supply, compared to about 30 per cent in the United States. To them, the bread ration was the symbol of sufficiency or the danger of starvation. We could only meet their needs to the extent that we could secure self-denial and elimination of waste on the part of the American people.

ORGANIZING TO MEET THE CRISIS

With these problems before us, we called meetings of the representatives of the grain dealers on May 15 to 17, 1917, and the flour millers on June 22. But until the Food Law was enacted on August 10, we had to stand by and watch the chaos.

On July 10, the President requested me to review the wheat situation. After describing the chaos, I could propose no constructive action except the passage by the Congress of the Food Control Act in the form we had recommended. When the Law was enacted, it embraced our recommendations concerning wheat. It provided a guarantee of two dollars per bushel for No. 1 northern wheat at the Chicago market, with adjustments for other grades, and an appropriation of $150,000,000 in working capital for the purchase and sale of wheat.

I selected Julius H. Barnes, a leading grain dealer, to head our Grain Division after he patriotically agreed to divest himself of all his interests in the grain trade.

THE FOOD ADMINISTRATION GRAIN CORPORATION

We had concluded that if the Food Control Law were passed as we had recommended, we would set up a Delaware corporation, wholly government owned, to conduct our grain and certain other commodity activities. To save time, a month prior to the passage of the law, Judge Curtis Lindley, chief of our Legal Division, had prepared articles of incorporation for the Grain Corporation with an initial $50,000,000 capital. The Corporation was registered on August 16, six days after the passage of the Act.

The principal officials of the Corporation were:

HERBERT HOOVER, *Chairman*
JULIUS H. BARNES, *President*
FRANK G. CROWELL, *First Vice-President*

There were fourteen other vice-presidents to head zonal operations.

Aside from our purchase and sale operations in wheat, the Corporation, by delegation from the Food Administration, had wide powers, which included the authority to act as the agent for other branches of the Government in food purchases and distribution.

FIXING THE PRICE OF THE 1917 WHEAT CROP

Although the Food Control Act authorized a minimum price to the farmer of two dollars per bushel for wheat from the 1918 harvest, it did not cover the immediate 1917 wheat then being harvested. It was therefore necessary to determine the price at which we would buy the current production and, if advisable, to set a higher price to the farmers than the guarantee—in order to secure the maximum production from the 1918 crop.

On August 14, I recommended to the President that he appoint an independent committee to determine these prices. President Harry A. Garfield of Williams College was appointed Chairman. He selected four members from farmer organizations, two from labor, two from agricultural colleges, two from industry, and two economists. On August 30, the committee voted unanimously that the price of the 1917 crop be fixed at $2.20 for No. 1 northern spring wheat at Chicago, with the usual differentials for other grades and markets. The same day, the President, on our recommendation, issued an executive order fixing the above price and added to the order:

> It is the hope and expectation of the Food Administration, and my own also, that this step will at once stabilize and keep within moderate bounds the price of wheat for all transactions throughout the present crop year, and in consequence the prices of flour and bread also. The Food Act has given large powers for the control of storage and exchange operations, and these powers will be fairly exercised. . . . the ordinary machinery of trade . . . can not function well under such disturbed and abnormal conditions as now exist. In its place the Food Administration now fixes for its purchases a fair price. . . . thereby it will eliminate speculation, make possible the conduct of every operation in the full light of day, maintain the publicly stated price for all, and, through economies made possible by stabilization and control, better the position of consumers also.
>
> Mr. Hoover, at his express wish, has taken no part in the deliberations of the Committee on whose recommendation I determine the Govern-

ment's fair price, nor has he in any way intimated an opinion regarding that price.[1]

WOODROW WILSON

We began to buy wheat on September 4, announcing that we would pay cash and sell for cash at cost to us, plus storage and a small differential to cover overhead. On September 14, 1917, we reached an agreement with representatives of elevators and storage concerns regarding the rate we would pay for their services. More than fifteen thousand elevators and warehouses signed up. The farm organizations, to save commission men's charges, requested that the Grain Corporation accept grain shipped directly to it. We agreed and charged 1 per cent to cover the expenses necessary to handle such shipments. We suspended all dealings in wheat or its products on all exchanges to end any speculation.

THE FLOUR AND MEAL MILLERS

Nine days after the Food Control Law was enacted, we set up the Milling Division of the Food Administration under James F. Bell and organized a committee that was representative of the trade. We submitted to this committee agreements with the Food Administration and with the Grain Corporation. By the end of November, 1917, a total of 85 per cent of the milling capacity of the country had voluntarily signed up. Others came in later, so that 97 per cent of the nation's milling capacity was eventually covered. We were

[1] Several years later, in a political campaign, I was charged with having fixed the price of wheat to the disadvantage of the farmers. In reply, Garfield, on July 10, 1924, addressed the following letter to Edgar Rickard:

"I think the mimeographed minutes of our meetings contain sufficient evidence to answer the absurd statements, that Mr. Hoover might just as well have had a higher price for the 1917 wheat crop, but the following are the facts: No one knew what the price would be until after the final ballot in the late afternoon of August 30, 1917. The first three formal ballots were taken on the 28th and 29th of August. The first intimation Mr. Hoover had was after our conclusion was reached on the afternoon of the 30th. So careful were we that no information of the agreed price should get out that no member of the committee nor its Secretary, Mr. Nasmythe, left the room until, having formulated our report, we all went to the White House at 5:30 that afternoon to report to the President."

compelled, however, to use our licensing power to stop the 3 per cent minority from black-marketing.

The agreements with the millers provided that they would not purchase grain at prices higher than the fixed price; that their profit margin should not exceed twenty-five cents per barrel of flour and fifty cents per ton of feed; that they would not contract for flour more than thirty days in advance or store more than thirty days' wheat supply; and that the Grain Corporation would apportion the export sales of flour over the entire trade.

The Milling Division, under Bell, established regional committees whose responsibilities were to secure maximum efficiency in the operation of the mills and in the distribution of flour and meals and to carry out certain conservation measures. This agency acted for our Division of Coordination of Purchase to distribute Allied and military purchases equitably. Agreements were made by the Food Administration's Wholesale and Retail Distribution Division, under Theodore Whitmarsh, with committees of the wholesale and retail trades in flour and meal concerning their profits or margins on sales. Thus the prices of flour and meal were stabilized all along the line.

The price of bulk flour at Minneapolis on August 10 (when the Food Law was passed) was reduced from about $17.00 per barrel to about $10.30, where it remained—until, to meet an increase in railway rates, we raised the price of wheat, which resulted in a price of flour of about $10.57 at Minneapolis. We held flour at that level until the end of the war.

BREAD

A few days after the enactment of the Food Control Law, we set up the Baking Division of the Food Administration under Alfred I. Esberg. About 60 per cent of our bread was baked in households, and thus for the nation as a whole, an average of 40 per cent was made in bakeries. However, the proportion of bakery bread in the cities was as high as 74 per cent. We proposed to the baking industry that they create the usual co-operating committee—which they did, under the name of the War Emergency Council of the Baking Industry.

The price of bread, however, could not be stabilized until we could set up a definite loaf weight that could be produced by all bakers. An investigation by the Federal Trade Commission, made at our request, disclosed that among 209 large bakeries there were eight different weights for the loaves, the general practice in the industry being to vary the size of the loaf according to the variations in the price of flour and other costs. Now that we had a stabilized price in flour and other ingredients, a standard weight for a loaf of bread and a reduced price became possible for the whole country, provided we could eliminate great wastes in distribution. In explaining this situation through the press on September 1, 1917, we said:

> . . . At the prospective prices for flour, it is improbable that a full one pound loaf can be delivered to the consumer for less than ten cents per loaf unless the consumer will join with the bakers and retailers in eliminating needless cost. It may be possible to reduce the cost of bread by about two cents per loaf if cooperation . . . can be secured and . . . wasteful practices which have grown . . . can be eliminated such as a reduction in delivery and certain credit practices. . . .

Voluntary action was taken by leading bakers to eliminate waste, but the trade was so competitive that this did not generally succeed. Therefore, on November 7, 1917, at the request of their committee, all bakers using more than ten barrels of flour or meal a month were placed under license in order to secure the savings. A little later (on January 30, 1918) we extended this requirement to cover all bakers using more than three barrels a month. It was necessary to issue 38,800 licenses covering the whole trade in order to bring the minority of small bakers into line.

With these arrangements, we were able to agree with the bakers committee on a one-pound standard loaf and an eight-ounce half-loaf, with certain tolerances. Wholesale prices were effectively established throughout the country at eight or eight and one-half cents, and the retail price was fixed at ten cents for the one-pound loaf.

We did not attempt to fix directly the prices of rye, oats, barley, or corn, believing that our various activities would sufficiently stabilize their prices without the enormous organization required for such action. Using April, 1917, prices at Chicago, the results were as follows (in cents per bushel):

	Wheat, No. 1 Northern, Chicago	Rye	Oats	Barley	Corn
1917					
April	325.0	135.6	61.5	102.3	113.4
Average (October to December)	200.7	168.2	63.5	113.0	149.7
1918					
Average (January to the Armistice)	203.6	180.9	77.3	127.5	151.7

CHAPTER 14

MORE STRINGENT CONSERVATION MEASURES

We were succeeding well in conservation with our household, public-eating, and elimination-of-waste measures, but as the 1917 crop year wore on, it became evident that in order to supply the Allies we would have to take many other steps.

BEER AND HARD LIQUOR

The Food Control Act required the suppression of all distillation of grain for beverage purposes. We stopped it on September 8, 1917. On our recommendation, the control of distillation was at once taken over by the Bureau of Internal Revenue (in the Treasury) because one of their lifelong preoccupations had been illegitimate distillation. They were also charged with the distribution of the stocks in hands of the distillers.

BREWING

The Food Control Act also authorized the limitation of grain used in brewing. The Prohibitionists waged a great campaign for the denial of all grain to brewers. On November 19, 1917, I presented the whole problem to the President, pointing out that (1) if beer were wholly suppressed, the country would go on a whisky-and-gin basis because of the large on-hand stocks of those potent liquors; and (2) the grain used in brewing resulted in a 30 per cent recovery as cattle feed. We proposed, as a middle way, that we limit the alcoholic content of all beer to about 3 per cent—the content of "light" beer—and by these means reduce the grain consumption by about 50 per cent.

The President, on November 20, agreed to my recommendations but raised the grain limitation to 70 per cent of the previous year's use. On November 26, I issued an explanatory statement to the press, the key paragraphs of which were:

> The President has approved the recommendation of the Food Administration that the alcoholic content of beer should be reduced in the first instance to three per cent maximum and that the volume of grain to be used in brewing shall be reduced to approximately seventy per cent of the amount formerly used. . . .
>
> The Food Bill provides for the . . . [suppression] of the use of foodstuffs in . . . [all] distilled spirits . . . and it was stopped on September 8th. There is, however, in the country from two to three years' supply of whiskey, brandy and gin, and other distilled liquors. . . .
>
> Those who wish brewing entirely suppressed should therefore bear in mind that if such a course were pursued the country would be placed on a whiskey[-gin] basis entirely and the amount of alcohol consumed would most probably increase. . . .

The Prohibition Party continued to agitate, and on June 4, 1918, in reply to their denunciation and demands, I issued the following statement:

> . . . If brewing were stopped today, beer would disappear from the liquor trade within one or two months. . . . The saloons would be left open . . . selling . . . . drinks carrying 40 or 50 per cent alcohol, with some small supplies of wine, instead of a large proportion of their customers being served with a drink of 2¾ per cent alcoholic content and therefore, from a temperance viewpoint, much less harmful. It raises . . . [a question for the prohibitionists] as to whether infinitely more damage will not result from such action than in a continuation of the use of this limited amount of foodstuffs in brewing.

OTHER MEASURES TO SAVE WHEAT

Our commodity divisions were systematically eliminating waste in processing and distributing. We set up, under the Grain Corporation, an organization of farmers to save waste in threshing and to get all the wheat in from the fields. The Corporation also set up measures to save waste in storage warehouses.

We established, through our millers committee, a requirement that all wheat should be milled up to about 78 per cent instead of the average of 74 per cent in their previous making of white flour. In this action, we ran into a group of advocates of 100 per cent milled wheat; they believed that such a product had great health values. Having tried this in the Belgian Relief with the consequence of a huge wave of dysentery in the population, we repelled this idea. In fact, the 100 per cent flour devotees did not know that the product sold in the markets as whole-wheat flour was in reality only 82 per cent of the grain. The millers eliminated much waste by standardizing packages, limiting stocks of flour in the hands of the trades, and simplifying distribution measures generally.

The conservation measures in the baking industry eliminated great wastes. The agreement on a standard weight for the loaf enabled the bakers to eliminate varied sizes of pots, pans, and oven space and to make savings in labor and materials. With the support of the bakers committee, we issued a regulation to the effect that the bakers should accept no return of bakery products from retailers. Returns could be used only for cattle feed. We also, in our licenses, limited the amounts of sugar and lard—or lard substitutes—which could be used. We called a meeting of the representatives of the trade engaged in handling all other bakery products—cakes, crackers, and other items—and agreed with them on rules for saving materials.

One of our major wheat-conservation measures was to persuade housewives and public eating places to use about 30 per cent of corn or barley flour in their bread. We made this compulsory for the bakers.

On January 26, 1918, as the crisis mounted, we secured from the

President an executive order expanding some of our conservation measures and introducing new ones. Our press release stated:

> These rules are effective from the morning of Monday, January 28.
>
> The effectiveness of these rules is dependent solely upon the good will, and the willingness to sacrifice. . . . In the last analysis the success or failure of any plan such as here outlined rests with the people. We are dependent upon the cooperation of the trades. We have but one police force, the American woman, and we depend upon her to organize in cooperation with our State and local food administrators to see that these rules are obeyed by that small minority who may fail. Part of the rules will be enforced under the Lever Food Act. . . .
>
> 1. As their part in reducing the consumption of wheat flour, the consumers of the country are called upon, in purchasing such flour, to buy at the same time an equal weight of the other cereals (corn meal, cornstarch, corn flour, hominy, corn grits, barley flour, rice, rice flour, oatmeal, rolled oats, buckwheat flour, potato flour . . . and meals). The housewife may use these products separately in making bread, cakes, and pastry, or mix them as she thinks best.
>
> The retailers are to sell wheat flour only with an equal weight of these other cereals.
>
> 2. Consumers will be able to obtain mixed cereal bread from their bakers, who will be required under the license regulations to mix 5 per cent of other cereals with their wheat flour, both in bread and rolls, and will be required gradually to increase this substitution until, beginning February 24, a minimum of 20 per cent of such cereals is to be used. The Food Administration strongly urges on consumers the buying of this bread, which will be known as "Victory bread," and will contain not less than 20 per cent of cereals other than wheat. . . . If you bake bread at home, use wheat substitutes; if you buy it, buy only Victory bread.
>
> 3. Manufacturers of macaroni, spaghetti, noodles, crackers, breakfast foods, pie, cake, and pastry are not to purchase to exceed 70 per cent of the wheat flour they used during the corresponding months of 1917. These manufacturers will be performing a patriotic service by using cereals other than wheat in their products.
>
> 4. Wholesalers will be required, under license regulations, not to buy more than 70 per cent of their purchases of flour from millers as based on their purchases for the corresponding months of the preceding year, and their sales to the retail trade must be in the proportion of 1 pound of

wheat flour to 1 pound of other cereals, this being the same proportion in which the retailer sells to the consumer, unless the wholesaler satisfies himself that the substitutes have been already purchased from another source.

A ruling has been made that in making any combination sales under this program, dealers shall name a price for each of the articles so sold which shall not represent more than a normal prewar profit on any one of the articles sold.

5. Millers of flour are to distribute their output through their customary channels and markets in such a manner that each city, town, and district may receive its usual proportion. The wheat millers have been required to produce 1 barrel of flour (196 pounds) from 264 pounds of wheat. This is a white flour and represents 2 to 4 per cent higher extraction than from last year's harvest.

6. To assist further in conservation, Monday and Wednesday of each week are to be observed as wheatless days, and one meal of each day as a wheatless meal. This applies both in the home and in the public eating place, and on such days and meals no crackers, pastries, macaroni, breakfast foods, or other cereals containing wheat should be used. The only exception to this is such small amounts of flour as may be needed for thickening soups or gravies or as a binder in corn bread or other cereal breads.

7. On wheatless days, and at wheatless meals, the Food Administration urges that bread baked in the home be other than wheat bread. Where bread is purchased either for use in public eating places or in the home, Victory bread should be used, if no [other grain] . . . substitutes can be found. . . .

We endured unending advice to require the substitution of corn bread for wheat or rye bread. The American people were, both in their homes and in eating places, accustomed to corn bread, and many people preferred it; but it could not be made universal. There were infants and invalids, to whom corn bread was not adaptable. It could not be made and distributed from bakeries fast enough to prevent it from becoming stale—and 40 per cent of our people were dependent upon bakeries for their bread. Excluding some parts of Southern Europe that continent was not familiar with corn products, except for fodder, and in any event, since their baking was done almost wholly in bakeries, the imposition of corn bread on Europe was unfeasible—despite the urgings of several Congressmen and others. The inquiries on this subject became so voluminous that we had to set aside a secretary to deal with them.

MORE STRINGENT CONSERVATION OF SUGAR

Housewives and public eating places under our Conservation Division unquestionably reduced sugar consumption. There were, however, other forces which coincidentally increased it. War wages increased buying power, with a resulting greater demand for candy and soft drinks. There were more than four million men in uniform, and they were naturally left unrationed in their consumption of sugar products. The servicemen also had money in their pockets for the purchase of additional candy and soft drinks. They were generous in giving sugar products to their more restricted relatives and friends, both at home and abroad. Moreover, the representatives of the Salvation Army, the Knights of Columbus, the Young Men's Christian Association, and the Red Cross gave candy to men in uniform. The Army and Navy consumed large quantities of canned fruit, jam, and jellies, all of which contained much sugar. Our rough estimate, based on military purchases and those of the charitable organizations, indicated a sugar consumption at the rate of about 120 pounds per annum per person in uniform, while the national civilian average was less than 80 pounds.

So more drastic measures were necessary. Through the Sugar Equalization Board, we ordered candy and soft-drink manufacturers to reduce their consumption of sugar by 20 per cent of the previous year's use. Because this regulation did not produce the hoped-for results, manufacturers were required to obtain certificates from the Food Administration stating the amount of sugar they were allowed. As the sugar situation grew more desperate by the needs of the Allies, the retailers were limited to sales of not more than two pounds of sugar per week per family.

Finally, through the Sugar Equalization Board, we restricted supplies from the Board to all non-military users by allotting a quota to each state on a per-capita basis. The operation was carried out through the issuance of certificates by the state food administrators to the county administrators and by them to the trades.

The Allied food authorities, joined by certain well-intentioned Americans, again raised a cry for the forcible rationing of the American people. Although it is somewhat repetitive, I give a condensation of a standardized statement we made at various times on this subject:

> Any system of card-coupon rationing of the United States bristles with difficulties. Forty per cent of the population are either food producers or live in intimate contact with the farmer and therefore cannot be fully restrained in their consumption by card rationing. Our industrial population varies greatly in its habits. The consumption of any given commodity varies in different parts of the country. For instance, the Southern worker consumes perhaps not more than two pounds of wheat products per week per capita, whereas in some parts of the North . . . [the worker] consumes eight pounds. Rationing of wheat on any broad national line would increase the consumption beyond necessity in the South and decrease it below necessity in the North. We should need [to] print probably 40,000,000 tickets with a long line of coupons attached for each commodity. We would need [to] create a rationing committee in every ward and village. And we would need a long line of inspectors, snoopers, and prosecuting lawyers. To adopt such a rationing system would increase the expenditures of the Government 50 to 100 million dollars annually and would produce less savings. The answer lies in the sense of service and voluntary action of the American people.[1]

[1] Despite these sound reasons and this experience, card-coupon rationing was adopted in World War II. Hundreds of millions of cards or coupons were printed, thousands of rationing committees created, and snoopers, informers, black marketeers, and prosecutors abounded. The cost to the government for comparable periods was two hundred times greater than in World War I. The effective restriction of consumption proved to be less than resulted from the Food Administration's appeal for co-operation on moral and patriotic grounds. This experience in World War II will be examined more fully later in these memoirs.

CHAPTER 15

THE WORST FOOD YEAR OF THE WAR

The bad crop of 1917, which I have described in Chapter 4, piled upon us continuous difficulties, which made it a year of great strains, much anxiety, and some hysteria. In addition, the losses from the submarine war had so reduced shipping that food surpluses in the Far East, Australia, and the Argentine were in large part isolated. The fall-winter period of 1917–1918 was the coldest in several years. Our railway transport was often crippled and at times totally immobilized. The Great Lakes were frozen for the longest period in many years, and thus the movement of supplies from the Northwest and Canada was slackened during the time of our most critical need. Added to all this, we had the worst influenza epidemic in all of our history. Nearly 20 per cent of the whole working force of the nation was in bed or convalescing. The death rate at home was greater than that of the war.

With all of these troubles and problems, it was vital for us in the administration to know accurately the food and shipping situation around the world—including that of the enemy. In order to be able constantly to evaluate the situation, we built up a strong Statistics Division under Dr. Raymond Pearl and Frank M. Surface. We also built up a strong division on Allied needs under Alonzo E. Taylor and Dr. Vernon Kellogg. We posted representatives in each country where the situation was critical to keep track of national stocks and consumption.

Since the food needs of any nation can be safely gauged by stocks on hand, supplies en route, caloric intake, and other less important criteria, we estimated the needs of each of the Allies and Neutrals every month. We also had to make a monthly appraisal of our own food stocks in order to judge the progress of our own conservation and the amount of our exportable surplus to the Allies. None of these statistics was comforting, either to us or the Allies, during this worst year.

The Allied food authorities were at times hysterical over their prospects. Naturally, they not only wanted assurances of supplies from North America, but their civil servants in charge of these matters also wished to avoid more and more drastic conservation measures for their own peoples. Tempers on both sides at times reached the boiling point.

The Allied representatives became insistent that the United States give them a firm commitment to meet their needs until the next harvest. They said that this commitment was necessary to maintain the morale of their people, who were frightened at the world food situation. I refused to give such guarantees. Such an action might plunge us into disaster at home. But of more importance, our information service in Europe advised us that this was merely bureaucratic desire to demonstrate efficiency; as will be shown later, there was no need for drastic action.

One of the matters which bothered us was that the Allies had about 3,400,000 tons of merchant cargo ships engaged in commercial trade in the Mediterranean and the South Atlantic, Indian, and Pacific oceans. They felt that continuation of this foreign trade was necessary to sustain their economic strength, and we sympathized with this idea. They were also using some of their passenger tonnage and some refrigerator ships to transport meats and fats from the Argentine and Uruguay—for which we felt our increasing supply of pork products could be substituted.

In view of all these complexities, we decided to send Alonzo Taylor to Europe, along with competent assistants, to examine these questions with the Allies on the spot. Dr. Taylor had long served with us and was familiar with the whole world food situation. Colonel

House was going abroad in November for a special conference on military and financial questions, and he agreed that Dr. Taylor should go along as part of his mission.

On October 27, prior to the Colonel's departure, I wrote to him, describing the situation as we saw it and the measures which ought to be taken. A condensation of my letter is:

MY DEAR COLONEL HOUSE:

I have one or two ideas on the present world's food situation which I would like to set out to you.

Taken broadly, there is a larger supply of food in the world today than is needed for the Allied countries. . . . great stocks of food rest in . . . the Argentine, India, and in Australasia. The supplies in North America, however, are considerably less than the total requirements of the Allies. . . .

It appears to me that . . . the present demands for foodstuffs from the United States will exhaust our entire surplus long before the next harvest, and it will then be critically necessary for the Allies to go to the markets further afield . . . primarily, the North American food hoard should be held on to until the last, because with any unexpected increase in the loss of shipping, the journeys, further afield will be hopeless, and this nearby reservoir should be held in reserve as much as possible. . . .

Therefore, the conference should first determine the world's food supply; should, second, determine the world's available shipping; and . . . every possible agency should be brought into play to increase the transport from markets furthest afield, the whole to be designed with view to reserving as large a stock of food in the United States as may be possible. . . .

HERBERT HOOVER

On Dr. Taylor's arrival in Europe, the Allied Food Ministers presented him with their estimated food needs until the next harvest. Their estimates did not include supplies for the Belgian Relief, the minor Allies, or the Neutrals. At Dr. Taylor's suggestion, the Ministers agreed to set up an "Inter-Allied Commission on Alimentation," comprising eight nutritional experts—two each from Britain, France, Italy, and the United States. Dr. Taylor advised me that as the result of the studies of the Commission, the Allied demands were reduced by about 25 per cent. The Commission, however, had based its estimates upon a daily caloric intake of more than 3,000 per person. This was only about 5 per cent below prewar normal. Bearing in mind our Belgian Relief struggles to maintain 1,800 calories per capita per diem, we concluded that the Allies would have to undertake more belt-tightening—or, alternatively, they would, in an emergency, have to go to the East or to the Southern Hemisphere for part of their supplies, even at the sacrifice of their other economic programs.

On November 8, we instructed Dr. Taylor by cable to insist that they immediately obtain part of their wheat supplies from the Southern Hemisphere. The use of only a part of their cargo tonnage engaged in commercial trade could make up their deficit in the emergency. Dr. Taylor advised us that the Allies still clung to the idea of the short journey for North American supplies. Therefore, on November 13, we again cabled him, urging that the Allies tap these more remote sources. Dr. Taylor advised me that the Allied food authorities then agreed temporarily to draw on the more distant markets. With this arrangement, we thought we were on our way out of the crisis. But the Allied shipping authorities now stepped in and insisted again that they be supplied from North America; this was not only the shorter voyage, but the route was also safer because of the protection offered by convoys.

The Allies became more insistent. They seemed to believe that we could produce miracles out of a statistical vacuum and ignored our need to keep some wheat for our own use during the period until the next harvest. They even suggested to Dr. Taylor that we substitute corn for wheat all along the food line in the United States. While I would have been more than happy if we could have given what they asked, we could do no more than promise to tighten our belts further, to maintain only the minimum necessary to protect the American people, and to ship the Allies every possible ounce.

BUREAUCRACY-INDUCED HYSTERIA

A few examples will suffice to show the hysteria among the Allied food officials. On November 24, our Food Administration representative in London, L. P. Sheldon, cabled on behalf of the British Food Minister, Lord Rhondda:

> I am seriously alarmed by your cable and Dr. Taylor's confidential statement that the total exportable wheat surplus from United States and Canada will not exceed 133,000,000 bushels. Unless Allies can rely on North American exports considerably in excess of these figures and upon a larger amount of grain than is now being allocated we shall be confronted with a situation of extreme gravity.

Lord Rhondda, however, had misinterpreted Dr. Taylor's statements; Taylor was referring to only two months' shipments—January and February.

The next person from whom I was to hear was the Premier of France, Paul Painlevé, through the French Ambassador in Washington.

> I must call your attention to the present situation of our cereal supplies, which is very serious. Our crop does not reach 3,900,000 tons and the average crop of the last ten years before the war was 9,400,000 tons.
>
> As you see we face an enormous deficit. With the amount immediately necessary for sowing, that is to say, 800,000 tons, and the stock for domestic consumption, there is practically nothing to save the large cities from starvation or to supply the needs of our armies from today onward. . . .
>
> We have a large deficit of our wheat imports in August and September. The threshing is very slow, in spite of our activity; we have already been obliged to consume our wheat imports. There is no available wheat today and we are living from hand to mouth.
>
> With regard to the cereals which we are using as substitutes for wheat, the situation is causing us great anxiety. The crop of these cereals will reach only 500,000 tons.
>
> So we have decided to use all the available ships in North America to

transport cereals prior to any other kind of cargo. It is urgent to obtain the same . . . [amounts] from the United States.

. . . The help that the United States can give us must be 200,000 tons [of] shipping a month for three months, over and above the quantity we transport by our own means.

If the United States Government agrees to our request and decides to order some ships to transport our cereals, kindly let me know immediately the name and positions of these ships which will be communicated to the Wheat Executive.

Mr. Hoover will have to be told the situation so that he will increase the quantities to be delivered to the Wheat Export for the Allies, and we ask you to second Mr. Robson of the Wheat Export with your personal influence with Mr. Hoover.

At this morning's sitting the "Conseil des Ministres" decided to send you this cable, asking you to settle this matter prior to any other as the situation is so extremely serious. Even go and see President Wilson for I must repeat that the situation is very grave not to say perilous.

PAINLEVÉ

I had known the emotional Painlevé, and I was convinced that the crisis was being exaggerated to him.

On December 22, Lord Rhondda cabled me:

The food position in this country and as I understand it, in France also, can now without . . . exaggeration be described as critical and anxious.

On December 28, K. B. Stoddard, Vice-President of the Wheat Export Company, just back from London, wrote to Julius Barnes:

The Wheat Executive impressed upon me that unless the program . . . could be fulfilled it would mean disaster for the Allied cause.

Since these statements did not conform to our information about Allied reserve supplies or their need to maintain such a high caloric intake, we did not succumb to panic. Moreover, it was not entirely our short wheat crop that was causing the trouble. When, by a

Herculean effort, we prepared to meet the December program of 1,100,000 tons (about 37,000,000 bushels) of grains from the United States, we received word that the Allies would provide only 850,000 tons of shipping. On December 24, I cabled Sheldon:

> First, the Allies have only provided 850,000 tons shipping for December which amount will be loaded despite some railway difficulties due to universal blizzard and if allotted steamers actually available in time.
>
> Second, we have provided full amount 1,100,000 tons [of grain for] January 10 [at] various ports and there will be no difficulty loading but we are informed that full complement of shipping is not assured.
>
> Third, all foodstuffs . . . will receive every . . . [priority] in railway and port movement.
>
> You can assure authorities that if we receive the shipping and barring of course unforeseen accidents of war we will load not only the cereal program [January] but 100,000 to 200,000 tons of foodstuffs for [other destinations]. . . .

By now the severe winter had tied up navigation on the Great Lakes, and the bulk of Canada's crop could not be moved to seaboard until spring. The Allies proposed that we advance them our stocks, which, if necessary, would be replaced from Canada when transportation reopened. To this we readily agreed and confirmed it on January 1 in a letter to their representatives.

In spite of all our efforts, the unprecedented rigors of the weather, together with a coal shortage, almost brought about a collapse of rail transportation. By the middle of January it became evident that the supply program for the Allies for that month could not be met because of railway difficulties. On January 15, the Allied representatives in New York wrote me as follows:

> We are very greatly concerned to hear, today, from the Milling Division of the Food Administration that, at present, they see no prospect of their being able to allocate to us sufficient flour to fill our programs for January and February.
>
> This position of affairs is nothing short of disastrous and we beg of you to take urgent and immediate steps to see that our steamer program for

January and February is filled, *as guaranteed by you* on the 28th December and the 1st January.

I had never "guaranteed" anything. I had promised that we would do our best and send them every ounce the railways could deliver to seaboard during the next weeks. I cabled Lord Rhondda on January 25:

. . . We will export every grain that the American people save from their normal consumption. . . . We believe our people will not fail to meet the emergency.

On January 24, the Allied food representatives in New York sent me an elaborate bill of complaints, some in offensive terms. We in the Food Administration were no less anxious and worried about the winter difficulties than the Allies, and our conferences on ways and means to alleviate the crisis lasted far into the nights. In answer to this new pressure, I replied on January 28:

I do not think anyone can charge the Food Administration with not having made every possible effort . . . to supply the Allies with [their real needs in] foodstuffs. Even today, as you will notice by the press this morning (the President's Executive Order of January 28), we are endeavoring to reduce the wheat consumption of our people to a point below that which the English Government have reduced their own consumption. I do not think that anyone could ask us to do more.

As to precise times of movement, and as to the precise character of foodstuffs, that we can place at seaboard at a given time, we can do no more than is physically possible in view of the railway . . . and weather conditions in this country.

It does appear to me that if Allied shipping had been directed to the Argentine at the first of January, supplies would in turn have been available from that quarter during the month of March. That the Allied shipping authorities have failed in this particular should not, I think, make us responsible. We shall do what we can from our side to correct this failure. . . .

The statistical information in the hands of our staff and other tests of Allied stocks did not justify any such hysteria. The staff drafted more paragraphs referring to British continuation of brewing beer, distilling liquor, and other items, but I concluded that they would probably not add amiability, ships, or food. The winter situation was discouraging enough without verbal snowballs. Instead, we suggested that our ham, bacon, and lard production-conservation program was exceeding our hopes and that the British could reduce their Argentine meat imports by substitution of these supplies.

A new *dramatis persona* now entered the hysterical scene. Lord Reading had been sent to the United States as British High Commissioner, superior to all other British officials. In the latter part of February, he took over the job of demanding a guarantee to meet British needs until the next harvest. He enlisted the Italian Ambassador and the French High Commissioner in Washington to bombard us similarly. These three officials sent me lengthy messages on what I had to do to save their countries from disasters which would cause the loss of the war. Reading had been a most able lawyer in London, and his method was to beat an opponent to pulp with words. He naturally knew nothing about food. He flung inaccurate statistics at us. He seemed at times to consider himself still the Viceroy of India.

It was, of course, the duty of subordinate Allied officials and those of Neutral nations to avoid disagreeable conservation measures for their people. And it is human nature to demonstrate prowess to superiors—even to set up scarecrows to beat someone down.[1]

[1] The disclosures in official British publications after the war amply confirmed the reports of our European staff.

The French also published elaborate books on their food experience which hardly justified the hysterical statements made to us. Their publications showed that in the worst period during the critical year, they still had an intake of 2,800 calories daily, as compared to 1,800 for the Belgians.

The Italians normally had a much lower level of caloric intake than the British and a somewhat lower one than the French. Their imports proved ample to maintain public health.

The British bureaucracy's hysterical complaints and urgings had no basis in fact. Fortunately, for the record, a book was published by the economist of the British Food Ministry, Sir William Henry Beveridge. His book shows that the British daily caloric intake per man during this critical period was:

Prewar (1909–13)	3,442
1917	3,320
1918	3,358

THE WHOLE SCENE SHIFTS

In late March, 1918, the entire military situation took a bad turn. The Germans, having forced the surrender of Communist Russia, shifted their eastern armies to the Western Front. They repeatedly crashed through the Allied lines.

The morale of the French and Italian armies and the civilian popu-

---

Beveridge shows that weekly bread consumption per pound per capita increased steadily from prewar to 1918:

Year	Pounds
Prewar	4.28
1916	4.33
1917	4.69
1918	4.80

His statements of stocks of cereals on hand were (in tons):

	1915	1917
January	2,168,000	1,816,000
November	2,589,000	2,852,000
December	2,309,000	2,469,000
	1918	1919
February	1,893,000	2,765,000
March	1,732,000	2,359,000
April	1,513,000	1,802,000

Besides this confirmation of our information, Beveridge shows that the British consumption of breadstuffs actually increased over prewar.

Year	Tons
Prewar average	4,520,000
1917	4,930,000
1918	5,050,000

That North America carried the major burden of provisioning the Allies is shown by the percentage of their imported supplies which were received from us and the Canadians:

	1917	1918
Wheat, and wheat products	80.1 per cent	77.4 per cent
Meat	16.3 per cent	36.2 per cent
Bacon and ham	82.7 per cent	98.9 per cent
Lard	93.8 per cent	97.0 per cent
Dairy products	35.3 per cent	58.4 per cent
Sugar	54.6 per cent	63.5 per cent

lations fell badly under these blows, and the press carried alarming rumors about their food situations. Early in April, we in the Food Administration decided to take a bold risk to lift the morale of these two countries. We advised them that we would fill with food any ship they sent us. The risks on our part were considerable. However, by the end of April, our winter-wheat harvest looked promising; savings from our conservation measures were producing monthly surpluses beyond our highest hopes. As we should be harvesting in sixty days, we then included the British in these assurances.

By the first of July, 1918, during this year of a statistical vacuum, we were able to measure the amount of self-denial of the American people in grains. The figures of our exports were as follows (in tons):

Commodity	Prewar Average	1917–1918
Wheat and rye	3,720,398	4,590,928
Other cereals	1,607,296	4,584,633
	5,327,694	9,175,561

And this was in spite of our statistical vacuum.

At no time during this worst year of the war did the Allied food situation approach a famine stage. No one on the Allied side was ever hungry, except the Belgians—and they survived.

A RUSSIAN EXPEDITION

I introduce the following incident here because it was part of our problem during the "worst year." In June, 1918, Secretary of State Lansing and Colonel House decided that a strong gesture of amiability toward the Communist Government of Russia to help solve their food problems might pave the way to better relations. They proposed that I head a mission to Russia. The Secretary addressed the following letter to the President on June 13, 1918:

I suggest the creation of the "Commission for the Relief of Russia." This Commission to be organized generally along the same lines as the

"Commission for the Relief of Belgium," except that all of the funds required should be furnished for the time being at least out of your War Fund. This would obviate the necessity of going to Congress for the present for an appropriation.

An announcement by you that in order to give some tangible evidence to the world that the United States proposes to stand by Russia and to assist the Russian people in the circumstances in which they find themselves, you had concluded to create this Commission and to request Mr. Herbert Hoover to act as its head and that the Commission would act in close conjunction with the State Department and be guided in all questions of foreign policy by the State Department. . . . I feel sure that Mr. Hoover's appointment to head such a Commission would be widely acclaimed as another evidence of the determination of the United States to assist the Russian people toward the establishment of an orderly Government independent of Germany. The creation of this Commission would, for the time being, dispose of the proposal of armed intervention. The British, French, Italian and Japanese Governments could be told that armed intervention would have to depend on Mr. Hoover's recommendations after he had proceeded further with his work. Armed intervention to protect the humanitarian work done by the Commission would be much preferable to armed intervention before this work had been begun. I know that you will hesitate to take Mr. Hoover from his present work. I have learned, however, that the organization of the Food Administration has proceeded to such an extent that, while much work remains to be done, nevertheless another man could easily step in and effectively continue the work. No doubt Mr. Hoover has told you, as he has me, that our food supply at the present time is most satisfactory and that the present problem will be to dispose of properly the enormous supplies we have acquired through stimulation of production. . . .

LANSING

Colonel House addressed the President on the same day supporting Secretary Lansing. Bernard Baruch, on July 13, 1918, added his urgings in a letter to the President:

As Russia's greatest enemy, in my opinion, is going to be hunger and privation, might I suggest (and I do so most hesitatingly) that Mr. Hoover should head the mission. If anything at all has trickled into their minds from the outside world, the Russians will realize in sending him you are sending someone to help, not to conquer.

Although I was willing to do anything the President wished, I had little faith that the Russians would accept the necessary stipulation for cessation of their purposes in order to receive our relief—especially since the harvest of their crops would begin within a month. I was greatly relieved when the President, on July 15, replied to Baruch as follows:

I agree with you in your estimate of Hoover, but I cannot, without dislocating some of the most important things we are handling, spare him from his present functions.

CHAPTER 16

PROVISION OF FOOD FOR THE NEUTRALS

Before I leave the problems of furnishing food to the Allies, I should relate our coincident food and shipping relations with the Neutrals, which also added to our difficulties. Much of that relationship concerned the Food Administration. Because of much misrepresentation of the attitudes and actions of the United States toward the Neutrals during the war, the testimony of a daily eyewitness has some historical importance.

I had had constant dealings with the Northern European Neutrals in connection with the Belgian Relief and was familiar with their hardships arising from the coincident Allied blockade and pressures from the Germans. During the time the United States was at war, we did our best to assure their food supplies, but we also needed their co-operation in shipping. One of our purposes in the war was to save the small nations from extinction; however, we had scant co-operation, except from the Norwegians.

The major European Neutrals were Holland, Denmark, Sweden, Norway, Switzerland, and Spain. All required large imports of certain commodities for their own support, while at the same time they had surplus production of other sorts. In Holland, Denmark, and Switzerland, the agricultural economy was largely based on the import of feed grains and the export of meat and dairy products. Sweden also exported some surplus animal products. Norway, in addition to these commodities, exported large amounts of fish, whale, and fish oils, which were then the base of oleomargarine. All of the Neutrals were dependent upon considerable imports of breadstuffs, feed, petroleum products, coal, coffee, sugar, tea, and sundry other commodities.

Each of these countries possessed a merchant marine larger than was required for transport needs. Their populations and seagoing gross tonnages, when we entered the war in April, 1917, were about:

Country	Population	Total Tonnage	Required for Their Own Supplies	Surplus
Norway	2,565,000	1,968,000	300,000	1,668,000
Sweden	5,756,000	853,000	300,000	553,000
Holland	6,588,000	1,302,000	400,000	902,000
Denmark	2,940,000	688,000	300,000	388,000
Switzerland * .	3,910,000	...	...	...
Spain	20,750,000	706,000	300,000	406,000
Total		5,517,000	1,600,000	3,917,000

* The Swiss would give us no information regarding the merchant ships they acquired or their charters—but we estimated they were ample for their needs.

The use of the Neutrals' surplus of ships by us and the Allies was vital to winning the war. The very life of the ten million hungry people in Belgium and Northern France also depended upon ships. Therefore, the Food Administration, through agents in each country, kept track of available tonnage and its use. We also kept a complete check on food production and exports, including amounts of food furnished the enemy and import needs.

Holland, Denmark, and Switzerland had adjoining frontiers with Germany; Norway and Sweden lay only across the straits. These small nations were ground between the dangers of German invasion and the Allied blockade. They were subjected to great pressures by the Allies to charter their surplus ships and by the Germans not to do so. Both the Allies and Germans wanted whatever food surpluses they produced. The Allies possessed the pressure weapon of the food blockade; they, together with the United States, Japan, and China, controlled all bunker coal in the world outside Germany.

Thus the Allies could control the Neutrals' homeward voyages with supplies and their foreign trade in the distant seas.

In view of the tough year (1917–1918) ahead of us and the Allies, it was imperative from the beginning of the Food Administration that the Neutrals go to the more remote food sources, such as the Southern Hemisphere, where there were abundant supplies. But they wanted to obtain supplies via the short journey to North America, thereby saving their own ships for lucrative trade opportunities in the Pacific, South Atlantic, and Indian oceans. Furthermore, they disliked the dangerous voyages to the Allies.

When the United States entered the war, we had an overseas merchant fleet of less than three million tons, which was not sufficient to maintain our own vital imports and, at the same time, to transport and supply our military forces in France. In fact, we were compelled to stop our own imports of many key materials from distant countries and to increase our drastic controls of consumption.

I have already described how the Neutrals, fearful of the state of world food supplies after the submarine war began in February, 1917, rushed into our markets, accumulating large stocks as protection for the future. The four-month delay of the Congress in passing the Food and Embargo laws facilitated these activities. This flood of buying contributed to the demoralization of both our grain and animal markets.

In Volume I of these memoirs and in this chapter I frequently refer to our endeavors to secure neutral charters for the Belgian Relief. The major reason for these urgings was, of course, to feed the Belgians, who were dependent upon a small fleet of Belgian-flag ships but mostly on Neutral charters. The Relief Commission's charters had a guarantee of immunity from attack from both Germany and the Allies, and our repeated urgings to the Neutrals to charter the large tonnage offered them the opportunity to serve without danger of German opposition.

I have quoted in Volume I of this memoir a vigorous letter which I wrote to Secretary Lansing a few weeks after I became Food Administrator. It states that in exchange for our furnishing food to the

Neutrals when our own situation was most difficult, the Neutrals should reciprocate by at least chartering their ships to the Belgian Relief. On June 7, 1917, I wrote a further note to Secretary Lansing, saying in part:

DEAR MR. SECRETARY:

. . . It appears to me that it is necessary for this government to food-ration the whole neutral world. This is an obligation to humanity, but as this country and the Allies are fighting for the freedom of the world, we must ask the neutral world for a much larger degree of services than the mere payment of cash for this rationing, and only on this basis could we justify the appeals we are making to our people to [work] overtime and to self-denial in their own food supply.

HERBERT HOOVER

After our entry into the war, in a discussion with Mr. Wilson concerning Neutral activities, I stated my belief that under Allied threats the Neutrals lived in constant fear of starvation, with resulting animosities and unwillingness to co-operate. I suggested that we might obtain more help from the Neutrals if we informed them of three policies:

First, we would assure them such a place at the world food table that they need not fear starvation.

Second, we would assure them that if they would undertake the longer voyages to the Southern Hemisphere food markets, we would facilitate supplies of bunker coal and allow such ships to pass the blockade.

Third, in return for this co-operation, they should be willing to charter ships to us, the Allies, or the Belgian Relief.

After the President created the Export Council, of which I was a member, in July, 1917, I notified the Neutrals, on the Council's authority, that the Allies needed more foodstuffs than could be supplied from North America and that they, the Neutrals, should go to more distant markets. Following this notice, with the approval of my colleagues, I informed each of their ambassadors or ministers of the policies which had been approved by the President. They all professed great relief at these assurances. I explained our critical food situation and described their excessive holdings of food in American ports and suggested that they deliver the excess amounts to the Belgian Relief at Rotterdam. I will relate how these various policies worked out.

THE NORWEGIANS CO-OPERATE

The Norwegians were always co-operative. They owned about 1,668,000 tons of ships over and above their own needs. In the panic over the submarine war, they had accumulated by July, 1917, a large amount of food on board ships and in storage in our ports. In August, we disposed of part of their holdings to the Belgian Relief, and part was released for their own uses. We also obtained a number of charters from them for both the Belgian Relief and the Allies.

In mid-November, 1917, our newly created War Trade Board, on behalf of the Allies and our Government, began negotiations with the Norwegians for charter of the remainder of their surplus tonnage. An agreement was reached for a large tonnage of charters to the Allies and some to the Belgian Relief.[1]

Also in November, the War Trade Board made further arrangements with the Norwegians in which they required food from us, despite the desperate year ahead. The amounts allowed were as follows (in tons):

Product	Last Half of 1917	First Half of 1918
Oleo oil	7,953	387
Pork products	4,148	13
Lard	1,617	161
Wheat flour	70,078	2,105
Oil cake and oil cake meal	35,907	....
Cottonseed oil	16,796	286
Barley	50,762	13,368

We filled these requirements and after the harvest of 1918 met all Norwegian demands.

[1] Herbert Hoover, *An American Epic* (Chicago, Henry Regnery Company, 1959—), Vol. I, Chap. 44.

HOLLAND

The Dutch had little fear of invasion. They had a substantial army, and although they could have been invaded by the Germans, it would have been a useless and costly operation. The Allies could, of course, have occupied the rich Dutch East Indian empire—at the possible cost of Holland's joining with the Germans in the war.

The Dutch were required by the Allies not to transship imported goods or their equivalents to the Germans. And by agreement, their surplus native produce, mostly animal products, was divided between the Allies and the Germans. This amounted to five thousand tons a month for each side.

Like the other European Neutrals, Holland had bought large quantities of food and feed from the United States and elsewhere at the beginning of the submarine war and had landed considerable amounts in Holland prior to our embargo. Before opening negotiations with the Dutch, we made our usual appraisal of their food needs. Our investigation revealed that they had ample animal and sugar production for their own use and that their population would suffer no privation if they were allowed to import 300,000 tons of grain during the harvest year 1917–1918, plus a supply of coffee, cocoa, and certain non-food commodities, including petroleum products.

Soon after the embargo was imposed, Dutch authorities asked for license to export their holdings in the United States. It developed that they had some sixty ships in American harbors with the following food on board (in tons):

Wheat	18,500
Corn	64,900
Barley	16,600
Oats	42,500
Linseed cake	52,000
Total	194,500
Ships in ballast	85,000
Total ship tonnage	279,500

We later found that they also had food in warehouses.

At a meeting with the Netherlands Minister early in July, 1917, I set forth the President's policies toward Neutrals and asked for Dutch co-operation. We had further meetings, and on July 31, I wrote the Netherlands Minister the following review of our situation and made a proposal to him:

July 31, 1917

YOUR EXCELLENCY:

I beg to confirm our conversation of today. That the immediate difficulty in this country is our totally inadequate supply of . . . [food] grains and fodder material to carry over the . . . [Allies] and their animals until the arrival of the new harvest [1918]. That we are informed that the people of Holland have sufficient supplies to carry them over until the arrival of the harvest [of 1917] and that thereafter they will be in a perfectly safe position for some months. That the reports which have reached us of the actual starvation in Belgium fill us with the greatest anxiety and are due in fact to our inability to secure the transport of foodstuffs for the Belgian Relief. That while we feel a great humanitarian obligation to the people of Belgium, we also feel that this has been for an equal time uppermost in the minds of the Holland Government, as shown by the devotion of the Dutch people toward the Belgian people since the beginning of the war.

With view to saving the drain on our food supply which would otherwise ensue if we supplied Belgium from our present stocks, I have to suggest that two-thirds of the grain still in good condition, now in Dutch shipping, should be delivered by the Dutch Government to the Belgian Relief Commission at Rotterdam, the remainder, of course, being delivered to the Dutch Government itself. The portion delivered to the Belgian Relief Commission will of course be subjected to inspection and will be paid for by the Commission at cost, and the charter money and insurance will also be paid by the Relief Commission.

I feel that you will agree that this arrangement would solve a great humanitarian problem and meet our situation as well, and that I could secure the adherence of all the interested Governments.

HERBERT HOOVER

The Minister replied on August 3, 1917, confirming this arrangement.

I have not failed to submit the proposal contained in your note of July 31st to my Government who declared in principle to agree to transfer to the Belgian Relief Commission two-thirds of the cargo at the actual time loaded in Netherland ships in ports of the United States.

However, the Netherland Government has thought it advisable to consult the Belgian Relief Commission itself concerning your proposal and informs me now that the Commission does not consider advantageous an arrangement by which it is to receive two-thirds of the cargoes now loaded in Netherland vessels in the United States as among those cargoes are barley, oats and linseed cake, which would be of no use for the Commission. Therefore the Netherland Government and the Belgian Relief Commission have in accordance with the spirit of your proposal agreed on the following points:

There are now in the different ports of the United States 42 Netherland vessels with an aggregate cargo space of about 195,000 tons and loaded with about 18,500 tons of wheat, 64,900 tons corn, 16,600 tons barley, 42,100 tons oats and 52,400 tons linseed cake. At the disposal of the Belgian Relief Commission is to be placed two-thirds of this total cargo space or about 135,000 tons. The Commission is to receive its proposed part of the above mentioned amount of wheat and corn already loaded, or about 50,000 tons, whereas the balance of 85,000 tons due to the Commission could be made up by 14 Netherland vessels lying empty in the United States ports with an aggregate cargo space of 65,000 tons and other vessels with an aggregate cargo space of 20,000 tons, also of Dutch registry, ready to be sent from Holland at first notice.

It is understood that all the above mentioned vessels can sail without delay of any kind and that the United States authorities secure the adherence of all the interested Governments. The Belgian Relief Commission agrees to it that the price be fixed at cost and the cargoes delivered at Rotterdam.

W.L.F.C. Van Rappard

I was greatly pleased with this settlement, and, on the same day, I replied:

Your Excellency:

I am indeed obliged for your letter of the 3rd August, and will take the matter up with the Export Council.

I will be glad to know, however, if the Holland Government has any foodstuffs purchased or in warehouses in the United States which could be used to fill the 85,000 tons which you mention as a further supply to the Relief Commission, and I assume, of course, that only cargoes will be delivered to the Relief Commission which have passed inspection as to quality and character.

HERBERT HOOVER

The Minister again wished to discuss these matters. I confirmed our conversation as follows:

August 10, 1917

YOUR EXCELLENCY:

With regard to our conversation upon the assignment to the Commission for Relief in Belgium of certain cargoes lying in American ports, I have now had an opportunity of consulting the Export Council and they are disposed to recommend—

First. That all of the wheat cargoes and 40,000 tons of the corn cargoes be delivered to the Belgian Relief at Rotterdam.

Second. In that case export permits to be issued for Holland for 13,500 tons of barley and the balance of the loaded corn up to 37,000 tons.

Third. The cargoes to be inspected in American ports and those accepted by the Relief to be assigned to them.

Fourth. The Commission for Relief in Belgium to pay the cost and original charter money and insurance for the cargoes assigned to them, without demurrage.

HERBERT HOOVER

The Minister confirmed his Government's agreement to this proposal on August 13. I then instructed the New York Director of the Belgian Relief to have the cargoes examined by the Department of Agriculture inspectors. The inspection revealed that the cargoes had fermented and were unfit for human consumption. The Relief Commission broke off the transaction.

On September 4, the Netherlands Minister sent a long protest to the State Department. When it was referred to me, I made the following reply to the Assistant Secretary of State:

September 6, 1917

DEAR MR. WOOLSEY:

With respect to the memorandum of September 4th from the Netherlands Minister, reciting his troubles, I have only one observation to make:

> . . . the business got up to a point where it was ready to be submitted to the Export Council for final approval. The ships were inspected for the purpose of seeing the condition of the cargoes, and it developed that there was practically only a small percentage of [fit] human food actually in them. There was no cargo that could be accepted by the Relief Commission in toto, although the whole negotiations started out on the basis of the inspection.
>
> The Dutch finally proposed to the Relief Commission a scheme of sharing the material that might be of some good for human consumption, and as soon as this came before the Export Board they refused to grant licenses for export.
>
> I do not myself see where any complaint comes in. In fact, my impression is that the Relief Commission can complain that their time was exhausted in negotiating for materials that the Dutch must have known were of no value for human consumption.
>
> The whole negotiations were based on securing [fit] human food for the Belgians. . . .
>
> HERBERT HOOVER

The delay of negotiations by the Dutch had resulted in the rotting of 195,000 tons of precious food.

In December, 1917, new negotiations for ship charters with the Dutch were taken up in London by the War Trade Board and the British. An agreement was reached on January 28, 1918, providing for the charter of 500,000 tons of shipping for the Allies, not to be used in the danger zone, of which 150,000 tons were to be assigned to the Belgian Relief. The agreement, however, required a large amount of food and feed to be supplied to Holland from the United States. We and the Allies were in the midst of our worst food crisis. However, under German pressure, the Dutch repudiated this new agreement.

The question of requisitioning the sixty Dutch vessels in American harbors immediately arose. The British had set a precedent by requisitioning Danish vessels, lying idle in English harbors, which the Danes had refused to charter for any service. The British now urged similar American action in the case of Dutch ships. In March, 1918, during the increased shipping crisis resulting from the German attack on the Western Front, the War Trade Board presented the matter to the President's War Council; the President agreed to the requisitioning. The Dutch officials and their press had much to say in protest, but they omitted all reference to the fact that America's purpose in the war was to save the independence of the small states from rape by German and Austrian militarists—such as had taken place in previous years in Poland, Bohemia, Serbia, and elsewhere.

The requisition of Dutch shipping in our harbors amounted to about 530,000 tons, and at the same time, the British requisitioned 124,000 tons. The Dutch still had ample tonnage to carry essential supplies. We secured part of this requisitioned tonnage for the Belgian Relief. Since both we and the British announced that we would pay the prevailing exorbitant charter rates, the shares in Dutch shipping companies rose enormously in price, indicating that there was no grief among Dutch owners. No one in Holland suffered from lack of food during our worst year of the war, 1917–1918, which confirmed our information that they had imported considerable stocks during the early part of 1917.

SWITZERLAND

The Swiss had a small fleet of merchant vessels which they had bought or chartered. They had arranged with the Germans for immunity for their vessels from attack, a guarantee similar to that given the Belgian Relief, and could therefore obtain additional Neutral charters. When the Swiss sought food from us, I suggested to Secretary of State Lansing that he give them our usual assurances that they would not starve—but that we expected co-operation from them. This he did on June 19, 1917. However, on August 15, 1917, an official delegation arrived in Washington, insisting that we obligate ourselves to find food for Switzerland and ships from the United States. We stated our difficult situation and urged the delegation to go to the Southern Hemisphere.

With the aid of Americans of Swiss descent and American residents in Switzerland, the Swiss launched a great propaganda campaign, demanding supplies and ships from us. They added to the clamor by sending to the United States a propaganda mission armed with many speeches on human freedom and on our obligations to them in its practice. As a propaganda stunt, they demanded that we affirm our respect for their neutrality and independence. The State Department agreed at once, but the propaganda continued.

In November, 1917, in the midst of our worst food crisis, the Swiss sent 15,000 tons of their own shipping to American ports and demanded that the ships be loaded with food. Although they had no need for food at this time, the Food Administration, at the insistence of the State Department, informed the Swiss Minister on November 26 that the 15,000 tons would be furnished. Since his countrymen could already have received these supplies from the Argentine, I expressed to the State Department my indignation over imposing this load of sacrifice on our own people and on the Allies at this crucial time.

In the meantime, the War Trade Board had been negotiating with Swiss representatives, and an agreement was signed on December 5, 1917. The agreement enumerated supplies for Switzerland during the following twelve months: 360,000 tons of grain, to be obtained somewhere at the rate of 30,000 tons a month. But there was a condition that these food supplies would be furnished only if "they were not required by the Associated Powers."

I promptly informed the War Trade Board that we had neither ships nor food to supply this program without depriving the Allies and that the Board would have to demand that the Swiss charter Neutral ships and go to the Argentine. But the Swiss propaganda agencies launched a bitter complaint that the United States was 60,000 tons behind the "guaranteed" program. The British claimed that under the agreement the Swiss had only "the right to buy 30,000 tons of food a month" from somewhere and therefore refused to furnish any tonnage—also insisting that the Swiss charter Neutral vessels and go to the Argentine.

Our constant and accurate information on Swiss food supplies showed that the Swiss were in no danger of starvation. However, their propagandists became even more excited and bitter. As a consequence, in late March, 1918, in the middle of the shipping crisis resulting from the German attack on the Western Front, the Shipping Board, at the insistence of the State Department, made available 60,000 tons of shipping. I agreed to load it, but I protested that it would deprive the British and French of just that many supplies and ships. The Shipping Board, then regretting its deal, stalled in sending the ships until May 3, 1918, when, as a counterpropaganda stunt, the Board dispatched two grain ships to the Swiss with a flourish and an unnecessary naval escort.

In September, 1918, the Swiss reminded us that we were now more than 90,000 tons short in our "guarantee"—which was, in fact, no guarantee. There was no hurry because their new grain crop would carry them for several months. We and the Allies were busy transporting Pershing's large army, and we gave them no ships.

One of our annoyances was that the Americans who received the hostile Swiss propaganda failed to reply that we were fighting a war to save such states as Switzerland. Also, it can be said that in spite of their unco-operative tactics and our shipping restrictions, no one in Switzerland starved during the war.

SWEDEN

Sweden had a surplus merchant fleet of about 500,000 tons beyond its need to transport essential supplies. The Swedes had an army of more than 400,000 men and were in no danger that the Germans would waste strength in attacking them across the Baltic. Moreover, they were shipping to Germany annually nearly 5,000,000 tons of a superior iron ore which the Germans could not do without. They were also shipping the Germans wood pulp, fish, and some animal products.

Under German pressure, Sweden had kept much of her merchant fleet idle at home or in refuge in foreign ports. The vulnerable point was Sweden's need for imports of grain, petroleum products, coffee, and other secondary commodities. Swedish food production had dropped because of the employment of agricultural labor in making industrial supplies for the Germans.

Sweden dispatched a special commissioner to Washington—Herman Legercrantz—who arrived on May 18, 1917. He was sent to me by the State Department, and as in the case of all other Neutrals, I assured him of our determination that no Neutral should starve. I made our usual proposal that the Swedes use their surplus shipping to get supplies from more remote markets, and that we would see that they secured bunker coal and permission to transport such supplies through the blockade. I asked that they co-operate with us in our problems, one of which was the immediate need of ship charters for the Belgian Relief.

The Swedes, like the other Northern Neutrals, had made large purchases of grain in the United States prior to our entering the war. Later, when the embargo was applied, we found that they held contracts for some 270,000 bushels of rye and nearly 700,000 bushels of wheat. Also, at this moment the British were holding up at Halifax about 370,000 bushels of American grain in Swedish ships. Our information showed clearly that the Swedes had substantial stocks at home and no immediate need for any such volume of supplies—and in any event they could have obtained them from the Argentine. At their request for export licenses, we proposed that they sell 550,000 bushels of wheat to the Belgian Relief and give that organization charters for six vessels, to which they agreed.

Later, the War Trade Board, jointly with the British, undertook negotiations with Sweden on various outstanding questions. One result was to get the United States entangled in the purchase of iron ore to prevent its going to the Germans. (It subsequently developed that the Germans had more ore than they could use at the time this purchase was made.) The negotiations dragged on until the tide of war began to turn in favor of the Allies in September, 1918, when the War Trade Board obtained a large amount of ship tonnage. At the insistence of the Swedes that 200,000 tons be employed on safe routes, we were able to secure this shipping for the Belgian Relief.

DENMARK

The Danes had no consequential military forces, and the Germans could have moved in at any time. The Germans knew that the blockade would stop all forage imports to Denmark, and thus their meat and dairy products from that source would vanish. Also, they knew that if they invaded Denmark, the Allies would seize the entire Danish merchant fleet on the seas, as well as their foreign territorial possessions. Denmark had a considerable merchant marine for such a small but highly enterprising nation—about 500,000 tons beyond its own needs.

The Danish food industry was built on animal products, for which they imported large amounts of feed grains. They also needed some bread grains, coffee, petroleum products, other minor commodities, and bunker coal. When our embargo was imposed in July, 1917, the Danes had 75,000 tons of cottonseed cake stored in our ports, which we detained. In line with our policies, I sent for a Danish representative and suggested to him that his country charter a substantial part of its merchant fleet to the United States or assign it to the Belgian Relief. To my disappointment, they flatly refused. Since the Danes, with their forthcoming harvest, would not be in acute need for food or feed, the Exports Commission refused them export permits.

By October, 1917, the embargo had begun to pinch, and Denmark started negotiations for food with the War Trade Board. The British, however, demanded more drastic restrictions on Danish food shipments to Germany, and matters were further delayed. On November 27, the Board laid before the Danes a proposed agreement on ships and food. Under German pressure, they refused to accept it.

Interminable discussions dragged on until March, 1918, when the War Trade Board issued a statement of its final terms, revolving principally around ships, but without results. When the tide of war began to turn in favor of the Allies in September, 1918, an agreement with Denmark was reached—just sixty days before the Armistice. This agreement provided for large food exports from the United States. As a result of our 1918 harvest, we were able to meet the food provisions. Under the settlement, Denmark was required to supply 265,000 tons of shipping to the United States and 200,000 tons to Great Britain. I secured some ships for the Belgian Relief.

No one in Denmark went hungry.

SPAIN

The Spanish had a fleet sufficient to supply themselves with food from South American markets—and did so. Their problems, therefore, did not concern the Food Administration. They had, however, a surplus of ships, which was a problem for the War Trade Board.

LATIN-AMERICA

The Latin-American countries secured their small import food needs from the Argentine. The only dealings of importance which the Food Administration had with the Latin-American states concerned Mexican sisal hemp for binder twine; we received little cooperation.

A SUMMARY OF RELATIONS WITH NEUTRALS

The history of our relations with the Neutrals during the war has been the subject of unending discussion and criticism of the United States, mostly from academic sources. Many of the critics were intent on proving American brutality and violations of the basic concepts of freedom.

Seldom has it been pointed out by these persons that, as I have already stated, the United States was forced into a very dangerous war by the German and Austrian militarists, who were bent on extinguishing all small nations on the Continent—as they had already done with Poland, Serbia, Croatia, Bohemia, Slovakia, and others. Seldom do the critics mention that our avowed purpose in war was to assure the freedom of small nations.

Also, these arbiters omit reference to the critical crop year of 1917–1918, when we were desperately straining to provide food supplies for the Allies, or to the fact that any food exports to Allies and Neutrals had to come from the self-denial of the American people. Nor do they refer to the fact that the Neutrals could have obtained unlimited supplies from the Southern Hemisphere and that their demands on us were aimed at effecting shorter voyages in order to carry more cargoes of profitable trade. Nor do these critics mention the extortionate rates which the Neutrals demanded for their ships—six voyages paid the original cost of a ship—and the other huge profits they made from the war. The Norwegians were the co-operative exception to this.

However, when the Neutrals did charter vessels to the Allies for war service, their crews gave outstanding proof of the physical courage of their people. Many of them perished in Allied service. And no doubt it is the duty of national officials to insure their country's interests and complain when they do not get their demands.

CHAPTER 17

THE END OF OUR ANXIETIES OVER FOOD SUPPLIES FOR THE ALLIES

Our anxieties regarding supplies for the Allies ended with the huge harvest of 1918. This harvest was the result of Food Administration, Department of Agriculture, and Canadian policies to stimulate production and save food. It was due to the hard work and longer hours of old men and boys on the farms and to the women who worked in the fields for the first time in their lives, including many women who volunteered from the towns and cities.

The estimated grain crop for 1918, with its improvement over 1917, was, in round numbers, as follows (in bushels):

1918 Crop	Production	Increase or Decrease from 1917
Wheat	921,500,000	+284,800,000
Corn	2,500,000,000	—600,000
Oats	1,538,000,000	—55,000,000
Barley	256,000,000	+44,000,000
Rye	91,000,000	+28,000,000
Total	5,306,500,000	+301,200,000

Although the 1918 corn crop was less, in bushels, than that of 1917, it was fully matured and of very much greater food value than the crop of the previous year. There were increases in rice and beans.

From our stimulation of animal production, we now had all the meat and fat supplies which the Allies could transport.

Our increased sugar production in the Western Hemisphere was sufficient to protect all of us, provided there were moderate restrictions on consumption in each country. Added to these supplies was an abundant harvest in Canada, which was due to the same hard work in the fields by Canadian men and women.

The problem of food for the Allies and Neutrals was now a question of available shipping—and that depended upon military strategy.

THE MEETING OF ALLIED FOOD ADMINISTRATORS IN LONDON IN JULY, 1918

In order to determine our food strategy and co-ordinate our operations with available shipping during the new crop year beginning in July, 1918, we arranged a conference in London in late July with the food ministers of Britain, France, Italy, and Canada.

I represented the United States, along with James Bell, Chairman of our Milling Division; James Jackson, Vice-President of the Grain Corporation; Joseph Cotton, Chief of our Meats and Fats Division; Dr. Alonzo Taylor, our European representative; Lewis Strauss, my secretary; and Hugh Gibson, who was assigned to us by the State Department.

Lord Rhondda, the ablest of the British Food Ministers, had passed away a few weeks before our arrival, and J. N. Cline, a member of the Labor Party, was appointed to the position. Cline's experience in food consisted of only three months as Lord Rhondda's Parliamentary representative, but he was an able man.

I SPEAK AT THE MANSION HOUSE

On July 23, the Lord Mayor of London gave a luncheon for us at the Mansion House. A condensation of my remarks on that occasion (partly ad-lib) is as follows:

YOUR HONOR THE LORD MAYOR AND GUESTS:

At the outbreak of war four years ago, we were startled with the realization that a mass of 10,000,000 people in Belgium and Northern France were in jeopardy of immediate starvation. Thus was announced to the whole world the vital relationship of food and war.

At the time of that call for help, we little realized that sooner or later the food supplies in the world of 2,500,000,000 people would be disturbed and that its problems would penetrate into every quarter of the globe. . . .

In normal times, the world possesses little margin of food supplies from year to year, for population presses upon the heels of food supply. With the higher standard of living among the Western races, there is some safety margin by decreasing consumption without damage to public health. Reduction of consumption in war is, however, an insufficient measure. [But true] . . . food strategy in war lies in the stimulation of production.

Also, food policies must be founded on the science of nutrition, a science which had long remained locked up in our laboratories, but it stands now silhouetted against a background of tragedy. And, as the control of food supply has thus gained in complexity and importance, normal methods of distribution have broken down. The feeding of peoples [in war] is no longer a matter of private initiative, but a function of government. Furthermore, the war problem of food, penetrating as it does three times daily into every home, gives rise to anxieties and fears in every heart. And it becomes one of the dominant problems in morale and steady partners in war.

Fourteen months ago when the United States entered the war, I was called by the President from Europe to undertake, under his personal direction, the supply of food to the Allies from the United States. The submarine menace had to be met by the short voyage from North America, and the best guarded highway. Other fundamental changes in food strategy were necessary to save tonnage. For instance, overseas transport of fodder must be reduced by allowing the production of meats and fats in the Allied countries to decline, provided we could quickly increase North American exports of these concentrated foods.

. . . From climatic causes, our 1917 harvest in the United States left us no statistical export surplus. Beyond this again, the great drain of foodstuffs to Europe during the previous season had exhausted our supplies to an extent never hitherto known and had even [encroached] upon our capital in animals. Yet we have, despite all these difficulties, during the last twelve months exported 15,000,000 tons of food from the United States including the West Indies, or nearly double our prewar exports.

I am happy to tell you that the . . . exertions of our . . . government and of our farm men, our women and boys . . . have borne such fruit that there is no need during the next 12 months for any restriction on the volume we can furnish our European Allies if we have the ships.

We can summarize our present position by stating that in the next 12 months we can, with pressure of saving by our people, export at least 20,000,000 tons, and to this Canada will add about 4,000,000 tons.

With these reserves in the nearest markets, with this saving in shipping, and this volume of supplies, we can say with assurance that all anxiety as to the stocks of food is now passed.

We can also note the situation of the enemy, for there is within the enemy lines one outstanding, dominating fact—hunger. A periphery of starvation rings about so-called German victories and among their occupied peoples.

I am the bearer of a message from the President of the United States:

"That the American people are gladly willing to make any sacrifice in consumption and production of foodstuffs that will maintain the health, comfort, and courage of the people of the Allied countries. We are . . . eating at a common table with them."

INTER-ALLIED FOOD ORGANIZATION

Upon my arrival in London, we agreed to set up an "Allied Food Council," comprising:

J. N. Cline, *British Minister of Food*
Victor Boret, *French Minister of Agriculture and Food*
Silvio Crespi, *Italian Minister of Agriculture and Food,* with Signor Bernardo Attolico, *his first assistant*
Herbert Hoover, *Food Administrator for the United States*
Dr. James Robertson, *Canadian Food Administrator*

The Council first convened on July 23. The Allied representatives made informal estimates of their needs. When I added the needs of the Belgian Relief, the minor Allies, and the Neutrals, the total came to 32,000,000 tons of food for the following year. These estimates could be fulfilled only by going to the Southern Hemisphere, and the ships required for food and other supplies would total more than 4,500,000 tons in constant use. This estimate, however, was based on the amounts which the various food controllers would have liked, rather than on the hard facts of the shipping world. It was suggested by the Italian representative, Silvio Crespi, that the European harvest should, if possible, be held in reserve for emergencies—and therefore that initial shipments from North America should be on a larger scale than the estimated monthly need. But this was impossible because it would require still more shipping during the early months.

In order to get down to the realities of the situation, we appointed a temporary committee to study these estimates. The committee was comprised of two representatives from each of the five governments, together with representatives of the Allied Maritime Transport Council, the Inter-Allied Finance Council, and the Inter-Allied Nutritional Commission. In reality, the program for the next year had little relation to these determinations. It depended upon the military strategy of the Allies in the coming months, which would determine the shipping we would have available. I decided to find out what this strategy would be, the account of which I give in the next chapter.

On August 8, I returned to London, and, in view of the shipping available, we quickly settled the American and Canadian food programs for the next year, should the war continue. The program of Allied supplies was (in tons):

Breadstuffs (wheat and substitutes in terms of grain)	10,400,000
Meats and fats	2,600,000
Sugar (from United States and West Indies)	1,850,000
Feed grain	2,700,000
Total	17,550,000

The Canadian Food Administrator and I stated that we could handle the program from North America alone. However, we found that we also required ships from the Belgians, the minor Allies, and the Neutrals. This program, considering inevitable port delays and the slow convoy system, implied the constant use of more than three million tons of shipping for food and other civilian supplies during the year. I informed my colleagues that any program we agreed upon would likely need to be changed with any alteration in military strategy and that we might have a rough time. The Food Council, at my suggestion, passed the following final resolution:

> Resolved that, while the increased production of the United States renders it possible to relax some of the restrictions which have borne with peculiar hardship upon all our peoples, yet it is absolutely necessary that rigid economy and elimination of waste in the consumption and handling of all foodstuffs, as well as increased production, should be maintained throughout the European Allied countries and in North America.
>
> It is only by such economy and elimination of waste that the transportation of the necessary men and supplies from North America to the European front can be accomplished. . . . stocks of foodstuffs can be built up in North America as an insurance against the ever-present danger of harvest failure and the possible necessity for large emergency drafts to Europe.
>
> We cannot administer the food problem on the basis of one year's war; we must prepare for its long continuance if we are to ensure absolute victory.

CHAPTER 18

THE REVOLUTION IN ALLIED MILITARY STRATEGY AND ITS EFFECTS ON FOOD SUPPLY

As the amount of food we could deliver depended upon the ships at our disposal and that in turn upon the military strategy, a knowledge of what that was to be was essential to any food action or policy. In my quest for information in London, both my food colleagues and the highest British authorities stated that the major line of strategy was not yet determined. With Hugh Gibson of our American Legation in London, I then went to Paris.

Our exploration of the military strategy in Paris was interrupted by the extension to us of many Belgian and French courtesies. Hugh Gibson's diary records that on August 1 we visited the King of the Belgians, at his request, at La Panne. On August 2, we attended a luncheon given by President Poincaré (with speeches). On August 3, we attended a public luncheon in Paris (with speeches); in the afternoon, we attended a reception at the Hotel de Ville (with speeches). On August 4, I called on Marshal Joffre, who, being retired and reticent as well, gave me no information. General Foch's staff stated that strategic plans were still unsettled.

An inter-Allied council generally known as the Supreme War Council had been set up in Paris. General Tasker H. Bliss was the American representative. General Bliss informed me that nothing had yet been determined and that General Pershing, not being a member of the Council, was in a position to more frankly describe the situation. I arranged to meet the General at the American Army headquarters at Chaumont on August 6.

Some background is necessary to make clear the reasons for the military indecision, what transpired at my meeting with the General, and the subsequent effect upon our food policies. In the early chapters of this memoir, I have reviewed the strategy of the Allied governments and their military leaders.

Their strategy had been based on a "wearing down" of the Central Empires by holding the trench front and the blockade. The Allies had opposed any idea of building up considerable American ground armies. Primarily, they had wanted naval and air support and materials from the United States and, for morale purposes, a few token divisions of infantry.

General Pershing, from the time he was given command of the American force, had constantly insisted that large American ground armies in France would be necessary to win the war. He had been told repeatedly that shipping was not available to transport such armies and at the same time support the Allies with naval and air forces, food, raw materials, and munitions.[1] On March 1, 1918, he had a total of about 250,000 American fighting men on the front line in France.[2]

The whole picture changed with the defeat of Russia under the hammer blows of the Germans. The Communists made peace with Germany on March 2, 1918. At once the Germans moved their armies from their Eastern Front to the Western, and late in March, they crashed through the British lines. In the face of this peril, the Allies, through the War Council, at last agreed on a single command and General Foch was appointed. On April 5, the Allied Prime Ministers cabled President Wilson:

"... General Foch has presented to us a statement of the utmost gravity. ... as there is no possibility of the British and French increasing the numbers of their divisions ... there is a great danger of the war being lost unless the numerical inferiority of the Allies can be remedied as rapidly as possible by the advent of American troops. ...

[1] See Chapter 3.
[2] Omitting service troops.

"We are satisfied that Gen. Foch . . . is not overestimating the needs of the case. . . .[3]

"D. LLOYD GEORGE,
"CLEMENCEAU,
"ORLANDO."

In May, the Germans smashed the French lines, reaching the Marne. On June 5, the Allies again cabled the President:

We recognize that the combatant troops to be dispatched in July may have to include troops which have had insufficient training, but we consider the present emergency such as to justify a temporary and exceptional departure by the United States. . . .

FOCH
MILNER
PERSHING

In this critical situation, General Pershing again urged that he be given shipping to transport still larger forces from the United States for an early all-out counterattack, since the German Army had been greatly weakened. The nature of his proposals is indicated by his letter of June 19, 1918, to General Peyton C. March, Chief of Staff, in Washington:

. . . The general situation here on the Western front indicates clearly to me that we must be prepared to strike with a very strong force as early as it is possible to do so. The German strength is undoubtedly on the wane and by early fall we should look forward to the possibility of assuming the offensive, to be continued early in the spring with all the force that we can get together. There are several reasons why we should do this. One is that our allies are becoming so war-weary that I do not believe they will hold out beyond another year. Another is that we should strike while the Germans are weakest and before they can recuperate by conscription in Russia, as now seems possible.

To this end, the most energetic measures should be taken to insure the flow of troops at the rate of 250,000 a month, beginning with August

[3] I am able to present this and subsequent military dispatches through the courtesy of our War Department.

and continuing at least until the first of April [1919] and thereafter, if necessary. . . . I believe it is much the wiser plan if it can be done. Our people are now at the top notch of enthusiasm and are anxious to have the war terminated successfully. Our losses would be much less than if the war were allowed to drag along for two or three years.

A letter from General Pershing to Colonel House dated the same day made similar recommendations, adding:

> More shipping is going to be needed but we should sacrifice some of our commerce if necessary and allot more tonnage to the army. . . .

On July 15, the Germans attacked the French lines at Reims, but the same day, the Allies counterattacked on the Marne. With the aid of Allied and American transport, by August 1, in the four months since the Allied Prime Ministers' appeal, Pershing's strength was increased to about 750,000 fighting men.

The primary problem in strategy-determination was ships. On August 1, our American merchant fleet totaled about 3,800,000 tons, but our great shipbuilding program had bogged down (see Chapter 2). General Pershing had most of the American ships in his service. We were even using old sailing ships and converted yachts for domestic-import purposes. As I have already stated, the British, French, and Italians had 3,470,000 tons of ships engaged in commercial trade in the Mediterranean and the Indian, South Atlantic, and Pacific oceans. They insisted, with justification, that this trade had to be maintained to hold their economic strength.

It was against these backgrounds that I met General Pershing on August 6. I explained to him that our food supply was much improved and that our information showed the food situation in the Central Empires to be so deteriorated that it was undermining the morale of their people, despite recent victories. I confessed that I was in a fog with regard to our food strategy because of our inability to learn anything of military plans for the next year, either in London or Paris. These plans would determine the shipping available to us for food and other supplies to the Allies.

The General said that he could understand my bewilderment because there were no plans yet agreed upon. He then informed me that the Supreme War Council would meet in a few days and would probably decide what to do. He stated that the military question was whether to make an early counterattack in the remaining months of 1918—carried, possibly, into the winter of 1919, provided the ground were still hard enough to move heavy equipment. The alternative was to defer the attack to the late spring or early summer of 1919, with the hope of ending the war in late 1919 or early 1920. The difference, as far as ending the war was concerned, might be as much as a year.

The General was adamant that the counterattack be made at once. One of the reasons he gave was that the Germans had suffered about 800,000 casualties in their attacks on the Western Front. Another reason was the steadily degenerating morale of the French and their army. He also explained that the deferment of the attack meant continued trench warfare and that the Americans would have to take over much larger segments of trenches from the French. He foresaw that we might have 1,000,000 American casualties in the trenches if the attack were deferred until the late spring of 1919.

In describing the effort needed, the General repeatedly used the expression "full power." He explained that "full power" meant the concentrated maximum military strength of the United States, Britain, France, and Italy on every front; that it necessitated bringing American troops quickly from the United States in order to build up his strength to a possible one hundred divisions, including air and other services, involving the immediate movement of two million men from the United States.

Pershing went on to say that considerable opposition to this strategy came from all British, French, and Italian military quarters, who contended that too large a proportion of American troops would be too inexperienced for immediate risks. He discounted the Allied views that our armies now in the United States could not be quickly placed on the front. He stated that the main resistance to his plan came from all Allied civilian agencies, who contended that there was not enough shipping under Allied control to transport and service the larger American armies he proposed and, at the same time, to transport food and other necessary supplies to the Allies.

I asked him what additional tonnage of ships he would need immediately to secure his "full power." He estimated 3,000,000 tons. I suggested to him that there were several possibilities for securing this 3,000,000 tons of shipping. I mentioned that the Allies still had those 3,400,000 tons of shipping in commercial employment in the more distant oceans and that he should be able to secure some of this for an emergency period.

But my strongest recommendation was that we had more than 3,500,000 tons of overseas shipping in constant use carrying food and collateral supplies to Allied civilians; they had their new harvest in hand and could, if necessary, live from five to seven months on it—provided we could retain about 1,000,000 tons to transport certain critical foods, such as meats and fats.

I emphasized that if the larger part of our food fleet were taken away for some months, the attack failed, and the war continued, we would be in trouble. To supply the Allies, after they had consumed their domestic production, would require an immense food fleet; and we would have difficulties in loading and getting such an amount through our railways and ports. I stated that to divert our food fleet imposed a huge risk but that we should take the risk if this dreadful menace to the human race could be eradicated a year sooner. I further stated that the Allies had considerable preharvest stocks of food and that there was room for more "tightening of the belt" in the Allied countries if necessary.

The General asked me for three things: first, to give my views to General Bliss at once, since the War Council was about to meet; second, to write him a letter which he could repeat to General Foch the next morning; and third, return to Washington as soon as possible and impress these views upon the President, Secretary Baker, and the Army General Staff.

I expressed some reluctance to write a letter which might get into circulation because I was well aware of the resentment by military officials of any advice from mere civilians; furthermore, my food colleagues might resent any action they had not approved. I stated that it would be impossible to secure their approval, except by disclosing strategic plans—which was unwise. But the General insisted that he needed the letter to aid him in his discussions with General Foch, that I should word it carefully in terms which he and Foch would understand, and that, in any event, it would be held confidential.

Hugh Gibson had not been present at my discussion with Pershing. By telephone, he arranged an appointment with General Bliss in Paris for late that evening. Gibson was with me at this interview with Bliss, and I can best illuminate this phase of the narrative with an entry from his diary.[4]

August 7, 1918: General Bliss says that Foch is now preparing the preliminary plans for the 1919 offensive campaign. He has found it necessary to make heavy demands upon the tonnage of the Allies for strictly military purposes, and all our military people are inclined to trim down the demands before passing them on to the civilian branches. H.H. was up in arms at this and told the General [Bliss] that there was no need to trim down a particle of the [military] demands; that we were now using our tonnage in a way that was certainly susceptible of being scaled down; that we and the Allies would have to get along without things that we now considered necessary . . . and that we could be made to do so if it was a matter of life and death. The difference between giving [or not giving] Pershing . . . what [he asked] . . . [might] readily prove to be another year of the war and the lives of a million American soldiers. We *cannot* stand for this, no matter what deprivation the civil population is called upon to make, and if the need is made clear enough, the civil population will increase its output of ships and reduce its demand [for food] . . . until the big job has been put over. If there is not enough resiliency in our whole system to make up the full budget of what [Pershing] . . . wants, we had better make up our minds now that we can't win and make such a peace as we [can] get in the fall.

H.H. besought Bliss to stand tight for the full list [power] and urge

[4] The diary of Hugh Gibson is in the Hoover Institution on War, Revolution, and Peace at Stanford University. The diary gives the date of the entry here referred to as August 7. The Pershing interview took place on August 6; my letter to the General was completed at 2:30 A.M. on August 7.

Pershing to insist on just what he needed for his task. After the General had gone, we sat and talked the matter out, and H.H. wrote a lengthy letter to Pershing, putting the matter up to him and strongly urging him to stand for no compromise.

It was 2:30 in the morning (August 7) when I completed the letter (dated August 6) in longhand. Apparently I kept no copy, since we could find none in my files when preparing this memoir. With the permission of General Pershing's son, F. Warren Pershing, I had a search made in the Pershing papers and found the original letter. It had not been necessary to spell out details for Pershing. Also, had it been written at any other hour, my grammar and punctuation might have been better. The letter read:

HÔTEL DE CRILLON, PARIS
Confidential

MY DEAR GENERAL:

I learn that Gen'l Foch will present to the Supreme War Council within a few days a programme; that this programme will be based upon . . . some hypothesis of strength against Germany on this front next year; that there are a number of programmes short of the maximum; that the voice of civilian necessity may temper these demands.

Could I suggest something to you? The programme that will give so far as human vision can foresee a finish of this business in [early] 1919 is the only programme that we are justified in receiving for the American people. No doubt a hundred civilian agencies will say it cannot be done; but if the programme is put forward on this basis of full power; if anything short means a certainty of another years war and the sacrifice of another 1,000,000 of American lives, then we must put over the full power programme. If the full power programme is 100 divisions of U.S. troops, we want that programme.

As between full power and part power there does not stand [in the way] *more* than 3,000,000 tons of shipping; perhaps at most 2,000,000 tons; if we stand in a position where there is not this margin of resiliency between 1919 and 1920 then we will never win for if we cannot find self denial in these 220,000,000 people . . . we will never last until 1920. Furthermore no group of civilians like myself can get anywhere in our complex problems unless we have a *definite* positive issue to hew at.

Nothing except a positive demand backed by a definite statement of the tonnage supplies and men that are needed—against the alternative of which stands the loss of 1,000,000 lives [—] will bring these negotiations bickerings and higglings to an end.

I believe there is more margin in this transport situation than the mass of aggregated views of officials zealous for their own jobs will indicate.

I am for the final and maximum blow and any tampering should be done after its demands have been fully stated [and] not before.

H. Hoover

Hugh Gibson's diary continued:

I agreed to take the letter to him [Pershing] and deliver it in person. The General read H.H.'s letter and snorted with pleasure. I added the part that was to be delivered verbally and that was received with equal pleasure. He [Pershing] said he was holding out strong for Foch's full program and that he would not be a party to scaling it down on this side. Said he had no patience with the people who said we must not send over any troops that we cannot fully supply with our own tonnage. . . .

I was asked to thank H. for his letter and say that he had supplied the General with . . . ammunition. He seemed much pleased with H.'s stand and said he was a most valuable supporter. . . .

The verbal part of my message to which Gibson refers was a more detailed statement of the German food situation, about which Gibson was fully informed, to which I added:

. . . the German . . . morale could well collapse with any hammer blow and the certainty of German fears of further food shortage during the coming winter. It might reach to the extent of a revolutionary explosion.

In confirmation of Allied opposition to the immediate attack, I cite a telegram from Prime Minister Lloyd George to Premier Clemenceau—sent prior to my visit to General Pershing—which implied that for shipping reasons any general attack would have to be delayed. The Lloyd George telegram to Clemenceau is quoted in a letter from General Pershing to General March and reads as follows:

". . . Because of the serious character of this information I immediately made a preliminary study of the questions with the Minister of Naval Transportation, Sir Joseph Maclay. I regret to declare that we shall not be able to continue our help as far as cargoes of merchandise are concerned and that we shall probably have to cut down the tonnage assigned for troop transportation. In the last few months we have lost several troop transports of large tonnage, notably the Justicia, which could carry 5,000 men and 10,000 tons of material per trip. As far as merchandise shipping is concerned we are already grappling with serious difficulties. Every day Australia and New Zealand ask for a help we are unable to give them. . . . The coal question is giving me the greatest anxiety because the situation in France and Italy as well as our own munition production depend upon a suitable coal supply. By reason of the lack of coal a large number of ships have been subjected to delay in our ports and our whole program of naval transport has been shaken up by this fact. This increases our difficulty to help the Americans in executing their program with regard to merchant shipping. While continuing naturally to do our best . . . in the future, as we have in the past, I think it best to let you know without delay what difficulties we may meet in attempting to realize the American program in its entirety."

A letter from General Pershing to the Secretary of War on August 17, 1918, ten days after our talk at Chaumont, expressed almost exactly the same ideas as those in my letter of the seventh to him:

. . . The food question, in general and in particular, must, of course, be given every consideration, but after all the fact remains that we are not making war in a country destitute of food supplies and that France has fairly good crops this year. . . . Of course, I realize that all in all it is going to require considerable sacrifice to make the necessary saving in allied food, but with 220,000,000 people in the allied European countries the supply of 2,000,000 or 3,000,000 men, even though our contribution might be limited, is not likely so to deplete stocks as ever to bring us anywhere near the danger point of starvation. Therefore the question of food should not frighten us off.

I returned to Washington on August 22, 1918. I went directly from the train to call upon Secretary of War Newton Baker. General

Douglas MacArthur was present, being on a short military visit.[5] The Secretary asked many questions about my proposal to General Pershing. While engaged in this discussion, I received a call from the White House that the President wished to see me at once. I expressed to the President the same views that I had already given Pershing, Bliss, and Baker. The President told me that the American Army, in "full power," would be shipped to Europe. Although I was relieved that General Pershing's viewpoint had prevailed, I had a deep foreboding over possible consequences in food supply.

General Pershing began his successful attack on the St. Mihiel salient on September 12. The general attack of all Allied armies was begun on September 18; on October 4, the Germans asked for an armistice; on October 17 the Allies reached Lille; in October, a revolution, under the leadership of Prince Max of Baden, began in Germany; on October 20, the German armies were retreating all along the front; on October 31, Turkey surrendered; on November

[5] I may well add to this phase of the narrative a letter written to me by General MacArthur some thirty-nine years later. We had discussed the date of our first meeting, and he recounted the conversation at Secretary Baker's office. As a check on accuracy, I submitted this chapter to him. His letter is as follows:

12 November 1957

DEAR MR. PRESIDENT:

Thank you so much for giving me an opportunity to read Chapter 79 of your experiences in World War I. I have found it most interesting. This is especially the case as it was during this period that I first met you.

It was in the office of the Secretary of War, Newton D. Baker, some time in the latter part of August. You had just returned from Europe and apparently were on your way to the White House to report to President Wilson. I was a member of the General Staff at the time and was discussing with the Secretary the burning question of the minute—how large a force the United States could and would send to Europe. After introducing me and greeting you the Secretary explained what we had been discussing and asked you how large a force you thought could be transported to Europe and supplied there; the crucial item, of course, being shipping. I shall never forget your immediate reply to the effect that you could send and support as many millions of troops as were needed. To me it was an inspirational assurance of victory.

In retrospect, how different was our action in the Korean debacle when, with success within our grasp, we weakly adopted the policy of appeasement, in violation of the world-tested principle that a great nation which enters upon war and fails to see it through by accepting a stalemate will ultimately suffer all the national consequences of defeat. In this case we already see as one of the calamitous results the emergence of Communist China as a great military power which threatens to destroy the international balance against the free world. . . .

DOUGLAS MACARTHUR

9, the Kaiser abdicated; and on November 11, the Germans signed the Armistice. By that time, Pershing had more than two million fighting men on the front and more in reserve.

The food shortage in Germany played a large part in causing the revolution there.

I cannot claim credit for the great shift in military strategy which brought the war to an early end. That honor belongs to General Pershing. It was his confidence and courage which ended the war a year sooner than Allied plans contemplated. He prevented at least one million American casualties—which would have occurred in another year of trench warfare.

For any assistance I might have given General Pershing, I was repaid by him many times. His co-operation aided us greatly in the solution of many difficulties of the European famine after the Armistice.

CHAPTER 19

THE FOOD ADMINISTRATION GOES ON

While all of these momentous events were taking place, the Food Administration had to continue its domestic duties—and face many problems. One of the latter was an act of the Congress on July 6, 1918, increasing the price of wheat to $2.50 per bushel. Secretary of Agriculture Houston and I recommended that the President veto the act, which he did, because no further stimulant to production was necessary. And in any event, the matter could be reviewed in the spring of 1919, when the world situation would become clearer.

Another problem was the farmers' rushing wheat to market after the harvest of 1918 because they had nothing to gain by retaining it on the farms. The volume to be handled required that we increase the capital of the Grain Corporation to the full $150,000,000 authorized by the Congress; and in the end, to handle the flood, we had to borrow $385,390,000 from the banks. But our wheat holdings were an invaluable treasure with which to meet the inevitable European famine.

In August, General Pershing began his demand for ships from our overseas food transport; our food shipments from North America fell to 700,000 tons a month.

During the weeks from August to early October, my Allied food administrators and I lived long days and nights of anxiety, lest the war might go on for more months and our task of filling the Allied vacuum become exceedingly difficult. No one welcomed the Armistice more than I.

One result of our reduced exports was to fill our warehouses to overflowing. The farmers were sending more grain and animals to market every day.

With the beginning of the German retreat in October, the Allied Wheat Executive became fearful of what might happen to its wheat supply, in competition with the imminent postwar famine demands from all Europe and much of Asia and the Middle East. The Allies requested a commitment from us to supply 100,000,000 bushels of wheat against this contingency. We signed the contract on October 31, stipulating that the wheat was not to be delivered until after February 1, 1919, in order that we could take care of early famine demands. In addition to this reserve they stated their monthly requirements of 100,000,000 bushels for November and December.

The Allies also requested commitments of hundreds of millions of pounds of meats and fats for the coming three months. We agreed to all of this.

THE ARMISTICE

The signing of the Armistice on November 11, 1918, was a day of world-wide rejoicing. It brought a lift of spirit to all nations. Americans believed that they had played a great part in winning the most important crusade for liberty in all history.

Fear vanished. Hope swept in like a desert sunrise. Our men on the front emerged from the dugouts into the sunlight. They scraped off the trench mud and the lice for the last time. They sang and shouted. They surveyed No-Man's-Land and the enemy trenches curiously. They talked with the enemy and gave him a smoke—soldiers respect good soldiers. Victory had come to a billion people, and sons, husbands, and brothers were coming home. Youths began again to plan their lives. Good cheer, smiles, and laughter met at every crossroad, every street corner.

This was to be the last great war. The burdens of fear and arms would be lifted. Liberty, freedom, democracy, and lasting peace were the watchwords of the day. Revolutions all over enemy-controlled Europe broke the old chains; everywhere people expelled old leaders, declared their independence, and adopted governments with guarantees of personal liberty.

But in the shadows behind this rejoicing was the record that the world's combatant armies had absorbed 59,000,000 men. And of them, there were:

Dead	7,782,000
Wounded	18,681,000
Prisoners or missing	7,080,000
Total	33,543,000

Before the Armistice was signed, President Wilson requested me to go to Europe to negotiate terms concerning the Allied organization through which American participation in the relief and reconstruction of Europe would function. The day after the Armistice, I issued a statement to our staff. The essential paragraphs follow:

TO ALL REPRESENTATIVES OF THE FOOD ADMINISTRATION:

Your work during the last year has had more to do than you may realize in the achievement of the American people which will be one of the remembered glories of this titanic struggle. That achievement was not only the provisioning of the armies and the Allies unto victory: it was the demonstration that there was no power in autocracy equal to the voluntary effort of free people.

The essential feature of . . . [our work] was that individual conscience should rule under . . . local leadership. It was, then, your work which made the devotion of twenty million households fruitful.

As we come to the end of that undertaking, we are summoned to a still larger task—to provision the Allies and the liberated nations of Europe which face not hunger alone but the collapse of all that holds civilization together unless a steady stream of food supplies can be kept flowing to them to repair their gravest deficiencies, and in far greater volume than . . . last year.

The President has asked me to take charge for this Government of this relief work; to perfect and enlarge the arrangements for foodstuffs to the populations of Belgium and France now being released, and to organize and determine the need of provision to the liberated peoples of Eastern Europe to prevent such debacle as has taken place in Russia.

I am asking the Federal Food Administrators to join forces with the new organization of relief . . . [so] that the same splendid support which was given to the prosecution of the war may be devoted to establishing the peace and security of the world.

HERBERT HOOVER

CHAPTER 20

SOME IMMEDIATE PROBLEMS OF THE FOOD ADMINISTRATION AT THE ARMISTICE

With the signing of the Armistice on November 11, 1918, the Food Administration had to be reoriented—from the problems of food supplies for 230,000,000 people among the Allies and Associated Powers and the Neutrals to the inevitable food shortage or famine among more than 600,000,000 people in Western Europe and Russia. The change in scene greatly affected our domestic food policies. We no longer had to maintain many regulations. Almost overnight, we re-established private enterprise by repealing most of the legal restrictions on the food trades.

At the Armistice, the number of men and women working for the Food Administration in Washington and in the states totaled about eight thousand, of whom more than six thousand were volunteers. Since the average annual salary rate prescribed by the Civil Service Commission to the paid employees was $1,274.83 per year, they, too, in the face of rising prices, were making a great sacrifice.

In order to carry out our guarantees to farmers and to serve in the organization of relief in Europe, we retained the Grain Corporation, the Sugar Equalization Board, the Meats and Fats Division, and the Purchasing Division—which controlled imports and exports. Those divisions needed some 600 staff members. But for our other duties, within sixty days the staff in the United States was reduced to less than 150 employees, directed by Edgar Rickard, whom I had appointed Assistant Food Administrator in Washington. We moved the headquarters of the Food Administration to Paris, taking fifteen experienced men and otherwise recruiting our new staff from the American Army and Navy.

Before closing this account of our major activities in Washington, it is fitting to pay tribute to the high character of some of my associates in the war.

Secretary of War Newton D. Baker was modest, courageous, methodical, and helpful. He surrounded himself with able men, irrespective of party, and left an eminent name in the annals of American public service.

Secretary of the Navy Josephus Daniels was an honest, considerate and devoted man.

We naturally had daily contact with the War Industries Board, which was headed by Bernard Baruch. He was a fine gentleman and a great administrator, with a special talent for choosing men, such as Alexander Legge, Arch W. Shaw, Daniel Willard, Julius Rosenwald, and Judge Robert S. Lovett. Baruch had two other qualities: a capacity for friendship and loyalty and an ability to listen patiently to complicated discussions and produce a penetrating, successful solution to the problem. The latter, at times, seemed to be a sixth sense.

Another outstanding war administrator was Vance McCormick, Chairman of the War Trade Board. David Houston, Secretary of Agriculture, was a most helpful colleague. He was an able, austere man with a fine co-operative spirit. Franklin K. Lane, Secretary of the Interior, was lovable, loyal, and able and a source of strength in many battles. Robert Lansing, Secretary of State, was always considerate and helpful.

To indicate the work of the Food Administration, I introduce at this point a table showing the total exports from the United States to the Allies and Neutrals during prewar years and the calendar years 1917, 1918, and 1919. This table, drawn up in round numbers, was compiled from publications of the Department of Agriculture, the Department of Commerce, and the Food Administration. There are differences among these authorities because of classifications and conversions of weights, but as an expression of American support to the Allies and Neutrals during this period, the table is sufficiently accurate.

The exports of food were (in tons):

	Prewar Average	1917	1918	1919
Wheat	3,009,000	6,066,000	6,266,000	8,013,000
Corn	1,262,000	1,596,000	1,318,000	1,448,000
Oats	201,000	1,818,000	2,097,000	1,081,000
Rye	24,000	411,000	457,000	1,134,000
Barley	202,000	606,000	549,000	1,309,000
Rice	16,000	104,000	84,000	188,000
Beans	10,000	56,000	72,000	168,000
Pork Products	498,000	820,000	1,535,000	1,310,000
Beef Products	73,000	320,000	390,000	560,000
Dairy Products	13,000	290,000	560,000	751,000
Vegetable Oils	165,000	70,000	150,000	120,000
Sugar	2,243,000	3,880,000	3,950,000	3,040,000
Canned Goods	41,000	333,000	438,000	350,000
Dried Fruit	71,000	59,000	44,000	115,000
Fresh Fruit and Vegetables	350,000	260,000	510,000	405,000
Grand Total *	8,178,000	16,689,000	18,420,000	19,992,000

* In addition to the food listed in this table, 204,000 tons of tobacco were exported in the prewar period; 205,000 tons in 1917; 208,000 tons in 1918; and 388,000 tons in 1919.

West Indian sugar is included because the Food Administration guaranteed to purchase the crops at prices designed to stimulate production. A large part of the refining was done in the United States, and the resulting exports to the Allies and Neutrals were due in large part to American self-denial. The Allies were largely isolated from sugar supplies; the American sources sustained them.

The table being only possible in calendar years does not indicate "the worst year"—July 1, 1917–July 1, 1918—because both the first half of 1917 and the last half of 1918 were our drought period. Also, on a fiscal year basis, the exports for 1918–1919 would exceed 21,000,000 tons.

SECTION II

THE AMERICAN VOLUNTARY CHARITABLE AGENCIES

INTRODUCTION

There has been no greater expression of American solicitude for suffering humanity than the activities of the American charitable organizations. Aside from their multitude of services within our borders, they served in all of our overseas wars.

During the war they brought food to the starving and provided medical aid and hospitals for the sick and wounded. They brought clothing to the destitute. They gave care to children and the aged. They gave protection to the persecuted. They rebuilt homes and villages and restored farms. They brought spiritual consolation to the bereaved. Those of the religious faiths gave courage and hope to those in despair. They contributed greatly to sustaining the moral and spiritual foundations of a troubled civilization.

As an indication of this outpouring of American compassion, I give the following list of these organizations:

THE CHARITABLE AND RELIGIOUS ORGANIZATIONS 1914–1923

American Allied Ambulance
American Allies Cooperative Committee
American Artists Committee
American Baptist Convention
American Central Committee for Russian Relief
American Child Relief Fund
American Commission for Relief for Vienna Children
American Commission to Serbia for Restoration of Serbian Youth
American Committee of the Allied Home

American Committee of the Argonne Association
American Committee for Armenian and Syrian Relief
American Committee of British and Allies Comforts
American Committee of the British Red Cross
American Committee Collecting for the Charities of the Queen of the Belgians
American Committee for Devastated France
American Committee for "La Renaissance des Cités"
American Committee of the International Reconstruction League
American Committee for Relief in the Near East
American Committee for Relief to Ireland
American Committee for Relief of Russian Children
American Committee for Training in Suitable Trades the Maimed Soldiers of France
American Committee in Aid of Italian Soldiers Crippled in the War
American Committee of Villages Libérés
American Field Service
American Free Milk and Relief for Italy, Inc.
American French Service Committee
American Friends of Musicians in France
American Friends Service Committee
American Fund for Charité Maternal
American Fund for French Wounded
American Godmothers' League
American Homes for Children in the Rheinpfalz, Inc.
American Huguenot Committee
American Ice Flotilla Committee
American Jewish Relief Committee
American Jugo-Slav Relief Committee
American Library Association
American McAll Association
American Medical Aid for Russia
American Memorial Hospital Committee of the American Fund for French Wounded
American Mennonite Relief
American Ouvroir Funds
American Poets' Ambulance in Italy
American Red Cross
American Red Star Animal Relief

American Relief Administration
American Relief Committee for German Children
American Relief Committee for Hungarian Sufferers
American Relief Committee for Sufferers in Austria
American Relief for Russian Women and Children
American Society for the Relief of French War Orphans
American Students Committee of the Ecole des Beaux Arts
American Women's Hospitals
American Women's War Relief Fund
Appui aux Artistes
Armenian Medical Relief Association of America
Armenian Relief Committee
Army and Navy Field Comforts Committee
Army Girls' Transport Tobacco Fund
Australian War Relief Fund
Authors' League Fund
Belgian Refugees Knitting Yarn Fund
Belgian Soldiers' Tobacco Fund
Blue Cross Fund
British-American War Relief Fund
British & Canadian Patriotic Fund
British Sailors and Soldiers Tobacco Fund
British War Relief Association, Inc.
Catherine Breshkovsky Russian Relief Fund
Central Committee for Relief of Germany and Austria
Central Committee for the Relief of Jews Suffering through the War
Central Relief Society formed in New York City
Chelsea War Refugees Fund
Children of Flanders
Children's Tin Box Fund
China Famine Fund
Christian Relief in France and Belgium
Christian Work Fund for Starving Children in Armenia
Christian Science War Relief Fund
The Church of Jesus Christ of Latter-day Saints
Cognac Fund
Comforts Committee of the Navy League
Commission for Relief in Belgium
Committee of Hope

Committee for Men Blinded in Battle
Committee for the Relief of Belgian Prisoners in Germany
Committee for Relief of Belgian Refugees
Committee for Relief of Jewish University Students in Central Europe
Committee of Mercy
Committee for the Rescue and Education of Russian Children
Committee on American Hostels for Belgian Refugees in Paris
Daughters of the American Revolution
Dollar Christmas Fund for Homeless Belgians
Duryea War Relief
Edith Wharton War Charities
Elizabeth Whitman Chain Letter
Emergency Aid Committee
Fatherless Children of France
Federal Council of the Churches of Christ in America
Federal Council Commission of France and Belgium
Food for France Fund
Franco-American Committee for the Protection of Children of the Frontier
Franco-Serbian Field Hospital
Free Milk for France
French Actors' Fund
French Heroes' Lafayette Memorial Fund Inc.
French Restoration Fund
French Tubercular Children's Fund
French Tuberculous Soldiers' Relief Committee
French Tuberculosis War Victims' Fund
Friends of Poland
S. R. Fuller Lecture Fund
Fund for the Aid of Protestant Churches
Fund for Relief of Men of Letters and Scientists in Russia
General Allen's American Committee for Relief of German Children
Gospel Committee for Work among War Prisoners
Hospital Under Three Flags
Imperial Order, Daughters of the Empire
Interchurch Committee for Christian Relief in France & Belgium
International Serbian Educational Institute
Italian War Relief Fund of America
Jewish Joint Distribution Committee
Kindergarten Unit

Kitchener Memorial Fund
League (Society) of the Ten Allies
Le Bien être du Blessé
Le Paquet de L'Orphelin
Le Pacquet du Soldat
Le Sou de Mutilé
Les Maisons Claires
Ligue Fraternelle des Enfants de France
Literary Digest
Lithuanian Central War Relief Committee
Mayfair War Relief
Mon Soldat
National Allied Relief Committee, Inc.
National Catholic Welfare Council
National Committee of the United States for the Restoration of the University of Louvain
National Fund for War Orphans in Italy
National Lutheran Council
National Polish Committee of America
National Special Aid
National Surgical Dressings Committee
National War Council of the Methodist Episcopal Church
Near East Relief
Needle Work Guild of America
New England Italian War Relief Fund
The New York Sun Tobacco Fund
Our Boys in France Tobacco Fund
Overseas Club in America and Patriotic League of Britons Overseas
P.S.D. Fund
Paderewski Fund for Poland
Patriotic Service League
People's Relief Committee for the Jewish War Sufferers
Permanent Blind Relief War Fund
Polish Children's Relief Fund
Polish National Department
Polish Reconstruction Committee
Polish Victims' Relief Fund
Prince of Wales Fund
Professional Classes War Relief Fund

Refugees Relief Fund
Refugees in Russia
Relief Committee for Greeks in Asia Minor
Roumanian Relief Committee
Russian-American Relief Association
Russian Famine Fund
Russian War Relief Committee
Salvation Army
St. Vincent de Paul Society
Save the Children for the France of Tomorrow
Scottish Women's Hospitals
Secours de Guerre
Secours d'Urgence
Secours Franco-American
Secours National of France
Serbian Aid Fund
Serbian Child Welfare Association of America
Serbian Hospital Fund
Serbian National Defense League
Serbian Relief Committee
Seventh-Day Adventists
Shamrock Fund
Siberian Regiments, American Ambulance
Siberian War Prisoners Repatriation Fund
Smith College War Service Board
Société de Secours aux Blessés Militaires
Society of Friends of Roumania, Inc.
Society of Serbian Mothers
Society to Relieve Distress in Germany and Austria
Students Friendship Fund of the World's Student Christian Federation
Stage Women's War Relief
Syrian Mt. Lebanon Committee
Trench Comforts Packets
Union des Arts
Union Nationale des Eglises Réformées Evangéliques de France
Vacation War Relief Committee
Vienna Children's Milk Relief
Villiers Fund
Volga Relief Society

War Babies Cradle
War Orphans of Italy Fund
War Relief Clearing House for France and Her Allies
Winifred Holt's American Committee for Helping Blind
Woman's Hospital Unit for Foreign Service
Woman's Naval Service, Inc.
Women's Apparel Association
Women's Overseas Hospital
World Alliance for International Friendship
Young Men's Christian Association of the U.S.A.
Young Women's Christian Association of the U.S.A.

In addition to the above, I must add to this record the great foundations, which, although they engaged in little direct relief, gave generous support to many other organizations:

Carnegie Corporation of New York
Carnegie Endowment for International Peace
Laura Spelman Rockefeller Memorial
The Commonwealth Fund
The Rockefeller Foundation

Thus there were at least 211 voluntary organizations, and they operated in forty-five countries or areas of people.

The activities of these organizations fall into four periods:

First, from the outbreak of war in August, 1914, to the entry of the United States into the war in April, 1917. In this period, most of the organizations followed the American Government's policy of neutrality and gave aid to all the combatants.

Second, during the United States' participation in the war—from April, 1917, until the end of the war, as marked by the Armistice in November, 1918. During this period, these voluntary agencies were an important supplement to the United States Government's relief agencies.

Third, during the Armistice period to the signing of the Peace in July, 1919. With the signing of the Peace, American Government activities ceased.

Fourth, from the Peace, when most of the agencies had concluded their work, until September, 1923. During this period, the major burden of relief fell upon the voluntary agencies.

This second volume of *An American Epic* deals with the activities of these agencies up to the Armistice. A large number of those on the above lists were organized after the end of the active war.

Volume III will deal with their activities—nation by nation—in more than 45 nations and their support of special groups.

Another large group consisted of the religious-denomination agencies, which, prior to the Armistice, engaged only in spiritual and morale-building activities, not in the physical provision of food, medical aid, clothing, or materials for reconstruction. However, most of them engaged in such relief after the Armistice and will therefore appear in Volume III.

Many of the voluntary charitable agencies devoted themselves exclusively to serving the American armed forces. While these activities were a generous expression of American charity, they do not fall within the scope of these memoirs, which I have devoted to the relief of overseas nations and groups.

As stated in the Introduction to this volume, I give frequently the monetary expenditure upon different services. Again, I may repeat that monetary sums are not the measure of the service given. They are presented only that the reader may have some grasp of the dimensions of the work. The sums have been calculated from the accounts of these agencies by my staff and are illustrative only.

There were certain of these agencies which engaged in actual relief prior to the Armistice and which I describe separately. They were:

The American Red Cross
The Near East Relief Committee
The Jewish Joint Distribution Committee
The Salvation Army
The American Friends Service Committee
The Daughters of the American Revolution
The Church of Jesus Christ of Latter-day Saints
The Christian Scientists

CHAPTER 21

THE AMERICAN RED CROSS

The American Red Cross needs little description for the American people. Its roots lie deep in American soil. From the day of its creation by Clara Barton in 1881, it has been a magnificent expression of American solicitude to human suffering from disaster. Its federal charter, granted by the Congress in 1882, has been frequently expanded to enable it to carry on vast relief programs, not only at home, but also abroad.[1]

The President of the United States heads the Red Cross as its president. The active administrator is the chairman of the executive committee and is appointed by the President. The Red Cross is supported by dues and gifts but has often administered special funds, voted by the Congress, to disaster areas.

At the base of the organization are "chapters" in almost every city and town in the United States. The chapters not only conduct the raising of funds, but administer relief in disasters which occur in their own regions.

[1] Rather than encumber the text with footnotes on the authorities used, I give a list of references in the Bibliography.

AMERICAN RED CROSS RELIEF FROM 1914 TO THE ENTRY OF THE UNITED STATES INTO THE WAR IN APRIL, 1917

Prior to the American declaration of war, Red Cross relief expenditures, both for civilians and for men in uniform, amounted to some four million dollars. Part of these expenditures were donations to the Red Cross societies abroad and to other organizations in the field. In keeping with Red Cross tradition, its major service was devoted to medical aid and hospitalization. In keeping with the Red Cross tradition of neutrality, its service, prior to the American entry into the war, was extended to all combatants.

At the outbreak of fighting in August, 1914, the Red Cross proposed to its sister societies in the warring nations that it supply the American surgical and nursing personnel to make up hospital units of three surgeons and twelve nurses each. The first complement—ten units—sailed from New York in mid-September, 1914, six weeks after the war began. Ultimately, the personnel of the hospital units abroad in this period totaled 75 surgeons and 225 nurses. There were two units each in England, France, Belgium, Russia, Germany, and Austria-Hungary and three units in plague-ridden Serbia. The units either supplemented established hospital staffs or set up their own bases. The latter group found themselves performing major operations in a former school of technology in Kiev, a theater in Germany, a converted casino in Southern France, and a tobacco warehouse in Serbia. By consent of both the Germans and the Russians, a combined American contingent from the German and Austro-Hungarian units was allowed into Russia to minister to thousands of German prisoners of war held near Moscow. Prior to the United States' entry into the war, the Red Cross made 341 shipments of supplies valued at $1,526,469. These supplies ranged from hot water bottles, bandages, sheets, and stretchers to drugs, chemicals, and bacteriological and sterilizing outfits. Of the total, 273 shipments worth $1,150,070 went to Allied nations, including England, France, Belgium, Italy, Russia, Serbia, and Montenegro; 55 shipments worth $358,449 were sent to Germany, Austria-Hungary, Bulgaria, Turkey, and their prisoners of war in South Africa and Siberia; and 13 shipments went to Poland, Armenia, Syria, and Mesopotamia. The expenditures of the Red Cross in the Central Powers prior to our entry into the war were:

Germany	$170,005
Austria-Hungary	22,917
Albania	599
Bulgaria	6,000
Turkey	106,513
Total	$306,034

One of the achievements during the early years of the war in Europe was in Serbia. Three Red Cross hospital units were dispatched in the autumn of 1914 to care for wounded Serbian soldiers. These units soon had to meet problems of typhus and cholera in the civil population, and two of their surgeons perished from these infections. With the first German invasion of Serbia by the Central Powers, Dr. Edward W. Ryan, director of that unit, was given charge of all the Belgrade city hospitals, including those for the insane. He was also given the responsibility for feeding some six thousand Belgrade residents. Early in 1915, with the continued spread of typhus, the Red Cross organized a sanitary commission under the direction of Dr. Richard P. Strong. This commission temporarily beat back the menace.

AMERICAN RED CROSS RELIEF AFTER THE UNITED STATES' ENTRY INTO THE WAR

To prepare for American Red Cross service in the war, President Wilson, on May 10, 1917, appointed the seven-man Red Cross War Council, headed by Henry P. Davison. The Council administered the affairs of the Red Cross from July 1 of that year to February 28, 1919, when control reverted to the permanent Central Committee, of which Dr. Livingston Farrand was chairman. Dr. Farrand was succeeded by John Barton Payne in October, 1921.

The Red Cross accounts do not separate expenditures for the eighteen-month period prior to the Armistice from the four subsequent months, since they follow the period of the War Council. However, in order to visualize the extent of Red Cross service in various countries, I have had made from the accounts fairly accurate calculations of its expenditures in each country prior to the end of 1918, which fairly approximates the Armistice in November. I give these calculations a little later.

I may, however, at this point give the two years' work of the War Council as an indication of the enormous expansion of Red Cross activities under its administration. In December, 1914, there were 107 chapters and 16,000 members within the United States; by May 1, 1917, it had grown to 562 chapters and 486,194 members. The day the Council relinquished its job, there were 3,724 chapters with a membership of about 20,000,000. Together with more than 11,000,000 junior members, this represented nearly one-third of the population of the United States.

Two months after the United States entered the war, the Red Cross national headquarters had on hand a balance of $3,134,904.33. From that date to February 28, 1919, when the War Council was dissolved, its revenues totaled $260,002,589.34 as a result of fund drives managed by a special war-finance committee, appointed by President Wilson, under the chairmanship of Cleveland H. Dodge. Beyond these sums raised by the national headquarters, the local chapters directly expended approximately $91,000,000 in cash and $28,000,000 in chapter-produced articles bringing the total to about $379,000,000, a considerable part of which was expended upon the armed forces within the United States.

In preparing for organization in the different countries overseas, the War Council dispatched commissions comprising experienced physicians, surgeons, child-care experts, and business executives. Such commissions were sent to England, France, Italy, the Near East, and Siberia and to aid the Belgians outside the German-occupied areas.

GREAT BRITAIN

Red Cross aid to Britain was mainly through contributions to existing British charities and institutions. Among them were hospitals, aids to soldiers' families, workshops for unemployed women, and pay-care for shell-shocked youngsters. My calculation of such support prior to December 31, 1918 comes to $10,834,861.

FRANCE

France was a major center of Red Cross overseas operations. The eighteen-man commission to France, under Major Grayson M-P. Murphy, was the first to arrive in Europe, reaching Paris in June, 1917. With this nucleus, Red Cross personnel expanded rapidly until by the end of February, 1919, there were 5,860 Americans at work for the organization in France, of which 5,058 were paid a living salary, the rest being volunteers. They organized civilian relief in four directions:

First, in August, 1917, they set up in France a children's bureau, which was devoted to all aspects of children's problems in war. By February, 1919, twenty-five children's hospitals and convalescent homes and 99 mobile dispensaries and clinics were in operation, with more than 200,000 patients treated; 32,000 school children were served food in canteens; 519 French institutions and societies for children were given financial support; seven traveling expositions, at which proper methods of child hygiene were demonstrated, were conducted jointly with the Rockefeller Foundation.

Second, for the relief of French soldiers' families, the Red Cross operated a "home service." Cash to meet desperate needs was distributed to 87,652 families. Another aspect of its work was the physical and occupational rehabilitation of men discharged from the service because of disability, primarily tuberculosis, and the *mutilés* (those maimed in the fighting). The Red Cross set up a factory near Paris where artificial limbs were manufactured in cooperation with the French Government; six hundred men were supplied with artificial arms and legs. It also helped finance a re-education program for the blinded and crippled, setting up a Red Cross model center to train them in self-support.

Third, the largest and costliest Red Cross activity in French civilian relief was direct emergency aid to 1,726,534 refugees, mostly from the German-invaded area in the North of France. This mass relief operation, conducted in conjunction with French agencies, comprised hospitalizing, housing, and afterwards returning the people to their homes and giving them a new start. The Red Cross also engaged in provisional housing repair in seven villages. In the course of its refugee program, it operated sixty-seven hospitals and dispensaries, sixty-eight workrooms, and eight canteens. One of the major operations was the establishment of four great warehouses in the devastated areas behind the Allied lines which extended from Belgium to Switzerland. Here were stored quantities of relief articles imported from America, thousands of tons of food, clothes, bedding, kitchenware, medical supplies, garden tools, and farm machinery—some four thousand separate items in all. These were distributed either by co-operating French societies or upon requisition from the Red Cross itself.

Fourth, the Red Cross, in a main-line action in French civilian relief, fought a tremendous battle against tuberculosis; this was financed by the Rockefeller Foundation. The Red Cross directly operated five TB hospitals and a number of mobile educational units which set up local anti-TB dispensaries. In addition, it gave aid to 847 TB institutions under French auspices, which included financing of supplies, completion of unfinished sanitoriums, and systematic enlargement of bed capacity. Some of these activities stretched into the period after the Armistice, but my calculation of the expenditures of the Red Cross in France up to December 31, 1918, is $61,401,877.

ITALY

The Red Cross commission sent to Italy returned home in October, 1917, and reported a relatively small need for relief. Within a few weeks, on October 25, 1917, to be exact, the Austro-Hungarian breakthrough at Caporetto ignited a mass flight of soldiers and some 500,000 civilian refugees. Relief workers and supplies were rushed from the Paris headquarters, and, with the help of both Italian emergency committees and American Consuls in various cities, immediate supplies of food, clothing, shoes, mattresses, blankets, and medical items were distributed. Canteen service and temporary lodgings were provided and rehabitation work undertaken.

In January, 1918, the Red Cross set up a large program of care for Italian children in co-operation with private and official Italian agencies. Centers were created in 141 cities and villages from the Alps to Sicily. Within the next year, an estimated 155,000 children were cared for in orphanages, special kitchens, day nurseries, schools, playgrounds, health centers, and summer colonies partially financed by Red Cross funds and, in some cases, managed by its personnel. Relief in the form of cash to soldiers' and refugees' families was distributed to 326,000 destitute families, and employment was provided in workrooms for the repair and manufacture of clothing.

The scope of Red Cross service to Italian refugees may be gauged by the fact that up to March, 1919, some 891,000 garments, 148,000 pairs of shoes, a million yards of cloth, and 971,000 bedding and household articles had been distributed and three hospitals, three dispensaries, 50 kitchens, 88 workrooms, and five refugee colonies were being operated. A colony was established near Pisa at which the Red Cross furnished two thousand residents with food, housing, medical attention, schooling for their children, and employment in factories especially constructed for the production of war materials.

My calculation of Red Cross expenditures in Italy is $16,819,897.

BELGIUM

The Commission for Relief in Belgium served German-occupied Belgium. The Red Cross concentrated its work in the small corner unoccupied by the Germans and on the estimated 600,000 refugees in France, Holland, Switzerland, and England.

As it did in France through French organizations, the Red Cross worked primarily through Belgian relief agencies and societies, an estimated three hundred in all, for which it provided financial and other support. In Unoccupied Belgium, milk was distributed free through fifteen Red Cross centers. Some four hundred outfits of baby clothing were distributed monthly in Belgian refugee settlements around Le Havre. An estimated twenty thousand youngsters were evacuated from refugee centers to school colonies in France, Holland, and Switzerland. Two of these school colonies, financed by the Rockefeller Foundation, were under Red Cross management, and the rest were aided with supplies and medical supervision.

About 300,000 Belgian refugees were concentrated in France, and for them the Red Cross established and maintained nine hospitals, provided visiting nurses, and where needed, furnished food, clothing, furniture, housing, and livestock. By way of economic help, a sawmill was provided for making building materials, and sewing machines were supplied to women refugees.

Our calculation of Red Cross expenditures in Belgium up to December 31, 1918, is $3,295,447.

RUSSIA

A seventeen-man Red Cross commission arrived in Petrograd in August, 1917, the Kerensky Government then being in power. The commission had scant time in which to put a relief program into effect because within six months, the boiling Revolution and the subsequent Communist peace treaty with Germany, removed Russia from the Allied ranks, but the commission lingered on until October, 1918. During the Kerensky regime, the commission furnished a 125-car ambulance unit for the Russian Army; some $200,000 worth of medical and surgical supplies for Russian hospitals; food, which was distributed to 25,000 Russians employed on the railway link between Petrograd and the port of Murmansk; and $20,000 in cash relief for the families of officers, soldiers, and workmen in Moscow. After the Communist surrender to Germany, several thousand tons of food, drugs, and soap—to a total value of about $1,560,000—were furnished to prisoners of war returning from German and Austrian internment.

The Allies retained control of Archangel and Vladivostok. Red Cross units were sent to these ports, and they provided aid for hospitals and other services. Relief posts were established for Russian civilians around Archangel and for the hordes of refugees advancing eastward to Siberia to escape the Communists.

The work of the Siberian Red Cross commission assumed its greatest proportions after the Armistice in November, 1918, and will therefore be discussed in Volume III.

Our calculation of the Red Cross expenditures in Russia up to December 31, 1918, is $809,820.

RUMANIA

The Red Cross commission to Rumania arrived in September, 1917, accompanied by twelve doctors, twelve nurses, and quantities of medical supplies, serums, vaccines, and foodstuffs. Rumania had already been occupied by the Germans and Hungarians. All that remained of that free nation was the province of Moldavia, bordering on Russia, and into this area, normally inhabited by a million people, were jammed an additional two million refugees and retreating soldiers. Cholera, typhus, and pneumonia were everywhere, together with a shortage of clothes, shoes, and food.

The commission opened headquarters in Jassy, the temporary capital of Rumania. Food was distributed, along with garments, medicines, bandages, serums, vaccines, and surgical instruments. The commission fed forty thousand persons a day, maintained an orphanage, and ran two hospitals—one, for civilians, at Jassy and another, for soldiers, at Roman, with dispensaries attached. In March, 1918, the Rumanians made a separate peace with Germany, and the commission was compelled to withdraw.

Our calculation of Red Cross expenditures in Rumania up to December 31, 1918, is $809,392.

SERBIA

The Red Cross commission to Serbia arrived there in August, 1917. Serbia had been invaded by the Central Powers, and all that remained when the commission arrived was a narrow strip of territory around Monastir, near the Greek border, which now lodged some fifty thousand Serbs who were wholly dependent upon charity. The Red Cross commission provided them supplies. Six farm experts from the United States were sent along with a supply of seeds, tractors, and other farm machinery, to restore production in the remaining 21,000 acres.

An estimated 150,000 Serbian refugee families were scattered through Northern Greece, Macedonia, and around Salonika. To these, the Red Cross supplied clothes, food, temporary dwellings, and medical care, both in established institutions and by setting up and staffing a small hospital. Six dentists were brought from the United States, together with ten complete sets of dental equipment.

Our calculation of Red Cross expenditures in Serbia up to December 31, 1918, is $1,616,349 and in Montenegro (up to December 31, 1918) $1,212.

PALESTINE AND THE NEAR EAST

Prior to the British Army's advance from Egypt to Jerusalem in early 1918, the Red Cross contributed substantially to other organizations which were aiding Palestine and the Near East. In June, 1918, a Red Cross commission established headquarters at Jerusalem, with doctors, nurses, sanitary engineers, and a cargo of food and medical, surgical, and sanitary materials. By the time of the Armistice, it had established a general dispensary, a children's clinic, and a hospital, was managing two orphan asylums, and had begun a program of industrial service work, furnishing employment in weaving, knitting, and sewing.

Our calculation of the Red Cross expenditures in Palestine and the Near East up to December 31, 1918, is $4,414,507.

SWITZERLAND

In Switzerland, where it operated its service on behalf of 3,604 American war prisoners in 72 German camps, the Red Cross also helped to lighten the burden on the Swiss imposed by the great influx of refugees, interned soldiers, and families whose sons or fathers were in the American Army.

Our calculation of the expenditures of the Red Cross in Switzerland up to December 31, 1918, is $2,108,804.

POLAND

Poland was also helped in late 1917 by a donation of $289,858 to a Polish relief committee whose headquarters was in Vevey, Switzerland. Arrangements were made through the American Legation at Berne to use the money solely for food and clothing for destitute children. The Archbishop of Warsaw was appointed administrator of the relief.

OTHER COUNTRIES

The work of the Red Cross prior to the Armistice by no means exhausts the story of its service. It expended $540,287 in Greece; $15,600 in Holland; $61,461 in Lithuania; $6,618 in Iran; and $6,000 in Portugal.

TOTAL EXPENDITURES

The following table reviews our calculations of Red Cross expenditures overseas up to December 31, 1918 (approximately the Armistice):

Country or Region	Expenditure in $
Albania	599
Austria-Hungary	22,917
Belgium	3,295,447
Bulgaria	6,000
Canada	500,231
Europe (general)	413,378 *
France	61,401,877
Germany	170,005
Great Britain	10,834,861
Greece	540,287
Holland	15,600
Iran	6,618
Italy	16,819,897
Lithuania	61,461
Montenegro	1,212
Palestine and Near East	4,414,507
Poland	289,858
Portugal	6,000
Rumania	809,392
Russia	809,820 †
Serbia	1,616,349
Siberia	4,280,875 †
Switzerland	2,108,804
Turkey	106,513
Total	108,532,516 ‡

* The major part of this item, $402,368, represents expenditures all over Europe from January 1, 1917, to June 30, 1917, prior to the change in American Red Cross accounting procedures from a calendar-year to a fiscal-year basis. The amount was not broken down but includes relief to France, Belgium, England, Italy, Serbia, Rumania, Portugal, Bulgaria, Austria-Hungary, Germany, and Greece.

† Both the Russian and Siberian totals include $32,623 in aid to German prisoners of war prior to our entry into the war.

‡ Of the total expenditures, $54,023,717 represents appropriations for the six-month period from July 1, through December 31, 1918. This calculation is based on Red Cross reports, but the reader should know that in the earlier years, reports on different countries did not include personal services or operational costs. No separate breakdown is possible between services to American military forces and those to other supports overseas. The items in the table concerning the Central Powers refer, of course, to spending in those nations prior to American entry into the war.

CHAPTER 22

THE NEAR EAST RELIEF COMMITTEE

One of the greatest of American charitable relief efforts was the organization which subsequently became known as the Near East Relief Committee. In time, its activities embraced the southern provinces of Russia—Armenia, Georgia, and Azerbaijan—practically every part of the Turkish Empire, and also Persia.

The roots of the Near East Committee also lay deep in American soil. For more than a century, American religious groups and educational institutions had spread universities, colleges, schools, hospitals, and orphanages over the Turkish Empire and Persia. Thousands of Americans were serving in these institutions.

In the background of the Committee's work were the sharp shifts in the war alignments. Turkey had joined the Central Powers against the Western Allies and Russia in October, 1914, two months after the outbreak of the war. When the United States joined in the war in April, 1917, the Turkish Empire became one of our enemies. Turkey surrendered to the "Allies and Associated Powers" with the other Central European powers shortly before the Armistice in November, 1918.

The Communist Revolution in Russia of November, 1917, followed by the Communists' peace with Germany in March, 1918, did not materially affect the Committee's work in the South Russian provinces until 1922.

Beneath the relief problems in Turkey and Persia lay tense conflicts in religious faiths. These nations were predominantly Moslem; there were minorities of Christians and Jews in each nation. To these religious conflicts were added the emotions evoked by war. No more emotional situation had ever confronted American enterprise in compassion.[1]

OPERATIONS IN TURKEY

Early in 1915, the Turks, asserting their fears of disloyalty among the non-Moslem minorities, decreed that many of them be expelled wholesale from homes which had been theirs for generations. Included in these persecutions were the Christian Armenians, Syrians, and Greeks and Jews. For months following the decree, terror and the rigid censorship of internal and external communications prevented the large community of resident Americans from informing the world of these horrors and of their own inspiring relief measures. The first real disclosures and stir to action came in telegrams from Henry Morgenthau, the American Ambassador to Turkey. He cabled Louis Marshall, a prominent Jewish leader in the United States (further details of which I will take up in the next chapter), and sent the following telegram, dated September 3, 1915, to the State Department:

> The destruction of the Armenian race in Turkey is rapidly progressing. . . . The Turkish Minister of War has agreed to permit the departure of those Armenians to the United States whose emigration Mr. Morgenthau will vouch for as being bona fide.

Ambassador Morgenthau's message was forwarded by the State Department to Dr. James L. Barton, Secretary of the American Board of Foreign Missions. On September 16, Dr. Barton arranged a meeting in New York, and a temporary relief committee, called the Armenian Relief Committee was set up. It included Cleveland

[1] In order to avoid a multitude of footnotes for authentication of each incident and each activity of relief, I present a list of the extensive literature on the subject in the Bibliography of this volume.

H. Dodge, Arthur Curtis James, Charles R. Crane, and other prominent Americans. In October, the Relief Committee for Armenians in Persia was formed by this group; it was followed within a few months by the Committee for Armenians in Syria.[2] The initial officers of the Armenian Relief Committee included:

JAMES L. BARTON, *Chairman*
CHARLES R. CRANE, *Treasurer*
SAMUEL T. DUTTON, *Secretary*
WALTER H. MALLORY, *Field Secretary*

The Committee at once authorized the raising of $100,000, of which $60,000 was pledged on the spot. Mr. Dodge volunteered to provide personally all solicitation and administrative costs, thus enabling the Committee to assure potential givers that "100 cents of every dollar go for relief—none for expenses, which are met privately."

The original $100,000 was met and the money cabled to Ambassador Morgenthau within a month after the Committee's formation. Further funds were raised as information concerning the enormity of the crisis became widespread.

The immediate targets of the expulsion decree were the Armenians. There were an estimated 2,000,000 of them in the Turkish Empire, there being also 1,500,000 in the Russian provinces of Armenia, Georgia, and Azerbaijan, and about 500,000 scattered throughout other areas, including Persia. Some Armenians, because of the sympathy of local Turkish authorities, managed to evade the decree. About 400,000 managed to escape to the Southern Russian provinces. For the rest, there was little escape. The reports of the resident Americans state that a fury of pillage and murder attended the decree. Many women and girls were carried off to harems; the number of able-bodied men massacred or driven to death was esti-

[2] For brevity, I use the term "Near East Relief Committee" to include all Near East relief groups in this narrative, although the various subcommittees were not consolidated until August 16, 1919, when they were incorporated by Congressional act under the above title. The Near East Relief Committee continued under this name until 1930, when it was transformed into the Near East Foundation for continued educational, social, and economic aid in this area of the world.

mated at nearly a million. The remnants, mostly women, old men, and children, were stripped of everything except what they could carry and were forcibly set on marches of hundreds of miles through snow and mountains—north into Russia, south and east into exile in the Syrian and Arabian deserts. The youngsters abandoned en route, or left on American mission doorsteps, formed the nucleus of the Near East Relief's subsequent orphanage program.

THE OTHER CHRISTIAN MINORITIES

Of the other Christian minorities, some 100,000 Greeks were deported into the interior from seacoast settlements. Although they were less maltreated than the Armenians, all their homes and other property were seized without compensation.

A third refugee bloc developed with the Turkish invasion of Persia, which event caused the flight into the Caucasus of 29,000 Nestorians and Armenians, the vanguard of later and much larger numbers.

ORGANIZATION AND RELIEF OF TURKEY PRIOR TO AMERICA'S ENTRY INTO THE WAR

Fortunately, the Near East Relief Committee was able to operate because of the monetary remittances to the American institutions in Turkey which were in a position thus to purchase supplies. These institutions had their American personnel to direct the work and their facilities provided buildings and compounds, some large enough to accommodate thousands of refugees. Also, with their normal functions disrupted by war, the parent educational and religious bodies in the United States continued to pay the operating expenses of these institutions and, until the Armistice, the subsistence of the American staffs. The American residents included doctors, nurses, and teachers who were familiar with Near East customs and languages, experienced, from past crises, in dispensing relief, and eager to stay at their posts. Their value to organized relief was all the greater because Turkey would not permit the entry of relief workers from abroad.

These Americans set up their own residents' committee to coordinate their work with the Near East Relief Committee. The extent of these ready-made resources of plant and personnel can be measured by the fact that through these affiliations, they were able to set up and maintain representations in more than fifty centers in the Near East without calling for a single relief worker from home during the period prior to the Armistice.

The American Residents Committee's relations with the Turkish Government were reasonably harmonious, mainly because of the trust engendered during the generous prewar American service to Turkish students and the sick. The Committee extended aid, not only to the Armenian, Syrian, Assyrian, Greek, and Nestorian minorities, but also, in critical cases, to Turks, Kurds, Tartars, and Persians. The harmony was also partly due to the scrupulous neutrality of the American Residents Committee and the Near East Relief Committee in aiding the needy, irrespective of race or creed. To insure against difficulties in this regard, the Committees did not include among their members nationals of any of the groups requiring relief.

Against this background of complexities, the American Residents Committee set about filling the most basic wants of an estimated 1,500,000 people in acute distress in an area 2,000 miles west to east from Constantinople to Teheran and 1,300 miles north to south from the Caucasus Mountains to Cairo. Relief activities primarily took the form of organizing refugee camps, usually in mission compounds converted for the purpose; providing food, clothing, and medical care; furnishing employment for able-bodied men and for widows; and giving special segregated attention to orphans and mothers with dependent children.

One of the wise policies of the Committee—and the action reaped dividends in good will from the Turks—was that where possible, recipients of relief who were capable of doing so were required by the Committee to give labor in return. Paved roads, new irrigation ditches, repaired buildings, reclaimed land, and a handiwork industry were some of the tangible results of this policy, but a far greater boon was the restoration of the dignity and self-respect of legions of the war's most wretched victims.

TURKEY AFTER AMERICA'S ENTRY INTO THE WAR IN APRIL, 1917

When diplomatic relations between Turkey and the United States were broken upon the United States' entry into the war, the American Residents Committee was still allowed to carry on in the guise of attachés to the Swedish Legation, which at that time took over management of American diplomatic affairs.

The Near East Relief Committee's task during this period was in one sense simple and in another formidable. Its work was limited to raising funds and transmitting them to the American Residents Committee, now presumably Swedish. On the ground, however, the practical problems were enormous.

To the minorities continually on the move, dispensing aid was difficult enough, and in the particular case of the Armenian deportees, it was, virtually impossible, since on their forced marches they were kept under heavy guard while passing through communities where Americans lived. Help for those who had found refuge or who, in Turkish territory, had been herded into encampments often depended upon the whim of local Turkish officials. Even where no man-made obstacles were thrown up, the bad roads and bridgeless streams created a problem of access to the more remote sections. Inadequate rail and other transport complicated delivery of supplies, making food amply available for purchase by the Residents Committee in some areas but scarce and subject to speculators' prices in others.

At the time the United States declared war, there were an estimated 300,000 Armenians directly on the relief list, and another 200,000 Armenians and Greeks required aid. The Residents Committee continued the use of the American colleges as refugee centers, and systematic medical aid was given by the American hospitals. In

Constantinople, the Committee was maintaining a hospital, three orphanages, and eleven soup kitchens; it distributed 1,400,000 rations in the last half of 1917.

NEAR EAST RELIEF IN SYRIA

In Syria, prior to the European war, a large minority of Jacobite Christians and Maronite Roman Catholics had amicably co-existed with both their Moslem neighbors and the ruling officials. Syria had enjoyed considerable freedom within the Ottoman Empire, but with the coming of war, the Residents Committee reaped a harvest of woes. The Allied blockade cut off Syria's trade with the outside world, a locust plague ravaged some of its crops, and it was a strategic corridor where the Turkish troops were poised for fighting the British armies.

Added to these troubles was the influx of about 500,000 Armenian deportees—dumped around Damascus, Aleppo, and Deir-ez-Zor, with no provision for their reception or care by either the central or local governments. It was to these unfortunates that American relief efforts were primarily directed.

By order of Turkish Military Governor, Jemal Pasha, a foreigner giving food to a native was subject to arrest. Thus no formal American relief committee could be set up. Instead, an unofficial distribution agency was created by staff members of the American University at Beirut and by field workers of the Presbyterian Board of Missions, which had established a number of schools in Syria. Jemal Pasha's decree was surmounted by mutual acceptance of the fiction that all relief funds from America represented contributions from former Syrian nationals—and indeed, they did contribute about one million dollars in individual remittances through the Presbyterian Board of Missions prior to the entry of the United States in the war.

In 1916, an attempt was made by the Near East Committee to send a Christmas cargo of food, clothing, and medical supplies to Syria on the U.S. Navy collier *Caesar*. After the ship's departure, Jemal Pasha insisted that the cargo be consigned for his personal distribution. The ship was diverted to Alexandria, then occupied by the British, and the supplies were bought by the American Red Cross for use in Serbia. The proceeds went to Beirut for relief purposes.

In time, with the unspoken relaxation of the Turkish restrictions and the use of Syrian and Armenian graduates of American schools as relief investigators and dispensers, the Committee's efforts in Syria were gradually stepped up. Food was distributed to refugee encampments through soup kitchens, relief centers were maintained in coastal villages, some two thousand orphans were sheltered and cared for in Aleppo churches, a number of orphanages were set up elsewhere, and employment for destitute women was provided by way of the creation of a factory for the manufacture of clothing materials.

NEAR EAST RELIEF IN SOUTH RUSSIA

From the outbreak of the war in 1914 to the Communist Revolution in 1917, Russia was on the Allied side. At that time Russia, except for occasional outbreaks against the Jews, was generally a tolerant nation. Its prewar population combined some thirty races and a dozen minority religions.

The Russian authorities raised no obstacles to the Armenian, Assyrian, Nestorian, and Persian refugees who flooded their southern provinces. The Russian Government furnished emergency rations and army doctors in the fight against starvation, destitution, and epidemics among the refugees. However, these aids were far from adequate, and the American Consul at Tiflis, F. Willoughby Smith, appealed to the Near East Committee for help. Within a month, some $40,000 was en route, a prelude to far greater funds.

There had been no substantial American missionary activities in Russia, and thus there was little American personnel available to the Committee. However, some Americans from their institutions in Turkey and Persia accompanied the refugees from those countries, and later, additional American staff was sent from the United States.

A local volunteer committee of Americans was formed, with Samuel G. Wilson, previously in Persia, as chairman, and Consul Smith as treasurer. They joined a British relief committee which had been created under the chairmanship of Lord Bryce. In return for monthly rations from the committee, some 130,000 Armenian refugees were set to work repairing irrigation ditches and rebuilding roads and sanitary systems. Factories were set up and some 2,500 refugee women were employed—at spinning wheels and looms built by refugee carpenters—turning out cloth both for relief use and for public sale. Families were resettled in rural areas and provided with seed and animals; they soon became self-supporting. More than 15,000 orphans were apprenticed to refugees in 450 villages under a subsidy arrangement.

With the Communist Revolution in November, 1917, the Russian Government aid ceased. Medical supplies were unobtainable, and epidemics of typhus and relapsing fever raged among the refugees. However, the White Russian armies to the north provided a shield against the Communists, but the Germans and Turks began invasions from the south, and the American workers had to be temporarily evacuated. To prevent a total break in the relief efforts, supplies and funds were left with local committees, while thousands of orphans continued to be cared for under the supervision of John Elder, a Young Men's Christian Association worker who had been unable to leave because of illness. Elder and a companion who had remained to nurse him obtained funds for their effort by selling drafts on the Near East Committee in New York to local merchants. Although unknown to the Committee at the time, this device was approved by it *ex post facto* and the drafts honored. Such was the relief in Russia at the Armistice.

NEAR EAST RELIEF IN PERSIA (IRAN)

Persia was an independent and supposedly neutral nation. A Moslem country, it contained a sizable Christian minority of Armenians, Nestorians, and Assyrians, largely living in the Urmia and

Tabriz districts of the northwest provinces bordering on Turkish Kurdistan and Russian Armenia.

American missionary endeavors in Persia had begun in 1811 and by 1914 were represented by seventy-five medical, educational, and religious institutions maintained at six stations in Tabriz, Urmia, and Teheran. To administer the funds sent from the Near East Committee, this personnel combined with the United States diplomatic staff into committees at Teheran and Tabriz, headed by the American Consul, Gordon Paddock.

However, Persia was drawn into the war by military invasions from both Turkey and Russia. Except during 1916 and early 1917, when the Russians were in occupation, northeast Persia was an incessant battlefield of the Russians and Turks; in the meantime, the Kurds pillaged the Christian towns. Some of their inhabitants took refuge in safer interior cities, such as Teheran and Hamadan. Others fled to Russia. The inevitable result of these battles and general uncertainties of life was famine, not only in the northwest provinces, but all over Persia.

Among the emergency programs operated by the American residents' committees were the shelter and feeding of fifteen thousand Persian Christians within the mission compound at Urmia for a five-month period in 1915 following a Turkish victory in the area and the maintenance on monthly rations of hundreds of thousands of refugees in Teheran and Hamadan during 1918. In each temporary cessation of the crisis, the refugees were given tools, lent animals, and provided with seed in an effort to restore their self-support.

The orphan problem was relatively minor. Three small orphanages were maintained at Tabriz, Hamadan, and Kermanshah.

PERSIA AFTER THE UNITED STATES ENTERED THE WAR

Soon after the United States joined in the war, we stationed a contingent of American troops in Persia. The American Residents Committee already had public works under way, widening and paving the streets in Tabriz, Teheran, and Hamadan. With the co-operation of the American Army, these works were continued and expanded. From Army contracts, workrooms were established where thousands of refugees were employed in making underclothing and stockings for the troops.

The last great American relief project in Persia prior to the Armistice was a successful battle against typhoid, typhus, and cholera. Waged originally by medical-missionary personnel, the fight was joined in the summer of 1918 by reinforcements from America attached to a special thirteen-man commission headed by Dr. Harry Pratt Judson, President of the University of Chicago. This commission had the broad purpose of bolstering Persian neutrality through such tangible evidences of American good will as help to fight famine and undertaking rehabilitation in devastated areas. The commission was authorized by the Near East Relief Committee to buy foodstuffs, drugs and medicines, automobiles, and other transportation equipment. Arriving in Persia by way of Bombay and the Persian Gulf in the summer of 1918, the commission was able, by the Armistice, to report its mission accomplished on both humanitarian and political scores.

OTHER ACTIVITIES OF THE NEAR EAST RELIEF COMMITTEE

On the fringes of the Near East Relief's major wartime areas of operations, refuge had been given in Egypt and Macedonia to numbers of Armenians, Syrians, and Greeks from the Ottoman Empire. The Committee provided funds for their support.

FINANCE OF THE COMMITTEE

From its beginning, the Near East Committee was dependent upon appeals to the generosity of the American people. Subscribers came from every religious faith, from every walk of life, from the native and foreign-born, from fraternal societies, labor unions, women's clubs, educational institutions, synagogues, churches, and Sunday Schools, whose young pupils alone donated a total of one million dollars the first year.

Support for these efforts was provided by a Congressional resolution of July, 1916, and a subsequent proclamation by President Wilson setting aside two days in October for contributions. To supplement public giving, the Committee secured substantial sums from the Rockefeller Foundation and from the American Red Cross.

The extent of the Committee's efforts is indicated by the funds raised and those expended in the years prior to the Armistice:

	Receipts	Expenditures
1915	$ 176,929.51	$ 134,100.00
1916	2,227,209.77	1,665,742.62
1917	4,520,087.75	4,386,058.93
1918	7,021,972.78	6,712,215.98

The following is a geographical breakdown of the Near East Committee's relief appropriations from its inception in late 1915 until the Armistice:

Country	Amount Appropriated
Turkey	$ 4,443,179
Egypt	35,764
Greece	5,500
Japan (Armenian refugees)	3,000
Mesopotamia	90,000
Palestine	670,000
Persia	3,439,930
Russian Provinces	2,763,304
Switzerland (Armenian refugees)	10,000
Syria	1,572,760
Total	$13,033,437

I continue the narrative of the Near East Committee during the great famine which followed the war in Volume III of *An American Epic.* But I may mention here that this Committee, during its fifteen-year span of life, raised and expended about $117,000,000.

Sums of money give some indication of the magnitude of the Near East Committee's labors, but they cannot convey either the sacrifice in dimes and dollars of the American people or the one million human lives saved by devoted men and women who worked among a thousand difficulties, hardships, and dangers. Engaged in all of these endeavors were one thousand American workers. In the war and its immediate aftermath, twenty-seven of them died of typhus, cholera, pneumonia, and exhaustion—and one from a bandit's bullet.

CHAPTER 23

THE JEWISH JOINT DISTRIBUTION COMMITTEE

The First World War brought great suffering to the Jews. They formed part of the people in practically every country at war. In addition to the calamities which fell upon all peoples involved in the war, they were singled out in Germany, Poland, Austria-Hungary, Turkey, Bulgaria, and some parts of Russia for systematic persecution. These persecutions were not only economic plunder, but also included the terrors of eviction from their homes, wholesale deportations, starvation as refugees, and death from pogroms.

When the war broke out in Europe, there were about 13,000,000 Jews in the world, of whom more than 9,500,000 lived in the belligerent countries. Their major source of help from overseas came from their fewer than 2,400,000 American co-religionists.

I have reserved this narrative to follow that of the Near East Relief Committee because that record gives graphic evidence of the terrors which the Jews suffered in common with the Christians. In that chapter I have mentioned the relief of the Jews in the Middle East only briefly and have reserved the more complete record for this chapter.

Soon after the war began, appeals for American help resulted in the creation of two major and one minor relief committees. The first of them was the Central Committee for the Relief of Jews Suffering through the War, created on October 4, 1914, by the Union of Orthodox Jewish Congregations in America under the chairmanship of Leon Kamaiky.

The second committee, created a few weeks later, was the American Jewish Relief Committee, with Louis Marshall as chairman. It was set up in response to an appeal for aid to Palestine by the American Ambassador to Turkey, Henry Morgenthau.

A year later, a third organization, of no great financial strength, was created—entitled the Jewish People's Relief Committee—under Congressman Meyer London, representing Socialist groups.

The first two committees received substantial sums from their appeals, and at once there arose the problem of how to distribute the funds in more than a score of places where the terror was in progress. This problem was solved by a proposal from Felix M. Warburg to consolidate the distribution of the funds raised from American Jewry into one organization named the Jewish Joint Distribution Committee—the J.D.C. for short. The Committee was organized on November 29, 1914, under Mr. Warburg's chairmanship. It was destined to become one of the world's greatest voluntary relief agencies. The Committee proclaimed its purpose to be purely humanitarian, with no political objectives, and stood ready to aid all races and creeds in the areas in which it operated. It never deviated from these principles.

FINANCE

The J.D.C. did not appeal directly for funds. The raising of financial support was conducted by the two major committees singly and at times jointly. The first year's goal of $5,000,000 was announced at a meeting in Carnegie Hall in New York City on December 21, 1915. In that meeting nearly $1,000,000 was raised. Impetus was given the drive when, in line with a Senate resolution, President Wilson designated January 27, 1916, as Jewish Relief Day. Another $1,000,000 was raised on that day. By the end of 1916, the total of funds raised was $4,750,000.

On December 21, 1916, on the anniversary of the Carnegie Hall meeting in 1915, another meeting was held in the same place at which a $10,000,000 joint appeal for 1917 was announced. An impressive spur toward this hitherto unprecedented goal was provided when Julius H. Rosenwald of Chicago offered personally to contribute up to $1,000,000 on the basis of the total collected by November 1, 1917—a goal that was met. In New York alone, $5,000,000 was collected over a period of ten days.

These contributions resulted in the ability of the J.D.C. to make the following expenditures in the years prior to the Armistice:

Year	Amount
1914	$ 61,000.00
1915	1,904,749.48
1916	4,249,561.95
1917	2,827,785.29
1918	5,894,687.27
	$14,937,783.99

ORGANIZATION

Except in a few special instances, the J.D.C. did not itself engage in shipment or distribution of supplies. Its method was to make monetary contributions to already-existing Jewish organizations overseas and to secure the creation of such organizations where none had existed previously. These committees either purchased their supplies locally or imported them.

Aside from such major operations, the J.D.C. conducted a number of special services. One was its Transmission Department, which forwarded remittances from individual American Jews to relatives overseas, the regular channels of exchange to many nations having been cut off by the war. Thirty-five offices were established by the J.D.C. in American and Canadian cities where a person could deposit dollars and have the J.D.C. make payment to a designated recipient in local currency through its foreign affiliates. A total of $10,300,000 was transmitted during the six years from 1914 to 1921.

A second special J.D.C. service was the establishment of bureaus whereby societies among American Jews who had emigrated from the same European locality or city could transmit funds to their former home towns, which disbursed the money in ways specified by the donors.

A third special service was the Personal Service and Location Department. It ascertained the whereabouts of refugees and dealt with such problems as government allotments to soldiers' families, desertion cases, and inheritance matters.

The major activity of the J.D.C. was monetary support to the Jewish organizations in Germany, Poland, Austria-Hungary, Turkey, and Russia. It was within these countries that ruthless persecutions were rife, with consequent great masses of refugees and great suffering from disease and starvation. There were some minor areas elsewhere, but 90 per cent of the J.D.C.'s charitable resources prior to the Armistice were required in the above-named countries. The following regional narrative indicates the labors of the J.D.C. affiliates.

OPERATIONS IN PALESTINE

The appeal of Ambassador Morgenthau, which sparked the American relief activities for Palestine, was met initially by contributions from individuals and the relief committees to the extent of about $90,000 prior to the creation of the J.D.C. in November, 1914. The J.D.C. took a hand in these early activities by chartering the U.S. Navy colliers *Vulcan* and *Sterling* in late 1915 and early 1916 for immediate dispatch of food and medicines. Thereafter, however, the J.D.C. acted through a committee set up at Jerusalem under the chairmanship of American Consul-General Otis A. Glazebrook. For some unknown reason the Palestine Jews were not subjected to the Turkish Government's 1915 expulsion decree of religious minorities. However, they were strictly confined; they were without resources with which to live, and Jewish groups from elsewhere in Turkey were loaded upon them.

The Palestine Committee set up soup kitchens, where bread or flour was also supplied. Bread was distributed to the schools and to the destitute. Aid was given to educational, charitable, health, and child-care institutions. Cholera and typhus epidemics were combated, and in 1917, some ten to thirteen thousand Jews expelled from Jaffa and environs by the Turks were cared for. Loans were granted to farmers and workers; shops in which food and petroleum were sold at cost were set up; and, through a public-works committee, refugees and others were employed to lay out streets, repair pavements, and perform drainage and irrigation work.

With the British Army occupation of Palestine in December, 1917, the American Red Cross took over such relief as was necessary, and the J.D.C.'s activities gradually gave way to other Jewish organizations concerned with long-range objectives. The J.D.C., however, continued to support some special agencies, notably in the care of some four thousand war orphans and the financing of a malaria-eradication drive.

OPERATIONS IN GERMANY

Support for the Jews in Germany by the J.D.C. was established through co-operation with the German Hilfsverein der Deutschen Juden, which had been organized long before the war. The Hilfsverein der Deutschen Juden included German Poland in its activities, but with the German occupation of Russian Poland, it was prevented by the authorities from operating in that area. I take up the subject of the Jews in this region in a later section on Poland.

OPERATIONS IN RUSSIA

In Russia, the J.D.C. initially operated through EKOPO, a Jewish organization, supported by Russian Jews long before the war, which had even received subsidies from the Czarist Government. But soon after the outbreak of the war, the German-Austrian invasions of Russia created, from a relief point of view, two Russias: "Occupied Russia" and "Unoccupied Russia."

OPERATIONS IN "OCCUPIED RUSSIA"

The major problems of relief in German-occupied Russia were in Poland and the Baltic States. It must be remembered that Poland, a century before the First World War, had been partitioned among Germany, Russia, and Austria. The Germans quickly occupied Russian Poland, which along with their prewar segment constituted all of Poland except for the Austrian section. With their enlarged Polish area, the Germans controlled the greatest aggregate of Jews in all Europe, and their invasion included the Baltic States and the Jewish communities therein, the largest of which was in Lithuania.

The Germans barred the use of funds of the Hilfsverein der Deutschen Juden in Russian Poland and the Baltic States; consequently, the only hope of Jews in German-occupied Russia lay in the J.D.C. The J.D.C.-affiliated organization in this area was the Jüdisches Hilfskomite für Polen und Litauen, a group formed in Berlin soon after the German advance into Russian territory.

At the peak of the invasion, the Hilfskomite maintained ties with the Jewish communal and special relief groups in 252 cities and towns. Kitchens for both adults and children were opened, and bread, potatoes, clothing, and wood for fuel were distributed. For those who could pay, provision stores were opened where food was sold at fractional cost. Nursing of the sick was undertaken; hospitals were subsidized; orphanages and kindergartens were set up; religious schools were supported; refugees were placed in private homes or, where possible, repatriated; unemployment relief was granted; and workshops were maintained for homeless girls. Artisans and merchants were given loans through credit associations established for the purpose. At one point (February, 1916), 700,000 Jews in Poland, Lithuania, and the Baltic States were entirely dependent upon the J.D.C. for their continued existence.

OPERATIONS IN "UNOCCUPIED RUSSIA"

In Unoccupied Russia, the J.D.C. adopted EKOPO as its affiliate to receive aid. The J.D.C.'s funds were transmitted to EKOPO partly via the Europe-wide Jewish Colonization Association and partly via the American Ambassador at St. Petersburg, David R. Francis.

Jewish distress in Russia mounted rapidly with the war. The Russian front extended from the Baltic to the Black Sea. The Czar's armies sometimes moved forward, but for the most part, they were beaten back. With their advances and retreats came an estimated 800,000 Jews—uprooted from their homes or in flight from persecution. Of these refugees, some 100,000 were from the Austrian segment of Poland, mostly Galicia, and from Bukovina. The remainder were fugitives from Poland and the Baltic States. The Russian Government gave a sparse ration to all refugees, but the burden on the J.D.C.'s affiliate became enormous. EKOPO, through its 142 local committees (and through its "correspondents" where no local organizations existed) helped evacuate these Jews in orderly fashion, transported them, supervised them en route, and undertook the creation of new settlements in the Russian interior. It also undertook to restore life in these settlements by building schools, orphanages, and hospitals. It gave manual training in workshops. Artisans were given instruments, and mechanics were given tools.

But the Communist Revolution intervened to stifle the efforts of the J.D.C. Their contacts with the EKOPO quickly weakened and finally that organization was dissolved by the Communists. Of the 500,000 who remained in Russia after the Revolution, some two-thirds were homeless and stricken with sweeps of contagious diseases, and little help came to them until the great famine in Russia in 1921, when the Soviet Government appealed to the free world for help. I resume the work of the J.D.C. on that occasion in Volume III of these memoirs.

OPERATIONS IN AUSTRIA

In Austria, the major reliance of the J.D.C. for administration of relief was the Israelitische Allianz of Vienna. The recurrent advances and retreats in the battle with the Russians over Galicia and Bukovina resulted in masses of Jewish refugees, not only in Russia, but also in Austria. An estimated 400,000 Jews fled from Galicia and Bukovina into the interior, clogging Vienna, Budapest, and other large cities. For these, and for the Jews in Russian territory occupied by Austria-Hungary, only the barest relief was possible.

The J.D.C. funds were furnished to the Allianz to supplement the government aid by the provision of clothing, money for more foodstuffs, emergency barracks for shelter, and wood for fuel. People's kitchens and tearooms were set up. Special shelters housed orphans. Rabbis, teachers, students, and schools were given direct financial help. Some aspects of reconstructive work were undertaken by way of establishing employment bureaus and providing artisans with the tools of their trade.

The J.D.C.'s final appropriation for Austria-Hungary was made in February, 1917. After the United States broke off relations with the Central Powers, American relief efforts had to be restricted and new arrangements made by the J.D.C. With State Department approval and with the good offices of neutral Holland, the J.D.C. set up a committee of Netherlands Jews which received J.D.C. funds under a license from the American War Trade Board, apportioned them for the enemy areas, and arranged for their transmittal to local Jewish relief committees via the Netherlands Embassy officials in the countries concerned, including Austria.

In Palestine, after we entered the war, the task was taken over by S. Hoofien, manager of the Anglo-Palestine Bank and a Netherlands citizen, who acted on behalf of the J.D.C.'s Holland branch.

THE PEOPLES SERVED

The widespread activities of the J.D.C. and the great dimension of its efforts prior to the Armistice are indicated by a statement of expenditures as of August 30, 1918:

Russia	$2,612,300
Poland	5,780,662
Austria-Hungary	1,583,700
Palestine	1,646,485
Turkey	656,004
Alexandria (Palestinian Refugees)	56,394
Greece	91,021
Serbia	22,500
Serbian Jews in Switzerland	2,000
Rumania	135,900
Bulgaria	18,500
Tunis, Algiers and Morocco	9,000
Students and Writers in Switzerland	11,200
Destitute Families of Russian Jews in France	5,000
Spain, Turkish Refugees	8,000
Japan, Russian Refugees in Yokohama	80,000
Persia	26,700
Kosher Food for Jewish Prisoners of War in Internment Camps	15,500
Advanced a/c Refugees from Palestine	12,298
Transmission of Individual Remittances Throughout the World	607,808

In addition to the above amounts, the Central Committee for the Relief of Jews Suffering Through the War remitted the following sums directly:

For Refugee Rabbis, Teachers and Children in Yeshivas and Talmud Torahs	$ 59,915
For Austria-Hungary Relief Committee	5,307
For Palestine General Relief	13,659
For Palestine Institutions	9,515
For Palestine Funds	18,500

It transmitted donations:

Designated for Institutions in Palestine	$270,979
Designated for Individuals in Palestine	181,939
Remitted by People's Relief Committee to Dienensohn's School, Warsaw	10,000

(The total expense of the Joint Distribution Committee and its constituent committees, for collecting and distributing these funds during the four years since the outbreak of the war, amounts to less than two and one-half —2½—per cent.)

With the fall of the German, Austrian, and Turkish empires and Bulgaria in November, 1918, the whole relief scene shifted for the J.D.C. With the triumph of the free nations, major persecution of the Jews ceased. Some oppression and persecution continued in Communist Russia, but that country was practically inaccessible. After the Armistice, the J.D.C. joined in the relief of many countries from the great famine. An account of this is given in Volume III of these memoirs.

The dimensions of the effort from 1914 to 1923 is indicated as about $58,500,000. This amount came almost wholly from the Jewish communities in the United States, of which there were then fewer than 500,000 families.

But the saving of life and the alleviation of suffering and moral decay cannot be measured in dollars.

It was a magnificent demonstration of human compassion.

CHAPTER 24

THE SALVATION ARMY

When the European war broke out, the Salvation Army[1] was known to practically every adult American. It had given more than thirty-four years of life and hope to the lowly, the discouraged, the dissolute, and the forgotten men and women in the slum areas of American cities.

The organizational structure of the Salvation Army was a complete anomaly and contradiction in American life. It was an oligarchy of a single but distinguished family with a military-type setup. There was no system of the checks and balances usual to American organizations. It had, however, the strongest of all controls—conscience, devotion to human service, and the words of Jesus Christ.

After the outbreak of hostilities in 1914, the Salvation Army was one of the first American organizations to prepare for overseas aid. A month later, in September, 1914, it established its War Service Department under the direction of:

EVANGELINE C. BOOTH, *Commander-in-Chief*
COLONEL WILLIAM PEART, *Chairman*
COLONEL GUSTAVE S. REINHARDSEN, *Secretary and Treasurer*
LIEUTENANT COLONEL WILLIAM S. BARKER, *Director in France*

[1] The parent organization of the Salvation Army was an East London Mission founded by the Reverend William Booth and his wife, Catherine, in 1865. Thirteen years later, the name was changed to the Salvation Army. The American branch of the organization was formed in 1880.

The British Salvation Army had already established branches in the Protestant countries on the Continent, but such branches were either non-existent or weak in the Catholic countries.

Prior to the United States' entry into the war, the American Salvation Army preserved a rigid neutrality. It not only followed President Wilson's urgings to the American people for such conduct, but so did its affiliated organizations in every combatant country on both sides of the struggle. Moreover, it had thousands of members serving in opposing armies.

At the outbreak of war in Europe, Commander Booth announced the establishment of a "War Fund" and made a public appeal for donations. The Army immediately sent Colonel Mary Murray and two experienced associates to Belgium to devise help for refugees. In December, 1914, the Army gathered up and shipped thousands of Christmas presents for the war orphans in many countries. It also made an appeal for old clothing, which it renovated in workshops it had equipped. The first shipment of clothing was dispatched on December 19, 1914, and its receipt was acknowledged on March 2, 1915, by the American Minister in Brussels on behalf of the Belgian Relief Commission. The Army also began the shipment of clothing and other supplies to the American Relief Clearing House in Paris, which on March 14, 1915, acknowledged the arrival of twenty-nine cases.

One of the Salvation Army's earliest actions was an appeal for old linen. This it laundered, sterilized, cut in strips, rolled into bandages, and shipped to armies on both sides of the conflict. By December, 1914, six thousand bandages had been shipped and the Army had to make a public appeal for funds to enable it to expand its work. The collection of dimes and quarters mounted slowly. The Army's weekly journal, *The War Cry,* reported a total of only $18,821.75. By July, 1915, the Army had laundered, sterilized, stitched, and rolled about one million bandages and had established its own laundry and sterilizing plants. An issue of *The War Cry* of August, 1915, records an acknowledgment on June 25, by American Ambassador James W. Gerard in Berlin, of the receipt of eighteen cases containing bandages for wounded soldiers. *The War Cry* notes the arrival in France on July 24, 1915, of 173,410 articles for the use of the wounded as the result of the "old linen" campaign.

Prior to American entry into the war, the Salvation Army added to its overseas work by the dispatching of missions, mostly to France, comprised of both men and women who operated ambulances, constructed and established service centers, known as "huts," for rest and recreation and aids to enlisted men behind the lines, created receiving homes for destitute children, and gave aid to families in trouble.

THE SALVATION ARMY DURING AMERICAN PARTICIPATION IN THE WAR

When the United States declared war in April, 1917, the neutrality of the American Salvation Army ended.[2] Its full strength was devoted to service for the American Army and Navy, both at home and overseas. Although this was a magnificent and devoted service, it falls outside American aid to foreign nations and therefore the purpose of this memoir. But as an indication of the importance of this service to the American Army, General Pershing incorporated the Salvation Army staff as an attachment of the American Army, with a special—and for the women attractive—uniform.

A few items from Salvation Army records demonstrate its devotion—and they include some incidental service to foreign civilians:

77 motor ambulances manned by Salvationists

87 hotels for use by soldiers and sailors

107 buildings in the United States placed at the disposal of the Government

199 service huts and 300 rest stations with recreation rooms equipped with papers, magazines, books, etc., established at Army camps

[2] One of the best accounts on civilian service to our armies ever written is *The War Romance of the Salvation Army,* by Evangeline Booth and Grace Livingston Hill (Philadelphia, J. B. Lippincott Company, 1919). This book deserves a high place in American literature. It is an inspiring account of American women serving the American Army in France, not in the towns and cities, but scarcely out of the reach of shellfire—and many times even there. Seldom has there been such a portrayal of the human side of war—and of human goodness.

15,000 beds in hotels close to railway stations and landing points at seaport cities supervised for soldiers and sailors going to and from the front

100,000 parcels of food and clothing distributed to soldiers and sailors

100,000 wounded soldiers taken from battlefields in Salvation Army ambulances

300,000 soldiers and sailors in daily attendance at Salvation Army canteens

45 chaplains serving under Government appointment

2,184 war widows assisted by legal aid or other aid or visited

2,404 soldiers' wives cared for, including medical help

442 war children under Salvation Army care

3,378 remittances by soldiers amounting to $196,081 forwarded

600 parcels supplied to prisoners of war

1,300 cables sent for soldiers

40 military hospitals regularly visited

147 ships with 324,052 men on board met

35,845 telegrams sent for soldiers

And incidental to these activities, the Salvation Army established receiving homes for destitute children and provided for the children while the mothers worked; poor children were taken out of the bombardment areas and cared for in the country.

The Salvation Army raised and expended more than seven million dollars.

The Salvation Army's overseas service did not end with the Armistice. I again return to its activities in Volume III of this memoir.

CHAPTER 25

THE AMERICAN FRIENDS SERVICE COMMITTEE

The Quaker tradition of service to suffering humanity is as old as the Quaker faith itself.[1] Beginning with the Great Plague of London in 1665, soon after the "Society of Friends" came into being, its members have helped alleviate distress wherever they have found it. In the Franco-Prussian War of 1870–1871, they raised a fund for the relief of both French and German civilians and distributed considerable supplies. Their men and women in service at this time wore a mark of identity by way of a red and black double star, which some of their workers in the foreign field still wear.

The Society of Friends has never been a large religious sect, its number in modern times being about 160,000 each in the United States and in England, with a few scattered meetings in other nations.

By their faith the Quakers are pacifists. However, important officers and officials in the Revolutionary War, the Civil War, and the First World War were Quakers, and many served in the ranks in all wars. A considerable number, however, stoutly refused to enter combat service and suffered greatly because of their resolution.

The American Quakers, ever since William Penn set up their refuge from persecution in Pennsylvania in 1692, have been a thrifty and enterprising people. Over the years, they built up great in-

[1] I have omitted the multitude of references to authorities in order not to encumber the text. I give a list of sources in the Bibliography.

surance, banking, and industrial concerns and fertile farms. They therefore furnished a recruiting ground for skilled administrators of never failing integrity. In consequence, beyond their own direct relief enterprises, they were called upon to manage large relief operations financed by other organizations.

THE FRIENDS' ACTIVITIES PRIOR TO THE UNITED STATES' ENTRY INTO THE WAR

Prior to our entry into the war, the American Friends' activities were largely in support of, and at times jointly with, the Friends in England. The British Friends, in September, 1914, established a threefold service: a volunteer first-aid and ambulance corps on the French Front, aid to enemy aliens interned in Britain, and relief to tens of thousands of refugees from Occupied Belgium and Northern France. American Friends volunteered for service in these activities, and the American Quakers made monthly contributions to support their British brethren during this period.

THE FRIENDS AFTER THE UNITED STATES ENTERED THE WAR

On April 30, 1917, within a month after we went to war, representatives from throughout the country met in Philadelphia to explore possible avenues of wartime service. They issued this declaration:

> We are united in expressing our love for our country and our desire to serve her loyally. We offer ourselves to the Government of the United States in any constructive work in which we can conscientiously serve humanity.

On May 28, 1917, this group formally organized the American Friends Service Committee. The Committee's first officers were:

RUFUS M. JONES, *Chairman*
ALFRED G. SCATTERGOOD, *Vice-Chairman*
VINCENT D. NICHOLSON, *Executive Secretary*
CHARLES F. JENKINS, *Treasurer*

Later on, I served as their honorary chairman for some years.[2]

In July, 1917, the Committee assembled one hundred conscientious objectors at Haverford College for a rigorous training course in relief and reconstruction work overseas. The training included instruction in language and history, first aid to the injured, road-building, building construction, the maintenance and repair of automobiles and farm machinery, and farming. This group, selected from twenty states, included engineers, doctors, architects, mechanics, social workers, farmers, and carpenters. They were furloughed by the War Department for service to the Committee. In September, 1917, the first contingents landed in France.

The members of the pioneer unit merged with the British Friends already on the scene. The Americans, directed by Charles Evans, engaged in five activities: medical aid, driving ambulances, the building and reconstruction of homes, farming, and the care of refugees.

In the medical field, the joint British and American committees provided clinical and dispensary help for the wounded and for refugees. They staffed and maintained two children's homes, two convalescent homes, a home for aged women, and two general hospitals. The most celebrated of the eight institutions was a maternity hospital at Châlons-sur-Marne. Prior to the close of this institution at the end of the war, it had provided facilities for 981 births and nursing care for 1,909 other children.[3]

[2] Organized for the immediate emergency, none of the members of the Committee could have foreseen that their organization would still be active in humane service to the date of this narrative—more than forty-three years. They were awarded the Nobel Peace Prize in 1947 jointly with the British Friends.

[3] As a war memorial, the Quakers built a new hospital at Châlons and dedicated it in June, 1922, leasing the buildings and land to the Marne Government and providing enough endowment to pay staff salaries for ten years.

In the agricultural field, the American members undertook restoration of land from havoc wrought by explosives, barbed wire, and weeds. They established several centers which lent new farm equipment to the peasants, set up shops for its repair, and furnished seed and binder twine. In addition, squads traveled from village to village with tractors, gang-plows, harrows, and threshing machines. In this aid of peasants, these members took part in the actual labor. Also in their agricultural relief, they furnished sheep and goats and set up rabbit-raising centers and poultry and dairy farms.

The French authorities forbade the return of refugees to their ruined villages until housing could be provided. The British Friends had established a factory for the production of two- or three-room prefabricated houses with interchangeable parts. The American Friends built a second factory with financial aid from the American Red Cross. By the end of the war, a total of 544 houses had been turned out at the two factories. In addition, the factories made doors, windows, furniture, barns, and barracks. They furnished the Red Cross with two hundred houses for a TB settlement.

During the great German offensive in the spring of 1918, the Friends evacuated whole villages under heavy fire, providing transport, food, and lodging until the people could return home. Among the evacuees were many aged, crippled, sick, and insane-asylum patients, whom they took to safety in the Pyrenees.

The American Friends Service Committee sent a mission of six women to join the British Friends in Czarist Russia. Their work was largely concentrated at Samara, where the local population of eighty thousand had been swelled by twenty thousand refugees. All of the Russian doctors had been drafted for military service. The Friends provided hospital care, workshops for refugees, and care for orphans until the Russian doctors returned in October, 1918.

I return to a description of the further activities of the American Friends Service Committee in Volume III of this memoir.

The Friends raised funds among themselves and from the public, and they were generously supported by other charitable organizations and even by governments. I may mention here that of their expenditures of about $25,200,000 during the war and its aftermath, they received from the following sources the amounts indicated:

American Relief Administration	$5,400,000
German Government	4,500,000
American Red Cross	500,000
Jewish Joint Distribution Committee	500,000

Perhaps their greatest contribution was this group of highly cultural men and women, undertaking any task, no matter how lowly, in their gentle way and with glowing kindness. Wherever the Friends went, they spread a ray of sunshine into the despair and suffering which was the backwash of war.

CHAPTER 26

OTHER CHARITABLE AGENCIES PARTICIPATING IN RELIEF PRIOR TO THE ARMISTICE

For brevity only, I group the following devoted organizations into one chapter.

THE DAUGHTERS OF THE AMERICAN REVOLUTION

Upon our declaration of war, Mrs. George Thacher Guernsey, President-General of the Daughters of the American Revolution, appointed a permanent War Relief Service Committee, with Mrs. Matthew T. Scott as chairman and Mrs. Albert S. Burleson as vice-chairman. The Committee financed itself through the D.A.R. members.

The relief activities of the D.A.R. prior to our entry into the war included contributions in cash amounting to $67,484 to the National Surgical Dressings and the American Red Cross. They made for the Red Cross and other organizations 20,538 hospital garments, 331,686 surgical supplies, and 328 knitted garments, or a total of 352,552 items. They made cash contributions of $27,680 to Belgium and $263 to France. They donated more than $300,000 to the Y.M.C.A., the Y.W.C.A., the Knights of Columbus, the Salvation Army, Jewish Relief, the American Library Association, War Camp Community Service, and other organizations doing war wark. They also contributed more than a million books and thousands of phonograph records.

The D.A.R. donated to the French relief agencies 64,896 refugee garments, 401 shawls, 200 layettes, and 5,581 other articles. They provided $9,135 for poultry farms, $17,737 for hospital beds, cafeteria equipment, and children's clothing, and $5,554 for miscellaneous items—a total cash contribution of $32,426.

To the other Allies, the D.A.R. donated 30,106 garments and 3,235 other items and provided $94,546 in cash contributions and gifts.

THE CHURCH OF JESUS CHRIST OF LATTER-DAY SAINTS

The Church of Jesus Christ of Latter-day Saints (colloquially the Mormons) inaugurated relief measures for Europe in 1914 under Sisters Sarah M. McLelland and Edna L. Smith and Sister Gates. They collected money and used clothing for distribution by their religious colleagues overseas. In November, 1917, they raised a $100,000 contribution to the building of a soldiers' home in Europe. They were also active after the Armistice.[1]

THE CHRISTIAN SCIENTISTS

In October, 1914, a "War Relief Committee" was organized by the Christian Scientists, and contributions were taken up in all Christian Science churches for the support of Christian Scientists in difficulties overseas. A total of $82,104 was raised and expended in England, Germany, France, and Switzerland. In December, 1914, a further

[1] While not directly connected with relief, an incident of devotion during the worst food year of the war is a part of *An American Epic*. A statement by the Sisters was:

> . . . [We have] turned over to the United States Government over two hundred thousand bushels of wheat—grain that was gleaned in aprons, bought with the difficult dimes and nickels of the faithful sisters, stored in their own or hired granaries for nearly half a century against a time of famine. . . . Yet, how proud we are to perform this service for our suffering. . . . Our hearts and prayers go with the gifts. . . .

amount of $29,155 was raised through church collections for relief to non–Christian Scientists in England, Holland, France, and Switzerland, and monetary aid was given, regardless of religious affiliation, to civilians in Armenia, Syria, Belgium, Poland, Rumania, Serbia, Lithuania, Russia, and Turkey.

ACTIVITIES OF THE CHRISTIAN SCIENTISTS AFTER THE UNITED STATES' ENTRY INTO THE WAR

Following America's entry into the war, a "Comforts Forwarding Committee" was organized. It consisted of more than a thousand groups of Christian Scientists throughout the United States. They provided more than a million knitted and sewn garments for soldiers, sailors, and civilian refugees. These garments were distributed through various agencies, including the Belgian Relief Commission, the Italian War Relief Committee, the American Fund for French Wounded, the Serbian and Polish Relief committees, the Russian Relief, and the Wellesley and Smith College units. In addition, a considerable quantity of yarn was supplied in bulk to small French factories which employed widows and dependents of French soldiers.

The total amount contributed to war relief by the Christian Scientists from October, 1914, to the formal closing of the fund on June 2, 1919, was $1,988,000.

THE GREAT CHARITABLE FOUNDATIONS

The great charitable foundations played a most important part in relief during the whole of the war and its aftermath. They were:

Carnegie Corporation of New York
Carnegie Endowment for International Peace
Laura Spelman Rockefeller Memorial
The Commonwealth Fund
The Rockefeller Foundation

These foundations did little with regard to direct shipments of food, medicine, and clothing and reconstruction aid or its distribution. They did, however, contribute great sums of money to the relief organizations. Before the Armistice, such contributions were:

Carnegie Corporation of New York		$ 2,100,000
The Rockefeller Foundation	(in excess of)	17,000,000

The Carnegie Endowment for International Peace and the Laura Spelman Rockefeller Memorial did not begin their contributions until after the Armistice. The Commonwealth Fund was organized just before the Armistice, and its contributions began after that date.

The grants mentioned above were made to organizations engaged in both domestic and foreign work connected with the war. They were a source of hope and encouragement to many organizations in time of need.

SECTION III

ORGANIZATION BEHIND THE FRONT TO MEET THE FAMINE IN FORTY-FIVE NATIONS

INTRODUCTION

When the Armistice quieted the killing of men over the world on November 11, 1918, the curtain was lifted on the greatest famine of all time. It was inevitable that it would follow the greatest war of all history up to that time. Practically every country in the world had been involved in the war. With the diversion of manpower to war, the use of fertilizers for explosives, the shifting of the manufacture of agricultural implements to munitions, there came into focus forty-five nations or peoples and a dozen special groups to whom overseas food, medical supplies, clothing, and reconstruction materials alone would save the lives of hundreds of millions of people.

The organization of supplies and their distribution would have been difficult enough had one nation possessed all the supplies, all the credits, all the ships, and all the raw materials—and had there been enough supplies for all the needy. But they did not exist.

The day of the defeat of the Central Powers by the Allied and "Associated" Powers, food supplies became one of the dominant weapons of political action, and a just distribution of the stock was imperative. And with four nations being jointly in command, with many different objectives, organization to meet the gigantic problem was difficult enough, and in any event, it was a complex undertaking.

The front line of the battle was to save these lives. That had to be undertaken nation by nation and could be won only if there were effective organization "behind the front."

This section of Volume II is devoted to a narrative of the immensity of the problems, the negotiations, the difficulties of co-ordination of effort, and the agreements concluded to assure the organization behind the front.

Following President Wilson's injunction of December 10, 1917, that the United States was not an ally but an "associated power," when I refer to the "Allies" I am referring to Britain, France, and Italy only. Where the United States was involved, I specifically indicate it.

CHAPTER 27

WORLD FOOD SUPPLIES AND NEEDS

The end of the war was evident when, by Reichstag action on October 4, 1918, Prince Max of Baden was made Chancellor of Germany. On October 6, he requested an armistice from President Wilson. The President demanded the demobilization of the armies of the Central Powers and proposed the terms of peace, to both the Allies and the Germans, which culminated in the signing of the Armistice with Germany on November 11, 1918. In the meantime, the old Austrian Empire, Bulgaria, and Turkey had asked for an armistice; the President imposed upon them the same terms—surrender and demobilization of their armies and the terms of peace.[1]

Even before the Armistice was signed it was obvious that a gigantic famine would follow and that food supplies of many nations would be affected. In mid-October, the Food Administration began a world food survey to determine both the world supplies available for overseas export and the minimum of needs for imports. Communist Russia was not included in this survey because we could obtain no reliable figures regarding its food situation. However, Russia did come into the famine picture later on. On November 4, 1918, I presented the result of our survey to the President:

[1] I give a detailed account of these negotiations in my book *The Ordeal of Woodrow Wilson,* Chaps. 5 and 6.

DEAR MR. PRESIDENT:

We have now completed a broad survey of the food supplies available in the world in case of an early peace, together with the world's necessities. We have calculated the supplies as being the surplus in any given commodity exportable from any country and have assumed the total export of such a surplus. In the matter of . . . [need] we have formulated our estimates on the basis of the preservation of public health and tranquillity, not upon the restoration of conditions to normal; that is, there would be an increase of food supply to the area at present controlled by the Central Empires but no very consequential increase to the Allies. The period covered by these calculations is that until the next harvest. I will not trouble you with the elaborate details referring to each country.

The following table shows the results in tons . . . :

	Total Export Supplies	Total Import Necessities	Deficiency or Surplus	[Possible Exports] From United States
Breadstuffs	19,000,000	16,000,000	+3,000,000	9,000,000
Pulses and rice .	1,400,000	1,400,000	....	300,000
Feeds	8,000,000	11,000,000	—3,000,000	5,000,000
Beef	1,600,000	1,600,000 *	....	300,000
Pork products ..	1,700,000	2,400,000	— 700,000	1,300,000
Oils	800,000	1,200,000	— 400,000	200,000
Dairy products .	500,000	800,000	— 300,000	300,000
Sugar	5,000,000	6,700,000	—1,700,000	1,500,000 †
Coffee	1,400,000	1,000,000	+ 400,000	....
	39,400,000	42,100,000		17,900,000

* This being the limit of refrigerating ship capacity.
† Assuming Cuba as part of U.S. supplies as we own their crop.

The following general points stand out . . . [from] this survey:

1. The amounts given as "total import . . . [needs of food]" . . [stated at 42,100,000 tons are] probably 10,000,000 tons short of enough to provide normal pre-war consumption.

2. . . . there is a deficiency below what we consider is desirable to preserve health and tranquillity.

3. This situation will be politically somewhat ameliorated by the fact that there is a sufficiency of breadstuffs which indeed comprise fifty per cent of the food intake of European people and therefore largely dominate public mind.

4. The critical shortage is in the fats where the deficiency amounts, in our view, to about 35%.

5. The only deficiency in which the United States participates is that of sugar, and this will indeed present a serious problem.

6. Of the above quantities of exportable food, United States and Cuba will be furnishing about 50% of the total calculated world's import necessities.

7. With the inability to even complete this programme of necessities . . . it is positively necessary that we have a continuance of the embargo so that we may regulate the outlet, or every one of our foodstuffs will be overdrawn and our own people faced with . . . [no supplies] next spring.

8. Another and very pertinent reason for continuance of the embargo lies in the fact that with the whole world bidding in our market without restraint, we . . . [would] have an era of high prices, of profiteering and speculation, such as we have never yet experienced.

9. Some systematic arrangement will be necessary for the determination as to how our available surpluses are to be divided amongst the various nations and to see to it that these divisions are carried out without disturbing our markets.

10. Our surpluses might be somewhat increased by a continuation of conservation.

HERBERT HOOVER

In order that the reader may have some picture of the food situation, I introduce here a rough classification of the food needs of forty-five nations, which was made two months after the Armistice. The populations given were, at a time of shifting boundaries, necessarily only estimates.

PEOPLES IN URGENT NEED OF OVERSEAS FOOD BUT NOT IN ACUTE FAMINE

	Population
Britain	43,000,000
France	39,600,000
Italy	36,500,000
Belgium	8,000,000
Portugal	6,000,000
Greece	5,000,000

PEOPLES IN URGENT NEED OF OVERSEAS FOOD BUT NOT IN ACUTE FAMINE (*Cont.*)

	Population
Cape Colony	6,000,000
Transvaal	4,000,000
Holland	6,600,000
Denmark	2,900,000
Norway	2,600,000
Sweden	5,800,000
Switzerland	3,900,000
Spain	21,000,000
India	300,000,000
Azerbaijan	4,000,000
Georgia	3,000,000
Lebanon	700,000
Mesopotamia (Iraq)	10,000,000
Saudi Arabia	5,000,000
Egypt	20,000,000
Abyssinia	10,000,000
	543,600,000

PEOPLES WHOLLY OR IN PART IN ACUTE FAMINE

	Population
Finland	4,000,000
Estonia	1,100,000
Latvia	1,600,000
Lithuania	2,000,000
Poland	28,000,000
Bohemia	8,000,000
Slovakia	7,000,000
Serbia	8,000,000
Montenegro	2,000,000
Slovenia	3,000,000
Rumania	16,000,000
Albania	1,000,000
Dalmatia	1,500,000

	Population
Armenia	2,000,000
Syria	2,200,000
Palestine	800,000
Persia (Iran)	10,000,000
Communist Russia	140,000,000
"White" Siberia	10,000,000
Germany	68,000,000
Austria	6,500,000
Hungary	8,000,000
Bulgaria	6,000,000
Turkey	8,000,000
China	400,000,000
	744,700,000

There are forty-seven nations, states, or peoples on the above lists, but because of the subsequent consolidation of some of the areas mentioned, we use the figure forty-five throughout this volume. The populations in these classifications were about 540,000,000 people in urgent need of overseas imports and about 744,000,000 in countries where there was wholly or in part acute famine. And still other nations, or peoples, also required medical aid. They included such nations as Japan, Abyssinia, and Egypt.

I may mention that the Jewish Joint Distribution Committee gave monetary aid for purchase of local supplies and general aid to the following countries, or peoples, not entered in these lists:

Morocco
Japan
Algiers
Tunis

The American Red Cross gave medical aid to countries not mentioned in the above lists. They were:

Bosnia
Herzegovina
Japan
Canada

Added to these problems of food and medical supplies, there were many special relief and repatriation jobs which fell to the United States Government official relief and to the American voluntary charitable agencies. A list of them includes:

Belgian refugees in Britain, France, and Holland.

French refugees in Belgium and Holland.

Russian refugees in Constantinople, Poland, Greece, Finland, and Estonia.

Yugoslav refugees in Greece.

Armenian refugees in Russia, Turkey, and Greece.

Jewish refugees scattered over the world.

Impressed laborers from Belgium, France, Poland, Russia, Finland, and the Baltic States in Germany.

Impressed laborers in Austria-Hungary from Poland, Rumania, Serbia, and Russia.

There were war prisoners from the armies of France, Belgium, Britain, Russia, Serbia, Rumania, and Italy in Germany.

German prisoners of war in England and the United States.

German and Hungarian war prisoners in Siberia.

These groups of displaced persons probably amounted to more than fifteen million souls, who, except for German war prisoners held by the Allies, can be added to the numbers in "acute famine."

CHAPTER 28

WE PREPARE FOR THE FAMINE

Weeks before the Armistice, it was obvious that the Central Powers would surrender. In order that there be no delay in shipments to the more acute famine areas, I took up with the President the question of immediately loading ships with food and other supplies.

With the Armistice, the shipping situation across the Atlantic would be reversed: United States-flag ships would be bringing men and equipment home, returning to Europe in ballast. The President directed the War Department and the Shipping Board to co-operate with us.

On November 9, I addressed the President with regard to the arrangements I had made with these two bodies and my recommendation for a Congressional appropriation for some of the liberated areas:

DEAR MR. PRESIDENT:

In the matter of feeding the liberated peoples . . . I have had conferences with Messrs. Hurley [1] and Baker [2] and our own staff and, as a result, I have to propose to you the following measures, which meet with approval on all sides:

That the Army should hand to us certain cargo boats at once which we will load with foods at their expense. This food will be of a character

[1] Edward N. Hurley, Chairman of the Shipping Board.
[2] Newton D. Baker, Secretary of War.

that can be used by the American Army or the Allies in any event, and will be despatched in the first instance to Bordeaux for orders. . . .

I then outlined the temporary organization which we would establish in Washington to handle these matters and continued:

It appears to me that it will be absolutely necessary to secure an appropriation for the handling of this enterprise. . . . with the state of mind of the well-thinking people of this country that the government could agree to appropriate $200,000,000 for the feeding of the liberated populations in Europe—such a sum to be placed at your disposal. In the ordinary course of events, I would not think that much of this money would be lost, for, at least, obligations could be obtained from municipalities and governments for its ultimate re-payment.

. . . It is not necessary for me to mention how fundamental it appears to me that this is, if we are to preserve these countries from Bolshevism and rank anarchy.

HERBERT HOOVER

The President marked this letter "Approved W.W."

The day after the Armistice, on November 12, I transmitted to him the final agreement we had signed with the other departments for emergency shipment. The President returned this document marked "Approved W.W."

On November 14, I proposed to him that we expand our emergency food shipments still further:

DEAR MR. PRESIDENT:

The general food situation in Europe looms more strongly hour by hour through the various reports and telegrams that we are receiving. . . .

After referring to the previous arrangements, which included 200,000 tons of food which the War Department had in the ports, I continued:

In addition to this, and in view of the serious situation in Northern Europe, I am—in accordance with our discussions of yesterday—instructing the Grain Corporation to purchase and ship to English ports for re-direction, another . . . 140,000 tons of food to be used, probably in Northern Europe. We can finance this through the Grain Corporation up to the point of . . . [delivery at ports]. . . .

I then urged again an appropriation from the Congress, so that we could adequately serve countries not eligible under Congressional acts for loans from the Treasury, and went on:

> While it should be clear in such appropriation that it is not a gift, but to provide a revolving fund to enable us to carry on relief commerce, it should have a special provision that the foodstuffs may be used for philanthropic purposes if necessary.
>
> HERBERT HOOVER

The President marked this "Approved W.W."

The President also gave directions to the War and Navy departments to place at our disposal the several hundred thousand tons of surplus food and medical supplies, which they had accumulated as reserves against possible emergencies.

I reviewed the situation in relief to Europe in an address to our state food administrators on November 12, 1918, as follows:

> We have now to consider a new world situation in food. We have to frankly survey Europe. A Europe of which a large part is either in ruins or in social conflagration; a Europe with degenerated soils and depleted herds; a Europe with the whole of its population on rations or varying degrees of privation and large numbers who have been under the German heel actually starving. The group of gamblers in human life who have done this thing are now in . . . flight, leaving anarchy and famine to millions of helpless people. We have also to survey the situation in the exporting nations of the world, to see what can be done to . . . [restore] this mass of humanity back to health and to social order. Up to the collapse of the Germans the world that is allied against Germany has depended upon the North American continent for the margins of food that maintain their strength against the common enemy. The loss of shipping . . . [has] isolated the stores of food in the Southern Hemisphere and the Far East. Within thirty or sixty days the world should begin to release cargo ships from military duty and to send them further

afield for food, and before the next harvest arrives the entire world's food supply should be accessible. On the other hand, the cessation of hostilities will create an enormously increased demand for food and we must be deeply concerned that the starving millions who have been liberated from the German yoke shall have such supplies as will enable them to return to health and prosperity. The war has been brought to an end in no small measure by starvation itself and it cannot be our business to maintain starvation after peace.

All these considerations must change our domestic food policies, and this opens to us as a nation an obligation and an opportunity of service.

We must now take an account of the whole food resources of the world and we must take an account of the total demands. . . . we must make such changes in our policies as are fitting to the new situation. . . .

After reviewing the world food situation, I concluded:

At this moment Germany has not alone sucked the food and animals from all those masses of people she has dominated and left them starving, but she has left behind her a total wreckage of social institutions and this mass of people is now confronted with engulfment in absolute anarchy. If we value our own safety and the social organization of the world, if we value the preservation of civilization itself, we cannot sit idly by and see the growth of this cancer in the world's vitals. Famine is the mother of anarchy. From the inability of governments to secure food for their people, grows revolution and chaos. From an ability to supply their people, grows stability of government and the defeat of anarchy. Did we put it on no higher plane than our interests in the protection of our institutions, we must bestir ourselves in solution of this problem. There are millions of people now liberated from the German yoke for whose interests we have fought and bled for the last eighteen months. We dare not neglect any measure which enables them to return to health, to self-support and to their national life. . . .

CHAPTER 29

CONFUSION IN METHOD OF ORGANIZATION TO MEET THE FAMINE

Early in October, 1918, there was some preliminary discussion in the President's War Council about the kind of organization we would need for co-ordinating with the Allies the relief and reconstruction of Europe. We decided that we should deal with this subject after the completion of the President's "basis of peace" and Armistice agreements.[1]

On October 22, however, we received the following plan of organization, formulated in London by the Allied Maritime Transport Council, together with the Inter-Allied Food Council and the Inter-Allied Blockade Council, and approved by the British Cabinet. It was approved by the French and Italian governments. The important paragraphs were:

> . . . A General Economic Board should be established as the supreme authority over the whole organisation. This Board should take over much of the functions and machinery of the Allied Maritime Transport Council. A new Raw Materials Council and a new Finance Council should be established. These Councils, and also the Transport, Food, and Munition Councils, should become more purely technical administrative bodies, the Allied Ministers exercising control over their policy through the General Economic Board. Responsibility for economic policy in each

[1] For details, see *The Ordeal of Woodrow Wilson,* Chap. 9.

country should also be more completely concentrated in the hands of a single authority.

These suggestions apply equally to the period between the termination of hostilities and the conclusion of the definitive treaty of peace, except that the Raw Materials and Munitions Councils could then be amalgamated.

During this period the whole inter-Allied organisation should be maintained. The national controls on which it is based should be strengthened in order to prevent private purchases in primary markets. The adherence of our present enemies to these controls must form one of the conditions of the peace preliminaries, and another condition must be the cession of all enemy shipping to the Transport Council, pending its eventual disposal under the final treaty of peace. The adherence of neutrals must also be secured, and the machinery of the blockade must as rapidly as possible be superseded by the system of control administered by the inter-Allied organisation. Where possible negotiations with neutral Governments should at once be directed to prepare the way for this development.

The Policy of the Allies should be directed to facilitate as early a return as possible to normal conditions.

For some time after the definite conclusion of peace a nucleus of international organisation must be retained. This should consist of the General Economic Board, with two advisory committees under it on finance and transport. The Board will consider the [continued] grant of credits to countries in special need of assistance, and will control a pool of tonnage for their benefit. During the period when existing national controls are being liquidated, international consultation on many points will be desirable, and the programme committees should be retained as consultative bodies for this purpose.

Closer international control for a longer period may be necessary in the case of certain essential commodities, for instance, wheat, meat, and oil-seeds.

During this post-war period the international organisation must be more or less coterminous in its membership with the League of Nations, though not directly connected with it.[2]

[2] Italics mine. I have given a short summary of these incidents in *The Ordeal of Woodrow Wilson* and my *Memoirs,* but without documentation. The document cited here is an essential and useful bit of history and was important in subsequent negotiations. See also Suda L. Bane and Ralph H. Lutz, *The Blockade of Germany after the Armistice, 1918–1919* (Stanford University Press, 1942), pp. 832–33.

This proposal was not entirely clear. It seemed to imply an inter-Allied pool of food, raw materials, and credit during the Armistice, and, for some time after the peace, directed by a board in London as the supreme authority.

On October 24, I wrote the President:

Dear Mr. President:

I feel that despite the great burden of anxiety which you must entertain, it is necessary for me to present for your consideration one or two phases of the after-war situation . . . for peace-making might catch us suddenly. . . .

I then briefly outlined the likely food situation and continued:

The principal reason why this problem arises at the moment is that some members of the Allied Food Council are putting forward suggestions for . . . [inter-Allied] control of world distribution of food after peace. My own instinct is entirely against any such agreements . . . for, at least morally, any international body on this subject in which we participated would involve us in acceptance of their views and, practically, in acceptance of their distribution of our supplies.

. . . we could use our food supplies to level up, in a rough manner, the deficiencies that will ultimately arise from the general grab for the balances of the world's food. If we maintain our independence . . . we can use our resources to make economic exchanges which will maintain justice all round. . . .

. . . we will require some imports of raw material and if we maintain control of our own supplies of food and raw material we will be in [a] position to make such arrangements as will insure our own [and world] interests.

I should be glad indeed if I could have your views in this matter, for if you hold the view that we shall enter no entanglements whatever I shall take steps at once to maintain such a stand.

Herbert Hoover

A day or two after my letter, the President brought up the subject. I advised him that these matters could be better settled by conference in Europe with the Allies after the Armistice. He agreed and asked me to go to Europe to represent our Government in settling our part in the relief and reconstruction organization.

However, the Allies pressed for an immediate agreement. On October 30, I received a cable from our Food Administration representative in Europe, Joseph P. Cotton,[3] indicating that the Allies were taking further steps toward creating international controls. He asked for instructions and continued:

> These recommendations have been unanimously [adopted] by the permanent representatives of the Food and Transport Council. The same considerations would appear to apply to raw materials and other commodities generally, and so far as we have been able to consult those representing these commodities, they are in full accord with the above recommendations.
>
> This morning Colonel House stated he has no instructions on this point and would like the view of the Washington Government in regard to it. Similar information goes forward to McCormick and Hurley, and Summers will cable Baruch. . . . We cannot over-emphasize the need for prompt action. Kellogg joins in the recommendation.[4]
>
> COTTON

On November 4, we received two more cables from Mr. Cotton, one of which concerned this same subject. I forwarded them to the President, saying:

> DEAR MR. PRESIDENT:
>
> I have received the two attached cables from our representatives in Europe. The one on the subject of international control of distribution of food, raw materials and ships does seem to me to require urgent consideration. In the meantime I have directed Mr. Cotton, my representative, that he should in no form take any part in pledges that would even appear to commit our government.
>
> HERBERT HOOVER

[3] Cotton had been head of a most important division in the Food Administration until the summer of 1918, when he was transferred to London as our representative.

[4] Vance C. McCormick, Chairman of the War Trade Board and later a member of the Supreme Economic Council and Chairman of the Superior Blockade Council; Edward N. Hurley, Chairman of the United States Shipping Board; Bernard M. Baruch, Chairman of the War Industries Board and later a member of the Supreme Economic Council. Dr. Vernon Kellogg was in Europe, as the Food Administration's expert, examining food needs in the various countries.

On November 6, I discussed the matter with the President. He gave me the general line of his views to be transmitted to Cotton. We cabled Cotton accordingly and sent a copy to the President with the following covering letter:

7 November, 1918

DEAR MR. PRESIDENT:

Please find enclosed herewith a telegram which I am despatching to Mr. Cotton in respect to the proposals for the world's food . . . shipping [and other] supplies to be vested in the Inter-Allied Food Council and the Inter-Allied Maritime Council.

I believe this cable is in accord with the conclusions of our conference yesterday and I am wondering if you could see your way to despatch this same telegram to Colonel House, informing him that it has been sent to Mr. Cotton by myself and that it is with your authorization and, furthermore, if you could state to Colonel House that I will be leaving within the next few days for Paris . . . .

HERBERT HOOVER

The two important paragraphs of the cable were:

7 November, 1918

COTTON, LONDON:

For your general advice this Government will not agree to any programme that even looks like inter-Allied control of our economic resources after peace. After peace over one-half of the whole export food supplies of the world will come from the United States and for the buyers of these supplies to sit in majority in dictation to us as to prices and distribution is wholly inconceivable. The same applies to raw materials. Our only hope . . . [of] securing justice in distribution, proper appreciation abroad of the effort we make to assist foreign nations, and proper return for the service that we will perform will revolve around complete independence of commitment to joint action on our part. . . .

We cannot consent to the delegation of neutral buying in the United States to the Inter-Allied Food and Maritime Councils. We must continue to act with entire independence in our commercial relations with all neutrals and Belgian Relief. I trust, therefore, you will in representing this Government discourage any attempts to carry out the proposals of your . . . [cable].

HERBERT HOOVER

The cable was transmitted by the Secretary of State to Colonel House with the additional information that "the Department approves entirely the policy above set forth." [5]

Colonel House cabled the President from Paris on November 8, but the cable had obviously crossed the one sent with the President's instructions. It contained some constructive suggestions:

To the Secretary of State

. . . for the President. Probably the greatest problem which will be presented to us upon the cessation of hostilities is the furnishing of food and other essential supplies to the civilian populations of . . . [enemy and liberated people]. This relief work, together with the reconstruction of devastated regions, will have to be done almost entirely through American effort and with the use of American food, raw materials, and finished products. Difficult questions of priority and the allocation of tonnage will be presented. At one of the meetings of the Supreme War Council Mr. Balfour proposed that as a condition of the armistice to be offered Germany the large amount of German merchant tonnage now in German and neutral ports be handed over during the armistice for operation by the Allies and the United States under the general supervision and control of the Allied Maritime Transport Council now sitting in London. I advised that this be not made a condition of the armistice but be taken up as soon as the armistice was signed and Mr. Balfour acquiesced in this suggestion. I now advise that instead of adopting Mr. Balfour's suggestion, which presents obvious objections, that you, as soon as the armistice *with Germany is signed, propose to Allies and Germany the immediate formation of the "International Relief Organization."* I suggest that Hoover be placed at the head of this organization and that McCormick and Baruch be associated with him as American representatives and that two representatives each be named by England, France, Italy, and Germany. Germany should at once be asked to place at the disposal of this organization until the final peace treaty is signed the entire German merchant marine now in German or neutral ports. The organization should then be charged with securing food and other supplies immediately required for the civilian populations of the countries above set forth and in determining the priority of the needs presented. These sup-

[5] United States Department of State, *Papers Relating to the Foreign Relations of the United States, 1918* (Washington, United States Government Printing Office), Supplement 1, *The World War,* I, 616–17.

plies would necessarily have to be furnished by the United States and the Allies. It should be pointed out to Germany that only in this way will it be possible for her merchant marine to be placed in service from the inception of the armistice until the final peace treaty is signed and that her willingness to enter wholeheartedly into such a scheme of relief, which would include her own civilian population, would be the best possible evidence of her desire to alleviate the sufferings caused the civilian populations of all countries by the exigencies of the war. *In this way also the whole question of relief pending the signing of the final treaty of peace can be kept separate from the very keen struggle which will arise immediately following the signing of the armistice between the various belligerent nations for selfish trade advantage.* It is very clear that the terms of the armistice provide that the blockade shall be continued. The impracticability of this so far as food and other essential supplies are concerned, has already become apparent. Conditions in Austria and in Bohemia are of such a character as to make relief on a large scale imperative if serious disturbances are to be averted. I should appreciate very much an expression of your views on this most urgent matter.[6]

EDWARD HOUSE

The Allies continued to press for immediate agreement on some sort of international controls, and on November 8 and 9, I received two paraphrased cables from Cotton through the State Department, the important paragraphs of which were:

November 8

HOOVER:

Mr. Cotton states that in order to clear up the position as to cereals with reference to finance and storage, as part of the general plan, *he asks that Mr. Hoover consider the possibility of participating in this year's wheat pool of prices and supplies which will buy all of the wheat surplus of Argentine for next year, including that which is carried over from the present year, as well as Indian, Canadian and Australian, if any, and the surplus of the United States for the period for which Mr. Hoover is now obligated.* Mr. Cotton states that in some degree this plan would provide insurance against financial loss by the United States. Also, it would, without utilizing anything that looked like a blockade and without withholding bunkers, furnish the handiest method of persuading neutrals to

[6] Italics mine.

act as they should and to retard an increase in prices. He further states that it would furnish means by which reasonably fair distribution of bread could be insured amongst the poorer or newer nations which are unable to obtain it now and which, under the existing relations regarding credit, cannot pay for it. *He states that in London there is being formulated such a plan.* We have, he adds, of course given no assent and shall do nothing more than to see it in shape and transmit it. . . .[7]

November 9

HOOVER FROM MR. COTTON [THROUGH THE STATE DEPARTMENT]:

Mr. Cotton states that he just heard of Mr. Hoover's intention to come to London. . . . He states that in the meantime, even during the next two weeks, plans must be crystallized somewhat for carrying on this feeding. All sorts of Americans are messing in it and the matter will not be held open entirely until Mr. Hoover's arrival. So far the proposed plans tend to put the machinery in British hands although all foodstuffs, practically, must be [obtained from the] United States. He states that it is extremely desirable that they should have some inkling of Mr. Hoover's desires before he arrives, if for no other reason than to prevent clashes later.

I forwarded Cotton's cables of the eighth and ninth to the President with these comments and recommendations:

DEAR MR. PRESIDENT:

I enclose herewith two cables which I would be grateful if you could find time to peruse.

. . . [The idea of] our entering into a joint inter-Allied pool for the purpose of distributing all of the world's wheat until the middle of 1920, fills me with complete horror. Of all the import wheat in the world, seventy per cent must come from the Western Hemisphere, and I assume that we would be called upon to finance it. . . . [This would] place the distribution of it in the hands of a body that we could not control. . . .

Both of these telegrams bring me to express to you the urgency of a definition of our principles in these matters, to be conveyed to the Allied governments in order that I and the other agents of . . . [our] government in Europe may be able to act in entire unison with your own views. . . .

HERBERT HOOVER

[7] Italics mine.

I was preparing to leave for Europe to direct relief work as head of the "International Relief Organization" mentioned in Colonel House's cable of November 8. A formal announcement of my appointment to that post was announced through the administration's *Official Bulletin* of November 11, 1918:

> The President has requested Mr. Hoover to take charge for this Government of the organization of measures for the food relief of the liberated people of Europe and to proceed at once to Europe as the Government's special representative for the determination of measures of relief in coöperation with the various Governments concerned. . . .

On November 12, in a meeting with the President, we settled on a cable to be sent to Cotton; the important part follows:

13 November, 1918

COTTON, LONDON:

With regard to various telegrams yourself and Cravath[8] on Relief to areas lately under German control on further consultation with President he authorized the following further statement to be made to our officials in Europe for their guidance, but not for communication and asks that a copy should be sent to Colonel House and Cravath—statement begins—we consider ourselves as trustees of our surplus production of all kinds for the benefit of the most necessitous and the most deserving. We feel that we must ourselves execute this trusteeship, that we are not unmindful of the obligation which we have to the sustenance of those who have fought with us against Germany . . . together with the necessities of those populations released from the German yoke we feel that they may well deserve a priority in our distribution. On the other hand, we cannot undertake any cooperative arrangements that look to the control of our exports . . . and furthermore and equally important, that the Inter-Allied councils hitherto set up in Europe were entirely for the purpose of guiding Inter-Allied relations during the period of the war and that any extension of their functions either by way of their control of our relations to other nations or the extension of their present functions beyond peace cannot be entertained by us. All relationship involving the

[8] Paul Drennan Cravath, advisory counsel of the American mission to the Inter-Allied Council on War Purchases and Finance. Cravath had been urging adoption of Allied proposals.

use of American food or credit for the people of other nations than the Allies themselves must await Mr. Hoover's arrival in Europe. . . .

You can inform Sir Worthington Evans [9] that the form of organization involving coordination of the United States Government . . . can only be settled upon my arrival, that the United States Food Administration is taking steps to at once largely increase the volume of American food stores at various points in Europe in order that the material may be available for earliest possible action after my arrival and that we have every desire for proper coordination of all efforts.

HERBERT HOOVER

On November 14, the Shipping Board received a message from the Secretary of the Allied Maritime Transport Council:

LONDON, 13th November 1918

The British Government has decided to suggest to the Governments of the United States, France, and Italy *that it is desirable to revise the representation and functions of the Allied Maritime Transport Council so as to make it a General Economic Council, which would co-ordinate the work of the various Councils, and, through them, of the Programme Committees.* It is also suggested that the various Raw Materials Programme Committees, together with those now grouped, and the Munitions Council, should be grouped under an Inter-Allied Raw Materials Council just as the food programme committees are grouped under the Inter-Allied Food Council.

I am authorised to transmit to you semi-officially, for such confidential use as you may consider desirable, the enclosed memorandum, which was before the British Government when they decided to make the above proposal, and may be taken as indicating generally the considerations influencing them. It must not, however, be understood that the Government have arrived at a decision in regard to all the detailed recommendations included in the memorandum.[10]

J. A. SALTER

Salter's "memorandum" proved to be an elaboration of previous plans to about six thousand words, again embodying proposals for a "General Economic Board" subject only to the Supreme War

[9] Sir Worthington Evans was British blockade minister.
[10] Italics mine.

Council, in which the United States had one vote in four. It again proposed control of shipping, credit, finance, purchase, and distribution of food and raw materials among the "Allied and Associated Powers, Neutrals, enemies and liberated people" during the Armistice and for at least a year after peace was made. We made no reply to this, since I was sailing for Europe the next day.

On this voyage I was accompanied by key members of the Food Administration staff, including Julius H. Barnes, President of our Grain Corporation; James F. Bell, head of our Milling Division; John Hallowell, chief of the States Administration Division; Dr. Alonzo E. Taylor of our Nutritional Division; Robert A. Taft of our Legal Division; and Lewis L. Strauss, my secretary. We were joined in London by our European representatives, Joseph P. Cotton, E. Dana Durand, and Dr. Vernon L. Kellogg. We also had command of services of our experienced Americans in the Belgian Relief. My old friend Hugh Gibson was assigned to us by the State Department for diplomatic liaison. By good luck, Norman H. Davis had been appointed representative of our Treasury Department and was also aboard the steamer, ready to help in our negotiations with the Allies.

The ship's wireless gave daily accounts of revolutions and the rise of new nations from the old empires of Germany, Austria-Hungary, and Russia. The shape of a new map of Europe was already clear.

Discussions aboard ship are probably of little importance, but they served to clarify some matters and to indicate the approach we had toward a multitude of problems. Most of us were familiar with Europe and we believed that from our experience we knew how best to organize the relief.

We discussed the Allied proposals of a pool of all resources under a board in which we would have a minority voice. We believed that when they realized that the preponderance of supplies had to come from the United States and that we would have to furnish 85 per cent of its finance, the Allies would agree to plans of co-ordination and co-operation rather than "pools."

We reviewed President Wilson's triumph in establishing the basis of peace, under which independence of nations and freedom of peoples would come to mankind. We also talked of economic and social reforms that would come from the fires of idealism kindled by the sufferings of war. We thought that want would be abolished by the methods of increased productivity learned in the war and that wider doors of opportunity would be opened for the children with the spread of freedom.

We discussed far into the night the reconstruction measures that would have to be taken to get the world back to work. We believed that there would be a period of great difficulties and readjustment. But we were certain that the purification of men and the triumph of freedom would herald a new Golden Age. We were indeed proud to play a part in this rebirth of mankind.[11]

It was in this hopeful mood that we arrived in London on November 21.

[11] For the superstitious, I may mention that thirteen of us sat at the table at least twice a day for six days, and all have lived to a ripe old age.

CHAPTER 30

THE BATTLE OF POOL VERSUS CO-ORDINATION AND CO-OPERATION

The morning after our arrival in London, we went into session with Allied representatives. The British were represented by Lord Reading; [1] J. N. Cline, Minister of Food; and Sir Joseph Maclay and Arthur Salter, Chairman and Secretary, respectively, of the Maritime Council.[2] The French were represented by Etienne Clémentel, Minister of Commerce; Victor Boret, Minister of Agriculture; and Ernest Vilgrain, Minister of Food. The Italians were represented by Silvio Crespi, Minister of Agriculture and Food, and Bernardo Attolico, who acted for the Italians in various inter-Allied economic organizations. The Belgians were represented by their Ambassador in London. All of these men were professional public servants. I was accompanied by our staff members, who, except Hugh Gibson, were volunteers from professional and business life.

After the usual salutations, Lord Reading presented once more the Allied ideas of a long-term inter-Allied pool and a super-directorate in London—which they had repeatedly presented to us before the Armistice. Lord Reading insisted that only by such a

[1] Lord Reading (formerly Rufus Isaacs) was a leading British lawyer who had been brought into the British Government at the beginning of the war. In time, he was appointed Governor General of India and was advanced to the nobility for his able service.

[2] At the Armistice there were many organizations set up by the Allied and Associated Powers for wartime co-ordination and co-operation. I later give a full list of these.

centralization of economic power could peace and reconstruction be attained. He laid emphasis on the necessity for all relief and reconstruction to be accomplished jointly by the four governments in order to demonstrate complete political unity. His associates argued that such organization was required to impose the political pressures that might be necessary to secure an orderly recovery of economic life throughout the war-torn world—and to enforce upon some nations decisions of the Allies and Associated Powers.

The Italians added a new item by proposing that a toll be levied on all bunker coal. They presented the fact that the Allies, including China and Japan, and the former enemy states constituted practically all of the world's bunker-coal resources. In their view, this was necessary to insure that all nations everywhere, including Neutrals, would contribute large sums in order to compensate for Allied outlays in securing freedom from world-wide militarism.

In the course of discussion, Sir Joseph Maclay proposed that each of the Allied nations should operate some minimum tonnage of its own ships, the amount to be determined by the Allied Maritime Transport Council. He proposed that the tonnage above this minimum and the three million tons of German and Austrian refugee shipping should be operated by the Council, which, with the control of bunker coal, could force the charter of Neutral shipping and thus serve further the needs of each nation.

In reply to a question from me, Lord Reading suggested a name for the new organization: *The Supreme Council of Supply and Relief*. Their blueprints did not emerge all at once, but only after persistent questioning by Davis and me; and we confined ourselves mostly to asking questions.

It was clear that the Allied ideas of control of American economic resources and the method of organization of relief were a long way from anything that American public opinion, the President, the Congress, Davis, or I would be likely to accept.

After this first meeting, my old friend Lord Eustace Percy, who had represented the British Foreign Office with the Belgian Relief and the Food Administration, stated to me that Lord Reading and

Minister Clémentel had authorized him to offer me the chairmanship of this council "to control the economic world." I was to resign my official American positions and administer the new organization from London as the neutral chairman. He said: "It would make you the economic Foch of the world."

The same day, British Food Minister Cline came to me and suggested that we consent to a reduction of American food prices. I reminded him that we were committed to guaranteed prices to those of our farmers who produced wheat, rice, beans, sugar, meats, fats, and other commodities; that these guarantees had been heartily approved by the Allies as a measure to provide their necessities; and that we could not, legally in some cases and morally in others, jettison these undertakings. Cline pointed out that his country could obtain food for much lower prices in the Far East and the Southern Hemisphere and that it was considered unfair to the British people to buy the higher-priced American food. I suggested that except for the balance of specific contracts they had already made with our processors, it was right that they should go to the cheaper markets and that we should supply the Neutrals and the famine areas—if the blockade were taken down on food for starving people. I was not much impressed that this constituted a threat to the United States because the total of dammed-back supplies would not nearly cover Allied needs.

There were further meetings with protracted discussions. We also discussed these matters separately with some of the Allied leaders. We repeated that President Wilson fully supported the co-ordination and co-operation in reconstruction and relief measures but that the President's view of its functions would not include pooling resources.

We proposed that to meet their view of a unified front, each government should appoint a representative to each country in which we would be operating and that the group of them could act as a co-ordinating committee. This plan would provide the "united front" and allow each of the Allies to show its interest by supplying as much food and credit as possible to each needy country; the United States would try to take up as much of the slack as possible.

We pointed out, however, that in furnishing supplies to any given country, each Allied or Associated Power would, in any case, have to secure cash goods or obligations. Therefore, these very accounts would disclose the contribution of each of the Allies and Associated Powers, and thus the idea of a pooled political and economic front would not be impressive.

With regard to the former enemy states and the Neutrals, we stated that we assumed these nations could pay for their own food and reconstruction materials, that they should be supplied from each of the Allies to the extent they wished, and that the United States would try to take up the slack.

We described our loading of supplies, which had already begun, for the famine areas. We said that we assumed the blockade would be taken down at once in order not to hamper this movement of food to starving people and that food would soon be supplied to Germany as provided in the Armistice agreement. Davis, with his agile mind, restated each point at length and with energy.

At one point in the discussions, the Allied representatives suggested that if we could not accept the controls they proposed for a number of years after the Peace, these might be put into operation only until the Peace was signed.

Concerning the council they proposed to administer this gigantic undertaking, we pointed out that committees were warranted only for advisory or policy functions and that they were a departure from the whole experience of government and industrial life—which called for a single administrator. We stated that a committee could no more administer this project than a committee could conduct a battle and cited their appointment of Marshal Foch.

In order to convince the Allies that I was not seeking anything for myself, I informed their leaders that my only purpose in Europe was to aid in setting up an effective organization; that I personally did not intend to undertake any administrative job; that I had already given more than four years to war service; and that I wished to rebuild my professional life. I suggested that there be an American in the position of leadership of relief and reconstruction, since the United States would be the major provider of supplies and credit, and that the ideal choice would be one of the successful American generals in the war.[3]

Our impressions from these discussions were quite discouraging. Because of our knowledge that the Allies—all of them—were dependent on the United States for food and credits during the Armistice, we became convinced that behind this whole pool idea and this council organization there was something else troubling the Allied minds. We were fully aware of the reluctance of the Allies to accept President Wilson's "Fourteen Points and subsequent addresses" as the basis of peace. It was obvious to us that they were groping for some plan which would prevent the President from exercising his power to use supplies and credit for imposing his political ideas.

We did not want to bring the discussion down to a take-it-or-leave-it basis. Finally, after these meetings and side conferences, we said that we had to lay their views before our superiors, that I had scheduled meetings with the Belgian Government in Brussels to determine the future of the Belgian Relief Commission and with the French Government in Paris to consider their taking over the relief of Northern France, and that we would return within a few days.

We left for Paris on November 25. Before leaving London, I received this note from Lord Percy:

FOREIGN OFFICE
November 24, 1918

MY DEAR HOOVER:

I hear you are going to Paris tomorrow, but I write this line to say that, when you get an opportunity, I want you very much to have a quarter of an hour with Tyrrell here on various points.

[3] Hugh Gibson's diary, now in the Hoover Institution on War, Revolution, and Peace at Stanford University, contains the following entry for November 23, 1918:

> In the meantime he [Hoover] seems to have arrived at one decision which is that we must have unified control of food and relief work and that as we are to supply 60% of the food and 85% of the money an American should have the supreme command. He does not want to take it himself as he knows just how thankless a job it will be, but he thought there might be some American General who could handle it properly—he had Harbord in mind.

I want also to say that I very sincerely hope you'll remain on this side for a considerable time. You're the only prominent person in any way responsible for American policy—and one of the few people responsible for the policy of any Allied country—who has at this moment a sense of *facts.* Just now vagueness rules supreme everywhere—on not one of the urgent points of international policy which I am keen on can I get anything approaching to an answer from Washington—and in this atmosphere of vagueness, sentiment here has been deteriorating in the last fortnight more rapidly than at any period in the nine years during which I have watched Anglo-American relations. . . .

EUSTACE PERCY

After long discussions in Paris, Colonel House sent a cable to the President, setting out his and our ideas on organization. The Colonel proposed that the President go over the heads of subordinates, with whom we were carrying on negotiations, to the Prime Ministers.

November 27, 1918

FOR THE PRESIDENT

Hoover arrived in Paris Tuesday morning. I am fully advised of and in agreement with his plans. . . . The chief problem presented is the difficulty of devising a plan which will not antagonize the Allies and particularly Great Britain and at the same time permit single American leadership in relief to the civilian populations of Europe. I am sure you will agree that American leadership is essential taking into account the fact that we are the most disinterested nation and the other allies are affected by local political interests. Further the supplies to be utilized for this purpose must in the main be obtained in the United States and will dominate American markets. . . . The matters that Hoover and I have discussed will not permit of delay in reaching a decision and accordingly I suggest that the views of the United States Government be presented in writing to the three Prime Ministers at their meeting in London. I suggest that you send me a cable instructing me to present to the Supreme War Council the following plan: . . .

The Colonel then outlined our recommendations for a proposal to be sent by the President and concluded:

It is exceedingly important that I have your advices concerning this matter at the earliest possible moment.

EDWARD HOUSE

I have not given the text of this cable because the President's quick reply was the controlling document of American policies. It came on December 1, 1918. The President directed Colonel House to transmit it to each of the Foreign Ministers—Lord Balfour, M. Pichon, and Baron Sonnino. The letter to Balfour was typical:

PARIS, December 1, 1918

MY DEAR MR. BALFOUR:

The President has requested me to communicate to you for the consideration of your Government the following memorandum containing his views respecting the general question of furnishing relief to the civilian population of the European countries affected by the war:

"I have given much thought to the formulation of the most practical means of carrying into effect the resolution presented by Colonel House at the last meeting of the Supreme War Council at Versailles to the effect that the Supreme War Council in a spirit of humanity desired to coöperate in making available, as far as possible, supplies necessary for the relief of the civilian populations of the European countries affected by the war.

"In considering this matter, I have had consequently in mind the urgent necessity of the case and the fact that it is essential, in the working-out of relief of this character on a large scale, that there be a unity of direction similar in character to that which has proved so successful under French and British Chief Command in the operation of the Allies on the land and on sea respectively. I suggest that the Supreme War Council proceed along the following lines:

"In order to secure effective administration there should be created a Director-General of Relief whose field of activities will cover not only enemy populations, but also the whole of the populations liberated from enemy yoke and the neutrals contiguous to these territories.

"It is obvious that present inter-Allied administrative arrangements cover the Allied countries themselves and if the whole of the world's food supplies could be made available through sufficient shipping, there appears to be sufficiency to take effective care of these other populations provided that these supplies are administered with care, with economy, and with single direction.

"The one essential to this plan, in order that all world supplies may be brought into play, is that enemy tonnage shall be brought into service at the earliest possible moment. It would appear to me entirely just that the enemy shipping, in consideration of relief of enemy territory, should be placed in the General Food Service of all the populations released from the enemy yoke as well as enemy territory.

"I have carefully considered the suggestion made by Mr. Balfour to the Supreme War Council at the time the terms of armistice to be offered the enemy were under discussion, to the effect that the enemy should be required to place under the operation and control of the Allied Maritime Transport Council the enemy mercantile fleet in enemy and neutral ports. It appears to me that in practice there would be many embarrassments presented by this plan and that the principle should be maintained that this fleet be used as to its carrying capacity for purposes of relief and be under the direction of the Director-General of Relief. In order to secure its adequate operation, the Director-General should assign appropriate portions of this tonnage, first, for operations individually by Italy, France, and Belgium sufficient to transport the relief to actually liberated nationals of these nations. The administration of relief in the three above instances would then naturally fall entirely under the three Governments mentioned, and would not further interest the Director-General of Relief. Second: The remainder of enemy cargo tonnage, or such part of it as is necessary, should be placed under the operation of the British Ministry of Shipping and the United States Shipping Board in equal portions, these two institutions agreeing with the Director-General of Relief to deliver a quantity of cargo equal to the carrying capacity of these two fleets from such sources to such destinations as the Director of Relief may direct in supplying the balance of populations to be relieved. Third: The passenger tonnage, or so much of it as may be required by the United States Shipping Board, should be assigned to them, they giving the equivalent cargo capacity delivery to the Director-General of Relief. Under this plan it does not follow that enemy shipping would be employed directly in the transportation of this cargo, but that equivalent cargo should be delivered. This plan enables the use of enemy passenger tonnage in the transportation of the United States Armies homeward. This arrangement would in effect add materially to the volume of the world's shipping and release tonnage for the particular purposes of the individual countries.

"In the operations of the Director-General of Relief, he would of course purchase and sell foodstuffs to enemy populations and therefore not require financial assistance in this particular further than working capital. In the relief of newly liberated peoples such as Belgium, Poland . . . (including Jugo-Slavia), and Bohemia, it will no doubt be necessary to provide temporary advances from the Associated Governments to these recuperating nationalities with which they can purchase supplies from the Director-General, such arrangements to be worked out by the Associated Treasuries. In some cases public charity may have to be mobilized.

"In the Director-General's dealings with neutrals they of course would provide their own shipping and financial resources, and probably some tonnage and food, either directly or indirectly, for the purposes of the Director-General, they acting under his direction and authorization as to supplies and sources thereof, the Director-General, of course, acting in these matters in coöperation with the blockade authorities of the Allies and the United States.

"In order to prevent profiteering, the Director-General must make his purchases directly from the respective food administrations of the Associated Governments where his supplies arise from their territories, and where purchasing in neutral markets he should act in coöperation with the established inter-Allied agencies.

"It is evident that after the Allies have supplied themselves from their own territories at home and abroad and the balance from other sources, the only effective source of surplus supplies available for relief lie to a minor extent in the Argentine, but to a vast preponderance in the United States. The Director-General will have a large command of American resources and markets and will require the individual support of the American people in saving and productive activities.

"Owing to the political necessity of American control over American resources and the greater coördination and efficiency to be obtained thereby, I am sure that you will agree with me that the office of Director-General of Relief must be held initially by the United States Food Administrator and in case of necessity by such a successor as may be nominated by me. I would suggest, however, that the policies of the Director-General should be determined by the Supreme War Council, to whom he should report, it being our united policies in these matters not only to save life, but also to stabilize governments.

"All these arrangements [are] to be for the period of emergency and it is highly desirable for them to be liquidated as fast as practicable."

I shall be grateful to you if you will advise me as soon as practicable the views of the British Government concerning this matter.

E. M. HOUSE

In the meantime, I had spent November 28 and 29 in Brussels in consultation with the Belgian Relief staff and the Belgian Government.[4]

The Belgians were insistent that they did not wish their food or their economy placed under any such control as had been discussed in London, concerning which they had received a full report from their Ambassador to Britain.

Upon my return to Paris from Brussels on November 30, Ministers Boret and Vilgrain insisted that the Belgian Relief Commission continue to direct the relief of Northern France. In finally agreeing to carry on that difficult task temporarily, I expressed the hope that the United States would have French co-operation in adoption of the President's plan for the organization of relief and reconstruction.

I also met in Paris with Signor Crespi, the Italian Food Minister. It was obvious to me that he and I were discussing matters with wholly different purposes. We Americans were searching for an efficient, practical, down-to-earth method of meeting the food and reconstruction problems of four hundred million people, while the Italians, of necessity, had also to think on the level of political possibilities and effects.

In spite of our discouragement in presenting our point of view, on December 1, I issued an appeal to the American people from Paris, urging them to continue to save food. The essential paragraphs were:

The change in the foreign situation necessarily alters the details of our food program, because the freeing of the seas from the submarine menace, renders accessible the . . . supplies of India, Australia and the Argentine. The total food demand upon the United States is not diminished. . . . On the contrary, it is increased. In addition to the supplying of those to whom we are already pledged, we now have the . . . obligation of meeting the needs of those millions of people in the hitherto oc-

[4] I have given an account of those discussions in Volume I of *An American Epic*.

cupied territories who are facing actual starvation. . . . All these considerations mean that upwards of 200 million people, in addition to those we are already pledged to serve, are now looking to us in their misery and famine. Our appeal today is therefore larger than the former appeal to the "War conscience" of our people. The new appeal is the "world conscience," which must be the guiding inspiration of our future program. . . .

. . . No government or nation can stand if its people are starving. We must do our part if the world be not consumed in a flame of anarchy. . . .

HERBERT HOOVER

On December 4, I received this letter from Lord Reading:

MY DEAR MR. HOOVER:

Mr. Balfour received a letter from Colonel House informing him of the President's proposal with regard to the Relief of the civilian populations of European countries during the meeting of the Allied representatives yesterday.

The representatives were informed of its contents, but there was not time during their presence in London to go fully into the matter and it was therefore decided to ask Monsieur Clementel and Monsieur Bouisson, representing France, Signor Crespi and Signor Villa, representing Italy, and Sir Joseph Maclay and myself representing Great Britain, to examine in co-operation with yourself and Mr. Hurley the general question of the revictualling and supply of the enemy, allied and neutral countries in its economic, financial and other aspects, as well as the connected question of handing over to the Allies of enemy merchant ships, with a view to the preparation of a full Report for the consideration of the four Governments.

I hope very much that you will give us your valuable co-operation in this matter. . . .

READING

This wholly disregarded the President's plan, and the mention of Mr. Hurley did not contribute to our equanimity, since the Allied representatives advised us that he approved of their pool ideas. Moreover, he had no authority in these matters of relief and reconstruction. However, Davis and I arranged to meet again with the committee mentioned by Reading in London on December 5. The meeting was a long and tedious repetition of former discussions.

The Allied representatives steadily ignored Mr. Wilson's proposals and kept to their pool ideas. Davis and I stated repeatedly that we could not depart from the President's policies. In the hope that they would realize American importance in these matters, we suggested that the members of the Reading committee examine what financial support, what supplies, and what amounts of shipping each of the four governments could contribute to relief and reconstruction. They replied that they did not yet know the needs.

In a final effort at a meeting with this committee on December 10, Davis and I stated flatly that it was the American purpose to co-ordinate and co-operate with the Allies, that we could not accept any outside control of our economy, and that we supported the proposals made by the President and were open to any suggestions organizing co-operation and co-ordination within these limits. On December 11, I reported to Colonel House that we were getting nowhere and should await the President's arrival in Europe. He could deal with Prime Ministers. We were dealing with departmental civil servants—then colloquially known in Europe as "bureaucrats."

The obstruction to our proposals is partially clarified by a paragraph from Hugh Gibson's diary dated December 18, 1918:

> . . . Cravath and other Americans have been raising hob with our plans over here by running to the British with advance dope about what we were thinking and planning. In several instances too, Cravath at least has taken it upon himself to tell the British and French that the various provisions in our relief plan presented by the President did not emanate from him but were the machinations of Hoover. That of course has not made our task any easier. After we had stood about enough of it I was sent this morning to see the Secretary [Lansing had arrived in Europe]. . . . The Secretary waxed wroth. . . . [Cravath soon returned home.]

Behind all of these discussions was conflict between the ideals of the New World and those of the Old.[5]

Briefly, President Wilson had secured agreement from both the Allies and the enemy that "the basis of peace" should be his "Four-

[5] I have discussed these conflicts at length in *The Ordeal of Woodrow Wilson.*

teen Points and subsequent addresses." Within them were the stipulations of "independence of nations," "self-determination of peoples," and "freedom from domination." These stipulations were in keeping with American ideals but were in total conflict with the concept of empires.

The great empires of Britain, France, and Italy were the very embodiment of domination of peoples. Not only did the American stipulations conflict with pride of greatness, but the living standards in empires were dependent upon the economic harvest from territorial holdings abroad. Their statesmen believed that their recovery from war required not only maintaining their empires but expanding them. They equated the welfare of their empires with the welfare of the world. They honestly believed that with the enlightened development of colonies and empires, they were building a future for free men. The wrongs they had suffered from the war had raised fierce emotions of hate and revenge and demands for compensation for every injury, moral or economic. The terrible specter of war impoverishment haunted them, and every family mourned sons who had been sacrificed in their defense. No statesman who did not embody these emotions could survive in office.

Imperial leaders suspected that the President would use the economic power of the United States in food and finance to force them to carry out his proposals for the basis of peace. Their pool idea was one form of protection from such pressures. We could not convince them that Mr. Wilson, from the very idealism which dominated his terms of peace, would reject the use of threats of starvation and refusal of economic aid to force his ideas. Despite our sympathies with all the Allied difficulties, we could not go along with their views on the secondary but practical problem of relief and reconstruction; we rested upon our proposals to co-ordinate and co-operate with them.

The officials with whom we had to deal were delightful men personally. I should have been glad to win their affection by giving in to their every demand. Because of my understanding and sympathetic remarks on their sufferings and needs, at one time they misjudged my position as being different from that of the President. In any event, we got nowhere in these renewed discussions.

CHAPTER 31

AMERICAN RELIEF IN ACTION

In previous chapters I have described how, prior to the Armistice, we began loading ships with more than 600,000 tons of food for the acute famine areas. During our visit to Paris on November 26, we determined to open the American offices for relief and reconstruction in that city—since the leaders of all nations would be gathered there for the Peace Conference, including the President and Prime Ministers Lloyd George, Clemenceau, and Orlando. Hugh Gibson and Robert Taft secured for us a large furnished house on Rue de Lübeck for residential purposes and some temporary offices from which we later moved to a large apartment house on Avenue Montaigne.

Our ships were arriving, and the people in the liberated countries of Eastern and Southern Europe were starving. And starvation would not await the arrival of the President to arrange matters with the Allies. We concluded that, after all, the United States controlled its own economic destiny and that the American people did not need permission from anybody to deliver food to hungry people.

Pending the adoption of the President's plan of "co-operation and co-ordination" under American leadership, my authority stemmed from several sources. I was United States Food Administrator, Chairman of the United States Grain Corporation, Chairman of the Sugar Equalization Board, and Chairman of the Commission for Relief of Belgium and Northern France. As Food Administrator, I could determine all purchase and export of supplies from the United States, and, under the President's orders, I could draw on Army and Navy surplus supplies. In addition, we could secure, through the President from the American Treasury, loans to nations with which to pay for our food (i. e., nations which had participated in the war). It seemed altogether ample authority with which to start. It had not occurred to the hungry nations to ask whether or not our activities were visaed by the other governments.

When the President arrived in Paris on December 15, we had many pressing problems to take up with him besides inter-Allied organization. I met him on the evening of the fifteenth and again on the sixteenth. I described our organization for getting food in motion to the famine areas, and the President warmly approved it. We had a number of routine problems—and some major ones—which the President acted upon with his usual rapidity.

For instance, we had a tangle with the War Department over who would decide the destinations of our cargoes en route, and I had drafted a cable for Mr. Wilson to send to the Department, provided he approved it:

16 December, 1918

FOR SECRETARY OF WAR

In respect to the foodstuffs being shipped by the War Department for direction of Mr. Hoover, I would be indeed obliged if you would continue to forward these foodstuffs to such ports as Mr. Hoover may direct, and that the War Department continue to take care of the discharge and custody of these foodstuffs at these ports. The foodstuffs will not be released by the Quartermaster General's representative except as paid for by the Food Administration in Washington, arrangements for which are now being completed.

WOODROW WILSON

He marked this "Approved W.W."

We had an especially acute situation in Serbia. I suggested that credit could be extended to that country under the law. I informed Mr. Wilson that Norman H. Davis, the Treasury representative in Paris, had prepared a cable, by way of explanation, which he proposed to send to the Treasury and a draft cable from the President, authorizing a credit to Serbia of $35,000,000, as follows:

PARIS, 16 December, 1918

THE SECRETARY OF THE TREASURY

Mr. Hoover informs me that situation in Serbia and Jugo-Slavia is such that food supplies should be sent in there immediately in order to save life and maintain stability in the military situation, and Mr. Davis has shown me his proposed cable to you explaining the situation, and suggesting the establishment of a credit of $35,000,000 in favor of the Serbian Government to be used for relief of Serbians and Jugo-Slavs under Serbian Government, provided the Serbian Government makes application for such credit and agrees to turn over the funds to the Food Administration or the Grain Corporation for the purchase, delivery, and distribution of the supplies in question. If you therefore desire to establish this credit and to make advances thereunder as above indicated, you may consider this as my full approval.

WOODROW WILSON

The President marked this cable "Approved W.W."

I secured the President's approval to delegate to the Grain Corporation the purchasing, transporting, and accounting of all relief supplies and for the negotiating of contracts with foreign governments relative to conditions upon which supplies would be furnished. Since I did not have the executive order prepared, he said to "send it around."

We also had a most acute situation in Vienna, which city had less than ten days' supply of food. Under the law, loans could not be made to enemy countries. I proposed that the President furnish the Food Administration with five million dollars from his National Security and Defense Fund, which he had the power to dispose of at will. I had a cable drafted for him as follows:

16 December 1918

FOR SECRETARY OF THE TREASURY

Please pay at once to the U.S. Food Administration Grain Corporation five million dollars from my fund for National Security and Defense.

WOODROW WILSON

He marked the cable "Approved W.W."

I took up with the President the urgency of a special relief appropriation by the Congress for supplying the liberated countries which could not qualify under the law controlling Treasury advances to former Allies. I urged that this fund should be made available by charity instead of so-called loans. We especially wished to start a system for rehabilitating subnormal "children of famine"—solely as an American enterprise under the American flag. The system would be similar to the present operations for 2,500,000 children in Belgium and Northern France. The President at once directed that his administration in Washington request an appropriation of $100-000,000. I deal with this matter further in Chapter 37.

The President agreed to authorize General Pershing and Admiral Benson to assign us any members of their forces willing to join our work whom they could spare. I may interpolate here that General Pershing had more than two million officers and men idle in billets and camps, waiting to go home. Admiral Benson had a quarter of a million officers and men on ships, with no fighting prospects. Most of these men were prewar civilians, and among them was experience in every calling and profession.

When I called on General Pershing, he greeted me with a warm statement about my services to him in August, 1918 (see Chapter 18). On my request for permission to recruit some of his men, he said:

> Certainly—and besides, if you will let me know what background of experience you want, I will have some of them selected for you to choose from. If they wish to enter your service, I will keep them in uniform and keep up their pay until they wish to go home.

We found that most of the officers and men fitted for our work were glad to get out of tents and billets and serve with us.

Admiral Benson was equally co-operative. In the end, we had recruited into our organization more than four thousand able men from his and General Pershing's forces.

I had a further urgent problem to solve with the President. The

Allied blockade was still in force; we needed some relaxation to get food to the starving and to relieve our overcrowded warehouses, lest large amounts of perishable food spoil. To pave the way for action, I proposed to the President that Colonel House take up an immediate problem with the Supreme War Council. I drafted a letter for the Colonel to send to them. The President sent the draft to the Colonel with an accompanying note:

15 December, 1918

MY DEAR HOUSE:

The enclosed is the result of my conference with Hoover this evening. Would you be willing to communicate this paper to the Allied Governments, as you conveyed the original note about the relief administration to which this refers?

WOODROW WILSON

In this draft, I reviewed for Colonel House the arrangements which the Food Administration had made with the Allied Governments during the war; the great stimulants to production we had applied, with their full approval; the huge surpluses we had prepared for possible continuation of the war or, alternatively, to meet the inevitable famine. I stated that with the Armistice, the Allies would naturally wish to obtain food supplies from the cheaper stocks —dammed back in the Southern Hemisphere and the Far East for lack of transportation—and then continued:

Viewing the world's food situation as a whole, there is manifestly no surplus, even of American production, if the import of food into enemy neutral and liberated countries were released upon a normal scale. There would in fact be a shortage. . . .

This increase in food production in the United States is therefore still of the highest importance, for it becomes the supply through which the very life of many countries must be sustained, and the American people wish it used in a sympathetic manner for these purposes.

These foodstuffs, however, cannot at present reach many of these new areas freely, where they are so sorely needed, because of the blockade restrictions of many descriptions. The surpluses of American supplies are backing up and many of them are perishable and there is thus created a very threatening economic [and warehouse] situation.

The present situation, therefore, is one of two-fold character:

First. With literally hundreds of millions of underfed human beings in the world, the spoilage and waste of a large quantity of food in the United States cannot for a moment be entertained, either by the American public or by the Allies. Many of the American surpluses are of perishable character, and instant action is necessary to prevent waste as well as hunger.

Second. There must be instant expansion of . . . [export of the] American surpluses or there will be a great financial reaction in the United States. A review of the very large stocks now held and the large amount of banking credit advanced against these stocks creates a situation of the utmost danger. Any failure to find solution to this situation within the next few days would possibly precipitate financial difficulties in the United States, which would injure the hope of continued economic assistance to the Allies for a long time to come [because of possible failure of our guarantee].

No guarantees of any character have ever been at any time required to produce foodstuffs for the supply of the American people and all guarantees have been solely for the purpose of creating surpluses for the European Allies. . . . [our price] guarantees not only apply to the existing food supplies but also extend . . . [for many months ahead]. . . .

Therefore, I am directed to inquire if you will not recommend to your Government:

(a) That all restrictions upon neutral trading be at once removed in these commodities;

(b) That no objection be raised by the Allied Governments to direct or indirect sale and transportation [by them] to enemy countries or to the necessary financial transactions involved.

The draft was marked "Approved W.W."

The sum of all this was a request that the blockade on food supplies to the liberated countries and the Neutrals be taken down at once and that the Neutrals, under certain conditions, be allowed to trade food with the enemy countries.

Colonel House sent the letter to the Supreme War Council as suggested. His introduction to the letter was as follows:

The President has directed me to present these recommendations as matters of the utmost urgency and the key to many settlements which are to be presently attempted.

At the end of this session with the President on December 16, I stated to him that as soon as the organization of relief and reconstruction was straightened out and as soon as I had arranged for the Belgian and French governments to take over the Belgian Relief, I wished to return home and revive my engineering career. He remarked: "You cannot leave me with this worry in the hands of some new man and expect me to make peace as well." No one could forsake so co-operative and so burdened a man. I replied: "All right, I resign to my fate."

As I was about to depart, the President asked my estimate of the state of mind in Europe. I said: "You are the one hope of this enormous mass of people." I predicted that he would be confronted with great opposition from the Allied statesmen in making peace, even though they had formally accepted his basic terms. I stated that because of the emotional pressures and demands from their people back home and also because of their imbedded imperialism, he would find little idealism. He thought differently, saying that these were patriotic men who had fought a great war for a great ideal. (Three months later he referred to this conversation and told me wearily: "You were right.")

CHAPTER 32

THE AMERICAN PLAN FOR RELIEF AND RECONSTRUCTION IS ADOPTED

When the President arrived in Brest on December 14, he was met by Colonel House, who informed him of our failure to secure approval of his plan for the organization of relief and reconstruction. Two days before the President's arrival, I received the following letter from Lord Reading:

13 December, 1918

DEAR MR. HOOVER:

As soon as you have had time to consider the document I sent to you through the good offices of M. Clementel, I should like to know whether you accept its terms or in what respects you disagree with it.

After you left we devoted ourselves to putting the result of our deliberations into formal shape and trust that the outcome will meet with your approval. Of course I bear in mind that when you left no document had been prepared and that in so far as you expressed assent it was in a conversation which was not as precise as in a document.

Until I hear from you I fear no progress can be made.

READING

The letter had overtones of the Viceroy of India, and I could only surmise that it was prepared for the education of the President when he arrived. The "document" was of great length. It reiterated previous proposals and a rejection of the President's plan.[1] We were glad to have it in writing, since all of our discussions hitherto had been verbal, and it would confirm to the President any statement of mine with regard to their contentions.

When I met the President on December 15, I reported to him that only he could break through the London fog of power politics. I voiced my belief that the Allied pool proposals stemmed partly from fears of his use of pressures on their food supplies and partly from the wish to control food in the rest of Europe for political purposes. I suggested that he alone could free their minds from the idea that

[1] In the meantime, Colonel House had asked that I prepare an answer to the "document" which he could use. Robert Taft drew up the following memorandum, and I approved it for Colonel House:

The memorandum of the 12th of December, being a report to the Prime Ministers of England, France, and Italy . . . . The recommendations contained therein differ from the President's proposal in very essential matters.

The President's plan contemplates a single-headed administration of relief and a confinement of scope of relief to the immediate problem during [the] armistice so that human life may be saved and anarchy prevented without other objective. . . .

The Allied proposals amount to:

(a) A complete world control of food by an Inter-allied body, not limited to the armistice . . . action would be possible only by unanimity of agreement. . . .

(b) Through control of "source," quantity and distribution [of supplies] to all European countries there would in effect be a total control of the world's markets, including the U.S.

(c) The natural executive or administrative relations are minimized. Instead of confining the functions of the proposed Council or Board . . . to the determination of broad legislative policies for the guidance of the United States Administrative official, it is proposed that this legislative board assume most important executive functions.

(d) The principle that enemy tonnage is to be used for relief purposes is not accepted.

(e) No definite proposal is made for finance, and the impression is conveyed that objection will be found to the cash payment by enemy for food. In fact, in various discussions, Allied representatives have called attention to the fact that payment in cash or in exchange would result in depletion of German assets as against indemnities.

(f) The plan outlined would subordinate and jeopardize prevention of starvation until complete agreement of all four governments on every point—political, financial, transportation, and source of supply, instead of mere agreement on general policy as proposed by the President. . . .

There can be no question that there are situations in Europe requiring attention within days, perhaps within hours, and to obtain, with the political currents now flowing, inter-Allied agreement, in the sense expressed in this memorandum, on complex problems of organization, etc., with the rapidity necessary to prevent starvation and anarchy, will be entirely hopeless. . . .

our purpose was other than to save the starving and stabilize Europe. I expressed my conviction that most of these Allied notions came from highly developed bureaucracies and that I believed the Prime Ministers would have a broader vision. The President emphatically declared that he would insist on the American plan. I recommended that he ignore the "document" and allow Colonel House to undertake the negotiations with the Allied Ministers over the heads of the bureaucrats.

My conviction that the Allied Prime Ministers would agree to the President's plan was upheld by the overwhelming reception he received from the European masses. To them, he was a second Messiah, bringing national independence, personal liberty, and lasting peace. No Prime Minister could refuse the President his wishes on so secondary a question as the method of organization of relief and reconstruction.

On December 16, Colonel House addressed the following letter to each of the Allied Foreign Ministers—Lord Balfour, M. Pichon, and Baron Sonnino:

PARIS, 16 December, 1918

The President requests me to say that the discussions of his proposal of December 1st, submitted through me, for the creation of a European Relief Administration and the appointment of a Director General of Relief, have been reported to him. He entertains no doubt that he will receive in due course from the Allied Governments a reply to that note, but it appears from the discussion that some time will be required to reconcile the differences of view involved in the undertaking.

The objects of the United States Government in connection with food supply—which concern only the Armistice emergency—are to save life, to preserve order throughout the liberated, neutral, and enemy territories, and to create an efficient organization to accomplish these purposes. In these purposes he feels assured of your entire sympathy and cooperation.

Pending further discussions of the entire problem, however, the situation in certain areas is of so critical a nature, and requires such immediate emergency action that he wishes me to inform you that he is instructing the United States Food Administration to take measures at once to furnish food supplies and to establish an organization to this end in certain places outside of Germany.

Taking it for granted that you will also be anxious to undertake immediate action in these matters through your various food departments, and in order that there shall be full coordination in this task, he has asked Mr. Hoover to indicate to you these situations and the points at which he proposes to establish representatives for the administration of relief measures, so that if you see fit, you may also send your representatives to these points, and these gentlemen may mutually coordinate their various efforts.

EDWARD M. HOUSE

Balfour replied to Colonel House on December 19, again urging the Reading-Clémentel plan:

MY DEAR COLONEL HOUSE:

I have your letter of December 16th. I am sorry that the reply to your letter of the 1st instant forwarding the President's proposal for the creation of a European Relief Administration and the appointment of a Director-General of Relief was unavoidably delayed by the necessity for the discussions to which you refer in your letter of the 16th. The result of these discussions was, as you know, communicated to Mr. Hoover by Lord Reading, and Lord Reading was awaiting a reply to the letter which he sent to Mr. Hoover on the subject on December 13th.

I can assure you that the British Government are in complete accord with the objects of the United States Government as set forth in your letter though further discussion will be required for the purpose of arriving at a detailed plan of action. So far as I can judge from past discussions I do not think that any difference of opinion exists as to the necessity for the appointment of a Council of the four Governments *to take charge of and deal with the question of Relief to Europe*. I think that the best plan will be to set up this Council at once, without giving any special direction save that it is created for the purpose of dealing with Relief, and for each Government to nominate its representatives on the Council and leave *them to meet and deal with all questions including the extent of their own powers within the general limits prescribed in the document copy of which was sent by Lord Reading to Mr. Hoover*. If this plan is adopted I would suggest that the procedure to be followed would be that Mr. Hoover should at the first meeting of this Council make a full report of any action taken by him, that the same course should be followed by the representatives of the other Governments and that the Council would then get to work.

Perhaps you would kindly let me know whether this arrangement would meet the President's views. Then, if the French and Italian Governments also assent, His Majesty's Government would at once nominate their representatives with a view to enabling the Council to get to work at the earliest possible date.[2]

ARTHUR JAMES BALFOUR

However, a sudden reversal came from French Foreign Minister Pichon in a letter to House on December 23:

MY DEAR COLONEL:

The French Government has always been in cordial accord with the principles and the propositions mentioned in your letter of December 1st, regarding aid (revictualling) to be extended to the countries of Europe. The French Government accepts with equal willingness the proposition of the President that the Government of the United States should take the management of the administration of this aid (revictualling). The delay in making our reply arose solely from the necessity of holding various conferences in regard to the general questions raised by this proposition and for adapting the plan suggested to the following considerations which seem to us essential for the happy execution of the President's project. . . .

PICHON

He then continued with pious generalities echoing back to the "pool." They had little relation to the realities of the situation. The Italian Minister, Baron Sonnino, made a similar reply.

Colonel House replied, expanding Pichon's proposal:

PARIS, 1 January 1919

MY DEAR MONSIEUR PICHON:

I am in receipt of your letter of December 23rd, in reply to my letter of December 1st, relative to the European Relief Administration, and am glad to note that the French Government accepts in principle the plan proposed by me on behalf of the President.

The President is gratified that you desire that the United States Government should take the lead in this undertaking.

[2] All italics mine.

The President asks me to state that he accepts your suggestion that a special Council of two members, representing each of the Four Governments be . . . [established] under the Supreme War Council.

In view of the urgent action required in some territories, the President suggests that it is most desirable that each of the Allied Governments designate its representatives at the earliest possible moment and that at the first meeting of the Council it would be desirable that the representatives of each Government be prepared to state what participation and resources they will be able and willing to contribute to the common object.

He has therefore appointed Mr. Herbert Hoover and Mr. Norman H. Davis as the American members on this Council, and has asked Mr. Hoover, as Director General of Relief, as soon as possible to call a meeting of the Council.

With regard to the other considerations raised by you, it appears to him that these are matters which will necessarily come before the Council for consideration from time to time *and that while none of the Governments are releasing any freedom of action, all recognize that in setting up organizations of this kind there is a common desire to co-ordinate the activities of the different Governments in the directions outlined by yourselves.*[3]

E. M. House

The British said on January 1, in a telegram from the Foreign Office to the Earl of Derby, their representative in Paris:

Following Urgent Message for Colonel House

His Majesty's Government agree with suggestions put forward in French Minister for Foreign Affairs' letter of the 23rd ultimo to Colonel House commencing with words "with principles and objects stated in your letter of December 1st relative to relief in Europe." His Majesty's Government agree that that letter may now be considered as embodying their views in reply to proposals made by Colonel House in his letter of December 1st to Mr. Balfour.

If President Wilson concurs in proposals contained in M. Pichon's letter and so informs His Majesty's Government respective Governments will then have to nominate their representatives and His Majesty's Government will appoint theirs at once.

[3] Italics mine.

On January 2, Lord Reading emitted a final bark:

To Colonel House

With reference to the communication which Mr. Balfour made to you yesterday on the subject of the Council to be formed with a view to dealing with relief matters, *I am of [the] opinion that this Council ought to be appointed to consider and decide questions of general policy, while Mr. Hoover, as mandatory, should be entrusted with the actual administration of relief.* I suggest that as soon as the four countries have appointed their representatives a meeting should be held to determine all outstanding matters of emergency: finance should especially be dealt with, as this and political considerations are at the bottom of the difficulties of the problem which confronts us. . . .[4]

Colonel House replied to the British Ambassador again, setting matters straight:

Paris, January 4, 1919

My dear Lord Derby:

Would you be good enough to cable to your Government that I acknowledge receipt of the message addressed to me and contained in a telegram to you from the Foreign Office dated January 1, 1919.

I note with satisfaction that His Majesty's Government agree that the letter dated December 23rd addressed to me from the French Minister for Foreign Affairs may be considered as embodying an amplification of their views concerning the proposals contained in my letter of December 1, 1918, to Mr. Balfour.

On January 1, 1919 I sent you a letter addressed to Mr. Balfour containing a copy of my answer to Monsieur Pichon's letter of the 23rd ultimo. I hope very much that it will be possible for you to advise me in the near future of the names of His Majesty's Government's representatives.

I note that Lord Reading in the telegram from him, which you handed me yesterday states:

"I am of [the] opinion that this Council ought to be appointed to consider and decide questions of general policy, while Mr. Hoover, as mandatory, should be entrusted with the actual administration of relief."

I agree with Lord Reading that the Council should deal with ques-

[4] Italics mine.

tions of policy and that Mr. Hoover should have general charge of the undertaking. *The proposals that I have made at the direction of the President have never contemplated that the President's appointee for this work should act as the mandatory of an Allied Council. It is, of course, understood that the Director General of Relief, in coordination of efforts of the various governments, will in practice act on behalf of the Council.*

I shall be obliged to you if you would communicate the foregoing to your Government.[5]

E. M. House

On January 3, the American Commission to Negotiate Peace made an announcement, the key paragraphs of which were:

3 January 1919

. . . Since his [the President's] arrival . . . his discussions with the Prime Ministers of Great Britain, France and Italy respecting the general Peace settlement, he has been advised . . . the Governments concerning the method of organization for the relief of these populations.

The Allies and the United States are in agreement that relief . . . of this character on a large scale *necessitates a unity of direction similar in character to that which has proved so successful in French and British Chief Command in the operations of the Allies on the land and on sea respectively. The Allied Governments have advised the President that they desire that the United States Government should take the lead in the organization and administration of this relief.*

Under this arrangement between the United States and the Allies, a Council is being appointed of two representatives of each Government to secure co-ordination of food, finance and shipping resources in the solution of the problems connected with this relief. . . .[6]

My appointment as Director General was announced.

The net result of all these tedious negotiations was that the President's plan went into effect and many pitfalls to the American economy were avoided—albeit with many rugged experiences and sleepless nights.

[5] Italics mine.
[6] Italics mine.

CHAPTER 33

THE THEORY AND PRACTICE OF CO-ORDINATION AND CO-OPERATION

In order that the reader may understand somewhat more clearly the subsequent events in this narrative, I inject at this point a description of the inter-Allied organizational setup during the Armistice. At least it indicates the difficulties of co-operation, co-ordination, and action among the many nations involved in the war's aftermath.

No mortal man could know them all—and their functions. The reader, however, may better realize our problems from some description of them.

THE PEACE CONFERENCE

The organization of the Peace Conference was achieved by evolution. Its organization began with the election of Premier Clemenceau as President of the Conference and the creation of the "Council of Ten," which, theoretically, included only President Wilson and the Secretary of State, the Prime Ministers of Britain, France, and Italy and their Foreign Ministers, and two Japanese representatives. In sessions, however, these principals brought so many assistants with them that at times the Council of Ten seemed like a town meeting. Also, there was a constant leakage of information. When Mr. Wilson returned on March 15, 1919, from his visit to the United

States, he arranged that the three Prime Ministers and himself comprise exclusively what became known as the "Supreme Council" or, colloquially, the "Big Four," of which Prime Minister Clemenceau was Chairman. Thereafter, the Council of Ten continued under the four Foreign Ministers and the Japanese delegates. Secretary of State Lansing represented the United States on this body. Colonel House also sat in. The Colonel's relationship to the Peace Conference was never very clear, but he can best be described as the President's handy man. The Council of Ten, after the President's return, became a sort of "Court of the First Instance," sifting certain matters for the Big Four.

The work of the Peace Conference was divided among committees. The first concerned the League of Nations and was under the chairmanship of the President. Other committees were set up to deal with reparations; international labor legislation; international control of ports, waterways, and railways; financial and economic problems; territorial boundaries; and military and disarmament questions. All of these committees drafted proposed articles for the peace treaty along lines designated by the Council of Ten or, later, the Big Four.

THE PRESIDENT'S COMMITTEE OF ECONOMIC ADVISERS

One of the necessities on the American side was to have co-ordinated action among the Americans who headed our economic agencies. I made the following recommendation to the President early in January, 1919:

DEAR MR. PRESIDENT:

1. As you are aware, our Government has been represented in Europe upon various inter-Allied councils, relating to finance, food, shipping, and raw materials, war trade measures, etc. The purpose of these councils is rapidly changing and the American attitude toward them and the problems they represent must change. The matters involved are much interlocked and up to the time of the Armistice were co-ordinated

through the Council [the American War Council] sitting under your chairmanship. Messrs. Hurley, Baruch, Hoover, and McCormick are, or will soon be, in Europe. The working of these bodies still needs co-ordination . . . [by] the chief representatives here of the departments whose heads are still in Washington.

2. This same group is essential in determination of policies to be pursued by our Government in the peace negotiations.

3. It is recommended that a council be set up, comprising Messrs. Hurley, Baruch, McCormick, Davis, and myself . . . under your chairmanship, to discuss and decide such joint policies as are necessary in both these phases and to co-ordinate it with the Peace Commission by inclusion of Colonel House, General Bliss, and Admiral Benson, Colonel House to act as Chairman in your absence or inability to find time.

HERBERT HOOVER

The President sent back the memorandum marked "Approved: W.W."

The Committee was appointed by the President, with the above membership, and became known as the "President's Committee of Economic Advisers." Later, Hurley returned to the United States and Henry M. Robinson took his place.

Aside from its job of co-ordinating the American economic front among the multitude of inter-Allied economic councils and boards, the Committee was often drawn upon by Mr. Wilson for advice in other important matters, as will be shown later in this narrative. The Committee's meetings were generally informal and often held at mealtime. Minutes were seldom kept, and as far as there is a record, most of it will be found in Vance McCormick's diary and in our written communications with the President. It was fortunate that McCormick kept a diary. The other American officials keeping diaries were Lansing, House, Gibson, and Auchincloss (Colonel House's secretary); all of these men's diaries are intimate and continuous records. I could not find time to keep a diary, but I did dictate paragraphs daily on important proposals, interviews, and decisions which affected my organization.[1] Parts of the above statement appear in

[1] Copies of all of these diaries are in the Hoover Institution on War, Revolution, and Peace at Stanford University.

The Ordeal of Woodrow Wilson. In that book I also give short background sketches of the members of the Committee.[2]

INTER-ALLIED ECONOMIC COMMITTEES

A host of inter-Allied councils, committees, and boards for administrative purposes and co-ordination had sprung up during the war. Most of these continued during the peacemaking, and new ones were created for various purposes.

Under the plan of the President, agreed upon by the Allied governments, there was created an agency of co-ordination and cooperation called the "Supreme Council of Supply and Relief." It was limited to advisory functions and was comprised of representatives of the four governments with "ministerial powers" and a rotating chairmanship.

I called the first meeting of this Council on January 12, 1919. The "ministerial" representatives of the four governments sat at a central table in a large room at the French Ministry of Commerce, with some thirty to sixty Allied and American functionaries, armed with portfolios, sitting along the walls and periodically sending notes to their principals.

The Council served, temporarily, some useful purposes, such as the appointment of members of committees in Spa and Trèves to deal with blockade, shipping, and food problems with the Germans. It also served as a channel for the relief and reconstruction organization under my direction to keep the Allies informed of our activities. But it soon degenerated into a sort of chatterbox about minor matters and inaccurate information. By degrees, my American colleagues ceased to attend the meetings. In an effort to get more action, I secured the appointment of a subcommittee concerned solely with food matters, but it, too, faded away after some weeks.

[2] Pp. 84–86.

THE SUPREME ECONOMIC COUNCIL

When Lord Robert Cecil joined the British economic activities in Paris, I suggested to him that we do away with the whole Supreme Council of Supply and Relief apparatus and substitute a new organization, to be called the "Supreme Economic Council," with a preamble and an authority, the text of which I had drafted. Cecil fully approved and agreed to support its adoption by the Big Four. My draft was approved by them, with minor changes, on February 8, 1919. The text was:

(1) Under present conditions many questions not primarily of military character which are arising daily and which are bound to become of increasing importance as time passes should be dealt with on behalf of the United States and the Allies by civilian representatives of these governments experienced in such questions as finance, food, blockade control, shipping and raw materials.

(2) To accomplish this there shall be constituted at Paris a Supreme Economic Council to deal with such matters for the period of the Armistice. The council shall absorb or replace such other existing interallied bodies and their powers as it may determine from time to time. The Economic Council shall consist of not more than five representatives of each interested government.

(3) There shall be added to the present International Permanent Armistice Commission two Civilian Representatives of each associated Govt. who shall consult with the Allied High Command, but who may report direct to the Supreme Economic Council.[3]

We arranged that the chairmanship should rotate among the representatives of the four governments—and at times I served. The American members were McCormick, Baruch, Davis, Robinson, and myself.

The Supreme Economic Council, with no detailed constitution, no commitments, no rules, and few specific powers, served every needed purpose. It dealt with each problem on the facts and merits

[3] The original draft of the above in my handwriting is in the Hoover Institution on War, Revolution, and Peace.

of each case. We usually came to agreement, but not always. At least we developed the different points of view and presented them to the Big Four. The multitude of inter-Allied committees, boards, and councils which had been established during the war, and others added during the Armistice, were placed under the Council. Among them was the Superior Blockade Council, which had been created by Vance McCormick with the approval of the Big Four. It succeeded all previous blockade committees and councils. It was comprised of representatives of the United States, Britain, France, and Italy, under McCormick's chairmanship.

The Supreme Economic Council constituted a sort of second level of co-ordination and co-operation with the first level—the Big Four. The multitude of inter-Allied boards, commissions, and councils on economic subjects and missions constituted a sort of third level of co-ordination. And there was a fourth level in the joint missions to each country under relief and reconstruction.

Added to this complex were the internal boards, commissions, and councils within each Allied government; they decided the individual policies toward the inter-Allied agencies. At one time, our organization prepared a list of these agencies, but they frequently shifted in names and by consolidations. The list was:

The Supreme Council of Supply and Relief
The Supreme Economic Council (with sections on food, shipping, railways, coal and raw materials)
The Inter-Allied Maritime Council
The Inter-Allied Transport Executive
The Allied Blockade Council
The Superior Blockade Council
The Inter-Allied Food Council
The Sub-committee of the Allied Food Council
The Inter-Allied Wheat Executive
The Inter-Allied Meats and Fats Executive
The Royal Commission on Sugar Supply
The Inter-Allied Committee on Sugar Distribution
The Inter-Allied Adriatic Ports Commission
The Danube River Commission

The Commission for Relief in Belgium
The Commission for Relief in Northern France
The Inter-Allied Mission to Finland
The Inter-Allied Commission to the Three Baltic States
The Inter-Allied Mission to Poland
The Inter-Allied Mission to Czechoslovakia
The Inter-Allied Mission to Yugoslavia
The Inter-Allied Mission to Austria
The Inter-Allied Mission to Hungary
The Inter-Allied Mission to Roumania
The Inter-Allied Commission to Armenia
The Inter-Allied Mission to Bulgaria
The Inter-Allied Mission to Constantinople
The Inter-Allied Mission to Greece
The Inter-Allied Mission to North Russia
The Inter-Allied Mission to Trieste
The Inter-Allied Mission on Southeastern Railways
The Inter-Allied Mission on Northeastern Railways
The Inter-Allied Commission on Eastern European Coal
The Inter-Allied Committee on War Prisoners
The European Coal Council

In addition, there were inter-Allied committees whose duties cannot be indicated without some description, where available:

Name	Functions
Inter-Allied Permanent Armistice Commission (Spa)	General supervision of execution of Armistice conditions, formal communication with German Government.
Sub-Commission dealing with Clause 9 of Armistice (Entretien)	Recovery from Germany of costs of maintaining troops in occupied areas.
Sub-Commission dealing with Clauses 2 and 4 of Trèves Financial Agreement	Restitution of stolen and sequestrated securities.
Sub-Commission dealing with Clause 6 of the January Armistice renewal (Wiesbaden)	Restitution of stolen French and Belgian industrial machinery.

Name	Functions
Sub-Commission dealing with the handing over of agricultural machinery	Receiving from Germany agricultural machinery instead of rolling stock.
Commissions de Reception (Brussels and Metz)	Receiving from Germany rolling stock and raw materials handed over under the Armistice.
Calais Railway Commission	Control of Belgian railway system.
Field Railway Commission	Control of Luxembourg and German Rhineland railways.
Calais Navigable Waterways Commission	Control of Belgian and Northern France navigable waterways.
Field Navigation Commission	Control of the Rhine, Moselle and Sarre waterway navigation.
Commission for Postal Control	Control of correspondence, telegraphs and telephones in occupied areas.
Commission Economique (Luxembourg)	Supervision of distribution of raw materials to factories in the occupied area and output of goods, and regulation of economic relations in occupied territories.
Rhine Left Bank Committee	Dealing with blockade trade and other questions referred to it by the Army Command or the Luxembourg Commission.
The Shipping Commission at Rotterdam	Provision of channel of communication for settling practical details in handing over German ships.
Rotterdam Food Commission	Settlement of commercial and other details arising out of the sale of foodstuffs to Germany by the Allies.
Compiègne Finance Commission	Settlement of details of the financial arrangements between the Allies and Germany.

There were also five special temporary commissions of the Allied and Associated Powers appointed to negotiate the food and shipping question with German delegations at Spa, Trèves, and Brussels. In addition, we had to deal at times with the subcommittees of the Peace Conference.

There were probably other inter-Allied bodies in the economic field which are not listed. I was, at times, chairman of five or six of these organizations, and my organization appointed the chairmen and working staff of some twenty-five of them and had representatives on another ten.

My duties as Director General of Relief and Reconstruction were somewhat ill-defined. And also in this land-of-little-definition were my separate functions as administrator of the official American governmental relief and reconstruction agencies. In my capacity as Director General on behalf of the Allies, I had the duty of co-ordinating the activities of the various governments and answering for them to the Supreme War Council or the Council of Ten, as the case may have been.

In the inter-Allied missions and boards concerned with relief and reconstruction in the field, it was agreed that the Americans should appoint the chairmen and that the administrative work should be carried out by a staff of our appointment. On many of these committees or boards, especially those in the various countries and on special subjects, there was little for the Allied representatives, except the British, to do. Many members found reasons to hurry back to Paris, where the living was better and where they could "advise" equally well.

The co-ordination and co-operation of the American governmental relief and reconstruction activities with this multitude of committees, councils, and boards were a complicated performance. And in the first months of 1919, this involved many rugged experiences. But this narrative will show many instances on the brighter side. The previous and subsequent chapters indicate our difficult search for the Holy Grail of "co-ordination and co-operation." However, before our work ended, the Americans in my organization had won the confidence and friendship of our Allied colleagues.

In my capacity as United States Food Administrator and of all the United States Government's official relief measures, I had to direct 70 per cent of the supplies and 95 per cent of the actual relief delivered to the forty-five nations (or peoples) involved and to represent (or be represented by my staff) the United States on many inter-Allied organizations. Since this was wholly an emergency job, the titles and border lines of authority concerned us little.

The Food Administration had important responsibilities at home which, in turn, were related to the whole problem of co-ordinating world supplies to meet the famine. Our obligations included the guarantees to farmers and distribution of their products at home and abroad. We also had to control profiteering in world supplies and their equitable distribution. To accomplish this, we acted in two directions: The first was in the issuance of export permits from the United States (the predominant source), and we were guided by information as to supplies being imported from other sources and acted accordingly.

The second of these was to prevent competition, and thus chaos, in purchase of supplies from nations other than the United States. In a world short of food, there had to be some sort of order in the distribution of such overseas supplies. The American organizations under my direction were the only possible instruments for maintaining such order. Some nations felt that our requests for information about their purchases were an encroachment on their freedoms. But we, through our consular officials, secured reports of the important overseas shipments from each foreign port. We could, and did, regulate the flow from the United States in order to assure at least a minimum of food to each European nation. We continued to exercise this power until after the Peace.

In this job, however, I had a magnificent staff of experienced and devoted men from the Food Administration, together with the men drawn from the American Army and Navy in Europe. The task of recruiting staff was made easy by General Pershing and Admiral Benson, who co-operated as if they personally were part of our organization. As I have already stated, before our work was completed, we had about four thousand of the most able men from the American Army and Navy, with experience for every task, who were glad to take service with us until after the Peace was signed. They comprised generals, colonels, admirals, commanders, captains, lieutenants, sergeants, "doughboys," and "gobs."

In setting up our organization, we had the usual plague of theorists, who wanted to make charts with squares and circles showing the relation of each job to the other, along with descriptions of particular functions and authorities. Nothing could raise my temperature faster than charts for an emergency organization which shifted daily. As in previous emergency organizations, our invariable method was to choose a man to solve each specific problem and build an organization around him. I mention this here because in later years I have received repeated demands for the "Chart of Organization" of this enterprise in saving life. We had none. We did have men and women to whom pay, titles, and definitions of authority were immaterial and the opportunity to save life and get the world going again was a sacred call.

Because 94 per cent of the burden of supplies and finance to all of Europe except Germany fell upon the United States, the function of administrator of American governmental agencies was much more important than that of Director General of Relief. And superimposed upon all of my duties were many activities in the political field delegated to me by the Supreme War Council or by President Wilson.

Chroniclers of the President's work in Paris have mainly concerned themselves with the Peace Conference, its political struggles, its failures and accomplishments. But the activities of the American relief agencies constitute an important segment of any history bearing on Mr. Wilson. Their purpose appealed to his humane spirit, and to them he gave constant personal attention. Our activities were possibly second in their importance to the treaty-making. Mr. Wilson often referred to us as the "Second American Expeditionary Force to Save Europe."

The massive part undertaken by the American agencies in forty-five nations made it necessary for us to get the President's approval for many activities and to secure his intervention with the Council of Ten and the Big Four. At times, with the President's help, we had to appeal to those bodies over the heads of Allied officials. All of this constituted an extra drain on Mr. Wilson's vitality, but the results of our work were a constant satisfaction to him because our men—like those under General Pershing—never failed him at any point.

CHAPTER 34

WE OPEN A CRACK IN THE BLOCKADE AND GET A BAD SHOCK

The Allied tight blockade on food and other supplies to all Europe had ample justifications during the war. And they demanded its continuance during the Armistice for various reasons, including political control of all Europe. Theoretically, they did not wish to starve people, but practically, they made many difficulties.

On December 18, with the President's approval, I presented a proposal to the Inter-Allied Blockade Council. It specified the removal of all blockade restrictions on food to the newly liberated countries and to the Neutrals. It further proposed that the Neutrals could trade food to Germany for commodities not competitive with Allied exports—mostly chemicals.

The Blockade Council approved the plan on December 24, and news of its decision was spread through the world press. I notified each of our American Ministers in the Northern Neutral countries as follows:

25 December 1918

. . . The action of Allied Blockade Committee yesterday . . . not only releases any restriction on imports to neutrals but releases any restrictions on exports from them even to enemy countries. . . . It is our first movement towards feeding Germany. The only limit on neutral imports [of food] from U.S. is the amount we can spare and I will have to allot this when I know approximately the quantities wanted from different quarters. Would you have the American packers' agents in Sweden and Norway informed of these facts and that they can at once open relations with U.S. for imports. We wish to stimulate private trading as quickly as possible.

HOOVER

To quiet the nerves of our food processors, who were greatly agitated about their dangerously increasing stocks, I telegraphed Frederic Snyder, the head of our Meats and Fats Division in Washington, as follows:

. . . Yesterday Pork products were placed on the free list. This means that there is no restriction . . . on their re-sale even to the enemies. Please inform packers learning what they intend doing at once in reestablishing their business. If you have slightest trouble getting them ships from Shipping Board cable me at once. I wish to sell Northern neutrals through Grain Corporation if packers do not take prompt action.

HOOVER

I notified all the Neutrals and liberated nations of this action, and it was confirmed by the British blockade authorities in those countries. The Neutrals were in a hurry to obtain food for themselves and to trade with Germany. Immediately after the relaxation of the blockade, they contracted with the Chicago packers for about sixty million pounds of meats and fats for delivery in January. They made contracts with the Grain Corporation for large quantities of cereals, especially coarse grains for their long underfed animals, and they began negotiations with the Germans for purchasing chemicals and other goods noncompetitive with Allied exports.

On December 30, the Allied purchasing agencies, at their usual monthly meeting with our representative—Dr. E. Dana Durand—confirmed the Allied requests for American food supplies for the following months. The combined British, French, and Italian orders for American food totaled 175,000,000 pounds of meats, fats, and dairy products and 100,000,000 bushels of grain monthly for January, February, and March, 1919.

With these arrangements for the famine areas in Eastern Europe, the Neutrals, the Belgian Relief, and some parts of Germany—as required by the Armistice agreement—and the Allied programs of purchase, it seemed that we were on our way. Our only anxiety was that there might not be enough food in the world to go around.

With the German fleet safely in Scapa Flow, the Allies now dominated the Baltic. Some admiral had given orders that the Germans could no longer fish in these waters. On December 25, I requested Admiral Benson to intervene, saying:

MY DEAR ADMIRAL:

We have received recently many complaints from the Germans regarding the limitation on German fishing for food purposes, which has reduced their food intake so that they have even less food in this particular than before the Armistice. In view of the Armistice provisions assuring food supplies, it appears to me as the first matter to look into.

From a food production standpoint it would be highly desirable to permit this fishing, under any restrictions which may be deemed necessary by the Naval Authorities, but I am not familiar with the reasons which might lead the Naval Armistice Committee to take an opposite view. I should be greatly obliged if you could present this view of the matter to the American Member of the Naval Armistice Committee with a view to his urging upon the Committee the importance of this action.

HERBERT HOOVER

The Admiral reported that he was unable to persuade the British Admiralty to revoke the orders against German fishing—simply a stupid action of admirals ignorant of food problems. Benson expressed himself verbally to me in typical, outspoken sailor's language.

THE SHOCK

On December 31, a sudden joint meeting of the British, French, and Italian members of the Allied Meats and Fats Executive, the Wheat Executive, the Allied Maritime Transport Council, and the Allied Blockade Council, along with some of their Army and Navy leaders, was held in London. We received no notice, and our representatives in these organizations were not present.

This meeting ordered a reversal of the blockade relaxation of December 24 and reimposed a tight blockade on all Europe except the Allies. More astonishing still, they repudiated the Allied programs of supplies from the United States settled the day before. This included the cancellation of all outstanding Allied contracts with American processors for beef, pork, and dairy products and with the Grain Corporation for grain, cottonseed, beans, and other ground crops. Their contracts with our meat packers, involving hundreds of millions of pounds, called for special cuts and cures which were not marketable elsewhere.

We first learned of these actions in a cable from our New York office on New Year's Day; the cable stated that Allied buying agents had canceled all contracts with the packers—who subsequently were in a panic. A confirmation also came by cable from the chairman of the packers committee in Chicago:

> Hog price stabilization has reached critical stage. Arrangements made with Food Administration may break down unless hogs now arriving of correct weight and quality for English meats are so utilized. Unless European shipments are maintained, packers' storage facilities, now fully utilized, will make full killing impossible.
>
> THOMAS E. WILSON

It being New Year's Day, I had trouble getting Dr. Durand on the telephone but finally reached him. He said that he could not believe this story because he had just confirmed the large orders from the Allies the day before and that such a meeting could not have taken place without his being notified. It was hard for me to believe it also. However, Dr. Durand soon called me back to say that he had been informed by Signor Attolico, the Italian representative on the Allied agencies, that this action had been taken and that the British were primarily responsible. Attolico said the British argument was that the time had come to break the inflated prices of food over the whole world "in the common interest of everyone, including the American people." Attolico had vainly insisted that I be consulted before action was taken.

So that the reader may grasp the seriousness of this action, I again recall that the Food Administration had, with the approval of the Allies, guaranteed prices to our farmers and our food processors in order to create the huge surplus needed for the Allies. The guarantees on hogs and dairy products extended to the end of March, 1919; on cottonseed and rice to June 30, 1919; on sugar to the autumn of 1919; and on wheat to June 30, 1920. As I have said, we were in great danger of spoilage from lack of warehouse space.

I was far from agreement that this re-enactment of the blockade was in the interest of the hundreds of millions of starving people in Central and Eastern Europe. Nor did it strike me as in the "interest of everyone, including the American people."

This action of December 31, if it had succeeded, would have been certain to create a financial panic in the United States. Our farmers, on the faith of our guarantees, had borrowed heavily from their country banks in order to produce the food. The country banks had borrowed from the city banks. The Grain Corporation had borrowed enormous sums from the larger banks. And the food processors and merchants had also borrowed from the larger banks to finance the huge stocks in storage. The entire fabric of the American economy depended on the continuation of these wartime arrangements until we could organize their systematic liquidation.

The President was leaving at once on a speech-making tour through France, Italy, and England. I, however, did inform him of what had happened. He authorized me to act for him with the Allied governments and suggested that I consult with the American peace delegation members.

Secretary of State Lansing, General Tasker H. Bliss, Colonel House of the peace mission, and I were quartered in the same hotel. We had a hurried meeting on the afternoon of New Year's Day. We discussed the background of this action, and I stated that there was inherent economic folly in this Allied action. They might have broken world prices temporarily, but there would have been an enormous spoilage of precious perishables, a halt in production, and a suspension in American financial support to the Allies. The blockade was bound to come down sometime, and prices would then rise higher than fixed by our guarantees. (This proved to be the case in every one of the food commodities later on when our guarantees of prices had expired.) I stated my belief that this folly was merely an outbreak at the bureaucratic level, probably not even understood by the ministers concerned, and that we should deal with it at this level, provided we had the support of all American officials, which they assured me.

That evening, I convened the principal members of our staff, and we sorted out the effects of this action on our various food commodities. The Grain Corporation, aside from its capital of $150,000,000, had outstanding bank loans of more than $300,000,000 from its purchases of ground crops. Further finance of the oncoming grains did not bother us much. The wheat guarantees and the prices in force had been made by Congressional authority, and if necessary, the Congress would appropriate money to the Grain Corporation to maintain them. The price of rye, rice, beans, and some other ground crops had been assured by the Grain Corporation and it could find finance to protect them. These commodities were not perishable, and we could build temporary storage for the farmers' shipments. We were sure that we could hold this line until the increasing shortage and famine in Europe forced open the blockade.

As for sugar, the Sugar Equalization Board could finance the oncoming supplies at the banks, with the aid of American sugar refiners; and by removal of our restrictions on consumption, the American people would be glad to eat it. Moreover, if the Allies did not want sugar, the free markets in the world would take it all.

Our urgent problems thus narrowed down to two:

(1) We had about 700,000 tons of food en route to the acute famine areas and the Neutrals which might, under these Allied orders, be stopped by Allied navies.

(2) Our cold storage for pork and dairy products was already overcrowded. Without export outlet, the processors could not maintain our guarantees of those products and there would be great spoilage.

We cabled Washington to hold all our agencies steady and to assure the meat packers and milk processors that we would solve the matter in a few days.

We decided first to take up the subject with each of the Allied food ministers, since we believed at least some of them did not realize the effects of these actions upon their countries. On January 2, I sent a restrained (in view of my indignation) letter to each of the British, French, and Italian food ministers and had it delivered by messenger. I first reminded them of the historical background, stating that our guarantees had been entered into with their approval in order to meet their needs, and continued:

No guaranties of any character have ever been at any time required to produce foodstuffs for the supply of the American people and all guaranties have been solely for the purpose of creating surpluses for the European Allies. These guaranties not only apply to the existing food supplies but also extend to next year's wheat crop.

With the change produced by the Armistice, however, the markets of the Southern Hemisphere naturally open themselves to the Allied world, and the restriction of marketing from that quarter over four years has necessarily produced a lower range of prices than has been necessary to assure . . . the increase of production from the United States. Naturally, the Allies desire to seek the Southern Hemisphere markets with a view to securing the cheaper foodstuffs. . . .

Viewing the world's food situation as a whole, there is manifestly no surplus, even . . . [with] American production, if the import of food [stuffs] into enemy, neutral, and liberated countries were released upon a normal scale. There would, in fact, be a shortage. . . .

This increase in food production in the United States is, therefore, still of the highest importance, for it becomes the supply through which the very life of many countries must be sustained, and the American people wish it used in a sympathetic manner for these purposes. With literally hundreds of millions of underfed human beings in the world, the spoilage and waste of a large quantity of food in the United States cannot for a moment be entertained. . . . Many of the American surpluses are of perishable character, and instant action is necessary to prevent waste as well as hunger.

These foodstuffs, however, cannot at present reach many of those new areas freely, where they are so sorely needed, because of the [renewed] blockade restrictions of many descriptions. The surpluses of American supplies are backing up and there is thus created a very threatening economic situation. Any failure to find solution to this position within the next few days would possibly precipitate financial difficulties in the United States, which would injure the hope of continued economic assistance to the Allies for a long time to come.

The American people are most desirous of safeguarding the supplies to the Allies and wish to extend to them the full need for which they may call. Our present surpluses, however, in wheat, flour, barley, rye, pork products, condensed milk, and cottonseed-oils and various seed meals are above the demands of the Allied Governments between now and the next harvest. Other surpluses will develop later.

Therefore, I am directed to inquire if you will not recommend to your Governments:

(*a*) *That you indicate as nearly as may be the amounts of these commodities which will safeguard your position from January 1 to the end of our crop year—July 1, 1919.*

(*b*) *That all restrictions upon neutral trading be at once removed in these commodities.*

(*c*) *That no objection be raised by the Allied Governments to direct or indirect sale and transportation* [*of food*] *to enemy countries or to the necessary financial transactions involved.*

[(*d*) *That the food blockade on the liberated countries be removed at once.*]

The President has directed me to present these recommendations as matters of the utmost urgency and the key to many settlements which are to be presently attempted.[1]

HERBERT HOOVER

Because the British seemed to be at the root of our troubles, I further addressed the British Food Ministry as follows:

PARIS, January 2, 1919

THE BRITISH MINISTRY OF FOOD
LANCASTER HOUSE
LONDON

GENTLEMEN:

The problem of taking care of the surplus production from the United States is becoming acute and requires further solution, or alternatively

[1] Italics added.

we will have an economic situation arising that will be a disaster to all the Associated Governments.

In further amplification of the letter which I addressed today to . . . [all Food Ministers] on this whole subject, I would like to point out the pork product situation as a case in point.

The original British program under war conditions called for an import, according to the various programs, of somewhere in the neighborhood of 50,000 or 60,000 tons (100,000,000 or 120,000,000 pounds) a month of pork products. . . . The producing conditions in the United States were adjusted to this originally and from the necessity of advance manufacture, preparations were made by the American packers to supply the particular cuts required by the British public. As you are aware, this curing has to be started 60 days in advance. The [agreement as to the] program of over 400,000 tons (800,000,000 pounds) of these products for January–March was repeated and established as late as December 15 and confirmed to our Washington office.

On the faith of these programs the packers were assured by the Food Administration that they should go ahead and make the necessary provisions, and they state that this advance curing was also confirmed by your representative.

I am advised from Washington that they now find themselves with some 45,000 tons (90,000,000 pounds) of Cumberland cuts and some 30,000 tons (60,000,000 pounds) of Wiltshire cuts in hand, ready for delivery in January . . . [which are not marketable elsewhere].

. . . [We have no intention of asking] the British Government or the British public to take a product which they cannot consume, and we are extremely anxious to come to some adjustment in the matter which will protect both sides. I cannot but feel that there would be the same desire on your part to meet the changed conditions produced by the war [and Armistice] situation that there has been on our part to adjust supplies to the Allies' every need, and I would indeed be glad to know if you cannot suggest some further solution to this matter.

HERBERT HOOVER

On the same day (January 2), I telegraphed our New York office as follows:

Washington informs me that Pearson [the head of the Allied Purchasing Organization in New York] ordered packers to put down English cut, and upon his representation they have prepared 92 million pounds

Wiltshires and 72 million pounds Cumberlands for January shipment. Please ask what they propose to do about it.

HOOVER

Our representative was unable to get a reply from the Allied offices in New York. The American packers' representative in London confirmed that the blockade had been re-established on the Neutrals and that supplies en route and under contracts could not be delivered.

We were not without some power. To keep up the courage of the packers, we ordered the Grain Corporation and the Belgian Relief Commission to relieve the warehouse strain by purchasing a total of 100,000,000 pounds of pork and dairy products for immediate shipment to Europe, stating that we would name the destinations for the ships later on.

We then went into session with Admiral Benson, the commander of our fleets in Europe. I asked him if the Allies had any right to stop ships flying the American flag and carrying food to people dying of starvation in the liberated countries or foodstuffs previously contracted to Neutrals. Being a rough-hewn sailor, the Admiral replied: "Not as long as there is a ship left in our fleet." I suggested that he tell this to the Allied admirals. He relished his mission. Upon his assurance, we informed our Allied colleagues that the American-flag ships, some of which were already discharging their cargoes in Baltic and Adriatic ports for the acute starvation areas, would continue relief on a larger scale.

We also took these matters up with Henry Robinson, an old friend, who was the American Shipping Board representative in Europe. His indignation having risen to the level of mine, he assured me that adequate American-flag shipping would be made available to us to relieve any strain.

Having no reply from the British Food Minister, I inquired of Sir John Beale, British food representative in Paris, what he knew about the cancellations. He confirmed them but now gave as the reason that the American Treasury had notified the British Treasury that there would be no more credits to finance food purchases in the United States.

I at once inquired of Norman H. Davis, our Treasury representative in Paris, if this were true. Davis informed me that it was not. He stated that the British had an unexpended credit of more than $200,000,000 available for food purchases on January 1 and had made no application for further credits.[2]

On my informing Beale of this fact, he shifted to the statement that the British were overstocked with meat and fat products, had no further needs, and could get grain much cheaper from the Southern Hemisphere. We knew every item of their stocks. They had laid in a supply of pork products for some months before the Armistice as a protection against war contingencies. Although they had repeatedly reconditioned these commodities, many of these pre-Armistice stocks were inedible.

Our next action was to go into session, on January 3, with Ernest Vilgrain, Food Minister of France, and Silvio Crespi, Food Minister of Italy, both of whom were in Paris. I called their attention to my letter of January 2, asked if the cancellations by their representatives had been made because they did not need the food ordered from the United States the day before the cancellations, and asked if they needed any future shipments. I informed them that if this were the case, it would be my duty instantly to notify our Treasury representative in Paris to cancel all agreements for advances to them for food purchases—present and future. I added that if they did not need the food, I would divert it to the Neutrals and the starving areas in Central and Eastern Europe via American-flag ships under the protection of the U.S. Navy.

At once Vilgrain and Crespi protested that they had to have supplies, that they had no funds with which to buy from the distant markets, and that they had not realized the implications of the London action. They requested us to restore their programs, made with Dr. Durand the day before the cancellations, directly by our office in Paris instead of through the Allied Purchasing Commission. Crespi asked me if we could increase the supply of meats, fats, and dairy products to Italy beyond the December 30 requests because the Inter-Allied Food Council had held the supply below the actual

[2] This was confirmed by a letter from Secretary of the Treasury Glass to the Food Administration in Washington on January 29, 1919.

needs of the people. He also informed me that since the Italian Navy was enforcing the blockade in the Mediterranean, they would protect the discharging of our cargoes in the Mediterranean ports.

With these positions established, I wrote the British Food Ministry on January 8, challenging the entire conduct of the Inter-Allied Food and Blockade Councils:

GENTLEMEN:

I am advised . . . from Washington that they have been notified by . . . [the Allied Purchasing Executive that they] have been instructed by cable to cancel entire . . . [meats, fats, and dairy products programs] for January, February, March on behalf of [all the] Allied Governments. I am informed by the French and Italian Governments that this is not the case and that their orders are for . . . [200,000,000 pounds] for January delivery. I would also be glad to know if an order is being given by the British Government for 12,000 tons [24,000,000 pounds] in replacement [as agreed] of resales to Holland. I desire again to call attention to the fact that the refusal of the British authorities to accept the Wiltshire and Cumberland cuts prepared in accordance with [your own specifications] . . . for January, February delivery cannot but precipitate a situation which will do the most infinite damage.

HERBERT HOOVER

When the President returned from his speaking tour of Italy and England, he asked for a memorandum to lay before the Allied Prime Ministers. I gave it to him, describing all the counteractions we had taken.

Because our guarantees on pork and dairy products extended over the three months until the end of March, I complete the story here —although it overlaps in time with other important chapters.

Amid these discussions, Secretary of the Treasury Carter Glass entered the food scene. The correspondence by cable and letter is long and tedious.[3] The sum of it was that while he did not refuse more credits to the Allies for food purchases from the United States, he did say that the British had resources for financing these purchases themselves.

[3] This is available in the National Archives and in the Hoover Institution on War, Revolution, and Peace.

Secretary Glass held the view that we should remove our domestic food controls and allow prices to seek their natural levels. We pointed out that prices could not stabilize themselves as long as the whole Allied and Neutral buying was controlled by the various Allied purchasing agencies. We also pointed out our obligations to the farmers—to maintain their prices for certain periods, varying with the commodity. To this he replied that we should go to the Congress for appropriations to compensate the farmers. We pointed out that such compensation would have to be paid to more than fifteen million individuals and that the cost would be far greater than maintaining present guarantees.

However, Secretary Glass was a persistent official. On February 18, 1919, under his leadership, the Cabinet proposed a resolution to remove all controls within the United States and telegraphed it to the President in Paris. It recommended that the Congress be asked for an appropriation to indemnify all persons against losses. The President asked my advice. I wrote him on February 24, 1919:

DEAR MR. PRESIDENT:

It is my understanding of the suggestion of the Cabinet, that Congress should undertake the compensation of all those who become losers from the alteration of Congressional or moral guaranties. In order to do this, Congress would have to make provision in advance for liquidating payment to probably 15,000,000 individuals in the United States. Unless this advance provision were made, there would ensue the most disastrous financial collapse. Furthermore, taking a world view over the next four months, while some drop in prices might follow removal of control, the world situation . . . is such that even higher prices than the present might rule.

HERBERT HOOVER

The President agreed with me. No action was taken.

BACK TO THE FOOD SITUATION

During January and February, there were many sleepless nights for the leaders in the Food Administration. We were not only carrying the load of relief to Belgium and the North of France and using all energy to save the people in sixteen liberated countries, but we were also worrying about the consequences of failure to meet the guarantees to the American farmers and the possibility of financial calamity in the United States.

Added to our other troubles during January and February, the fifty packing establishments in the United States were in a state of jitters; they had a right to be, since they had invested hundreds of millions of dollars in the good faith and ability of the Food Administration. On at least three occasions, the packers warned our Washington office that they could not go on buying animals at our agreed prices. At each such critical moment, Mr. Snyder, the head of our Meats and Fats Division, and Governor Stuart of our Agricultural Advisory Committee met with the packers committees. We were at all times supported by Thomas E. Wilson, the chairman of the packers committee, whose arguments were interspersed with many kind words for our efforts. His view was that the packers could not be worse off if present prices continued and that the time would come when the world would empty its warehouses.

Finally, to resolve any doubt of meeting the guarantees to farmers and processors of pork and dairy products, I directed the Belgian Relief to buy and ship another fifty million pounds of these products —which, if necessary, we could later sell to the starving Germans. I also directed the Grain Corporation to buy any further amounts necessary to hold the guarantees and to ship such products for storage in Antwerp, Rotterdam, and Copenhagen. The packers' anxieties were thus lessened.

As will appear in a later chapter, we Americans, with the support of President Wilson, had carried on a continuous protest against the Allies' food blockade of Germany and the other former enemy countries. However it was not until March 12, 1919, by an agreement in Brussels, that the food blockade was finally lifted. At this time the Food Administration had on order, in transit, and in storage in these ports more than 300,000,000 pounds of pork and dairy products. When the food blockade was relaxed, we poured these supplies into Germany from every port.

March 30, 1919, being the date when our guarantees on pork products expired, we gladly announced that this operation was over. As I had anticipated, the world shortage caused prices to rise above those fixed by the guarantees. Within a few days the price of hogs at Chicago rose to $21.50 from our controlled level of $17.50.

Our guarantees of prices to the farmers on dairy products, cottonseed oil, rice, and beans extended to the spring of 1919. Problems concerning these commodities after the relaxation of the blockade in March, 1919, were easily solved by our shipment of supplies to the liberated and enemy countries.[4]

The holders of the dammed-back supplies in the Far East and the Southern Hemisphere were not unaware of the world shortage and quickly advanced their prices above our Food Administration–controlled levels. And the British asked us to restore their contract for 100,000,000 bushels of wheat, which they had canceled. We did so.

I wish to make clear that this discussion of our troubles with the British bureaucracies is not a charge against the high-minded men of the British Cabinet. It is merely a record of men in a bureaucracy gone wild with ideas of dictating the economic shape of the world. The British were absorbed in the stupendous problems of demobilization, unemployment, and peacemaking. As will be seen in Chapter 36, when Prime Minister Lloyd George became aware, on March 7, of his Cabinet's actions, he abruptly shifted certain men from the scene and placed Lord Robert Cecil in charge of British participation in relief and reconstruction. From that time on, we and the British enjoyed full co-operation.

THANKS FROM THE AMERICAN FARMERS

In the midst of our troubles I received the following letter from Governor Henry C. Stuart, Chairman of our Agricultural Advisory

[4] To those interested in further details, I recommend the following:
Frank M. Surface, *The Grain Trade During the World War* (New York, The Macmillan Company, 1928) and *American Pork Production in the World War* (New York, A. W. Shaw Company, 1926) and Bane and Lutz, *op. cit.*

Committee, which represented every branch of agriculture at the farmers' level:

March 10, 1919

MY DEAR MR. HOOVER:

. . . It is unnecessary, if indeed it is not impossible, for me to add anything by way of appreciation of your administration to what has already been conveyed to you through the medium of a resolution unanimously passed by the Live Stock Sub-Committee. . . . I wish, however, for myself and in behalf of the entire Committee to renew and emphasize our endorsement individually and collectively of your administration and of your splendid achievements as a most important factor in winning the war and now a factor of world-wide importance in the adjustment of the most acute of all the post war problems. I feel that I represent the sentiment of the Committee when I say that we feel ourselves greatly honored in having been co-workers with you in the great crisis through which we have passed, and now [that] our connection with your work has ceased we unite in an abiding [admiration]. . . .

H. C. STUART, Chairman

CHAPTER 35

THE BATTLE OVER THE BLOCKADE

The Allied blockade of Europe, from the Armistice to the signing of peace in June, 1919, was a constant plague to relief and reconstruction. Because of its stifling effect to every nation on the Continent, I deal with the blockade at this point.

The Allies held grimly to the blockade until peace had been made. Their primary reasons were to keep it for use as an instrument to force political and peace policies. This was nonsense as far as peace terms with the former enemy states were concerned. The enemy armies had been demobilized and disarmed under the Wilson stipulation and the Allies and "Associated Powers" still had some six million armed men on the Continent, ready for immediate call to action.

Another reason for the Allies' attitude was that they wanted to hold the blockade against imports of raw materials to Europe and exports of goods generally until they could recover their own trade.

Still another reason for the Allied attitude of holding the blockade, even on food, was that the Allied people had suffered irreparable wrongs, which they wanted righted before any aid was extended to the former enemy.

The President and the War Council in Washington held the view that the blockade generally should be relaxed and especially that the food blockade should be taken down at once.

There was a moral obligation upon the Allies and the United States to relax the food blockade on Germany.

The Armistice agreement, in Article XXVI, provided:

> The existing blockade conditions set up by the Allied and Associated Powers are to remain unchanged. The Allies and the United States contemplate the provisioning of Germany during the armistice as shall be found necessary.

This last sentence was not as strong as we Americans wished at the time, but in view of the known condition of starvation of the German people, it nevertheless constituted an obligation of immediate action.

My views on the blockade, indicated in an address to the state food administrators in Washington the day after the Armistice, did not fit the Allied state of mind. I said:

> . . . [This] is a problem of relaxing the watertight blockade, which continues through the armistice, sufficiently so that they may secure for themselves the bare necessities that will give stable government. Unless anarchy can be put down and stability of government can be obtained in these enemy states, there will be nobody to make peace with and nobody to pay the bill. . . .

I repeated this to the press.[1] The British press was most critical. When I arrived in London on November 21, I found the Allies stirred up by the American attitude. Sir John Beale of the British Food Ministry called upon me the day I arrived and urged that I not discuss the food blockade on Germany publicly any more, as they were opposed to relaxing it "until Germans learn a few things."

Soon after my arrival in Europe, I sent, through our military representative in Berlin, a request to the Ebert Government for a statement of Germany's economic and food situation. It arrived promptly in typically detailed German fashion. During the war, I had had reason to doubt many official German statements. Therefore I sent Dr. Vernon Kellogg, Dr. Alonzo Taylor, and Colonel W. B. Ryan, all of whom spoke German, to check this report on the spot.

[1] *The Christian Science Monitor,* November 18, 1918.

The first two men not only were food experts but, prior to our entry into the war, had frequently visited Germany on various food missions. Colonel Ryan was a competent observer of public phenomena. Investigations confirmed the statement of the new republican German Government.

This mission reported to me that as a result of the usual wartime diversion of manpower and industry, German grain production had plummeted from 30,200,000 tons prewar to 16,600,000 tons at the harvest of 1918. The bread ration of mixed grain had fallen to less than 1,800 calories per day per person, and even that could not continue without large imports. The meats and fats situation was even worse. The production of this category of food, about 3,300,000 tons a year before the war, had dropped to less than 1,000,000 tons. The population as a whole was 20 per cent under normal weight. The death rate in Berlin had increased annually from 13.5 per thousand prewar to 19.6 per thousand. The birth rate had decreased annually from 6.1 per thousand prewar to less than 1.0 per thousand. The mission estimated that the mortality of children had increased by 30 per cent and that of adults over seventy by 33 per cent; that a third of the children were suffering from malnutrition diseases; that crime was rampant; that demobilized soldiers were plundering the farms; that industry had almost stopped at the Armistice; and that unemployment was enormous. Railway car loadings had dropped to a bare 40 per cent of prewar normal. The country was short of coal and devoid of imported raw materials.

Worse still, our men reported that actual starvation had beset the lower-income groups in the cities, and that there were eight hundred deaths daily in North Germany from starvation or diseases caused by undernourishment. They reported that the food shortage was worse after the Armistice than before. The Germans could no longer secure supplies from the countries which they had occupied. Political disturbances and governmental breakdowns played hob with transportation. The weak governments could not keep the farmers from hoarding or hold in check the bootlegging of food to those who could pay. Rationing was breaking down.

Our mission also reported that the new Ebert Government was

weakening under Spartacist (Communist) uprisings, that machine guns were being fired in the streets, and that there was real danger of the Government's being overthrown by either the old military or by the Spartacists, who were playing on the emotions of the hungry.

In view of these findings, all of my American colleagues in Paris believed that continuation of the food blockade was a crime against women and children and a blot on Western civilization. No one who reads the records of those times will ever charge that crime against America. We have had to suffer from it.

In Chapter 34, I have related the minor relaxation of the food blockade on Germany with the Neutrals and the liberated countries which we secured from the Allies on December 24, 1918, and that it was reversed six days later, on December 31. Prior to the reversal, Colonel House and Secretary Lansing had requested me to prepare a memorandum on the food-blockade question. General Bliss, who had not been present at that time, wrote to me:

December 30, 1918

MY DEAR MR. HOOVER:

. . . I believe that it will rally the sentiment of the world in general to us if we now demand in the name of good business and in the name of common humanity a relaxation in the blockade against the Central Powers. I propose that we make a strong and direct appeal to get the President to formulate and push such a demand.

TASKER H. BLISS

I prepared the memorandum and handed it to the President on January 1:

1. In a broad sense, there is no longer any military or naval value attaching to the maintenance of the [food] blockade of enemy territory. Its retention has political value in the right settlement of ultimate political issues, but its principal incidence . . . require . . . [other] consideration. . . .

2. The problem of sustaining life and maintaining order in enemy territories revolves primarily around the problem of food supplies and secondarily around the gradual re-establishment of commercial life.

3. The . . . provision of foodstuffs in the volumes necessary entails the provision of financial resources . . . [which] must be drawn: (a) internally from these territories in the form of exchange securities negotiable throughout the world, or gold [Germany had about $600,000,000 in gold]; (b) by the provision of these food stuffs . . . [by loans] of the associated governments; (c) by the export of commodities and the consequent liberation of action to some degree of shipping and credit and communications. Even the first alternative of the use of internal resources is now entirely impracticable under the effective financial blockade. . . . The second alternative, of advances [loans to Germany] by Associated Governments, is impossible to contemplate.

4. It becomes necessary, therefore, to at once consider some modification of the present blockade measures that will establish production and exports with which to pay for food and some other imports at as early a date as possible.

. . . The first step suggested is provision that . . . [they] may trade to some defined extent with surrounding Neutrals and the Western Hemisphere.

5. Not only does this step forward in the restoration of commercial life in enemy territory imply a relaxation in absolute blockade measures . . . and it might be made coincident with the surrender to the Allies of a certain portion of enemy shipping for purposes of transportation of food to [them and the] liberated regions and for the return of the troops to the United States.

6. A relaxation of commodity, finance, shipping, and corresponding blockades is the only measure that will protect the situation against the evils which may arise from actual hunger. Even a partial revival of the ordinary activities of life within enemy territories will tend powerfully . . . [to check rising] Bolshevism and [bring] the stabilizing of governments.

7. It is not proposed that these measures proceed to the abandonment of [the whole] blockade prior to peace, but that certain agreed tonnage, agreed commodities for import and export; agreed avenues of credit operations and agreed channels of trade and communication . . . .

HERBERT HOOVER

To this statement the President added the following in his own handwriting:

To these conclusions I entirely agree.

W.W.

As a step toward compliance with the Armistice promise to Germany, I, as Director General of Relief, proposed at a meeting of the Supreme Council of Supply and Relief on January 12 that, subject to their handing over the refugee ships, the Germans should have an installment of 200,000 tons of breadstuffs and 70,000 tons of fats, with additional supplies later.

THE PRESIDENT TAKES A HAND

The President arranged for a hearing on the food blockade on enemy countries before the Big Four on January 13, 1919.

At the meeting, I sat in a small chair behind the President's right shoulder. The Allied officials likewise sat in chairs behind their Prime Ministers. In order to coach our champions in the debate, we had to poke our heads out from behind. This coaching of debate by the bobbing of heads was a little difficult.

The President made a strong presentation. The minutes of the meeting state:

President Wilson expressed the view that any further delay in this matter might be fatal as it meant the dissolution of order and government. They were discussing an absolute and immediate necessity. So long as hunger continued to gnaw, the foundations of government would continue to crumble. Therefore, food should be supplied immediately, not only to our friends but also to those parts of the world where it was to our interest to maintain a stable government. He thought they were bound to accept the concerted counsel of a number of men who had been devoting the whole of their time and thought to this question. He trusted the French Finance Department would withdraw their objection [to the use of German gold] as they were faced with the great problems of Bolshevism and the forces of dissolution which now threatened society.

M. Klotz [the French Finance Minister] said he would gladly meet President Wilson's wishes. But it was not altogether a question of food supplies. They were all fully agreed as to the necessity of feeding the Germans but he would appeal to President Wilson to consider also the question of Justice. He was quite willing to admit that German foreign securities should be earmarked for this purpose. But they were creating a new German debt. There were other Germans debts which were just as honorable and noble. Therefore, he would ask, as a matter of justice, why Germany should pay for food in preference to paying off debts incurred for the restoration and for the reparation of damage committed elsewhere. Why should exclusive priority be given to such a debt? As a solution of the difficulty he would agree that payment for this food should be made in foreign securities and values. But he would add that *"these assets shall be pooled and distribution shall be made by the Allies taking into account such privileged claims as the Peace Conference would admit."*

He would merely point out that it was not a question of food supply, it was purely a financial question and no delay need therefore occur in the supply of food.

President Wilson urged that, unless a solution for the immediate situation could be found, none of these debts would be paid. The want of food would lead to a crash in Germany. The great point, however, was this, that the Associated Governments have no money to pay for these supplies. Therefore Germany must pay for them, but if they were not paid for and supplied immediately there would be no Germany to pay anything.

An argument over details continued, but Klotz finally agreed, although he insisted that the method of payment be considered further.

M. Pichon [the French Minister of Foreign Affairs] said he thought that an agreement had now been reached. Everyone was agreed that payment had to be made. The Proposal could therefore be accepted. But the Conference could reconsider the question later on, should they wish to do so.

McCormick and I thought that at least a crack in the food blockade of Germany had been opened. Not so. The French insisted upon an Allied meeting with the Germans to determine the method by which the Germans could pay for this first installment of food. This conference took place at Trèves from January 15 to 17. My organization was represented by Howard Heinz. The following memorandum was agreed upon by the Allied and German representatives:

At Conference held at Trèves, on the 15th and 16th days of January 1919, the Delegates of the Associated Governments having referred to the needs of Europe for the importation of foodstuffs and the urgent necessity of increasing the total world tonnage from which the tonnage required for such supplies can be drawn, stated that it must be regarded as a condition precedent to the importation into Germany of a certain quantity of food that German mercantile shipping should be placed at the disposal of the Associated Governments. On the 16th day of January 1919 the clause appended to this document was inserted in the terms of the armistice renewed on that date. After further conference the German delegates accepted the following terms:

I. The whole of the German merchant fleet (including all passenger and cargo vessels other than those excepted by a commission which shall be set up by the Associated Governments) to be placed immediately at the disposal of the Associated Governments with a view to increasing the world tonnage from which the tonnage required for the supply of foodstuffs to Europe including Germany can be drawn.

The Associated Governments will take over the Administration of this fleet through the agency of the Allied Maritime Transport Council or of any other organ which they may create or designate for this purpose. . . .

Paragraphs II, III, IV, V, VI, VII, VIII, and IX related to details of the transfer of German ships.

Paragraph X stated:

Matters still outstanding of the nature referred to in the concluding paragraph of the armistice clause hereto annexed [revictualling Germany] shall be dealt with at a further conference to be convened as soon as practicable the Armistice Commission at Spa being used as the channel of communication.

The Delegates of the Associated Governments thereupon informed the German delegates that in the first instance the importation of the following supply of food would be permitted, namely: 200,000 tons of breadstuffs and cereals and 70,000 tons of . . . [fat] products, (but a portion of the foodstuffs to be prescribed by the Associated Governments may be replaced by condensed milk) in such manner and from such places as the Associated Governments may prescribe, and that the question of any further supplies of food would be referred to the Supreme War Council for decision.

The German Delegates agreed that the German Government shall from time to time arrange payment in a manner to be approved by the Associated Governments for such food as the German Government may import by permission of the Associated Governments.

Signed at Trèves, the 17th day of January, 1919 by the delegates of the Associated Governments

HURLEY	SALTER
ATTOLICO	VIBERT
CHARPENTIER	SIR JOHN BEALE
HEINZ	

Signed . . . by the Delegate of the German Government VANSELOW
Capt. für See und Mitglied der Waffenstillstandskommission

We again hoped that this would open a crack in the food blockade. Again not so. The French continued to impede every proposed method of German payment for supplies.

Although this obstruction was exasperating and destructive to the possibilities of ultimate world peace, I often wondered what the attitudes of the American people would be had they been invaded three times by a powerful, ruthless, destroying, plundering enemy. Would our people have been willing to make sacrifices in the hope that our invaders could be brought to co-operate in building peace for mankind? However, in this case, it seemed to us Americans that the course was clear—that we had to build on the one hope of support to the new Republic of Germany. The only alternative was Carthage.

This long debate and negotiation had another disagreeable aspect. The Americans, advocating the feeding of the Germans, were acting from sympathy with the suffering of a misled people and from common-sense statesmanship—not from any affection for the German militarists, who had been guilty of great brutalities. It wounded us deeply that the French should assert that we were pro-German or that we would promote German interests ahead of French.

On January 22, 1919, I offered the Supreme Council on Supply and Relief a suggestion concerning partial finance: call upon German nationals abroad, particularly in South America, to assist. The Germans in Germany held large investments in those countries, and food could be provided from these assets. According to the minutes, I said:

. . . If the Germans . . . could be induced to exert the full pressure of their credits in the Argentine and Brazil, it would not seem impossible for them to provide for the purchase of 200,000 tons of cereals [and 70,000 tons of fats] a month. Provision of moneys from Germany in this connection would then be limited to the cost of transportation to German ports.

The United States Government has certainly no wish to sell foodstuffs to Germany if they can be provided from any other quarter, and the above arrangement would be entirely satisfactory to it.

This idea was rejected by the Allied members of the Supreme War Council, who insisted that these assets should be held for reparations.

Since we were getting nowhere in our efforts, McCormick and I suggested three resolutions which the President might introduce to the Big Four. I also suggested to the President that if we exposed in the press the consequences of the delays, it might help. The essential parts of my letter to him were:

PARIS, 1 February 1919

MY DEAR MR. PRESIDENT:

Mr. McCormick will be sending to you the three resolutions which we are most anxious should be gotten through the Supreme War Council at its meeting on Monday or Tuesday. As you know, I have been advocating these points now for nearly two months . . . and I see no hope of attaining any such results except through strong intervention on your part.

. . . The French obstruct the notion of neutrals trading with Germany, although it would alleviate both the financial problem and distress. We have no justification in humanity or politics in debarring neutrals from buying all the food they wish for their own consumption now that we have ample supplies. The blockade on Mediterranean countries has no purpose whatever, except to serve detailed selfish interests. All these measures impose a much larger burden on relief than would be necessary if all these people could produce and trade . . . [commodities for] food.

There is so much obstruction that I despair even getting it past the Supreme War Council unless . . . world opinion is brought to bear, and I would like to have you advise me whether you do not think it is desirable for me to disclose the nature of these resolutions that you will propose, to the press . . . and I am sure there will be a reaction from the whole neutral world and a reaction from the United States in your support. . . .

HERBERT HOOVER

The President replied:

PARIS, 3 February 1919

MY DEAR MR. HOOVER:

I dare say it would be serviceable to discuss these matters with the press as you suggest, but how can you when the French press is so carefully censored by the Government that everything is excluded which they do not wish to have published. You could probably get it in the English and the American papers but could you get publicity for it anywhere else? . . .

WOODROW WILSON

On February 3, Mr. McCormick and I sent the draft of the three resolutions which we hoped the President would introduce to the Big Four. In a letter to the President, which McCormick approved, I explained our reasons for these resolutions:

PARIS, 4 February 1919

DEAR MR. PRESIDENT:

. . . I enclose herewith the resolution drafted by Mr. McCormick and myself, which we are anxious to get through the Supreme War Council. It has three main purposes:

FIRST. There is no right in the law of God or man that we should longer continue to starve neutrals now that we have a surplus of food. That is the object of the first part of the first resolution.

SECOND. The French, by obstruction of every financial measure that we can propose . . . [for] the feeding of Germany in the attempt to compel us to loan money to Germany for this purpose, have defeated every step so far for getting them the food which we have been promising for three months. The object of the second part of the first resolution and of the second resolution is to at least find some channel by which the Germans can help themselves by trade with neutrals and South America.

THIRD. The object of the third resolution is to allow the people bordering on the Mediterranean to get into production and trade with all their might and by so doing not only revive their commercial life but also to a large degree supply themselves with food and other commodities and thus take a large part of the burden of relief from the back of our government.

There is no possibility that with all the restrictions on trade taken off that the old Empire of Austria could ever resurrect any military importance. At the present time, we are actually furnishing food to points in [old] Austria at the expense of governments that could be taken care of by private individuals if they could revive their foreign credits. . . .

I have worked consistently since arriving in Europe on the 25th day of November to secure these . . . [objectives] and I have to confess that although they have been accepted in principle in first one department and one government after another, they are constantly defeated by one bureaucratic and special self-interest after another . . . I can assure you that the blockade against neutrals and the . . . [liberated countries] is being used today for purely economic ends. . . .

I realize that there is still some political importance in maintaining the blockade against Germany within certain limits, but it does not apply to the rest of Europe. I can see no hope of securing the removal of these restrictions except by a direct and strong intervention through yourself and mandatory orders given by the Supreme War Council.

. . . I am confident that no action is possible except of a mandatory character from the top.

HERBERT HOOVER

The President got nowhere in trying to persuade the Allied Premiers to adopt these resolutions. After many delays, meetings of Allied delegates with the German delegation were held at Spa, Belgium, on February 6, 7, and 8 to examine German food requirements generally and to work out the financing of them. Colonel J. A. Logan, Jr., represented my organization. The Germans asked for 400,000 tons of breadstuffs and 100,000 tons of fats monthly for seven months—until the next harvest, in August. Nothing came of that meeting either.

The Allies were occupying the left bank of the Rhine. Marshal Foch now delivered us an idea and a blast. His memorandum, insofar as it involved food, was:

> . . . in the course of the conferences which have just taken place at Spa, the supplying of Germany has only been considered as a whole.
>
> Speaking from an entirely military point of view, I have the honor to draw your attention . . . [to] the absolute necessity of considering the supplying of the left bank of the Rhine and its bridge heads independently from the supplying of the right bank for the following reasons—
>
> As I have already written to the Minister of Foreign Affairs, our chief arm at present is the blockade. . . .
>
> If we are obliged to use this arm, the supplying of the right bank of the Rhine must be independent of the supplying of the left bank, the supplying of which we must undertake in any event since we occupy it. . . .
>
> Under these circumstances, I request that a decision be taken immediately to arrange for the immediate supply of the left bank of the Rhine and of its bridge heads independently of the right bank.
>
> FOCH

This proposal was, in fact, a step toward a separatist movement within the German nation. I refused to comply unless ordered to do so by the Big Four.

McCormick's diary, under the date of February 11, contains the following illuminating note on a meeting of his Blockade Council:

> . . . Long, windy meeting afterwards on blockade relaxation. French seem to block every effort in this direction. . . .

At French and British demand, still another conference was held with the German delegates at Trèves on February 14, 15, and 16 to consider food, finance, and ships. McCormick's and my organization was represented by Mr. H. W. Harris of McCormick's staff. The United States Treasury was represented by Mr. Norman H. Davis. An agreement with regard to the Germans' paying for the initial 270,000 tons of food (part in gold and part in other foreign exchange) was reached. However, the French financial representative disagreed on the using of German gold for any further supplies and opposed all ideas of opening any trade between the Neutrals and Germany. Nothing came of this conference—except more delays.

I describe elsewhere the dissolution of the Supreme Council of Supply and Relief and the creation of the Supreme Economic Council. The first meeting of this Council took place on February 17. At this meeting, McCormick and I urged action concerning the blockade. The following is from the minutes:

> . . . The American Delegates reported that at the last meeting of the Superior Blockade Council the question of increasing the rations of the Northern Neutrals had been discussed, that it had been decided to submit to the Supreme Economic Council the question of increasing the rations of each country to their normal pre-war consumption, as the Superior Blockade Council had not been able to come to a decision owing to a question of finance.
>
> They further stated that the American Government was of the opinion that the blockade on those countries should be removed entirely on the understanding that the necessary guarantees regarding re-export to enemy countries were obtained.
>
> *It was agreed* that the matter should be discussed in detail at the next meeting of the Council.

Inasmuch as a recitation of the arguments, resolutions, counter-resolutions, speeches, and reports would take volumes, I can better illuminate this battle by quoting from McCormick's diary:

> FEBRUARY 17
>
> . . . Attended first meeting Supreme Economic Council at Ministry of Commerce. Clémentel presided. Klotz, Loucheur for France, Lord Robert Cecil, Sir John Beale for Great Britain, Crespi and Ciesa for Italy, Hoover, Norman Davis and self for the United States. Organized and agreed to let Inter-Allied organization remain intact. Discussed relaxation of blockade; did not get anywhere. Crespi said would not agree to any relaxation unless Great Britain or United States helped finance food for his distressed country. Meeting getting hot over Crespi's statement so Lord Robert adjourned meeting. Lord Robert very angry at Crespi's hold up game. . . .

On February 25, I again raised the blockade question in the Supreme Economic Council, saying, according to the minutes:

. . . I wish to point out with all emphasis the urgency of this situation. Foodstuffs to the amount of approximately $80,000,000 monthly must be delivered into Germany beginning with the first of March, and shipments must continue until one month after the blockade against Germany is withdrawn. It appears that the solution of the German financial problem could be reached either by (*a*) releasing the blockade; (*b*) allowing Germany to part with her liquid assets to the value of $80,000,000 a month; or (*c*) for the Associated Governments to consent to finance Germany to this amount for food.

The provision of some 30,000 tons of fats by the United Kingdom for gold and neutral currency is in progress, but, as will be seen by the above mentioned reports, this is but a very small portion of the absolute necessities.

I understand the Swedish Government offers to supply the German Government 50,000 tons of flour under their own arrangements, the Swedish Government making conditions to re-import to Sweden a similar quantity, which contract we should be able to effect. We strongly recommend that this should be done.

McCormick recorded:

MARCH 1

. . . Meeting of Supreme Economic Council at Minister of Commerce office. Trying to put through financial plan for permitting Germany to buy food. French blocked every plan. England and America dread consequences, as we seem living on a volcano. Two hundred million people not producing in the world and many hungry. . . .

The situation in Germany continued to degenerate. The Communists (Spartacists) were making steady progress by seizing control of several cities. The feeble German Republic was threatened with collapse.

On March 1, McCormick and I discussed the whole blockade problem with Lord Robert Cecil in Paris. We explained that because of the situation created by the Allies—reimposing the blockade on December 31 and canceling their contracts with the United States Food Administration—they had jeopardized the whole economy of the United States. We went on to say that in order to meet the situation we were compelled to store huge quantities of perishable food in all the Neutral ports around Germany—to await the inevitable opening of the blockade. We stated that the position in which we were placed was absolutely intolerable. I suggested that I draft some kind of new program, to which Lord Robert readily agreed. McCormick's diary says:

MARCH 3 (MONDAY)—
. . . Attended meeting of the Supreme Economic Council to prepare for Marshal Foch instructions on terms for feeding Germans. Agreed upon the terms of draft to be submitted at afternoon meeting. U.S. advisers lunched together to discuss details of same. Went to session again at 2:30. As usual, French again balked. Same old trouble, apparently political and financial. Regret French so shifty—hot meeting. Lord Robert got after Clémentel on a statement which looked like a threat. Finally agreed and delegates expected to leave tonight for Spa to meet German representatives. Hope they succeed as I believe we are facing another revolution in Germany and Bolshevism if they don't get food. . . .

At the insistence of the British and French, there was a further meeting of Allied and German delegates at Spa on March 5 under the chairmanship of British Admiral Hope. American delegates were also present. The gist of the meeting was that the Germans now refused to give up their merchant ships for any temporary food supply and demanded an assurance of continued supply for the balance of the harvest year (until August). They stated that rather than be coerced every month by the threat of starvation and lose their ships, too, they might just as well go Communist at once and end it all.

Admiral Hope's report of the meeting concluded with a quotation from the letter of German delegate Herr von Braun:

"I have the honour to report that a telephone communication I have just had with Weimar has once more asserted to me that they cannot alter their standpoint, because they cannot consider themselves justified to put the German mercantile marine fleet at the moment under the control of the Associated Governments without the food supply of Germany being assured to her at the same time. . . .

"If this proposed solution is not at the moment practicable for the representatives of the Associated Governments, the re-assembly of the conference would serve no useful purpose. . . ."

When Admiral Hope reported to Paris, I did not hesitate to state that the Germans were right in contending for a reasonable assurance of food until the harvest in consideration of their ships.

The state of affairs at this time is indicated by an entry from McCormick's diary under the date of March 5:

> . . . French still blocking food deliveries to Germany. Situation there alarming. Cables all show state of revolution. Americans in Germany being attacked. My opinion we are living on top of a volcano; if relief not immediate, bound to have trouble and will affect France. English fully alive to situation and fighting hard with us to better conditions. French agree but don't help and really hinder whenever possible.

On March 5, 1919, I gave Lord Robert Cecil a completed draft of a proposal which we subsequently referred to as an "understanding to end all former understandings." In it I proposed:

(1) That the Big Four take direct action on the entire matter;

(2) The Germans were to turn over all of their ships at once;

(3) They were to be paid a charter rate which was to be applied on payment for food;

(4) We were to assure, until the next harvest, such food monthly as was necessary and world supplies would permit;

(5) The Germans were to pay with any negotiable securities which they might have, and beyond that, they were to pay the balance in gold. Lord Robert approved the proposal and agreed that we devote the next meeting of the Supreme Economic Council (scheduled for two days later) to it.

The Supreme Economic Council met on March 7, with the American delegation comprising McCormick, Davis, Baruch, Robinson, and me. The British contingent was headed by Lord Robert Cecil, the French by M. Clémentel, and the Italian by Signor Crespi. Lord Robert presided. Admiral Hope's report on the meeting of the Allied and German delegates at Spa on the fourth and fifth of March was considered. Cecil said:

. . . Proposals had been made by the American Delegates and by himself and tentative conclusions reached. . . .

M. Clémentel asked Lord Robert Cecil if he could give an outline of the resolutions proposed.

Cecil outlined my proposals and called upon me for some explanation of the American point of view. The minutes, although not complete, record the following statement from me:

1. The food situation in Europe requires the use of the German Mercantile fleet at once.

2. Assurance of regular and limited food to Germany will not affect the political conditions of peace.

3. Germany can only pay . . . [in gold unless] her population can get into production, and export of commodities.

4. Germany will collapse and peace be impossible if such assurance of food and productivity is not immediately given.

I presented the following resolutions:

1. It is agreed that Germany must receive a regular monthly import of food until next harvest for humanitarian reasons and if order and stability of government are to be maintained, peace effected and reparation secured.

2. It is agreed that Germany must place her mercantile fleet in the service if she is to receive food, as this fleet must be used to effect the general provisioning of Europe as well as Germany.

3. It is agreed that Germany must pay for this food. She can pay (*a*) by exporting commodities; (*b*) by neutral credits; (*c*) by other liquid assets [including gold].

4. It is agreed that Germany needs approximately 300,000 tons of food per month. This will require the use of 7–800,000 tons of shipping in constant employment, or say one-third (?) of her total [merchant] tonnage.

5. It is agreed that Germany should be assured:

(*a*) That one-third of the shipping handed over shall be used in transport of food to Germany between now and next harvest;

(*b*) That Germany can export commodities (except [those on] a black list); the proceeds from the sale of such commodities to be used for food purchases;

(*c*) That she can use the outward voyage of the one-third of her shipping for the export of commodities as well as exports to surrounding neutrals and Allies;

(*d*) That she can use such credits as she can set up with neutrals or elsewhere to buy food;

(*e*) That she can convert into food purchases any currency she obtains from sale of commodities;

(*f*) That she can use hire of ships to buy food;

(*g*) In order to give immediate delivery of food before the above plan begins to materialize, part of the first 300,000 tons which Allies or neutrals can provide will be delivered in ratio to ships sent out under the present plan of finance.

The French and Italians objected to many of the points. The minutes reflect a long, desultory, and fruitless discussion. Finally the French delegates proposed the following delaying resolution:

. . . the Associated Governments are prepared to study the matter with German Delegates.

Since there had already been a dozen futile meetings with the Germans, we Americans refused to agree and demanded the adoption of the "understanding to end all former understandings."

CHAPTER 36

A CRACK IS OPENED IN THE FOOD BLOCKADE OF GERMANY

Prime Minister Lloyd George, having been informed of the impasse in the Supreme Economic Council, asked me to come to see him the evening of March 7, 1919. With him when I arrived was General Plumer, Commander of the British Army of Occupation in Germany. Plumer was in a state of emotion rare for a British soldier. He announced to me in tragic tones that Germany had to have food. That was no news to me. What he went on to say, however, was helpful. He declared that the rank and file of his army were sick and discontented and wanted to go home because they could not bear the sight of hordes of skinny and bloated children pawing over the offal from British cantonments. He said that his soldiers were actually depriving themselves to feed these children. Plumer added that the country was going Bolshevist. I supported all of his arguments and brought Lloyd George up to date on the latest Spartacist outbreaks in Hamburg, Munich, and Stettin, stating that machine guns were chattering in the streets of Berlin at that very moment.

After Plumer left, Lloyd George demanded to know why I had not sent food to Germany. He said that I had been appointed to that job and that the Supreme War Council had authorized it on January 13. Not often do I lose my temper, but this was too much. I was weary from constant obstructionism by day and constant work by night. In my explosion, I reviewed my efforts to co-operate with the British and stated that except for Lord Robert Cecil I had had little co-operation since my arrival in Europe. I reviewed the previous relaxation of the blockade on December 24 and the reimposition of it on December 31, as well as the repudiation of all Allied contracts for food with the Food Administration, which, together with the re-enactment of the blockade—even to liberated peoples—would have produced a panic in the United States and the end of all aid to Europe. I stated that we had been able to save the situation by strong action on our part. I stated that in order to protect our farmers and our financial stability I had been compelled to store three hundred million pounds of perishables, which would spoil in a few weeks, in Continental ports or in Belgium. I pointed out that since the Armistice the British Navy had been viciously and senselessly preventing the Germans from fishing in the Baltic. This had been one of their sources of food all during the war, and a ban would increase the burden on overseas supplies. I added a few sizzling remarks about a policy which starved women and children after a nation had surrendered in order to get food for them, and I said that no honest man could read the promises of the Armistice without a blush. I said that the Germans had not been sent a ton of food in the four months since that promise. I recalled that for those four months I had given warnings of the steady advance of the Communists among a hungry people and of the weakening of the new liberal German Government. I expressed the opinion that the Allies would be reduced to nothing better with which to make peace with Germany than the Germans had had with Communist Russia.

Lloyd George was a humane, overworked man. He had been helpful to me on every vital occasion over the previous four years. I immediately regretted this outbreak, apologized, and was about to leave. To my surprise, he mildly inquired if I would deliver "that speech" to the Council of Ten. I said that I would be delighted to do so but that if he agreed with me, it would carry much more weight if it came from him. He made some notes.

When I returned to my rooms and put on paper what I had said, I came to the conclusion that I knew the subject well enough to present it verbally and in softer terms.

President Wilson, in the United States at this time, was not able to attend the March 8 meeting of the Council. The United States was represented by Secretary of State Lansing, Colonel House, General Bliss, McCormick, Baruch, Davis, Robinson, and me. The British were represented by Lloyd George, Lord Cecil, J. M. Keynes, and others of their delegation. The French were represented by Premier Clemenceau, Foreign Minister Pichon, Finance Minister Klotz, Commerce Minister Clémentel, Marshal Foch, and others. The Italians were represented by Baron Sonnino, their Foreign Minister, Crespi, their Minister of Food, and others.

This meeting was a real occasion. The Big Three, together with Secretary Lansing, sat in judgment on a dais at the end of the room, with their various national groups scattered below. Since we feared that we might get emotional, and in any event were regarded as fanatics against the food blockade, McCormick and I, prior to the meeting, arranged for Lord Cecil to present the ideas of the "understanding to end all former understandings." Cecil restated the gist of what we had proposed, with minor changes in the "understanding to end all former understandings."

There ensued a long and heated debate among the British, French, and Italians. The published minutes are wholly inadequate, no doubt because the continuous shift of languages, the interpolations, and the rapid-fire questioning and reply confused the stenographers. But enough remained to describe what took place. Parts of these minutes have been published elsewhere. Not only is a more detailed record of importance to history, but this was a historical turning point, and any account of the relief and reconstruction of Europe demands that the record be given as fully as possible.

French Minister of Finance Klotz objected to certain immaterial matters, but he finally disclosed his real thesis. The French would not lift the blockade unless somebody, not they, would sell Germany food on credit. He charged the British with desertion and the British and Americans with trying to get German gold for food supplies, thus depriving France of her just reparations.

Clémentel, for the French, objected to any continued assurance of food to the Germans until the next harvest. He wanted a terminable, monthly ration and a monthly limit on the amount of gold which could be used by the Germans to pay for food. The minutes go on:

> MARSHAL FOCH held that Clause 3 [of Cecil's proposal] created a somewhat dangerous situation, since the Allies thereby bound themselves to supply food to the Germans until September 1st, unless, as stated in Clause 8, hostilities were renewed. Consequently, that Clause had the effect of disarming the Allies, who would be obliged to start hostilities should any difference arise with Germany, since, as long as the Clause remained, pressure could not be exerted by the fear of withholding food.
>
> MR. LANSING enquired what was the connection between the subject under consideration and the military situation.
>
> M. CLEMENCEAU replied that at the present moment the Allies possessed a method of applying pressure to Germany, without appeal to arms, but if the Clause suggested were accepted, the only method of exerting pressure would be the renewal of hostilities.

I entered the debate at this point. The minutes give a garbled account of my statement. The American stenographer gave me the gist of what I said as follows:

> The cold facts of the situation are: The Germans had been promised food at the Armistice; her women and children were starving when she surrendered; no food had been furnished her in the four months of winter; many of the German ships were in neutral ports and could not be obtained without her cooperation; the amount of gold or securities required were not one per cent of the sums to be levied in the reparations; the United States Congress, in its legislation authorizing loans and gifts to the Allies and liberated countries to supply them with food, had been adamant against any loans or credits to the former enemies; that we [Americans] had already supplied the Allied and liberated states with loans and credits to buy food amounting to ten times the amounts involved in the German transaction; that we could scarcely be charged with a lack of generosity; the morals of these delays were a strain on the Christian faith and civilization; and finally, that the political and social situation in Germany was such that if continued, the peace-making efforts of the Allies would be washed up within another sixty days.

Lloyd George now provided the emotional spark in his eloquent answer to the Foch, Clémentel, and Klotz arguments. The minutes record that he said:

. . . the Preliminary Terms of Peace would shortly be presented to Germany, and if Germany refused to accept those terms, that would put an end to the armistice. But when that happened, the Allies would be quite entitled to decide not to advance into Germany and to exert the necessary pressure by the stoppage of food supplies. Consequently, the only two contingencies when food pressure might be required, had been duly provided for. The Conference was therefore not parting with any potent weapon. On the other hand, he wished to urge with all his might that steps should at once be taken to revictual Germany. The honour of the Allies was involved. Under the terms of the armistice the Allies did imply that they meant to let food into Germany. The Germans had accepted our armistice conditions, which were sufficiently severe, and they had complied with the majority of those conditions. But so far, not a single ton of food had been sent into Germany. . . . [Their] fishing fleet had even been prevented from going out to catch a few herrings. The Allies were now on top, but the memories of starvation might one day turn against them. The Germans were being allowed to starve whilst at the same time hundreds of thousands of tons of food were lying at Rotterdam, waiting to be taken up the waterways into Germany. These incidents constituted far more formidable weapons for use against the Allies than any of the armaments it was sought to limit. The Allies were sowing hatred for the future: they were piling up agony, not for the Germans but for themselves. The British troops were indignant about our refusal to revictual Germany. General Plumer had said that he could not be responsible for his troops if children were allowed to wander about the streets, half starving. The British soldiers would not stand that, they were beginning to make complaints, and the most urgent demands were being received from them. Furthermore, British Officers who had been in Germany said that Bolshevism was being created, and the determining factor was going to be food. As long as the people were starving they would listen to the arguments of the Spartacists, and the Allies by their action were simply encouraging elements of disruption and anarchism. It was like stirring up an influenza puddle, just next door to one's self. The condition of Russia was well known, and it might be possible to look on at a muddle which had there been created. But, now, if Germany went, and Spain: who would feel safe? As long as order was maintained in Germany, a breakwater would exist between the countries of the Allies and the waters of Revolution beyond. But once . . . [the] breakwater was swept away, he could not speak for France, but trembled for his own country. The situation was particularly serious in Munich. Bavaria, which once had been thought to represent the most solid and conservative part of Germany, had already gone. He was there that afternoon to reinforce the appeal which had come to him from the men who had helped the Allies to conquer the Germans, the soldiers, who said that they refused to continue to occupy a territory in order to maintain the population in a state of starvation. Meanwhile the Conference continued to haggle. Six weeks ago the same arguments about gold and foreign securities had been raised, and it had then been decided that Germany should be given food. He begged the Conference to re-affirm that decision in the most unequivocal terms, unless this people were fed, if as a result of a process of starvation enforced by the Allies, the people of Germany were allowed to run riot, a state of revolution among the working classes of all countries would ensue with which it would be impossible to cope.

Clemenceau replied to Lloyd George. The essence of his remarks was, according to the minutes:

. . . he had already said, he was ready to give the food, whether promised or not. On the other hand, his information tended to show that the Germans were using Bolshevism as a bogey with which to frighten the Allies. If the Germans were starving, as General Plumer and others said they were, why did they continue to refuse to surrender their [merchant] fleet? The Germans certainly did not act as if they were in a hurry, and it was curious that a people who were said to be so hard up for food should appear to be in no hurry to assist in obtaining it by giving up their ships. No doubt very pitiable reports were being received from certain parts of Germany in regard to food conditions; but those reports did not apparently apply to all parts of Germany. . . . In his opinion, the Germans were simply trying to see how far they could go; they were simply attempting to blackmail the Allies. To yield to-day would simply mean constant yielding in the future. . . .

. . . In his opinion Marshal Foch should be instructed to meet the German Peace Delegates at Spa, and to tell them that the Allied and

Associated Powers refused to argue or to discuss matters concerning the accepted clauses of the armistice. The Germans had promised to surrender their mercantile fleet, and immediate compliance must be demanded. The Germans could at the same time be told that food would be sent, but the conditions of Article 8 of the Armistice of 16th January, 1919, must in the first place be fulfilled. It was essential that no signs of weakness should be displayed on the eve of the settlement of other large territorial, military and economic questions. The Germans must not be given any advantage to-day that might give them the impression that the Allied Powers could be intimidated and made to yield. Therefore, in his opinion Germany should be asked point blank: "Are you or are you not going to execute the conditions set forth in Clause 8 of the Armistice?" If his proposal were accepted, the position of the Great Powers would be extremely strong and promises to supply food could then safely be made.

Marshal Foch had made an objection which he (M. Clemenceau) considered to be very strong, but a slight amendment of the text would easily put that matter right. In regard to the manner of payment, he would be prepared to waive his objection to the ear-marking of gold for the purpose, provided he knew that the Germans would work for their food. This was not an unreasonable request, and it would be found to be in agreement with the teachings of Christianity. In conclusion, he could not too strongly urge his view that the Germans should be made thoroughly to understand that the Allies would allow no nonsense in regard to the minute observance of the terms of the clauses of the Armistice. As soon as the Germans recognized this fact, he felt sure his colleagues, M. Loucheur, M. Klotz and M. Clémentel, who were ever ready to be guided by feelings of humanity, would easily arrive at an agreement in regard to the supply of food to Germany, and the payment therefor.

The discussion turned to the French-proposed amendment to our memorandum, which would weaken the whole proposal. Lloyd George, becoming annoyed, said to Klotz:

. . . on January 13th exactly the same speech had been made by M. Klotz and he had then been overruled by the Supreme War Council. M. Klotz should . . . submit to the decisions then given by the Supreme War Council. . . .

. . . Nothing had, however, been done during those two months, and now the question had been brought up for discussion with all the old arguments. He would not have raised the matter, but for the fact that during the past two months, in spite of the decision reached by the Supreme War Council in January last, obstacles had continually been put in . . . way with the result that nothing had been done. He appealed to M. Clemenceau to put a stop to these obstructive tactics, otherwise M. Klotz would rank with Lenin and Trotsky among those who had spread Bolshevism in Europe.

Colonel House intervened, saying

. . . that it always made him unhappy to take sides against France. But the American Delegates had told him that they had gone to the utmost limits to meet the wishes of the French and unless Clause 4 were accepted practically as it stood, it would have no value.

M. CLEMENCEAU exclaimed that his country had been ruined and ravaged; towns had been destroyed; over two million men had lost their lives; mines had been rendered unworkable; and yet what guarantees had France that anything would be received in payment for all this destruction? She merely possessed a few pieces of gold, a few securities, which it was now proposed to take away in order to pay those who would supply food to Germany; and that food would certainly not come from France. In a word, he was being asked to betray his country and that he refused to do.

Finally, the debate cooled down, and our proposals were redrafted and accepted as follows:

1. As a preliminary to any discussion whatsoever with the German representatives, the principal representative of the Allied and Associated Powers is to make the following statement:

"On condition that Germany formally acknowledges and undertakes to execute her obligations under Clause VIII of the Armistice of January 16th, that is to say—

" 'VIII. In order to assure the provisioning of Germany and the rest of Europe, the German Government shall take all necessary steps to place the whole of the German merchant fleet, for the duration of the Armistice, under the control and the flags of the Allied Powers and the United States, who shall be assisted by a German Delegate.

" 'This arrangement shall in no wise affect the final disposal of such vessels. The Allies and the United States shall, if they consider this necessary, replace the crews either entirely or in part, and the officers and crews replaced shall be repatriated to Germany.

" 'Suitable compensation, to be fixed by the Allied Governments shall be made for the use of such vessels.

" 'All questions of detail, as also any exceptions to be made in the case of certain types of vessel, shall be settled by a special agreement to be concluded immediately.' "

The Delegates of the Associated Governments are authorised and directed to proceed upon these instructions as to revictualling.

2. Subject to the above undertaking by Germany the principal representative of the Allied and Associated Powers is authorised to make a communication to the German representatives. (On the basis set forth in Annexure 1.)

3. An Admiral, to be nominated by the British Government, will be the principal representative of the Allied and Associated Powers.

4. In order to avoid delay, the negotiations shall take place at Brussels.

The French Government [will] undertake to make the necessary arrangements with the Belgian Government.

An appendix was attached to this agreement. It reads as follows:

1. On grounds of humanity, the Associated Governments reiterate their decision to deliver to Germany the food now available in Europe for which payment has been arranged as soon as Germany shows her genuine intention to carry out her obligations, by sending to sea for that purpose the ships to be selected by the Associated Governments, and the Associated Governments will themselves provide (as quickly as transportation can be arranged) or will give permits for import from neighbouring neutrals for the balance of the month's supply, that is, of 270,000 tons agreed on, as soon as . . . ships have been similarly sent to sea, and as soon as payment for such food has been arranged.

2. She may import up to (300,000) tons of breadstuffs and (70,000) tons of fats monthly until September 1st.

3. She must pay for this food and may pay in any of the following ways:

(*a*) By the hire of ships.

(*b*) By the export of commodities and the sale of cargoes of German ships now in neutral countries.

(*c*) By credits in neutral countries.

(*d*) By the outright sale of foreign securities or properties.

(*e*) By the arrangement of advances against the use of foreign securities or properties as collateral.

(*f*) Further, gold also may be used as collateral or loans to be released as other means of payment provide means of liquidating such loans. The outright sale of gold can only be permitted in the event of its being agreed by the Associated Powers that the above named means of payment are inadequate.

The methods of payment provided in (*d*), (*e*), (*f*), shall not be resorted to beyond the sum of $200,000,000 (in addition to the financial arrangements already agreed upon in payment of the first 270,000 tons of food), until in the judgment of the Supreme Economic Council the possibilities of payment under (*a*), (*b*), and (*c*) have proved inadequate.

4. She may export commodities (except those on a black list) to any neutral or other agreed destination. The proceeds from these exports must, however, be converted into payments for foodstuffs.

5. A definite amount of the shipping handed over will be continuously available to transport food to Germany until next harvest.

6. She may purchase and import foodstuffs within the limits above stated, from neutrals who will, when necessary, be allowed to re-import equivalent quantities.

7. It is understood that the declaration of the Associated Governments under this communication will be null and void, should Germany break the terms of the Armistice.

It was agreed that we were to meet the Germans in Brussels on March 13, 1919.

Since these directions in the main complied with our "understanding to end all former understandings," I was sure they were workable. In the meantime, we made a further effort to get, from the British Admiralty, consent for the Germans to fish and to conduct coastwise trade with small vessels in the Baltic. These restrictions had increased the burdens on world supplies and had hampered our transportation for other nations. I again wrote to Admiral Benson:

PARIS, 12 March 1919

ADMIRAL W. S. BENSON
HÔTEL DE CRILLON
PARIS
MY DEAR ADMIRAL:

As you know, there are still limitations of many kinds on German traffic in the Baltic. This is having a most serious effect on the whole food situation in Germany. . . . It follows, therefore, that the Germans ought to be allowed to fish anywhere they like, either in the Baltic or the North Sea. In fact, I regard this as one of the vital questions in feeding Germany.

Furthermore, the limitations on the movement of coastwise traffic . . . greatly impedes movement along the German Coast, practically makes it impossible for them to cross the Baltic for fish and such articles as are allowed to them, has stopped up the movement of coal along the coast so that we are unable to keep the railway running at Danzig. . . . Subject to getting the German mercantile fleet, we are about to launch into a campaign to feed Germany which will cost the world, one way or another, one hundred millions of dollars a month. This could be enormously ameliorated if all these restrictions on German movement in the Baltic and the North Sea were taken off. . . . the time has now gone by when . . . [these restrictions] have even a political bearing on peace. . . .

If these restrictions were withdrawn, they could always be reimposed [if necessary]. . . . I would be . . . [glad if you would] take the matter up with Admiral Wemyss.

HERBERT HOOVER

Admiral Benson replied the next day:

MY DEAR MR. HOOVER:

. . . Since the early days of the discussion of the terms of the Armistice, I have stood out (and for a considerable portion of the time stood alone) for allowing the Germans fishing privileges and certain others. . . . It is my opinion that the Naval authorities of Great Britain will oppose a further relaxation until after the terms of peace are completed and signed.

W. S. BENSON

An extract from McCormick's diary at this period is of interest:

MARCH 12

. . . 10.30 Blockade [meeting] at Commerce Ministry. Tried to put through relaxation of blockade on Austria and Hungary complete, and eliminate machinery for bordering neutrals, blockading only Germany. Blocked by the Allies. Will keep at it and hope for success when we get at the men at the top. Little fellows still fighting the war. . . .

MARCH 13 (THURSDAY)—

Meeting War Trade Board. . . . I went to lunch with Attolico. . . . Italians worried over serious food situation and apologetic for action of Crespi in trying to force us into helping them by holding back their approval of blockade relaxation. Attolico—cleverest of the group—sees the mistake and is trying to correct error. . . .

THE AGREEMENT AT BRUSSELS— MARCH 13–14, 1919

The meeting with the Germans at Brussels took place on March 13 and 14. At the request of the British, who sent twelve delegates, Admiral Sir Rosslyn Wemyss presided. The American delegation, of which I was chairman, was comprised of Henry Robinson, representing the Shipping Board; Thomas Lamont, representing the Treasury; and Hugh Gibson, representing the State Department. My very capable secretary, Lewis L. Strauss, was also a member of the delegation. The French had nine delegates, headed by a general appointed by Marshal Foch. The Italians had three delegates. The Belgians had two delegates—my old colleague in the Belgian Relief, Emile Francqui, and an associate. The Germans sent fourteen delegates, headed by Edler von Braun.

The Allied delegates sat on one side of a long table and the Germans on the other. I had had dealings with Edler von Braun in Berlin during the Belgian Relief and knew him as an honest but stubborn man. Francqui and I sat together. He visibly hugged himself with satisfaction on hearing the very Germans of whom we had so often asked concessions for the Belgians, now on the other side of the table, asking us for food. In later years, he developed this incident into a great conversational drama.

The documents setting out the agreement with the Germans were long and technical. The terms were along the lines I had urged. They provided for an assurance of 300,000 tons of cereals and 70,000 tons of fats monthly—if world supplies permitted. The Germans were allowed to export certain commodities to the Allies and to trade with Neutrals, with certain limitations. Until the Peace, charter money for German mechant ships was to be paid by the Allies and credited to food. In addition, except for those payments for food furnished by the British, the Germans could pay in negotiable foreign securities or gold, to be deposited in the National Bank of Belgium and placed at my disposal as Director General of Relief. All available ships were to be handed over as rapidly as was physically possible.

I derived some humor out of inducing Admiral Wemyss to agree that the Germans might fish freely in the Baltic and conduct coastal traffic there with small ships. However, he could not swallow the idea of the Germans' fishing in the North Sea. He still had fears for the British Navy. We compromised by agreeing that the Germans could buy North Sea fish from the Neutrals without including it as a deduction from the monthly food program.

The delays in opening this crack for food, as promised in the Armistice, invoked many terrible consequences. Among them, a host of innocent people had died of starvation or from diseases resulting from lowered vitality. Had the Inter-Allied Blockade Council stuck to the original decision of December 24 on our proposal for trade between the Neutrals and Germany, much food would have flowed naturally into Germany and less gold payment would have been required. When the crack in the blockade was opened, the crisis in Germany was such that little payment could be made in trade, and practically the whole sum for food was handed over in gold. The French received fewer reparations than they could have obtained had they stuck to the agreement of December 24.

But there was a loss to the Allies and the whole world far greater than this. The Germans were for many long years unceasing in their denunciation of the continued blockade, and the effect was to poison the minds of their people and to sow the dragon's teeth of wars.

When the door to food was opened, I quickly found hate so livid in some of the British, American, and French press that I issued the following statement on March 21:

WHY WE ARE FEEDING GERMANY. From the point of view of my Western upbringing, I would say at once, because we do not kick a man in the stomach after we have licked him.

From the point of view of an economist, I would say that it is because there are seventy millions of people who must either produce or die, that their production is essential to the world's future and that they cannot produce unless they are fed.

From the point of view of a governor, I would say it is because famine breeds anarchy, anarchy is infectious, the infection of such a cesspool will jeopardize France and Britain, will yet spread to the United States.

From the point of view of a peace negotiator, it is because we must maintain order and stable government in Germany if we would have someone with whom to sign peace.

From the point of view of a reconstructionist, I would say that unless the German people can have food, can maintain order and stable government and get back to production, there is no hope of their paying the damages they owe to the world.

From the point of view of a humanitarian, I would say that we have not been fighting with women and children, and we are not beginning now.

From the point of view of our Secretary of War, I would say that I wish to return the American soldiers home and that it is a good bargain to give food for passenger steamers on which our boys may arrive home four months earlier than will otherwise be the case.

From the point of view of the American Treasurer, I would also say that this is a good bargain, because it saves the United States enormous expenditures in Europe in the support of idle men and allows these men to return to productivity. . . .

From the point of view of a negotiator of the Armistice, I would say that we are in honor bound to fulfill the implied terms of the Armistice that Germany shall have food.

Let us not befog our minds with the idea that we are feeding Germany out of charity. She is paying for her food. All that we have done for Germany is to lift the blockade to a degree that allows her to import her food from any market that she wishes and in the initial state, in order to effect the above, we are allowing her to purchase emergency supplies from [our] stocks . . . [in Neutral ports].

Taking it by and large, our face is forward, not backward on history. We and our children must live with these seventy million Germans. No matter how deeply we may feel at the present moment, our vision must stretch over the next hundred years and we must write now into history such acts as will stand creditably in the minds of our grandchildren.

I did not expect this statement to heal the wounds, the griefs, or the hates from four years of bitter war, but it served to stop any more complaints from my own countrymen.

But the battle of the blockade was not over and it was to continue until the ratification of the Peace Treaty by Germany on July 7, 1919. However, the food blockade on other former enemy countries was soon relaxed—but with restrictions.

During the Armistice there was staggering unemployment in all the countries of Europe, except in the three Allied nations and Belgium. This was to a great degree the result of the blockade restrictions on import of raw materials to these nations and on export of their products. We Americans unceasingly advocated the relaxation of these restrictions where such commerce would not injure the economic recovery of the Allies. Such action would relieve the burden of relief loans and charity, would make for economic and political stability, and would check the rise of Communism.

As this blackade has but an indirect bearing upon the activities and policies with which this particular narrative is concerned, to review this battle would require a book larger than this volume.

Vance McCormick led an unceasing battle to secure this relaxation of the blockade. We aided him when he was in need of support and we sometimes succeeded in minor fields. Students who are interested will find ample material in the Hoover Institution on War, Revolution, and Peace; and among this material is Vance McCormick's diary.

In Volume III of *An American Epic,* the continued blockade on each nation is necessarily devoted to a narrative of the famine—country by country—and the effect of the blockade on each of them is necessarily a part of the narrative.

If in this chapter, and in the records of the continuing struggle with this issue, we Americans were at times critical of the attitudes of our Allied colleagues, I bid American students to remember that we suffered few of the privations and cruelties that the Allies did. It was much easier for us to be objective. However, our objectivity did contribute to the mending of a war-torn Europe.

SECTION IV

THE UNITED STATES GOVERNMENT AGENCIES BEHIND THE FAMINE FRONT

INTRODUCTION

As the American people would need carry the major burden of relief and reconstruction of Europe, it was essential that we make our own organization as effective as possible. Britain also maintained an organization in Paris to deal with relief measures; it was under the general direction of Lord Robert Cecil, with Sir William Goode as director. The French and Italians took little except political interest in these matters.

To meet a food shortage and famine in forty-five nations, the first need for American action was a series of "behind the front" organizations stemming from our Paris headquarters. Since we had to carry on relief on the "front line" of forty-five nations and at the same time carry out political and economic missions for the Big Four, the description of the organization and the narration of incidents becomes somewhat complicated. For clarity, I have divided the section into five topics:

FINANCE
- The Treasury Loans
- The $100,000,000 Congressional Appropriation
- Financing Austria
- Our Use of Army and Navy Finance for the Sale of these Surplus Stocks in Europe
- Our Remittance Plan

HANDLING AMERICAN SUPPLIES

COMMUNICATIONS AND PASSPORTS
- Communications
- Passports

THE CHILDREN OF FAMINE

MISCELLANEOUS PROBLEMS

Clothing
Furnishing Economic and Technical Advisers
Displaced Persons
Barter and the Hoover War Library
The Hoover Institution on War, Revolution, and Peace

These activities overlap in time, but chronological description would produce an impenetrable maze.

CHAPTER 37

FINANCE

Under the laws enacted by the Congress as they stood at the Armistice, the Food Administration, its agencies, and the War and Navy departments had to be paid for any supplies they furnished to anyone else, including foreign nations. The Treasury, under the authorities vested in the President, was authorized to make loans to the nations which participated in the war against the Central Empires with which to pay for supplies. These nations included Britain, France, Italy, Belgium, Czechoslovakia, Portugal, Greece, Rumania, and Yugoslavia. Their total population was approximately 168,000,000.

The Neutral nations had resources with which to pay for their supplies, and four of the five enemy countries—Germany, Hungary, Bulgaria, and Turkey—had gold reserves and exportable goods to pay for their needs. The total of those who could pay from their own resources comprised about 153,000,000 people.

The nations in urgent need and not eligible for loans from the United States were Finland, Estonia, Latvia, Lithuania, Poland, Austria, and Armenia. They comprised about 45,000,000 people.

The British furnished helpful credits to some nations in Europe for supplies and—especially—transport. The French and Italians participated to a lesser degree.

All three of the Allies were dependent upon huge loans from the United States for the purchase of their supplies. The laws required that all purchases by loans from the United States Treasury had to be made in the United States. Of relief required by loans, the United States contributed about 94 per cent during the war and its aftermath and the three Allies 6 per cent. The Allied loans, as far as we have record of them, are listed in the various chapters of Volume III of *An American Epic.*

THE TREASURY LOANS

Secretary of the Treasury Carter Glass had a most sorrowful attitude toward lending money to any European country now that the war was won. His feelings toward the British, French, and Italian governments had not been improved by his full knowledge of their drive to envelop the whole American economy with a pool which would control our resources, including credits. On January 7, 1919, I received from the Food Administration in Washington the following:

HOOVER FROM RICKARD

Following letter received from Secretary of Treasury: "Treasury Department is now planning to discontinue loans to foreign governments as far and as soon as possible. I should be glad to know whether there are any outstanding questions with any government which your department would desire Treasury to take into account when making final arrangement with Allied governments or any other consideration affecting such arrangement which you desire to bring to its attention." . . .

The rest of the Secretary's letter was a lesson in primary economics, including our continued guarantee of prices to our farmers and his general reluctance to make loans.

On January 9, I instructed the Food Administration in Washington concerning its reply to the Secretary, the pertinent paragraphs of which were:

PARIS, 9th January, 1919

RICKARD [FOR GLASS]

. . . A certain amount of this food will be bought by neutrals, liberated and enemy countries and possibly some Allies, for normal exchange, but others must at least pending peace buy on credit. It is, of course, impossible to give but the roughest guess as to the proportions. . . . Our strong view is that the principle of extended credits should be adopted by the Treasury to all of the governments who have already been receiving loans from the United States. . . . It is our view that the food supply to Europe is a matter of vital importance to our national defense . . . [as] increasing disorder will make peace impossible and involve us in further military operations and that credits freely given . . . for food will greatly reduce this danger.

HOOVER

As a result of these communications with the Secretary, Mr. Davis advised that we seek no commitments directly from him or we would receive further lectures on economics. He suggested instead that we submit individual cases through the President.

A case in point arose regarding Rumania. Davis outlined the problem to Glass by cable:

PARIS, December 31, 1918

SECRETARY OF TREASURY

1. Reports from Roumania indicate necessity of immediate relief to prevent starvation and anarchy. See various cables to State Department and Hoover's cables to Food Administration. While it is difficult to proceed in situation apparently requiring action before full information is had and adequate arrangements are made for meeting same, it was decided advisable, in conference with Colonel House, General Bliss, Hoover, and others to take some temporary action to meet emergency before more definite plans and arrangements can be obtained.

2. Hoover states immediate situation could be relieved by an advance of $5,000,000 for expenditure through Food Administration or Grain Corporation to pay for cost of supplies now en route to Mediterranean which could be diverted to Roumania. This would only meet situation temporarily, but in meantime, other arrangements can probably be made including participation by England and France. In addition to food, Roumania reports indicate need of clothes and shoes, which they can probably get from England.

3. I explained the limitations of your power to make advances, but Secretary Lansing is of the opinion that Roumania's present state of hostilities brings her within those limitations and is so cabling you through

State Department, recommending importance of giving her financial assistance.

4. Hoover's information is that other sections of Europe will become desperate this winter unless assistance is furnished and if United States is to undertake this task, we should, it seems, obtain special legislation. . . .

8. This cable is sent with the approval of the President, who considers it advisable to establish now the credit of $5,000,000 in favor of Roumania if you can do so and are so disposed. In such event, the obligation could be taken here if Roumanian Minister is not there.

NORMAN DAVIS

The President confirmed to Glass his approval of the loan to Rumania and even forecast further demands. Glass still had reservations about the eligibility of Rumania for Treasury loans but began to weaken in his general attitude of opposition. He cabled the President:

WASHINGTON, January 15, 1919

FOR PRESIDENT FROM GLASS

. . . Your message regarding Roumania was received. Advance to Roumania will be made when essential requirements imposed by loan statutes are met. Wired Davis several days ago particulars and that Treasury would make advance whenever put in position to do so legally. Understand that State Department has cabled on subject.

. . . Appreciate importance of food supplies in relation to your policies and anxious to use powers of treasury to support them. Treasury has uniformly recognized supplies of foodstuffs to European Allies as a purpose for which loans could be made under existing law and will continue to do so until conditions change or you advise to the contrary. In no case has it refused to make such loans. . . .

On January 19, Secretary Glass replied to my communication of January 9. His reply was as Davis had forewarned—another lecture on economics. However, the pertinent paragraph from my point of view was:

I am satisfied that the supply of essential foods to countries at war with Germany is in the interest of the national defense and am prepared to exercise the powers of the Treasury for them. . . .

THE $100,000,000 CONGRESSIONAL APPROPRIATION

As this text shows, I had urged several times the necessity of a direct Congressional appropriation to provide for the newly liberated countries ineligible for loans under the President's authority. We especially needed to undertake the rehabilitation of famine-debilitated children of all nations. The President warmly supported this proposal. On January 1, I had drafted a message for him to Glass urging this appropriation. Its potent paragraphs were:

> Extended investigation and consideration of the food situation in certain parts of Europe discloses that especially the urban population in certain areas are not only faced with absolute starvation during the coming winter . . . they are utterly incapable of finding any resources that can be converted into international exchange for food purchases. . . . This applies more particularly to the liberated peoples [from Germany] of Austria, Turkey . . . and Western Russia. In these countries freedom and government will slowly emerge from chaos and require our every assistance.
>
> . . . from our abundance we can surely afford to offer succor to these countries destitute of resources or credit. The minimum sum upon which this work can be carried on for the next six months in the countries above mentioned will amount to at least 100,000,000 dollars. . . .
>
> The high mission of the American people to find a remedy against starvation and absolute anarchy, renders it necessary that we should undertake the most liberal assistance to these destitute regions.
>
> The situation is one of extreme urgency, for foodstuffs must be placed within certain localities within the next 15 to 30 days if human life and order is to be preserved. I, therefore, request that you should ask Congress to make available to me an immediate appropriation of $100,000,000 for the broad purpose of providing foodstuffs and other urgent supplies, for the transportation, distribution, and administration thereof to such populations in Europe, outside of Germany, as may be determined upon by me from time to time as necessary.
>
> I wish to appeal to the great sense of charity and good-will of the American people toward the suffering, and to place this act upon a primarily humanitarian basis of the first magnitude. While the sum of money

is in itself large, it is so small compared to the expenditure we have undertaken in the hope of bettering the world, that it becomes a mere pittance compared to the results that will be obtained from it, and the lasting effect that will remain in the United States through an act of such broad humanity and statesmanlike influence.

The President marked this "Approved, W. W." and I had it sent.

On January 11, the President sent a strong message to Senate and House leaders in charge of the legislation:

TUMULTY
THE WHITE HOUSE, WASHINGTON:

Please convey following confidential message to Senator Martin and Congressman Swager Sherley: [1]

"I cannot too earnestly or solemnly urge upon the Congress the appropriation for which Mr. Hoover has asked for the administration of food relief. Food relief is now the key to the whole European situation and to the solution of peace. Bolshevism is steadily advancing westward, has overwhelmed Poland, and is poisoning Germany. It cannot be stopped by force, but it can be stopped by food, and all the leaders with whom I am in conference agree that concerted action in this matter is of immediate and vital importance. The money will not be spent for food for Germany itself, because Germany can buy its food, but it will be spent for financing the movement of food to our real friends in Poland and to the people of the liberated units of the Austro-Hungarian Empire, and to our associates in the Balkans. I beg that you will present this matter with all possible urgency and force to the Congress. I cannot see how we can find definite powers with whom to conclude peace unless this means of stemming the tide of . . . [Bolshevism] be employed."

The Senate passed the appropriation, but Senator Henry Cabot Lodge secured an amendment excluding the use of any of this fund for people in any former enemy country, except Armenians and Jews in Turkey. I protested to the President as follows:

[1] Thomas S. Martin of Virginia, Chairman of the Senate Appropriations Committee, and Swager Sherley of Kentucky, Chairman of the House Committee on Appropriations.

27 January 1919

DEAR MR. PRESIDENT:

The Senate amended our $100,000,000 Relief Bill excluding Bulgaria, Germany, Austria-Hungary and the Mohammedan population of Turkey from the . . . [provisions] of the Bill. . . .

The Bill as passed by the House was in the form that we hoped the Senate would accede to. The large majority by which it passed . . . the House would seem to indicate some hope of getting it reviewed in conference without too much of a struggle.

HERBERT HOOVER

The President replied:

PARIS, 28 January 1919

MY DEAR MR. HOOVER:

I have sent a telegram to Glass along the lines suggested in your letter of yesterday in regard to the $100,000,000 Relief Bill.

WOODROW WILSON

The President's protest did no good. Lodge would not budge, and the Senate and House leaders accepted his amendment rather than cause further delay. Our special grief was that the Lodge amendment excluded our charitable rehabilitation of children in the former enemy countries. Since the appropriation act had to be sent to Paris for the President's signature, it did not formally become law, and we could not use the funds, until February 24.

The President interpreted the act as giving authority to establish the rehabilitation of children, except in enemy states, without repayment. At once, when the bill passed both houses, I addressed the President on an organization which I proposed to set up to administer the fund and otherwise simplify our operations:

PARIS, 25 January 1919

DEAR MR. PRESIDENT:

. . . I propose to set up a new organization, to be called the United States Relief Administration, and to transfer to this administration not only the $100,000,000 appropriation but also the accounting for the

$5,000,000 which I have already received from your Presidential fund. . . . I propose to enter into a contract between the Relief Administration and the United States Grain Corporation by which the Grain Corporation undertakes to deliver foodstuffs into various ports in Europe. . . .

. . . The Allies have proposed to us that our hundred million dollar appropriation should be practically placed in the Treasury of the . . . Supreme Council of Supply and Relief together with such moneys as . . . [the Allies] may contribute and the whole should be dealt with by this Council. I am legally advised that . . . we have . . . [no] right to do this and I feel strongly that . . . it would be a mistake . . . that we cannot allow. . . .

If you approve . . . I will have the necessary executive orders drawn to carry the Act into practical operation upon the above lines.

HERBERT HOOVER

The President marked this "Approved, W. W." We drafted the executive order covering the ideas we suggested, and the President signed it.

FINANCING AUSTRIA

Of the former enemy states, Germany, Hungary, Bulgaria, and Turkey could finance their food from their own resources. But there seemed no solution for Austria under the Lodge amendment. We were only days away from starvation in Vienna. The Communists were conspiring to take over that city as they had already done in several German cities. Aside from the other calamities involved, our railway inlet for relief to Czechoslovakia and Serbia would be cut off. I have already related the President's emergency advance of $5,000,000 to the Food Administration from his "security fund." Captain Gregory, our representative in Austria, discovered some $4,000,000 of good exchange in the Vienna banks, which, on assignment to us, brought our resources for supplies up to $9,000,000—but this was fast running out.

I suggested to the President and to Davis that I could see no way out except for the United States to lend Britain, France, and Italy

$30,000,000 each, which amounts these countries would in turn lend to Austria, from which that country would pay for supplies from our organization. We found the three countries willing, and Davis, with the President's approval, took up the matter with Secretary Glass by cable. However, to be prudent, Davis asked for $300,000,000 to be used in this way; he thought there might be other countries where such a method might be needed.

On February 28, Secretary Glass accepted Davis' full program—with "conditions." The important paragraphs of his reply, as far as we were concerned, were:

For Davis

. . . [Such] food supplies purchased by British, French and Italians from our advances . . . are not to exceed $300,000,000 in aggregate nor $100,000,000 to any one country. They need not be in equal amounts to each country.

. . . Trust it may be found possible to reduce amount of these loans. . . . It is . . . imperative that such advances be reduced to a minimum. . . .

. . . In case a lesser amount is loaned to any one of these countries for said purpose the loan to the others for said purposes must not be increased. . . .

As noted above, we had only asked for $90,000,000 for Austria, and we did not use all of that, as will be seen from our Austrian balance sheet.[2]

OUR USE OF ARMY AND NAVY FINANCE FOR THE SALE OF THESE SURPLUS STOCKS IN EUROPE

One of our great relief resources was the huge surplus stock of all kinds of Army and Navy supplies. As I have stated, the President approved the sale of these stocks on credit for relief, and I accord-

[2] As a matter of fact, this amount of such loans was never repaid to the United States by the Allies.

ingly made an agreement with the military departments on November 12, 1918.

The Army, especially, had accumulated great reserves of food, clothing, medical supplies, railway equipment, and other materials either for use or as protection against submarine and other sea-transport emergencies. And Army demands on this vast stockpile were steadily diminishing as our soldiers returned home.

General Charles G. Dawes had been appointed to organize the disposal of Army-surplus supplies. He had to return home, and the President, on February 11, 1919, created the United States Liquidation Commission under Judge Edwin B. Parker to succeed General Dawes.

The Army and Navy had no funds or authority to pay for transport to destinations, and that burden fell upon our organization. We paid for it and we had great help from the British.

The magnitude of the Army's surplus is indicated by its disposals through our organization, which totaled $381,721,094 and represented 823,202 tons of food, clothing, medical, and miscellaneous supplies.

The Navy also had some surplus stocks in Europe that were of great use to us. One of the Navy's notable contributions to our relief measures was the handling of the 1,500,000 refugees and prisoners returning home to the North of France or en route after the Armistice. Under orders from Admiral Benson, they erected a large number of barracks, furnishing them with beds and kitchenware. The Admiral delegated the officers and personnel to undertake this operation.

OUR REMITTANCE PLAN

Soon after we opened our Paris office, we were flooded with requests from individuals in the United States to help them transmit money to relatives and other persons all over Central and Eastern Europe. The currencies of these countries were in a mess. Many of the governments had inherited inflated currencies from the old empires; [3] they had currencies and were busy adding to them up to the capacity of the printing press. This situation resulted in stiff restrictions by the Federal Reserve Board on the banks making such remittances from the United States to Central and Eastern Europe.

Early in March, 1919, we decided that we could increase our resources for relief, reduce the burden of loans on the Treasury, and at the same time be of service to Americans wishing to aid their relatives or some hungry person abroad. To do this we organized a remittance bureau in our Paris office, with branches in our offices in New York and in the countries in Central and Eastern Europe. In this operation, we accepted dollar deposits in our New York office with which we bought food for shipment overseas. On receipt of advice of such deposits, we made payments in Europe, usually through the local banks, to the designated person. We obtained the local currency through the sale of food.

I secured Captain F. H. McKnight, an experienced banker, from General Pershing's army to manage the operation. Captain McKnight made an arrangement with the Federal Reserve Board by which American banks were allowed to accept such remittances in dollars and to turn them over to our office in New York with the names and addresses of the persons for whom they were intended. On May 12, we expanded the service to cover commercial remittances.

We started the operation in nine countries: Germany, Bulgaria, Czechoslovakia, Finland, Austria, Yugoslavia, Poland, Rumania, and Turkey. We found the working details extremely troublesome. Many of the designated recipients could not be found, and the money had to go back through a vast jungle of protective red tape. And the total of the remittances was disappointing.

Captain McKnight's division handled 17,216 remittances totaling $8,900,676.29, of which $2,428,820.14 had to be refunded, either because the payee could not be located or because satisfactory arrangements could not be made in the designated country. There

[3] The story was told in Vienna of a devoted father who had left a fortune of ten million kroner to each of his two sons. The prudent son invested in bonds which lost their whole value. The improvident son invested his entire fortune in wine and riotous spending. At the peak of inflation he sold his empty bottles for ten million kroner.

remained, therefore, a net total of $6,471,856.15, which relieved the Treasury by that amount.

We ceased these operations on June 30, 1919, with the official end of our American governmental relief agencies. However, we evolved from this experience a better method, called "Food Drafts," which we inaugurated as a voluntary relief organization after the Peace. It proved a huge success.

CHAPTER 38

HANDLING AMERICAN SUPPLIES

With the President's approval, I delegated the purchase, transport, accounting, and storage of supplies in European ports to the Food Administration's Grain Corporation.

I may repeat that the Grain Corporation was a United States–owned corporation of which I was Chairman and Julius H. Barnes President, with its head office in New York and its European office in London under Edward M. Flesh, its Vice-President.

The Corporation bought our supplies at various prices, and in order to simplify accounting, it made a uniform price to all nations. To provide against possible contingencies, we included a small margin in the uniform prices. This "margin" was subsequently to have great importance in relief of children.

We made a further step in simplification by a uniform contract with each recipient government—covering such questions as points of delivery, acceptance of our accounts as final, signing of notes payable to the United States Treasury, equitable distribution of the food among their people, and the method by which gold or goods were to be paid in cases where such sales were made. Our powers of enforcement of these conditions were simple: we could, and on one or two occasions did, stop supplies until these conditions were complied with. Our missions to each country were to have full freedom of inspection. It was a detailed and lengthy contract of which some paragraphs may have historical interest:

DELIVERY

Deliveries are to be made in warehouse or C.I.F. . . . at any . . . sea port in Europe to which the parties may agree. . . .

PRICES

The foodstuffs supplied will be delivered at cost, representing the purchase cost in the United States, plus all transportation, administration and other charges with a sufficient margin to protect the American Relief Administration or such agency as it may designate against loss.

ACCOUNTS TO BE FINAL

The agents of the American Relief Administration shall furnish the . . . [government] with statements of accounting which shall be accepted by the . . . [government] as final and conclusive. . . .

PAYMENT

The . . . [government] agrees . . . to pay in Washington for such foodstuffs out of the moneys received from loans made for that purpose by the United States Treasury. . . .

PAYMENT IN LOCAL CURRENCY

To the extent that the American Relief Administration can use local currency in the payment of expenses or for other purposes . . . the . . . [government] will pay . . . in local currency. . . .

With regard to payment for food other than through United States loans:

PAYMENT BY EXPORTS OR EXCHANGE

If the . . . [government] should be able to purchase foodstuffs from overseas through export of commodities or by the provision of international exchange in any other form, it agrees to offer such exchange to the American Relief Administration in reduction of these credits above, or in extension of purchases beyond the limit of said credits. . . .

CO-OPERATION AS TO PROGRAMMES

The American Relief Administration will consult with the representatives of the . . . [government] regarding the programmes for each month and will endeavor to meet the desires of the . . . [government]. . . .

THE AGREEMENT RETROACTIVE

This agreement shall supersede all former agreements between the United States government . . . and . . . [apply] to all deliveries made since January 1, 1919. . . .

THE FOOD TO BE DISTRIBUTED EQUITABLY

. . . the distribution of foodstuffs will be carried out subject to the general approval of the American Relief Administration and in accord with the dictates of humanity.

Each of the recipient governments signed this contract—except the British, French, and Italians, and the Belgian Relief, who made their own purchases in the United States under control of the Food Administration and arranged their own transport.

CHAPTER 39

COMMUNICATIONS AND PASSPORTS

COMMUNICATIONS

To accomplish our complicated job we needed a complete and rapid communications system. General Pershing had established a courier system over Europe to connect all American agencies with Paris. The couriers were sturdy sergeants who traveled by rail. They quickly learned that they could better themselves by trading in currencies between the different nations. This did not hamper the service because the more and faster the journeys, the greater the opportunities of making money. But the service proved to be much too slow for our purposes, since the journeys into Central and Eastern Europe required from a week to a month on the road.

Soon after our organization began work, Admiral Benson, on behalf of all the American organizations in Europe, established radio communication from Paris with important ports, in some cases assigning naval vessels for the purpose. Although the service was a great help, it gave us no direct contact with important internal points. However, the Navy had to go home, and we had to find another method of communications.

The telegraph systems of various nations were working normally within their borders. But the suspicions and hates over Central and Southern Europe were so intense that these nations would not allow international connection of their telegraph systems. Our telegrams, in these cases, had to be carried physically over frontiers by our staff and started again. Also, there were long delays from the rigid censorship imposed by every country in Europe. Some of our telegrams went through seven countries with wide-open ears.

At this stage in our difficulties, Colonel Logan proposed that we might secure personnel from the United States Army Signal Corps for operation of a telegraph system of our own—provided we could secure the assignment of circuits in each country, with freedom to connect over the frontiers.

To overcome the suspicions and hates among the twenty-six governments involved, we stated that all of our telegrams would be sent *en clair* and that their officials could read them in our offices at their leisure. With one exception—France—twenty-five countries responded favorably. Upon our presentation of the idea to General Pershing, he at once directed General Edgar Russel of the Signal Corps to organize the system and to staff it with telegraph operators from the Army in uniform and on Army pay. Originally, Major Frank H. Fay managed the system; he was later succeeded by Captain Paul S. Clapp.

The French insisted that all of our telegrams should go over their telegraph system. This meant the delays of censorship and that messages had to be carried over their frontiers by our representatives, in order to feed them into our widespread system, all of which was probably slower than sending carriers to the frontier points. However, General Russel solved this problem by using his own men to string connecting wires from our offices in Paris to General Pershing's headquarters in Paris, which had its own line to his occupying armies in Germany. At these points in Germany, we connected with thirty countries. The British gave us a special telephone wire to our office in London. We now had connections between our Paris office and every city important to us—from Helsingfors to Constantinople —and to way stations.

The *en clair* pledge quickly raised a dark cloud of trouble. Our men needed to transmit to us confidential information about the real needs of various governments, and they wanted to express their candid opinions of local officials. Spontaneously, they began to adopt American slang to express themselves. Soon they were using slang from baseball, football, colleges, stock markets, and service clubs. A difficult agreement with a foreign official was described as "he went through the hoop." Reprimands were "being on the carpet." A certain leader was a "fullback." A tricky move was a "slide to second base." A prospective dismissal was "three strikes." An easy agreement was a "snap course" or a "cinch." In the end, slang that had been dead for fifty years came to life.

American, British, and French press correspondents, having learned of our telegraph system, asked us to transmit their messages, which we were glad to do—provided they were all *en clair*. The American peace delegation in Paris and our Foreign Service over Europe also asked for our transmission to send their communications over our system. These were mostly in code. We agreed if they would get indemnity from *en clair* through the other peace delegations in Paris. They did so, but from their discussions, the various peace delegations learned of our system and requested us to transmit their telegrams also.

Since we were now involved in a large volume of long and tedious code messages and press dispatches, we concluded to earn a little money for our Children's Fund by requiring payment for all messages. We opened an office in Paris for that purpose and earned about five thousand dollars monthly for the children. Incidentally, the transmission of code messages removed stricken consciences of our Paris office over our own code system.

Late in June, the last of the Army Signal Corps was to leave Europe for home. Again our communications system was about to break down. In addition to our own needs, the State Department joined us in an appeal to General Pershing to keep the line operating to Coblenz and to provide substitutes for the servicemen who wished to return home. He arranged all this and the service continued for several months after the Peace.

PASSPORTS

Passports proved a real grief. The need to get visas from every country for every pass over frontiers—with all the red tape, investigation, and inspection by officials on each side of all frontiers—caused long delays and discomforts for our staff. Therefore, we proposed to all the governments that it would help us greatly if I could issue passports to our American staff (in terms similar to official passports) to be attached to our regular American passports and that they abandon visas. This provided our men with freedom from visas and surcease from delays and search at frontiers. Every government except the British and French agreed. These passports became a token of confidence that no other organization in history has ever possessed.

CHAPTER 40

THE CHILDREN OF FAMINE

The passage of the $100,000,000 relief appropriation enabled us to begin widespread rehabilitation of the children of famine. Those of us who had labored in the relief of Belgium and Northern France had witnessed the poignant degeneration of children in famine. The causes of this tragedy were clear. In famine, human beings eat the grain which would normally be fed to animals. Then the production of dairy and other animal products is reduced. The famine worsens, and people eat their productive herds. Moreover, the drastic rations in famine consist mostly of cereals and fats. These suffice for adults over a period, but children, the ailing, the aged, and expectant and nursing mothers wilt under such a regimen and quickly develop a host of bodily ills.

We found in Belgium that to sustain and rehabilitate these groups we had to give them a midday meal in canteens under medical supervision in order to make up their deficiencies. The canteen system was managed by devoted women. Before the war ended, the Belgian Relief was providing this extra meal to 2,500,000 children and others of the deficient groups in Belgium and Northern France. This experience had proved that not only were dedicated men and women at hand for this service but, with proper food, these devitalized children could be restored again to gleeful, chattering youngsters.

Our preliminary surveys after the Armistice showed that possibly ten to fifteen million children were already in a deplorable condition. In addition to the children wasting away in their own homes, there were millions of war orphans and waifs for whom homes or asylum had to be found and food provided if they were to survive. These children were not only pitiable little persons, but unless their degeneration could be remedied, those who survived would grow up to be a menace to their race and all mankind.

Beyond these impelling reasons for action, I hoped that the evidence of someone's concern for children might lessen the consuming hates that burned in the hearts of women in every country. Love of children is a biological trait common to all peoples. Around this deep emotion we could not only build our system for saving the younger generation, but we could also spur a renaissance of unity and hope among distracted elders of every country.

It was hopeless to get the job done through disorganized and inexperienced governments, whose resources, from borrowed money or elsewhere, could barely buy enough breadstuffs, crude fats, and vegetables to provide a basic ration. If the job were to be done properly, it called for organized volunteer action by the women of each country, and it had to be supported by free supplies from an organization that was completely independent of local governments.

Furthermore, we believed that this service should be a direct expression of the American people to these nations—and that it should be operated under the American flag. The Allied governments had neither supplies nor funds for such a service. Even before the $100,000,000 appropriation was available at the end of February we had inaugurated this service in some areas (from such funds as we could command) and had laid the foundations for a widespread organization.

Although we could deliver the needed supplies to any spot and could furnish skilled advice, we were loath to burden our overworked American staff in each country with further detailed administrative labors. We therefore sought the aid of the American Red Cross to administer the children's job—if we furnished the food free and delivered it to the spot of need. The Red Cross was already doing some sporadic work for children. I addressed a letter to them, soliciting administrative help and stating that we would deliver the food free of charge. However, after consultation with the Red Cross staff, it was obvious that organization had been so far demobilized that it could not help. We were thus driven to the decision that if these children were to be cared for, our organization had to do it.

Our first step in systematic organization was to establish a Children's Division in our Paris office and decentralize the work into special organizations in each nation where the famine was acute. We appointed A. E. Peden, who had been our state food administrator in Texas, to head this organization. However, he was soon called home, and we secured, through General Pershing, Colonel A. J. Carlson of the Army Medical Corps to take his place. His second in command was R. H. Simpson, an old Belgian Relief hand—and a good one. To direct the work in various countries, we were able to call for experienced and competent men from our staff in Belgium and Northern France. Among them were W. Hallam Tuck, Walter L. Brown, Maurice Pate, with Dr. Vernon Kellogg, and Dr. Alonzo Taylor of our missions already on the ground.

Our basis of organization in each country was the same. Our staff organized a national committee of leading women (and sometimes men) to undertake the work; these committees decentralized their own organization into local committees in every province, city, town, and village. The women at the local level set up the canteens for the midday meal, usually in schoolhouses. They found the equipment and the volunteer staff to do the work. In addition to food, we furnished free medical supplies and clothing. As it turned out, our free supplies represented about half the cost of operating the canteens. These committees of women also undertook the placement of waif children. Where asylums were already operating or specially created, we furnished their entire food supply without cost.

From our experience in Belgium we furnished criteria to women's committees to assist local doctors in selecting those requiring aid and tests for use when health had been restored. In this latter task, we received great help from Dr. Von Pirquet, a noted Austrian pediatrician.

The composition of our menu is best indicated by an analysis of total purchases for child-feeding. The contents, by weight, were:

Cocoa	5%
Sugar	10%
Condensed Milk	20%
Wheat Flour or Cereals	40%
Peas and Beans	10%
Other Fats	5%
Rice	10%

We also furnished vital mineral salts and authorized the purchase of meat at our expense, whenever it could be obtained, to enrich their soup. Each daily meal averaged eight hundred calories.

In a long life of administrative experience, I have never known an operation to go into action so rapidly, so efficiently, and with such devotion as did this effort on behalf of the children. There was a spirit of dedication in these women, fired by determination to protect the oncoming generation against great evils.

We had little trouble in connection with integration. The canteens served children of every race and religion in their neighborhoods. And this was the more remarkable along borders where their parents had recently been fighting each other.

Germany lay outside this organization. We could do nothing for the children of that country until the blockade was relaxed four months after the promise in the Armistice. Even with the relaxation of the blockade, Senator Lodge's amendment prevented us from using American Government funds. The condition of the children of the industrial and lower-income clerical workers was heartbreaking. We found a partial remedy by securing agreement with the Allied authorities that a large portion of the allowed German imports (for which they paid) should especially include food for debilitated youngsters. We found that the Germans were unable to meet the problem of children, even with these special imports. However, as this narrative will show, after the Peace was signed, we set up an efficient canteen system feeding many thousands of German children.

We had similar difficulties in Austria because of Senator Lodge's amendment. Nevertheless, we were able to get our canteen system established with an allotment from the President's emergency fund. By arranging for the Allies to lend funds—advanced to them from the United States Treasury—to Austria, we were able to sustain our canteen system there in full. We also avoided Senator Lodge's amendment by sales to Hungary of food for children for gold—that being legal under the general authorities of the Food Administration.

By the time Peace was signed in July, 1919, we were serving 3,500,000 children. I describe later the voluntary relief organization which we set up after the Peace. Before our activities in Europe had ended, we had served more than 16,000,000 children. As part of our preparation to continue this service after the Peace, I sent the following letter to the Prime Ministers of each of the countries to whom we had been supplying food, except the Allies:

June 12, 1919

SIR:

In the course of supplying foodstuffs . . . [the United States official relief agencies have] delivered all foodstuffs at fixed prices as near to the actual outlay as could be determined, with a sufficient margin to protect . . . [us] against loss arising from the unknown factors. . . .

The whole operation of relief to Europe has been by a coordination of shipping, finance and administration conducted as one operation and it has of course been impossible in advance to determine the exact cost for the contingent liabilities inherent in the operation. It is possible therefore that with the closing of the program in the month of July, and a final calculation of cost and liabilities incurred, there may be some profit accruing to the Relief Administration or its agencies.

Under the agreement . . . possible profits could of course be retained by the Relief Administration, but it is our earnest desire that no profits should be earned from the relief operations . . . if such a profit should exist, it will represent partially the saving effected through the sacrifice of the representatives of . . . [the United States official relief agencies], whose services are partially or wholly voluntary. Even when salaries are received they are usually paid by other departments of the United States Government without being calculated in the price of the foodstuffs. The prices fixed have therefore been less than commercial prices in a free market. Therefore such margins represent a gift of service to . . . [each government] by these gentlemen.

In these lights, I propose that any such total residual sum as may be determined by the Food Administration . . . to be in fact a profit after the completion of our total operations should be lodged with me or such organization as I may erect in New York to be added to public charity for the continued support of child relief. . . .

It is my intention to organize the supply of further funds by public charity in the United States and the addition of such residual amounts as above would give a substantial substratum and endurance to this effort.

It is very desirable however that such action should have the full approval of . . . [each] Government, and I would be glad if you would indicate that this course would meet with their approval. It is my intention to personally direct the organization and extension of such work in the United States if the above plan can be adhered to. It has been accepted by the other governments to which it has been submitted.

HERBERT HOOVER

All the governments accepted this arrangement.

CHAPTER 41

MISCELLANEOUS PROBLEMS

CLOTHING

There had been a large decrease in textile production for civilians over all Europe during the war. Moreover, Europe was dependent upon imports for a large part of its wool and hides and for all of its cotton. The wartime blockade had cut off all of these supplies to the enemy and the liberated states and had reduced the amounts which Neutrals could import. The war had drawn textile workers into the armed forces, and much of the textiles available had gone into uniforms.

It was astonishing how prewar clothing had been made to last during the war years. However, at the Armistice, the most pronounced styling was that of patches. The groups hit hardest, of course, were the poor.

Our United States official relief organizations could not undertake to supply substantial amounts of textile raw materials because our available funds had to be used for the great priority need—food and medical supplies. In only one instance did we furnish raw materials. That was the case of Poland in whose especially desperate situation we furnished five thousand bales of cotton.

Prior to the Armistice, the Belgian Relief had accumulated a large amount of second-hand clothing and new materials from all over the world. The Belgians were quick to import raw materials and start their textile mills. The American Relief Administration purchased the Belgian Relief stocks at out-of-pocket cost and distributed them throughout Europe.

The American Red Cross became interested in the problem, and on January 9, our Washington office cabled:

> . . . Red Cross states strong movement on part of people of liberated nations in United States, especially Jugo-Slavs, to collect and have Red Cross send used clothing and materials to their people. Red Cross inclined to accept goods. . . . Might expect 10,000 tons available for shipment April, May and June. C.R.B. old clothes should all be shipped by April 1st. If favorable cable something that could be used for publicity.

In response, I sent this:

January 11, 1919

FOOD ADMINISTRATION, WASHINGTON

> . . . I understand movement on foot in United States on part of our citizens who are originally from the liberated nations of Europe to collect and send through the medium of the Red Cross used clothing and materials to their stricken people on this continent. If this collection is efficiently done . . . untold suffering will be relieved. . . . I hope all haste will be made to encourage and expedite this good work.
>
> HOOVER

On January 15, the Paris directors of the Red Cross sought our aid in handling their clothing. We agreed to furnish free overseas transport on our food ships and to undertake distribution in areas where the Red Cross had no organization. In addition to these supplies, we obtained large numbers of new and worn uniforms, shoes, and other garments from the United States Army Liquidation Commission.

The total distribution of clothing by our organization during the Armistice period amounted to more than 417,000 tons; with probably a thousand garments per ton, this figure would represent more than 400,000,000 garments. The Allies also shipped such materials directly to different countries. I detail the quantities distributed to each country in Volume III of this memoir.

FURNISHING ECONOMIC AND TECHNICAL ADVISERS

It quickly developed after the Armistice that the newly created governments in Eastern Europe required economic and administrative advice. Their leaders were revolutionists with little practical experience in government. Saddled with huge problems in agriculture, rationing, currency, finance, railways, public health, and coal production, they had urgent need of experienced advisers and administrators. The political intentions of Americans were not suspect by these new leaders, and as far as I know, they sought such advisers exclusively from our organization. We thus built up a large technical staff of specialists and administrators attached to many of these governments. There were some one thousand such men, most of them in uniform. Some were officers of our Regular Army; many were prewar civilians we had recruited from the Army.

DISPLACED PERSONS

In Chapter 27, I have listed the many problems of displaced persons, whose number probably exceeded fifteen millions. During the Armistice, our official United States relief agencies were called upon to act to enable them to return to their own countries.

I have already related how our organization cared for the French refugees pouring into or through Northern France. A problem arose concerning one and one-half to two million Poles—part of whom were prisoners of war, part impressed laborers, and part emigrants—scattered over Southeastern Europe and in both the Communist and non-Communist parts of Russia.

For a time, the Polish Government conducted its own system of repatriation, but in June, 1919, it asked for our help with about 600,000 men, chiefly impressed workers, and about 400,000 more men, women, and children who had settled in some fifteen countries. We provided them free rides home on our trains and barges, with free food en route. Most of the Poles got home with this assistance.

At the Armistice, there were 1,500,000 Russian prisoners of war in Germany and a huge number of impressed Russian workers. There were also about 200,000 German and Hungarian prisoners in Siberia. They were our toughest problem. Our lawyers advised that under the Lodge amendment we could not support anything or anybody in German territory. The Germans, acutely short of food, at once laid the care of Russian prisoners in the Allies' lap—by the simple method of letting them starve.

On December 21, 1918, I was informed by American Army authorities that "the prisoners in Germany are dying wholesale from neglect"; they requested a supply of food through our organization. This seemed to me a job for the various Red Cross societies under the obligations of prewar treaties. The American Red Cross staff in Paris were inclined to my view but required assent from their directors in Washington. In support of the Paris director, I cabled the Assistant Secretary of State in Washington as follows:

PARIS, 21 December 1918

It is my view that the . . . [worst] suffering in Europe today is that of Russian prisoners in Germany and Austria. . . . They are dying wholesale from neglect. This is a matter of charity [which the American Relief Administration cannot handle] and it would seem to me a proper work for the American Red Cross . . . [and I understand that Commissioner here has put up to them the question as to whether their funds are available for that purpose].

HOOVER

The Red Cross authorities in Washington, however, declined the task on the ground that under the treaties, the Swiss Red Cross would have to take the initiative; the problem was tossed back to Paris. I will not encumber this text with an account of the many committee meetings, proposals, and shuttlings around of responsibilities among governments on this problem. The discussions comprise more than a hundred thousand words with regard to the Russian prisoners in Germany alone.

Some of the Russian prisoners, no doubt with German encouragement, were themselves finding a partial solution to their dilemma by walking home. On February 1, General Dupont of the French Army announced that the number of prisoners had decreased from 1,500,000 at the end of December to about 300,000. Alonzo Taylor of my staff reported from inspection on the ground that this figure was nearer 500,000.

The French and British military authorities at this time raised the point that if these Russian prisoners were repatriated, the Communists among them would join the Red Army and the non-Communists would join rather than have their throats cut. Thus the problem shifted to a military question; obviously, it became the job of the Allied occupation armies in Germany to feed these Russians if they wanted to keep them from their homeland for military reasons.

Since nothing substantial was being done, we tried to arrange a solution, which was set forth in a letter to General Pershing. The idea had been advanced that the United States Army should feed these prisoners and the French Government would pay for the food in francs, which our Army could use. My letter was:

PARIS, 5 March 1919

MY DEAR GENERAL:

As you know, General Harries, who represents you in Berlin in connection with the feeding of Russian prisoners, has continuously put before me the fearful situation of these prisoners and the obligations which he has entered upon towards them. While my organization has neither funds nor authority to do anything for Russian prisoners, we have tried to find some solution for General Harries, and as the result he seems to blame us with the responsibility of the whole thing.

We have, however, now arranged that if the American Army will supply General Harries with the foodstuffs necessary for these prisoners that the French Government will pay the American Army for the supplies so furnished. As you have to have French money to conduct your operations, this should be a fortunate arrangement. We consulted with the American Treasury officials here, who entirely approved the arrangement and absolutely nothing remains to be done in order to get General Harries out of his tremendously difficult situation except for you to issue orders to the S.O.S. to forward him the foodstuffs he requires. As he is in need of emergency supplies, perhaps it could be arranged to send him something from the Coblentz sector. I understand there are quite considerable supplies at Coblentz and as the total amount needed is probably not over 2000 tons a month, it does not seem to be very much of a job.

If you see your way to direct that this be carried out, would you see to it that your people act directly with General Harries instead of transmitting all of their communications through us, as we have insufficient knowledge of Army organization and do not pretend to have any authority over your officers!!!

The whole problem of feeding Russian prisoners is purely a military problem as it is desired to keep these prisoners from joining the Bolshevik. Otherwise, they could have . . . [gone] home. . . . In any event, as the French Government has now agreed to pay for their food, it seems to me the last obstacle is out of the road for the American Army to forthwith supply General Harries. . . .

The original undertaking of the French Government to pay for these supplies has been sent to General McAndrews and if any further assurance is needed that these arrangements will be carried out, I hereby guarantee through the American Relief Administration that the French Government will pay the American Army for these supplies.

I enclose herewith the last telegram which I have from General Harries, which is only one of a long series, equally impressive.

HERBERT HOOVER

General Pershing having approved, I sent the following telegram to General Harries in Berlin:

PARIS, 7 March 1919

. . . Quartermaster will deliver following supplies for Russian prisoners at Coblentz to your representative 1000 tons flour, 500 tons hardtack, 500 tons emergency rations, 200 tons sugar, 50 tons tea. General Pershing will secure authority for shipment through lines and you should arrange for transportation in Germany and send representative Coblentz to direct shipment.

HERBERT HOOVER

However, the French only complied with this agreement for a short time and then placed the matter back in our lap. We argued with the French that they were primarily responsible for keeping the prisoners in Germany and that they were merely furnishing supplies from money lent by the United States. Nevertheless, they insisted that they already had enough debts and refused to go on.

Finally, at this stage, finding that we would have a remnant of the President's previous five-million-dollar contribution from his emergency fund, we took on the job. We furnished 2,685 tons of food at a cost of $1,112,350 to carry on until our authorities ended with the Treaty of Versailles. But this problem of the Russian prisoners was to plague us for some months after the Peace, and I take it up again later on.

BARTER

In order to reduce overseas imports, our American missions in Central and Eastern Europe undertook extensive barter operations among the nations which had some variety of surplus food, or more coal, oil, or reconstruction materials than they could use. In most cases, the animosities of these nations kept them from dealing directly with each other. Some examples will indicate the importance of these transactions.

There was a surplus of food in the Banat province of Yugoslavia which could not, for transport reasons, be used by the starving in Serbia. The Chiefs of our mission, through Captain T. T. C. Gregory of our mission to Hungary, arranged for the purchase of some of this surplus for gold. They also arranged a trade for Banat supplies for coal from Czechoslovakia. They settled a trade to Austria of sugar and coal for railway equipment and machinery.

Altogether, our men negotiated the barter of more than 150,000 tons of food from surplus areas into short areas. We did not bother to incorporate these transactions into our accounts, since no American money was involved, but it would have run into more than fifty million dollars' worth of food supplies if shipped from the United States. I give more details of such transactions in Volume III of *An American Epic.*

THE HOOVER INSTITUTION ON WAR, REVOLUTION, AND PEACE

I mentioned in Volume I of *An American Epic* the enormous collection of historical documents in the Hoover Institution on War, Revolution, and Peace at Stanford University.

On one of my North Sea crossings during the Relief I read in one of Andrew White's writings that most of the contemporary literature of the French Revolution had been lost to history and that without such material it had been very difficult or impossible to reconstruct the real scene. Therein lay the origins of the Hoover Institution on War, Revolution, and Peace at Stanford University.

My original idea was to collect such fugitive documents and complete files of the major dailies and magazines in Britain, France, Germany, Holland, and Switzerland, to which countries I had continuous access, and to add to this any governmental or private documentation on economic and political matters. To do this efficiently, I engaged book dealers and some university professors as collectors and agreed to pay them in dollars after the war on a fair appraisal of their collections. The members of our Relief staff also plunged into this project with zeal.

After the Armistice we gathered up all collected material from these many countries—and I paid those to whom I had made promises. Thus soon after the Armistice the material already ran into millions of important items.

With my appointment to administer relief and reconstruction, the opportunities to expand this undertaking increased greatly.

With the Armistice I brought Professor E. D. Adams, the head of the History Department at Stanford University, to Paris to direct these collections. The organization which I directed now had four thousand able, intelligent Americans serving in every part of Europe and in close association with the high officials of the various governments. They took a great interest in building the collections. In time they developed a technique of securing important material. They found that the heads of revolutionary governments had little hesitation in allowing our men to select or copy documents from their predecessors' files. Also, they found that the expelled officials in these revolutions were glad to sell their documents or to place them in an accessible place for safekeeping.

General Pershing was greatly impressed with the importance of the project, and he assigned to Professor Adams some twenty former assistant professors and instructors of history from the Army. He kept them in uniform and maintained their salaries and expenses from the Army until it was able to send them home.

Our Paris staff secured all the public documents and volumes of material from the peace delegations—some of it confidential.

SECTION V

SPECIAL JOINT ACTIONS BEHIND THE FRONT

INTRODUCTION

I have segregated certain joint actions of the United States, Britain, France, and Italy in order that this narrative may more adequately demonstrate the co-operation of the four nations—and of many of the states suffering from the famine. They indicate the difficulties of organization "behind the front line" and great undertakings that were necessary.

These special joint actions were:

Overseas transport
Management and reconstruction of Eastern European railways
Management of inland waterways and ports
Management of Eastern European coal mines and securing petroleum products

These undertakings constantly involved the Supreme Council and the Supreme Economic Council. Through them all, the Allied and American leaders in the war participated in their organization.

Aside from the vital accomplishments in relief and reconstruction, these operations show many sidelights upon the history of those times.

CHAPTER 42

OVERSEAS TRANSPORT

As of January 1, 1919, the reports of the Allied Maritime Transport Council showed—exclusive of tankers, ships in military use, and ships under repair—a residue of the Allied and Associated Powers' dry-cargo vessels as follows (in gross tons):

British	9,266,989
French	899,647
Italian	604,676
Belgian	119,387
American	1,914,457
Total	12,805,156

The Neutrals at this time had remaining the following shipping of all kinds (in tons):

Norway	822,941
Sweden	403,634
Holland	551,154
Denmark	340,759
Spain	451,661
Total	2,570,149

Of this 2,570,149 tons, excluding passenger vessels, tankers, ships in repair, those needed for their new supplies, and those already requisitioned by the Allied and Associated Powers, there remained only about 250,000 tons of dry cargo ships which were available for food transport—that is, if the Neutrals had the mind to charter them.

The relief task was to transport—or supervise—about forty million tons of food, medicines, clothing, and reconstruction materials into forty-five foreign areas within nine months. We were slowed down in obtaining German and Austrian merchant ships by the four and one-half months' delay from the continued blockade. Moreover, ships were required to bring armies and their equipment home. Worse still, every nation was eager to restore its foreign trade.

In January, 1919, our estimate of the tonnage we required in constant use was:

	Shipping Required per Month [in Tons]
Baltic States	400,000
Belgium	400,000
Northern France C.R.B.	60,000
Poland	180,000
Czecho-Slovakia	180,000
Roumania	110,000
Serbia	60,000
Austria	200,000
Hungary	200,000
Jugo-Slavia	200,000
Bulgaria	25,000
Armenia	100,000
Turkey and Middle East	200,000
	2,315,000

In addition to this, when the food blockade was lifted, Germany would need about 400,000 tons of cargo ships in constant use—since some journeys must be made to the Argentine. The unending delays in securing German merchant shipping compelled me to raise our estimates. In any event, we were dependent on the American Shipping Board and the Allied Maritime Transport Council for ships.

THE AMERICAN SHIPPING BOARD

The American shipbuilding program had largely broken down during the war and it was not until the Armistice that consequential tonnage was launched. Most of these ships were so small that after carrying their coal, they had little cargo capacity. Our organization did use some of them, mostly for intercoastal transport in Europe, and we thus saved our larger ships for the longer journeys.

We had arranged, with the President's approval, for our American Shipping Board to furnish an average of 500,000 tons of cargo capacity per month, beginning February first. Our first disillusionment from this quarter came, in cable form, from Washington:

February 12, 1919

. . . Shipping Board agreed to supply 400,000 cargo tons sailing February. . . . They have to date assigned . . . 226,000 cargo tons. Of this amount we fear that 90,000 . . . tons will not clear by end month. . . . Shipping Board insist they are stripped to the bone but we are protesting vigorously that original agreement must be lived up to.

I was later informed that aside from the February deficiency, the Shipping Board had assigned us only 300,000 tons for March instead of the promised 580,000 tons. They advised that there were no assignments for April whatever. I cabled our New York office as follows:

17 March 1919

. . . Please express to Hurley [Chairman of the Shipping Board] the necessity of prompt firm assurance that Shipping Board will lift our programmes in order that we may present a strong front in our negotiations with the British to get them to do their share. . . . Also it is essential we be able to give positive assurance to the various peoples we are feeding upon which they can rely in setting up their rationing programmes.

I would like to suggest the following considerations arising out of the situation. . . . Mr. Rosseter [of the Shipping Board] agreed with us that if we would surrender all use of the army tonnage for relief purposes . . .

the Shipping Board would undertake to transport our programmes. We withdrew from the position where we could have had an unfailing use of a definite tonnage from the army . . . [but] the Shipping Board has not been able to fulfill its promises. . . .

. . . the President is in entire accord with the complete necessity of our continuing this sacrifice for the next three months by which time we shall have largely completed our national duty in the matter.

HOOVER

Edward N. Hurley was an efficient businessman serving his government at great personal sacrifice. But he could not resist the great pressure from American exporters for ships. He personally regarded the relief of Europe as secondary to our export trade. On March 18, in an interview with our New York and Washington directors, he found new excuses. A condensation of the New York report on this interview was:

. . . He states British are employing large tonnage in former trades moving ships in ballast or with part cargoes to maintain regular routes. Cites as example British tonnage moving large quantities cotton from Southern ports at double Shipping Board rates which they able exact because of lack American tonnage that trade. Also states British maintaining other commercial schedules our ports. . . .

States [that Italian] . . . ships are being used in commercial trades only. . . .

. . . Would not make promise of prompt allocations even if Army turned over additional tonnage immediately but definitely postponed final statement until above information obtained. . . .

Altogether, Hurley was in a bad humor. He did furnish a few ships, but failed entirely to carry out our agreed program. Things were getting desperate, and on March 24, the President cabled Hurley and Secretary of War Baker:

A review of the food situation in Europe shows that it is essential that transportation asked for by Hoover for April loading shall be furnished without fail. The human, political and military issues that revolve upon any failure of delivery of this program are incalculable. I therefore desire that the Shipping Board shall find the tonnage necessary and am confident that they may count upon the War Department to share the burden to the point of sacrificing all but the most absolutely necessary services. While it is probable that British Government has considerable duty in this direction, there seems little hope of their undertaking much service by April loading of ships and therefore we must take no risks and carry the burden for that month. I feel sure that a realization by our people of this, a service second only to the mission of our Army in Europe, will reconcile them to any sacrifice that is necessary for its execution. I am informed that the burden upon us will rapidly relax after the end of April and therefore the sacrifice is of temporary duration.

WOODROW WILSON

Two days later, our New York office cabled that Hurley and the War Department would not accede to the requests of the President, saying:

NEW YORK, March 26, 1919

HOOVER:

After joint conference War Department, Shipping Board, ourselves, Hurley states that maximum tonnage that can be allocated for relief shipments up to end of April is three hundred thousand tons deadweight. In securing this tonnage army has released some cargo boats carrying army supplies. . . .

. . . Shipping Board will absolutely make no commitments beyond end of April leaving this for future negotiations after we are advised as to availability of . . . [German refugee] cargo steamers. . . .

FOOD ADMINISTRATION

I promptly dispatched this letter to Mr. Wilson:

27 March 1919

MY DEAR MR. PRESIDENT:

I have received the attached telegram . . . in response to my request for 500,000 tons of food loaded in the month of April and in response to your direction to . . . [Hurley] and the War Department that he should find this tonnage. Mr. Hurley states that he will not find more than 300,000 tons.

In arriving at 500,000 tons, I took the theoretical necessity of the various peoples under relief, which amounted to 800,000 tons [to be contributed by the United States], and I reduced each single item to the lowest point that I thought was possible, and arrived at 620,000 tons but knowing the acuteness of Mr. Hurley's position I reduced it . . . to 500,000 tons. I wish to say that I simply cannot take the responsibility for this situation unless this tonnage is provided as we have requested. Every country that we have under relief is rumbling with social explosion. All the people in these countries are under drastic food regime[s] and to make a cut in the amount of 60% of their . . . [minimum] necessities can mean only a total collapse.

HERBERT HOOVER

Hurley made promises, but as before, the pressure on him by the export traders proved too strong. I was again compelled to ask for help from the President:

PARIS, April 25, 1919

MY DEAR MR. PRESIDENT:

I am extremely sorry to trouble you with any matter of lesser import than those which you are faced.

I then reviewed the Shipping Board's failures and continued:

. . . I am only able to eke out during the present month by borrowing [food] from other governments as against future replacements on an extremely expensive basis.

I feel that I have at least the right to inform you of my total inability to carry out the obligation that has been placed upon me in this situation. I have no desire to desert the post, but it does not seem to me fair that I should be given this responsibility and given assurances that would enable its execution, and then to be faced with this constant failure. When you consider that the American mercantile fleet delivered into Europe during the last days of the war nearly one million tons of commodities per month and that the Army is now . . . [requiring] only 100,000 tons per month of supplies, and when you consider the very considerable increase in our fleet, I think you will appreciate that I am not asking for the impossible. We have in effect asked that in the month of April—our most trying month—that we should have one-third of our fleet withdrawn from commercial trades in order to save Europe.

Incidentally, I hear that Mr. Hurley is about to assign ships for loading of coal to Italy, in order to enlarge employment of our coal miners. I would like to point out that if the same rates are charged on coal to Italy that are charged on food to starving populations, it will cost from $35 to $40 a ton to deliver this coal in Italy, out of which some $4 or $5 will be the purchase price of the coal on the . . . seaboard and from this amount the American miner will receive less than $2.00 a ton. The Italian credits are absolutely worthless and therefore in order to give $2.00 worth of employment in the United States, our Government is about to expend $35. The British have taken the obligation, and are performing their obligation, to furnish Italy with coal. It would occur to me that it . . . [would be] better to stem the tide of starvation in Europe and to devote the waste of $33 on sending a ton of coal to Italy to the employment of [American] workmen at shovelling sand on the beach.

HERBERT HOOVER

On April 28, the President wrote Henry Robinson, who represented the Shipping Board in Paris:

MY DEAR MR. ROBINSON:

Will you not be kind enough to . . . in my name make the strongest representations to the Shipping Board. . . . It is evidently, I think, a case of the unwillingness of the Franklin Committee [which assigned the ships] to divert ships from commercial routes which may promise large profits but in a matter of world exigency like this the Franklin Committee should be made to yield and cooperate. With regard to the arrangements for shipping coal to Italy . . . obviously this is not the time to further Italian industrial interests at the expense of feeding a distracted world. I am sure that you will agree with me in these matters.

The President informed me verbally that he had taken care of the problem. Whatever that care was, it was more effective than his previous efforts. Hurley assigned us a monthly average of 250,000 tons of ships, one-half of the promised tonnage upon which our whole structure of saving lives was based. Our deficits in deliveries to starving people were caused by the Shipping Board.

BRITISH SHIPS

Often in our negotiations for the organization of relief and reconstruction, the British had stated that while they could supply but little food because of their own import needs, their major contribution would be overseas transportation. They agreed to find us ships—from somewhere—amounting to 1,500,000 tons monthly. They more nearly complied with their promises than did the United States Shipping Board. Because our shipping needs for the subsequent months of April, May, June, and July increased to 2,800,000 tons a month, I presented a detailed statement of these requirements to the Supreme Economic Council at the end of March.

When Lord Robert Cecil became head of the British economic agencies in Paris, we began to receive real co-operation. For instance, we impressed upon the British food and shipping representatives the sheer nonsense and waste of their bringing many food supplies from the Far East and Australia—through the Suez Canal and thence two thousand miles to Britain—while at the same time we were sending food over the same route to the Black Sea and Adriatic ports. Lord Robert Cecil arranged to divert many substantial shipments through the Suez to the Black Sea, which helped Rumania greatly in the acute months.

GERMAN AND AUSTRIAN REFUGEE MERCHANT SHIPS

The German and Austrian merchant ships, which had taken wartime refuge in their own and Neutral ports, totaled about 2,600,000 tons. In his message of December 1 to the Allied Prime Ministers, the President had insisted that we have these ships for relief. And during all the negotiations with the Germans, from January to March, the Allied and American shipping representatives constantly urged upon them and the Austrians that their ships were required for relief purposes.

It was not until the Brussels agreement of March 14 that the Germans and Austrians began to deliver these refugee ships. However, the Big Four, without consulting our organization, handed the ships to the Allied Maritime Transport Council. This body promptly divided them among the Allies, with a recommendation that we be given part of them by each of the four governments. The division was as follows:

Britain	1,153,000 tons
France	486,000 "
Italy	596,000 "
United States	450,000 "
Belgium	8,000 "

We naturally pressed the different nations for these ships. We did not secure a ton from either the French or the Italians. Upon the President's orders, all of the dry-cargo ships in the American allotment were handed to us.

There were many delays because the refugee ships had to be manned by Allied crews and provided with bunker coal and voyage supplies. Those ships we were able to get only began delivery of food supplies to Europe at the end of April.

BLACKLISTED SHIPS

Another shipping matter also illustrates the bad headaches involved in the relief and reconstruction job. Since the French and British did not like certain Neutral shipowners because of their war crimes or for other reasons, they had blacklisted a number of their ships, thus keeping them off the seas. Although most of the ships were small, they could be of great use to us for reshipments from Rotterdam and Copenhagen to ports on the Baltic, thereby shortening the journeys of our larger ships. There were 348 of these blacklisted ships in Sweden, Norway, Denmark, and Holland—a total of about 80,000 tons. Through the efforts of Henry Robinson, we finally obtained most of them, but it required months of argument.

With the few ships from the American Shipping Board, the generous transport supplied by the British, and the Neutral charters we obtained at outrageous rates, we were able to meet the most acute situations. But hundreds of millions of persons suffered. Had it not been for our early loading of American ships in the month following the Armistice and our huge Army surplus, we would have met the complete disaster of mass starvation.

CHAPTER 43

MANAGEMENT AND RECONSTRUCTION OF EASTERN EUROPEAN RAILWAYS

Prior to the Armistice the railways in Eastern Europe had been co-ordinated within the systems of the old German, Austrian, and Russian empires. Some were government owned and operated; others were private enterprises. When these empires disintegrated, the railways were cut into disconnected segments. The systems of the old empires usually radiated from their major cities like spokes in a wagon wheel. With the division of the territory into new states, many of the spokes were cut off. For instance, the new state of Poland included parts of disconnected railway systems of Germany, Russia, and Austria. The new state of Austria still had the hub of its railway system radiating from Vienna, but now the spokes were in Poland, Hungary, Czechoslovakia, Yugoslavia, and Italy. Altogether, there were now eighteen different railway systems whereas originally there were three. Some cities could not be reached from the other parts of the same country without passing into foreign states and were therefore isolated.

Each new state at once created a railway ministry or department. The principal function of the new railway officials was to grab all the rolling stock they could lay hands on and refuse to allow its passage over their frontiers—for fear they would never see it again. These new governments also used their control of railways for political and trade pressures on their neighbors. Until we solved this problem, more than fifteen nations had incorporated these practices into their railway management. Some states had too big a share of rolling stock, some too little. There had been much war destruction and little maintenance. All the tracks and rolling stock were in bad condition. Never had there been such chaos and paralysis in the world of rail transportation.

Our first move on this front was, in December, 1918, to set up in our Paris office a railway section, under a staff of experienced railway men. The leaders were Colonel William G. Atwood, Lt. Colonel William B. Causey, Lt. Colonel William B. Ryan, Colonel J. W. McIntosh, and a host of able assistants from the American Army Engineers. After some tryouts, Colonel Atwood became chief of our Railway Division in Paris; Colonel McIntosh, in charge of Adriatic ports; Colonel Ryan, in charge of our Northeastern railway organization; and Colonel Causey, in charge of our Southeastern railway setup.

Because of the railway chaos, our supplies began, in mid-December, 1918, to pile up in the Adriatic ports—while inland cities were starving. Coal movements had slowed down so much that municipal services were being suspended. People were not only hungry but cold—and in the dark.

Initially, I had sent Colonel Ryan to Vienna, where he called a meeting of the railway ministers of five adjacent states, all of whom could speak German. However, it was the first time in a century that four languages had enjoyed equal dignity with German, and each minister insisted on speaking his own tongue and having the replies translated. The Colonel reported that it took an hour to say good morning—and even that was in offensive tones. By way of general comment on these meetings, he wrote:

> I have about come to the conclusion that the only way to handle Central Europe is a military dictatorship. These new nations cannot be made to work together by anything like moral suasion. They do not proceed on those tracks. The people in Paris don't know the hates in this territory.

I soon learned the hates. The new nations were taking everything they could get and doing every evil thing to their neighbors that they had hoped to do for centuries.

One of our worst jams occurred to the northward from the port of Trieste. In January, we sent Colonel Causey to succeed Colonel Ryan, whom I needed elsewhere. Colonel Causey had, for a short time before the war, been president of an uncertain, wobbly middle western railway system which I will call the C. & G. Z. He was a profane man. When he had been in Vienna about a week, freight was still being tied up, and he did not respond to our urgent inquiries. We finally sent a telegram to Captain T. T. C. Gregory, chief of our mission in Vienna, asking him to locate Causey and find out what he was doing and why he did not reply. A few hours later, we received this telegram:

> Saw Causey. He says . . . he also says he has been . . . busy. He says further these . . . railways are in worse shape than the . . . [C.&.G.Z.].
>
> T. T. C. GREGORY

Some paragraphs from the reports of our American railway men in Eastern Europe shed light on the consequences of war and are also very human documents. The following is a summary of a report to Captain Gregory from Lieutenant A. J. Barclay, one of Colonel Causey's men:

> PRAGUE, BOHEMIA, 20 February 1919
>
> 1. Pursuant to your verbal instructions, the following condensed log is furnished, descriptive of the passage of the first food train, Trieste to Prague.
>
> 2. The train left Trieste at 6:30 p.m., Sunday Feb. 16. . . . It consisted of 14 Cheko-Slovak cars loaded with 3,007 sacks of white flour. . . . With me on the trip . . . [was] Capt. John Tuther of Col. McIntosh's office. . . . The train, scheduled to leave at 3:00, was late, awaiting arrival of 25 Chek soldiers who were to guard it.
>
> Two Italian engines . . . were used at the start, with an Italian train crew. These engines were captured Austrian stock, and were not very powerful, and also badly needed overhauling. The grades outside of Trieste are steep (averaging about 2½%) and these two engines barely made it, with 200 tons load.
>
> First night passed without incident or delay, except that the Italian

train crew went to sleep on their brakes, and the train ran wild down the long hill between Opcina and Reifenberg . . . before they could get it under control. Fortunately we did not meet anything and stopped on the next uphill grade.

Arrived Podbrdo, the Yugo-Slav frontier at 9:30 a.m. Feb. 17, where a Yugo-Slav crew was put on. Engines were also changed, giving us one Austrian "Decapod" . . . which was quite powerful and well adapted for mountain work. We were delayed here about 3 hours, because the Italians would not let go of the passenger coach in which we were riding. It seems the Yugo-Slavs have been stealing Italian cars, (and vice-versa) and neither party will allow any equipment to get out of their hands. This is a point that should be kept in mind. . . .

At Feistreich-Woch were delayed about an hour making out "way bills" (or Italian equivalent) as freight had been paid to Italians up to the border. From here on it is paid at Prague.

This part of the line was handling 55–60 trains a day before the war. Now they are handling four, two each way. . . .

After a day's going over heavy mountain grades, arrived at Assling at 4:00 p.m. No particular delays were encountered, except the stopping at nearly every station until the line could be cleared. This took usually about one-half hour.

. . . At Assling . . . we had . . . about 2 hours delay account of hot-box, and had to unload one car of flour into a good car. . . .

Just beyond Assling there is a tunnel 8 kilometers long. This had been wrecked by the soldiers during the war, but is now repaired and in operation. We were the first train through since the repairs were made. This is fortunate, as it not only saves about 6 hours run . . . but also avoids re-entering and leaving of Italian territory . . . with attendant delays.

In this connection, I am today informed that the Yugo-Slavs and the Austrians are fighting again near the tunnel, and are using artillery. The extent of this trouble cannot now be ascertained. Will write it as I learn of it.

At the Rosenbach end of the tunnel Austrian guards were put on, one guard to each Yugo-Slav trainman, for the purpose of watching them. The train crews were changed at Rosenbach, and the guards left.

Beyond the tunnel is German-Austrian territory. . . . Was told that there are no passenger trains running, and that we were the first train through since January 6. At Rosenbach . . . before the war there used to be about 65 trains a day through this station, but now 4 is a big day.

At St. Veit had about 5 hours delay account of inability to get coal for the engine, and also because the Austrians put a foreign car into the middle of the train, and there was a lot of switching done with our engine. This use of food trains to carry local freight is a fruitful cause of delay, and should be strenuously objected to. . . .

At Knittelfeld there are large car shops, and considerable yard facilities. The car shops are not running, as nearly as I could learn, at all. There are a very large number of "dead" engines standing around. I was told that there are 102 locomotives here, of which about 20 are fit for use. This is borne out by appearances. Coal is extremely scarce, and some of the engines are burning wood. The yards were practically empty of cars, not over 20 being seen. . . .

Before the war about 30 trains a day passed this point. Now there are 6, 2 passenger and 4 freight.

At St. Michael arrived 1:25 p.m. Lost about an hour changing engines. . . . Here we picked up 5 foreign cars loaded with wood for various points.

Arrived Selzthal 5:00 p.m. . . .

Grades very steep on both sides of the town. Enginemen tell me that these Decapod engines can pull 900 tons north and 500 tons south from this point. In view of the performance of our engines I should say 500 and 300 would be a closer guess.

We lost about 2 hours at Selzthal. . . .

. . . Am informed that there were only 17 engines at this point, of which 4 were unfit. This information is not assured, as I don't believe the man knew much on any subject, although appearances bore him out.

Picked up onto our string here, 12 cars various freight. We put in a protest, but the Austrian officials said they knew nothing of ours being a special train.

Arrived at Freistadt 8:00 a.m. Feb. 18. During the night . . . we lost about 5 hours switching and picking up foreign cars. In the morning our string was 44 cars, of which about 12 were loads of pig iron, which held us back considerably. Further protests were wired to Prague, to stop this practice.

Arrived . . . at Oberhaid, the first Cheko-Slovak town at 10:00 a.m. At this place lost 2 hours account of customs officials collecting *on the freight that was not ours.* This customs office delay can be avoided by running special trains for the food, and is worth doing.

Arrived Budweis 2:00 p.m. . . . (They had a band to meet us at the station.)

Lost 2 hours here on account of customs officials, who have more than the usual amount of "official inertia." This man took our papers to his uptown office for consideration, and it took about an hour to get permission for the train to proceed. This fellow will have to be watched. There is no hostility but a large amount of typical Austrian officiousness.

At Budweis we got rid of our foreign cars, and got orders to run express to Prague. Left Budweis 4:00 p.m. and ran rapidly to Prague, arriving without further incident at 10:30 p.m.

3. The following notes may be of value in future shipments:

. . . The Yugo-Slavs are in sympathy with the Czechs, and no hindrances outside of the usual "hookworm" [slow action] should be expected.

The German-Austrian country is a different proposition, and one that will have to be handled carefully and tactfully. The Austrians are very hostile toward the Yugo-Slavs, and not especially friendly toward the Cheko-Slavs. . . . (Cigarettes will . . . help, judiciously used.)

Around St. Michael and Selzthal, children boarded the train several times, begging for bread. This seems significant. I was told that the bread allowance is 1-½ pounds per head *per week* around here.

In Cheko-[Slovakia] . . . the food situation is acute. Babies are dying daily in large numbers because of lack of milk. All shipments of fats should include a large percentage (40–50) of milk. Generally speaking, however, the crying needs are for (1) flour (2) meats and fats. There is also great need of soap, medical supplies, coffee, rice and lean meats. Here in Prague many of the butcher shops have gone out of business and closed up.

. . . On the whole of our trip up I saw only 6 or 8 trains pass us, and those well along on the way. . . . the line will hold practically any amount of traffic we can put on it, as it is now hardly carrying any. About 4 trains a day is the average over the whole distance. . . .

Nowhere on the line was any appreciable number of cars seen. The yards are all practically empty, and there are no cars standing on sidings along the line. Those that I did see were all in active use, apparently.

There are lots of engines in Austria, but whether enough of them can be used is a question. They are reported all in bad shape, but a detailed inquiry will be necessary to settle the question.

A representative of the Cheko-Slovak government should be on each train. This is essential. He should speak German and Czech, and Italian would also be useful. The presence of an American officer lends great eclat in Austria, and will probably be justified. A guard will always be needed.

Food trains should be run as special trains, and any admixture of "foreign" cars strictly forbidden, as it causes endless trouble and delay.

Much care should be exercised on the trips that no food cars are stolen from the back end of the train. This can readily happen.

The customs officials (which should not be a necessity in shipments of this character) should be watched, and kept hot after, to avoid useless delay.

The Austrians should be tactfully handled. . . . They greatly need tobacco, and a few tins of "Prince Albert" might go a long ways to save valuable time. . . .

4. In conformity with instructions I have included herein much detailed information, and comments, which have come under my observation. It is a very detailed subject and has made the report rather long. But I believe the details . . . are not non-essentials, in as much as they illustrate the situations encountered.

A. J. Barclay
1st Lt. Engrs. U.S.A.

Captain Tuther, who was along on the trip, reported that at a conference with the staff of a Czechoslovak transportation ministry, he was told that the Austrians claimed a shortage of cars and live locomotives. He made the following written statement:

. . . [Concerning] the division of locomotives . . . [formerly under] Austro-Hungary, the . . . [Czech] proportion numbered 2,000, but that only 1,000 had been secured, and of that 1,000 [locomotives] 600 were being used for the transportation of troops, leaving 400 locomotives available. When questioned why a larger number of the locomotives available were not . . . sent to Trieste, the Minister stated that 10 had been sent and that others would be sent promptly and in sufficient number.

The officers of the convoy called on President Masaryk and informed him of the obstructive actions of the Italian railroad authorities at Trieste. The President promised that he would take up this matter vigorously and at once with the Italian Ambassador at Prague and would instruct his representative in Paris to act. Returning from Prague to Trieste, Captain Tuther observed at Tarvis—150 kilometers from Trieste—two trains containing thirty-two cars of flour and fats which had been three days en route, with no immediate prospect of continuing the journey.

The Italians became one of our great trials. They had been given certain guarantees for expansion of their empire as a consideration for joining in the war. With the course of events at the Peace Conference, there seemed little likelihood of performance. The Adriatic ports were occupied by their armies, and railway connections to Austria, Czechoslovakia, Hungary, and Yugoslavia were in Italian control. In their discontents, the Italians made free use of these weapons on their neighbors. We had set up an "international food commission" for that area, hoping, by Italian inclusion and Allied help, we could solve local problems. I give some quotations, indicating what Italians were doing. On February 12, I sought the aid of President Wilson:

February 12, 1919

DEAR MR. PRESIDENT:

The feeding of the Czecho- . . . [Slovaks, Austrians] and Serbians all revolves around the use of port facilities and a single railway running out of Trieste. The Italians have taken such an attitude towards these other peoples that the operation of the railway is practically hopeless for the distance that it traverses Italian occupied territory. They have also stopped all communication through to Trieste from these territories and we are not even able to send the most commonplace telegrams with regard to food. They are apparently driving all of the other races than Italians out of Trieste and the consequence is that we have little reliable labor for discharging ships.

We have used every argument possible with the Italian authorities and there is in my view but one solution: that is . . . the operation of such docks and railways as we need for feeding these interior people . . . [should] be placed under the direction of the Interallied Food Commission . . . and the actual executive control vested in the American member. Their attitude . . . is such that I . . . protest most strongly against any further Treasury advances to the Italian Government until this . . . fearful injustice is put right. If you approve, I will ask Mr. Davis to make it a condition of further advances with the Treasury that this situation shall be straightened out to my satisfaction.

HERBERT HOOVER

Mr. Wilson replied:

PARIS, 14 February, 1919

MY DEAR HOOVER:

I think this may be a very useful piece of advice to give Mr. Davis in advising him how he is to handle this exceedingly important matter.

WOODROW WILSON

However, Davis' efforts did not cure our Italian trouble. On February 14, Captain Gregory telegraphed me from Trieste:

. . . During all this time the [Italian] Military authorities here refused to recognize the existence of the [Relief Mission]. . . .

. . . It is . . . clear . . . to see . . . the . . . effect of control of Trieste and Fiume . . . on the commercial future of . . . [Czecho-Slovakia], Austria, Hungary and Jugo Slavia which trade through Trieste and Fiume. Italian military forces . . . occupy a strip which gives them control of sixty miles of railroad, and this with the possession of the ports gives them an absolute strangle-hold on all the business moving in and out. . . .

. . . While perhaps we may not be interested in the conditions which are permanently to exist here, we are . . . vitally interested in them in relation to our food movements inland, and I can assure you right now that unless the Italian military regime here is given a heavy jolt . . . we will never . . . [fulfill] our shipping program. . . .

On February 18, I received another report from Captain Gregory in which he stated that our food was being held up by orders of the Italian Chief of Staff at Trieste. We fired off a vigorous telegram to Gregory, directing him to show this officer that he was violating orders of the Supreme War Council. On February 19, I wrote to the American peace delegation, protesting Italian obstruction:

We are compelled to use the port of Trieste for the supply of foodstuffs to [Austria], Czecho-Slovakia and to large parts of Jugo-Slavia. . . . We have placed large quantities of food at the disposal of these interior peoples and we have asked them to send their railway trains and officials to take delivery of it. The Italians have stopped every effort on their part to reach Trieste with their railway equipment. They have stopped our communications. . . . Italy receives advances for all the food she requires from the United States. . . . I consider that the time has arrived in view of this attitude that Italy should be notified that all her advances from the United States will cease immediately unless she is willing to receive directions from the . . . [Relief Organization] with respect to . . . the management of port and railway facilities running out of Trieste for the feeding of these people.

General Bliss privately advised the Italian delegation of the contents of my recommendation. This had no effect.

On February 22, Colonel Causey wrote, in a memorandum to Captain Gregory:

. . . On my arrival in Vienna, I found a new demand had been made on the . . . Austrian Government by the Italians for 177 engines and for some 3,000 railroad cars. The claim was made that this equipment is due the Italians in conformity with the armistice conditions. The Italians threatened that . . . the number of food trains being run into Austria daily would be immediately reduced from four to three and if the entire demand was not complied with by February 25, the movement of all food trains by the Italians into German Austria would be discontinued. . . .

. . . The Food situation in Vienna is, if anything, worse than ever. This week has been a meatless week in Vienna. The coal situation is worse than it was when we arrived in Vienna the first of January, the shipments of Bohemian coal having been gradually falling off since the first of February. The statement that food trains have been unable to move because of lack of coal for locomotives was correct. . . .

. . . The coal supply for domestic use in Vienna has become so diminished that thousands of households are now entirely without coal.

. . . The promise made me at Laibach on February 19 . . . by the Jugo-Slavs to deliver four engines to the Italians at Loitsch at 1 P.M. February 20 was not lived up to. . . .

. . . The whole question is in a terrible and inexcusable tangle. . . .

. . . An unfortunate occurrence at Laibach . . . has caused the . . . Italian Army to order that no food trains would be permitted to go via the Southern Railway . . . [from] Trieste. The Italians claim direct insult to their flag . . . the Jugo-Slavs disclaim responsibility. . . .

After the parties for the conference had assembled at the Italian Railway Director's Office at 4:00 P.M. the Director announced that he could not go in conference with the Jugo-Slav Representatives as diplomatic relations had been broken between the Italians and the Jugo-Slavs. . . .

. . . This means that until diplomatic relations are re-established between the Italians and the Jugo-Slavs, that all food trains out of Trieste must go over the single track line via Gorz, Udine, Tarvis and Villach. . . .

. . . Up to the present time seven (7) food trains have moved out of Trieste for Bohemia. I understand that two of these trains are held up at the Jugo-Slav border. . . .

W. B. Causey

On February 23, Colonel Causey made a further statement:

If the foodstuff now in Trieste is not to be allowed to rot in the warehouses, the . . . Food Administration must be given authority to operate southern railway between Trieste and Vienna or to dictate the manner in which the railway should be operated and have the proper forces to insure the non-interference with the scheme.

Up to the present time only 1340 metric tons . . . have moved out of Trieste for the Czechs. . . .

. . . The breaking off of relations between the Italians and the Jugo-Slavs has closed the former avenue of approach [to Trieste] for empty equipment. . . .

We had just as well realized now that this situation must be taken hold of by an iron hand, otherwise there is no possible chance of moving the foodstuff out of Trieste or relieve what we know to be actual suffering among the peoples for whom the food was brought to Trieste. . . .

. . . we are sitting here absolutely helpless and that the situation can never improve until there is some power to force proper operation of the transportation system. . . .

. . . there has [not] been more than one week of actual operation with a total movement of only seven trains. . . . More ships are on the way to Trieste and I am informed that . . . the warehouses are full of foodstuffs already.

. . . I feel it my duty as the Transportation member of this organization to endeavor to bring this question to a head immediately. Further delay . . . is simply courting disaster. . . .

W. B. Causey

Since the Italian Chief of Staff at Trieste persisted in hampering all of our efforts, I took the matter up directly with the Italian delegation in Paris. A telegram from Captain Gregory showed the results:

ROME, 25 February 1919

. . . The action which you took in Paris had the desired effect and the reason for the removal of the Chief of Staff at Trieste is well known and understood by all now or hereafter to be concerned so that once we get going again I think we will have no difficulty whatever with the local authorities.

Our load was lightened for only three days. Then the Italian Government officially announced that diplomatic relations with Yugoslavia had been broken off and stopped all our movements of supplies into that country from the Adriatic. On February 25, Captain Gregory went to Rome to appeal to Prime Minister Orlando. He reported that the Prime Minister would do nothing until the Yugoslav incident was settled. It was obvious that drastic measures had to be taken to prevent millions of deaths, plus anarchy in five nations.

On February 28, the American mission cabled the President (who was in Washington), after a conference with me, as follows:

28 February 1919

FOR THE PRESIDENT

Hoover informs us that since February first he has had large supplies of food at Trieste and has been strenuously endeavoring to obtain its distribution by railway inland to [Austrians], Jugo-Slavs and Czecho-Slovaks but that by one difficulty after another in inland transport less than one-third the needed supplies have been moved during the month of February. . . .

The telegram described the situation in detail and continued:

You will see the situation has come to a head and the only possible solution seems to be for you to authorize us to notify the Italians that we do not propose to have foodstuffs used further as a political weapon in Southern Europe, and that we cannot be expected to continue financing

Italian food supplies if this situation continues, and that we expect the Italians not only to consent but earnestly to support the proposal of Hoover that the amount of railway rolling stock formerly belonging to the railways running out of Trieste, including the stock recently demanded from Austria, shall be assigned to him as Director General of Relief to be operated at his direction under Interallied Commission at Trieste, for the sole transportation of food and that every facility shall be given at the port of Trieste and other Italian occupied territory for its movement.

[LANSING]

On March 3, I was so advised:

DEAR MR. HOOVER:

. . . President directs me to state that he approves of the action proposed. . . .

J. C. GREW
[Assistant Secretary of State]

On March 5, I asked Secretary Lansing to arrange for me to present the situation to the Supreme War Council. At this conclave he and Colonel House represented the United States in Mr. Wilson's absence. Premier Clemenceau attended. Mr. Balfour represented the British and Baron Sonino the Italians. The minutes show that I spoke about the piling up of food in the ports, the total inability of our representatives to get the co-operation of the Italians, and the complete chaos of the Eastern European railways in general. I reported that people were dying of starvation and that action by the Council was critically necessary to control interior transportation. In conclusion, I stated:

The solution which I propose, after elaborate investigation by American Railway Engineers, is one that I not only believe is feasible but will meet the various exigencies of the political situation. To this end the following plan is proposed: (*a*) all the states of the old Austrian Empire, including the areas held by the Italians on the Adriatic, should be called upon to furnish a definite contribution of railway rolling stock; (*b*) This rolling stock should be marked as belonging to the Relief Administration and used solely for its purposes; (*c*) The Director General of Relief should be made the mandatory for the disposition of this rolling stock; (*d*) A regular train service should be established under his direction that will carry out the necessary programmes of food to the different localities; (*e*) This service should have entire freedom of movement over all railways regardless of political boundaries and in complete priority to other services; (*f*) The railway servants of any nationality may be employed in operations over any territory regardless of nationality or political boundaries; (*g*) Definite portions of port facilities should be assigned to the Relief Administration at Trieste and Fiume for the consummation of these ends; (*h*) The rolling stock should not be demanded by any of the . . . Governments until this service is completely equipped; (*i*) That the railways officials of each state and port officials in each port should be called upon to co-operate in maintenance of this service.

The minutes also record in the following discussion:

Mr. Hoover added in regard to his recommendation (*c*) that he proposed that one person should be made Director . . . [of the railways] because he did not think that any inter-allied body could give the requisite executive punch to a situation of this kind.

However, the British, French, and Italians demanded an inter-Allied commission. I was glad to agree, provided that I could appoint the chairman and his staff from experienced American railway men. We were also glad to have the British, French, and Italians witness our woes.

On March 7, the Supreme War Council issued the following directions:

[Mr. Hoover's Proposal as finally amended and accepted by the Council of Ten.]

(*a*) All the States of the old Austrian Empire, including the areas held by the Italians on the Adriatic, should be called upon to furnish a definite contribution of railway rolling stock.

(*b*) This rolling stock should be marked as belonging to the Relief Administration and will be given priority for that purpose.

(*c*) The Director-General of Relief *working through the Communica-*

tions Section of the Supreme Economic Council should be made the Mandatory for the disposition of this rolling stock.

(*d*) A regular train service should be established under *his* direction that will carry out the necessary programmes of food to the different localities.

(*e*) This service should have entire freedom of movement over all railways regardless of political boundaries and in complete priority to other services except military, and within the Italian frontier this will be carried out in co-operation with the Italian authorities.

(*f*) The Railway servants of any nationality may be employed in operations over any territory within the old Austrian empire, regardless of nationality or political boundaries.

(*g*) The Italian authorities will assign definite portions of port facilities to the Relief Administration at Trieste and Fiume for the consummation of these ends.

(*h*) In general the rolling stock should not be demanded by any of the Allied Governments until this service is completely equipped without prejudice to the ultimate ownership thereof.

(*i*) The Railway Officials of each State and Port officials in each port will co-operate in maintenance of this service.

The head of the communications section of the Supreme Economic Council, Colonel Atwood, was one of our American staff in Paris.

On March 20, I addressed a letter to each of the Prime Ministers of the countries formerly comprising the Austrian Empire. The following are the important paragraphs:

EXCELLENCY:

I have the honor to enclose herewith for the information of your government a "Direction of the Supreme War Council of March 7th upon the operation of food traffic in the old Austrian Empire." . . .

It is hoped that under the authority conferred by the Supreme War Council, a great improvement will result in the movement of supply trains in this area with a resulting benefit to the various interested peoples. . . .

It would be very much appreciated if you would bring this matter to the immediate attention of your government. . . . It is needless to point out to you the importance of this matter . . . [to] the well being of your country and your people.

I feel confident that Colonel Causey . . . will be given every assistance by your government. . . .

HERBERT HOOVER

All of these governments agreed.

OUR SOUTHERN RAILWAY DIVISION

We established a Southern Railway Division, which was made up of about ten thousand miles of railways connecting the countries dependent on the Adriatic ports. Colonel Causey was in complete charge, with his efficient staff of railway men from the American Army. Our files contain documents of many thousands of words with regard to the working of our new railway setup, but suffice it to say here that the result was revolutionary. The new system was working by March 23. For weeks previously we had moved an average of only seven hundred tons of supplies daily out of Trieste. From this time on, we moved an average of about eight thousand tons daily. On April 1, we switched the sending of part of the Czech supplies to the canal from Hamburg.

These southern railways, however, needed much more than our special food trains. They needed a completely co-ordinated operation in the transport of all commodities if there was to be economic recovery in this area. Therefore, in addition to our controlled food and coal trains, we proposed to the state railway authorities in this area that they run their locomotives and cars across frontiers to final-destination points in other countries and that our organization would guarantee the return of the rolling stock. They all accepted this guarantee, and we placed an American Army officer at each frontier crossing to check the locomotives and cars passing in each direction. As a further step, we set up a clearinghouse for distribution of freight and passenger payments, which were in local currencies—occasionally of value.

Our next rehabilitation proposal was that surplus cars and locomotives in some countries be sold to nations which did not have enough. We carried out many such trades, but the quality of rolling stock delivered and the reliability of the undertakings to pay were equally doubtful. Where there was no credit and the currency was no good, our men arranged for payment by exchange of commodities. One day we received a telegram in Paris from Colonel Causey in Vienna: "Have arranged sell Galicia ten locomotives for eggs. How many eggs go to a locomotive?" Our railway section replied laconically: "Does not matter. We have no confidence in the age of either."

One of the first requirements in rehabilitating these railways was new rolling stock. We undertook that also. About 1,500 German locomotives and 5,000 cars had been assigned to the American Army by the Armistice agreement. There was also a large number of hard-used American locomotives and cars which were useless to return to the United States. General Pershing made most of the German rolling stock available to us without payment. We arranged with the United States Army Liquidation Commission to sell on credit the American rolling stock, amounting to about 1,800 locomotives and 26,000 cars. By all of these devices, we got the Southeastern European railways into better operation than the C. & G. Z.

THE NORTHERN RAILWAY DIVISION

Under our railway authority we established, on March 13, our Northern Railway Division under Colonel T. R. Ryan, with headquarters at Warsaw. It comprised about 20,000 miles of line in old Poland and its newly incorporated areas, together with trackage in Estonia, Latvia, and Lithuania. Colonel Ryan estimated that there were originally about 77,000 cars and 6,500 locomotives there and that the number had decreased to 30,000 cars, 20 per cent of which were out of action. Furthermore, of the remaining 2,125 locomotives, 40 per cent were crippled. He requested us to find him about 22,000 cars and 1,300 locomotives. We sent him 300 "Armistice" locomotives and arranged for the purchase on credit of 700 Army locomotives and 4,000 cars from the Liquidation Commission.

We were not able to furnish much rolling stock to the Baltic States. However, they maintained some interstate service on our guarantees to return rolling stock and vigorously repaired their tracks. In any event, most of our supplies for them were brought from overseas to their many ports.

Colonel Ryan and his American staff were faced with great difficulties in operating what the Colonel referred to as "the greatest show of railway junk on earth." Nevertheless, there were fewer conflicts among the Northern governments than those bedeviling Colonel Causey in our Southern Division.

To show our desire for full co-operation with the Allies, we proposed an inter-Allied railway mission for the Northern areas. The Allied appointees were content to allow Colonel Ryan to remain chairman and his American staff to do the work. He had the full co-operation of the local governments with which he worked, and he created as effective a management as the times permitted.

But our problems and difficulties with railways continued, as will be shown in Volume III.

CHAPTER 44

MANAGEMENT OF INLAND WATERWAYS AND PORTS

We were in constant turmoil over inland-waterway transport, again because of the fragmentation of the former empires. The Danube and its tributaries provided transportation all the way from Germany to Czechoslovakia, Hungary, Austria, and Rumania. With the Armistice, the Allied military authorities seized sections of the river and all of its tributaries. These governments held onto all the barges they could lay their hands on and refused to allow them to pass their frontiers.

On April 23, 1919, Colonel James Logan, our Chief of Staff in Paris, gave me the following memorandum describing the total chaos on the Danube and proposed that we set up an inter-Allied Danube River commission:

April 23, 1919

To Mr. Hoover

The entire river traffic of the Danube is today under the military control of the Allied High Command at Constantinople. This Command has recently ordered the sub-division of the control of this river in the following manner, viz:

So much of the river as in Roumanian territory is under the immediate control of a French Naval Captain, whose office is at . . . [Bucharest]; the balance of the river is under the control of the British Admiral . . . [Troubridge] whose office is at Belgrade. Commercial traffic on this river today is practically suspended. Great fleets of river barges, of boats, etc., are tied up at various points, resulting in a complete paralyzation of the normal economic activities of this great and important economic artery. . . .

The quicker we can set up some organization to take this matter in hand and to completely open up the river for unrestricted commercial traffic, the better it will be for all concerned and for the peace of the neighboring nationals. . . .

The Colonel then explained the conflicting Allied military commands over the river and recommended that the authority of the Big Four

. . . should be exercised through the Director General of Relief and by a Danube River Economic Commission, comprised of a British, French, Italian and American representative. . . .

I presented the following resolution, which was agreed upon, to the Supreme Economic Council:

(a) That, judging from the information before them, the Council is of the opinion that all traffic on the Danube except in the case of certain prohibited articles should be free.

(b) That the Communications Section should be notified of the above decision and requested to prepare for submission to the Council at its next meeting a scheme for carrying it into effect.

However, because of the obstruction arising from French political objectives in the Danube states, we got nowhere until I appealed over the heads of the Supreme Economic Council directly to the Supreme War Council on May 13. I secured its endorsement of our plan, and the Inter-Allied Danube River Commission was established. I proposed that British Admiral Sir Ernest C. T. Troubridge be chairman and named Henry James as our American representative. On May 22, I wrote to the Admiral concerning policies:

My dear Admiral Troubridge:

This letter will introduce to you Mr. Henry James whom I have appointed as the American Representative on the Inter-Allied Danube

River Commission, and of which Commission you have been designated as Chairman. . . .

My primary interest in the Danube River is to see it completely opened for commercial traffic at the earliest possible date. The resolution, as adopted, gives your Commission every authority to proceed rapidly to this end. . . .

Your Commission can arrange through the intermediary of Mr. James with Colonel Goodyear and Colonel Causey for the allotment and delivery of coal required in the operation of the Danube River equipment. . . .

I am sending a small group of [American Army] officers with Mr. James. These officers will be useful, working under Mr. James's direction, in establishing liaison with these [various American and] allied Missions which are endeavoring to re-establish the economic life of the countries adjacent to the Danube. . . .

There is no more important situation now facing the Associated Governments than the complete and immediate opening of the Danube River to unrestricted commercial traffic. In my opinion, there is no single measure facing the Great Powers that will tend more to re-establishing good order throughout this territory than the complete opening of this great economic artery.

You can always rely on my giving every possible support to this great undertaking, and if at any time you feel that you need such support, do not hesitate to call on me.

HERBERT HOOVER

Admiral Troubridge replied:

BELGRADE, 26th May 1919

DEAR MR. HOOVER,

Mr. James arrived yesterday bearing your letter, and I was glad to welcome him as a colleague. . . .

It is hardly necessary for me to tell you that I am entirely in agreement with you in your view that the navigation of the Danube is today of the first importance. Until we can restore freedom of navigation upon this great waterway we remain on the edge of a precipice. . . .

As was usual with non-American-headed inter-Allied bodies, the Commission was very slow to take action. Also, it failed to secure compliance from the various governments with the Supreme War Council's decision. Finally, to get our supplies (including coal) moving, we were compelled to set up our own organization of barge service in the same manner in which we had set up our special food trains. Hungary, however, had gone Communist under Bela Kun, who periodically restricted our barge movements until he fled in August, 1919.

The Treaty of Versailles provided for a permanent Danube Commission, with powers, but our temporary organization carried on for some months after the Treaty was signed and made many improvements.

THE RIVER ELBE

In January, 1919, we tried to open the River Elbe for traffic to Czechoslovakia, but the Germans refused to agree until they had obtained assurance of their own food supply. This delay was just another of the many consequences of Allied continuation of the food blockade on Germany for four months after the Armistice, which I have already discussed. The traffic was opened by the Brussels agreement of March, 1919. On April 10, I was able to report the first shipments via this route to the Supreme Economic Council:

> . . . As a further security to regularity of supplies arrangements have been made for shipment through Hamburg *via* the Elbe into Bohemia. The first shipments from Hamburg were dispatched on the 3d of April.

On May 7, I wrote our New York office:

> . . . I am in hopes that we can maintain the supplies of Czecho-Slovakia from now on through the Elbe, so that our ships on Southern Relief should materially decrease. . . .

Early in April, we completed arrangements for barge shipments from Danzig to Poland on the Vistula, which helped to relieve our Northern European railway system.

MANAGEMENT OF PORT FACILITIES

We assigned the management of our European port facilities, except in the Mediterranean, to our London office under Mr. Flesh. Admiral Benson gave the superb assistance to Mr. Flesh of naval officers at every Northern European port.

I have already mentioned our difficulties at Fiume and Trieste, where our ships began to arrive in December, 1918. I requested aid from Admiral Benson for Colonel McIntosh, our Trieste representative. The Admiral's instruction to Admiral Bullard, who commanded the American fleet in the Mediterranean, were:

December 21, 1918

ADMIRAL BULLARD

The United States Food Administration is sending vessels with food into certain eastern Adriatic ports, probably Ragusa, Cattaro or Attavari. . . . Food Commission has appointed Colonel McIntosh with a staff to take charge in the name of Mr. Hoover of supply bases being established at Trieste and possibly at ports mentioned above. . . . It is anticipated that these gentlemen will experience considerable difficulty in moving around in Adriatic and getting their respective organizations established. You will please issue such directions as you may consider necessary to insure the complete co-operation of naval vessels and naval personnel with the work of these commissions and assist them in any way practicable consistent with the duties of your force.

BENSON

However, it was not until we had obtained (on March 7) the order of the Supreme Council—giving our organization a definite part of the ports—that we really began to function.

As a sidelight on the political situation in the Adriatic, I give a telegraphic report from Colonel McIntosh of December 26, 1918:

. . . Political conditions are exceedingly chaotic at all ports up and down this coast and it will not take much to touch off a fight. . . . The Italians have about 15,000 troops in and about Fiume, the Americans 1000, French 1000, and the British about 800. The Serbians have quite a number of men just outside the city but information is vague as to the exact numbers. The sympathies of at least 60% of the people of Fiume are for the Serbians. . . .

. . . The Italians also furnished some food to the inhabitants on the Islands of Plasman and Ugli. In return for this food they compelled them to sign papers stating that they were in favor of Dalmatia coming under the Italian flag and the next day the Italians posted it in all public places, reading "The undersigned have declared themselves in favor of Italian citizenship." . . .

Despite all our difficulties, our intrepid Americans sent a total of about 800,000 tons of supplies through Adriatic ports.

CHAPTER 45

MANAGEMENT OF EASTERN EUROPEAN COAL MINES AND THE SECURING OF PETROLEUM PRODUCTS

Coal and petroleum products were just as essential to relief and reconstruction as food and the management of railways, waterways, and ports. The dismemberment of the Old Empires, which had demoralized these other services, had also demoralized the production and distribution of coal and oil. Aside from the need for coal in cooking and in keeping human beings warm, all public services of light, gas, and railway transport were threatened with collapse as a result of the degeneration of production and distribution of these essential fuels. Not only were some Eastern European states separated from their former sources of supply, but those without coal fields had little money with which to buy coal or few commodities to exchange for it. Even when coal was available the breakdown of the railways blocked its distribution. In states which had coal mines, the miners had grown inefficient through hunger, and Communism was making great headway. Also, the coal supply became an instrument of power politics among the new governments of Central and Eastern Europe. The story of coal and oil is, incidentally, a contribution to the history of the small wars in progress in parts of Eastern Europe.

After an inspection trip through the area, Dr. Alonzo Taylor reported to me in April, 1919:

. . . There must be an allocation of coal. Ninety percent of the coal is produced in the Silesian Basin. The other mines are scattered, of low output and inferior quality. If Czecho-Slovakia and Poland withhold coal, they can ruin Austria, Hungary and Greater Servia absolutely. . . . [some one] should decide on the coal needs of the different countries and in the fairest possible manner divide the short available supplies. Wise men in Prague and Warsaw realize that it will do them no good to force their [domestic] industries and [thus] drive Austria and Hungary into Bolshevism. But the problem is so intricate and feelings so tense that an allocation of coal cannot be accomplished except under guidance from without. . . .

A major battle was in progress in the Peace Conference at Paris over the division of Silesia among Germany, Poland, and Czechoslovakia. And pervading all was the French determination to dismember Germany on any excuse. Undercover or open wars were being waged for possession of parts of the Silesian coal areas. Agents of contending governments were being sent in to foment strikes, revolutions, riots, and murder. The Supreme Economic Council was undecided about who would get certain coal fields, and the rival claimants were engaged in the old game of *fait accompli* by seizures.

One of the major political conflicts stifling the coal supply concerned possession of the old Duchy of Teschen. The Duchy occupied a corner which was now partly in Czechoslovakia, Poland, and Germany and was one of the important coal sources in Eastern Europe. The Poles and Czechs were not only fighting in Paris to get Teschen from the Peace Conference, but their nationals and the Germans were battling it out in the streets and villages of the Duchy itself. Production had dropped to 25 per cent of normal. Prime Minister Paderewski of Poland told me on April 21, 1919:

You know the whole district is in an uproar. About eighty per cent of the miners are on strike and the situation is getting worse every day. As our government has no authority and as the authority of the Miners' Organization [a German agency] is annihilated, it is necessary that a new authority step in and take the reins. As far as I can see the only authority in which . . . our people have any confidence is the authority of the American Relief. They are the men who can bring us back to good order again, if they have the power. . . .

At a meeting of the Supreme Council on April 27, with President Wilson's approval, I proposed that I be given a mandate by the Big Four to control the management and distribution of all the coal mines in Eastern Europe. The Council agreed, subject to the usual appointment of an inter-Allied mission—which we gladly accepted, provided we could appoint the staff, with an American as chairman.

The French and Italian members of the mission soon evinced a marked preference for Paris as the scene for co-operation.

Because our immediate difficulty in the Duchy of Teschen was the three-way war going on, I sought the good offices of Secretary of State Lansing and proposed that the Czech and Polish activities in the Duchy be postponed until the matter had been disposed of in the peace treaty. This worked in Paris, but not in the Duchy.

To administer the whole Eastern European coal job, I asked General Pershing "for the best combined coal and railway man in the world, who is in the Army." He assigned to us Colonel Anson C. Goodyear, who in civilian life was both a railway man and a coal operator. Colonel Goodyear was a cheerful person, and on his appearance at my desk, the conversation ran something like this. Introducing himself, the Colonel said, "Thank goodness, somebody dug me out of this dead Army and gave me to you. So what can I do?" I replied, "For one thing, I have appointed you 'Duke of Teschen.' " "Where is the Duchy? However, I accept the Dukedom, wherever it is." I told him he also had the job of getting coal in motion all over Eastern Europe with a staff of as many officers from the American Army as he needed. The Colonel asked, "What are the Duke's powers?" "A letter from me to the Prime Ministers of Czechoslovakia, Poland, and Austria and the President of Germany, asking for full co-operation of their government officials and everybody else." He seemed unconvinced of the potency of letters. I suggested that if they did not bear fruit, the food supplies of any one of these countries could be stopped on a telegraphic recommendation from him as we could not have continued chaos among millions of people and consequent starvation. Or the food supply could be increased in the coal districts if needed. The Colonel brightened up at once.

The following is a condensation of my instructions to him covering his charge of all the Eastern European coal fields:

PARIS, 2 May, 1919

MY DEAR COLONEL:

I enclose herewith letters which have been addressed to the various governments, officially advising them [that we are coordinating the coal production and distribution]. . . . As soon as you arrive at Vienna, I request that you transmit these letters, with a covering letter from yourself, to the different governments, so as to definitely fix your position. In view of the fact that the Teschen coal fields not only supply coal to the territory of our Trieste Mission, but also to the territory of our Warsaw Mission, it is not considered advisable to place your work under either Colonel Grove, or Captain Gregory, or Colonel Causey, as . . . [you are not directly dependent] upon any one of these officers. . . .

Your Mission will, therefore, report directly to me. I, however, desire to point out that the success of your work is entirely dependent on the establishment . . . of co-operation . . . [with all our American missions in that area]. . . .

Your work is absolutely non-political and should be directed with the sole endeavor to stimulate the production of coal and to insure a prompt and equitable distribution of this coal between the various dependent nationals. . . .

The importance of this work you are about to undertake cannot be over-estimated from the standpoint of the re-establishment of order. The supply of coal to the railroads and the water communications is naturally of primary importance to this end. However, only secondarily in importance to the opening of the railways and water ways, is the question of supplying coal to the factories and shops, engaged in work of an economic advantage . . . [and thus the employment of] idle labor. . . . It is not reasonable that manufacturing of, for example, war materials [in a particular country] should take precedence over the operation of factories where clothing, shoes, etc. [are produced]. . . .

HERBERT HOOVER

Colonel Goodyear recruited sixteen officers from the American Army, mostly engineers, together with an American clerical staff. The officers were Lt. Col. F. H. Newberry; Majors H. R. Gabriel, W. S.

Brand, and L. A. Barton; Captains M. C. Sturtevant, A. P. King, A. M. Butcher, F. B. Watterson, A. G. Fish, and J. A. Stader; and First Lieutenants F. E. d'Amour, H. G. Wilson, G. E. Greer, and R. W. Howard. He also chose Sergeants R. F. New and H. J. Heiman and five American civilians for the clerical staff. The Colonel established his mission's headquarters in Teschen.

The important paragraphs of the letter I gave Colonel Goodyear for the Prime Ministers of the states in this area were:

PARIS, May 2, 1919

EXCELLENCY:

I have the honor to enclose . . . [the order of the Supreme War Council]. You will note . . . that, as Director-General of Relief, I am charged for the present with all matters in connection with the endeavor to increase . . . coal production and with the supervision of . . . distribution. . . .

It is needless to say that this great and important work can only be successfully accomplished by the hearty co-operation of your government and the other interested governments. I would appreciate it very much if you would have the necessary instruction to this end issued to the various ministers and representatives of your government. . . .

HERBERT HOOVER

The Colonel was such a charming and efficient person that all the governments soon co-operated with him to dissolve the chaos. Although he had few troubles with government officials, he had plenty of others. By firm but fair treatment he settled the strikes and street warfare in the Duchy. He was equally successful in the other fields, which included Kattowitz and Upper Silesia in Germany; Dumbrowa and Galicia in Poland; Brux-Teplitz-Komotaw, Falkenau, Kladno-Raconitz, and Pilsen in Bohemia and Czechoslovakia; Leoben and Koflach in German Austria; Trifail in Serbia; and Dorog and Salgotarján in Hungary. In one month the Colonel and his men had doubled the coal production in Eastern Europe. Even so, the output was still insufficient for all the needs, and we lived with the coal problem until we withdrew after the Peace. Nevertheless, the people were pulled through without too much hardship.

One of the incidents concerning Colonel Goodyear which was

long treasured by our Paris staff was a telegram from him asking that we send him $10,000 worth of tobacco. Our staff replied: "We have neither $10,000 nor tobacco." To which the Colonel replied: "I have already sent you $10,000 in American gold certificates, which the banks here had left over [from before the war], and Mr. Hoover knows a miner cannot perform without a smoke!" We got his tobacco from American Army stocks.

The Colonel's troubled life in the distribution of coal among these nations could be depicted in a host of lengthy documents. I give only one as a sample. Like the others, it is illustrative of the problem and the political relations involved. I have transposed the Colonel's indirect references to himself into the first person for clarity. His report read:

> . . . when . . . [we] reached Mahrisch-Ostrau, there existed only one contract covering the delivery of coal from one country to another.

He then described this contract, by which the Czechoslovak Government furnished Poland 3,683 tons of coal and 800 tons of coke, and continued:

> Very shortly after our arrival . . . a strong complaint was received from the Austrian Government regarding the delivery of coal from the Ostrau-Karwin district to the Vienna Gas Works. A meeting was held in Prague on May 13th, 1919, at which an agreement was reached calling for the shipment of 1100 tons of gas coal daily to the Vienna Gas Works. . . .
>
> On May 28, 1919, a meeting was called in Prague by . . . [myself] for the purpose of arranging a contract between the Austrian and Czecho-Slovak Governments for the delivery of coal to Austria [for general purposes]. After several days' negotiations an agreement was apparently reached, providing for the delivery of a total of 241,675 tons of coal per month to Austria. . . .
>
> Payment for the coal was to be made partly in the currency of Czecho-Slovakia and partly by . . . materials manufactured in Austria. . . . [I] was informed that the agreement was concluded and that the contract would be signed within an hour, as it was then being typewritten. With this understanding I left Prague for Berlin. . . .
>
> . . . the contract has not yet been ratified by the Czecho-Slovak Govern-

ment. Three clauses were inserted in the contract, one of which . . . provided for the delivery of certain munitions, including machine guns and artillery ammunitions to Czecho-Slovakia. . . .

At this time the Czechs were defending themselves against an invasion by Bela Kun's Hungarian Communist Government. The Colonel continued:

The delivery of munitions to Czecho-Slovakia, it was feared might bring about the downfall of the Austrian Republic and the establishment of a communistic government [by their local communists]. The Austrian Government stated that it was powerless to deliver these munitions as the workers in the factories producing them and the soldiers guarding these factories had strong communistic tendencies and would not permit the delivery of munitions to Czecho-Slovakia which was at this time engaged in hostilities with the Hungarian Soviet. The Czechs were suffering severe reverses and were being driven back by the Hungarians due to a lack of artillery and ammunition and they, therefore, declined to enter into any contract unless the munitions were delivered. . . . [I] did not insist upon the execution of the contract but at the same time required the Czecho-Slovak Government to continue . . . [supplies to] Austria.

The situation became more acute and meetings were held in Prague in the early part of June and three in Vienna on June 18th and 19th, which resulted in an agreement on the part of the Austrian Government that the munitions should be delivered to the Italians at Innsbruck and by the Italians in turn to the Czecho-Slovak Government. It was understood that the delivery should begin immediately; none were received in Czecho-Slovakia until the early part of August. When the munitions were received the government of Czecho-Slovakia executed and sent to Vienna a contract which was not in accordance with the understanding with [me]. . . .

A final meeting was held in Prague on August 18th, at which an agreement was reached and a contract executed. . . . Three and one half months have elapsed since the original negotiations at which it was stated by the contracting governments that an agreement had been reached. . . .

There are several thousand more words in reports from the Colonel on his distribution woes, but he overcame most of these. In the end, the Colonel effected the needed co-operation between producing and consuming nations and during his time of service produced and distributed more than 50,000,000 tons of coal to the needy spots. Our coal problems extended beyond the end of our official life on July 1, 1919, and the Colonel stayed on. I take the subject up again in the next volume of this memoir in chapters devoted to political assignments from the Big Four after the Peace.

OIL

The petroleum problem in Eastern Europe at this time in the world's history was not a shortage of fuel oil, for which coal could be substituted, but a shortage of gasoline for trucks, kerosene for lighting, and lubricants to keep the railways and the other productive wheels turning.

Rumania possessed the major oil field in Eastern Europe. There was a smaller field in Poland and some production in the Ukraine. Wars had flared between Poland and the Communist Ukraine and between Czechoslovakia and the Hungarian Communists; the Rumanians had invaded Hungary. Despite all of these disturbances to economic co-operation, it was imperative that we secure petroleum products from these fields; otherwise, we would have to import them from the United States, using relief funds.

As an indication of the progress of Eastern European wars, and incidentally of petroleum products, I give a condensation of a report to me from Colonel Causey:

VIENNA, 5 May 1919

DEAR MR. HOOVER:

The supply of . . . [lubricating] oil for use on the railroads in . . . Austria is practically exhausted. There may be enough of this oil to permit the railroads to operate for two weeks, possibly twenty days. The supply of other oils for railroad use is also very limited.

This same situation applies to the Czecho-Slovak state. . . . [Austria] advised that they have an arrangement with the Ukrainians for the purchase of practically a train load of oil in tank cars, the compensation being goods manufactured in . . . Austria. . . .

. . . A conference was held this morning in my office attended by the Ambassador to the . . . Austrian State from Ukrainia, by two other Ukrainian representatives, by Dr. Burger representing the Czecho-Slovak railroads . . . [and an] Austrian railroad repesentative and myself.

. . . the Poles and the Ukrainians have their forces arrayed against each other in the Lemburg district, and their lines extend southward from the Lemburg district around the oil fields to the Czecho-Slovak border.

The Ukrainians evidently realize that the Poles are superior in men and armament, particularly in artillery. Just here it might be well to mention that the Ukrainian Ambassador made the statement that within the last few days several batteries of Italian artillery had been identified on the Polish front and further stated that the Polish movement was being directed by a French officer.

It is true that during the past two or three weeks train loads of material, chiefly artillery supplies, have passed through. . . . Austria in the direction of Poland. This matches with the statement made by the Ukrainian Ambassador.

In the city of Vienna, however, the most friendly relations exist between the Ukrainian and the Italian missions. A statement to that effect was made today by the Ukrainian Ambassador.

Owing to the extreme shortage of oil in . . . Austria . . . I agreed to furnish an American officer to convoy a train of empty tank cars and the loaded cars of Austrian products to be used in payment for the Ukrainian oil. . . .

In order to reach the Ukrainian border it is necessary to pass through a small part of Hungary. This portion of Hungary, however, is beyond the zone of activities of the Hungarians, and both the Czechs and the Ukrainians claim that there will be no interruption to the movement of traffic through this territory.

A bridge was destroyed recently, however, on this route when the Hungarians retreated before the Ukrainian advance, and this bridge will not be in operation before the middle or latter part of this week. Advice received from Prague within the last hour, stated that a company of French engineers was at work on this bridge to re-establish communication.

The Czechs have also purchased oil from this Ukrainian field, which until now they have been unable to move because the Poles obstructed communication through Poland and until now the fighting between the Roumanians and the Hungarians prevented the movement through Hungary. . . .

It was suggested at the conference this morning, and the suggestion was accepted by the Ukrainian Ambassador, that the Ukrainians at once move all of the loaded tank cars, of which there are a large number, to the Ukrainian border, so that they would be out of reach of the Poles in case of a quick advance, and with the hope that the Czechs could reach this point and pull the cars into Czech territory before the Poles could interfere.

This contest over the Ukrainian oil fields at Drohobycz is a most unfortunate affair, and may result in the entire destruction of the field. The Poles have announced publicly their intention to take this field, and object to any effort to bring out the oil which had been purchased by the Czechs and the Austrians, because they claim that the compensation for this oil should come to the Poles instead of the Ukrainians. Therefore the necessity for using the round-about southern route which I have indicated above.

This oil field is the only available source of supply, with the exception of a very limited production further west in Poland, for this section of Europe, and this will continue until the Roumanian oil fields are accessible.

These facts are brought to your attention with the hope that some action may be taken whereby the activities of the Poles and the Ukrainians might be suspended until such time as the line between the two peoples is established.

The Ukrainians indicated today that they would stand by any line that was established by proper authority, but they will fight to the death the unauthorized advance of the Poles into this oil field, and it is my opinion, that if the Ukrainians are forced to retire, that they will destroy the oil fields. . . . As the Poles are practically advancing now, if any action is taken it must be taken quickly.

W. B. Causey

Our organization could do many things—but Colonel Causey's request for peace between Poland and Communist Ukraine was too much for us.

A week later, Causey further reported to our Paris office:

VIENNA, 11 May 1919

. . . In the past ten days the Czecho-Slovak advance into Hungary has opened up a route to the Ukrainian fields. . . . I had a conference with the Ukrainian minister, with a representative of the Czech Government and a representative of the . . . Austrians, and I have arranged to send a train of empty oil cars under convoy of an American officer, accompanied by a representative of the Czechs . . . Austrians and the Ukrainians to the Ukrainian border at Sianki, and also at Baskid. . . . The latter town is in Hungarian territory occupied by the Roumanians, but only a short distance east of the Czecho-Slovak line of advance.

It is expected that the Czecho-Slovaks will send a train of empty oil tank-cars at the same time that the Austrian train goes, [in order] to have the benefit of the American Relief Administration convoy.

I endeavored, by consultation with the Polish representative in Vienna to run this oil train through Galicia via Oderberg and Krakau, but it became evident at once that the Poles would not permit this transaction.

The line which we propose to follow from Vienna through Pressburg and thence on through Slovakia, is not so desirable as the line through Galicia, but as oil must be had if we are to keep our transportation lines open . . . the train leaves Vienna tomorrow evening, May 12th.

Captain Gregory is sending Colonel Jones and a small staff on this relief train to the Ukrainian boundary . . . and report on the possibility of obtaining both food and oil in the Ukrainian territory. . . .

W. B. CAUSEY

Through our American mission in Rumania, we urged that Government to get its fields into greater production, but without much effect. Colonel Causey and our mission finally arranged for three trainloads of petroleum products to go into the surrounding states in exchange for commodities or currency. Also, the Colonel tried to set up a petroleum-exchange bureau, but there were too many local wars going on for any systematic organization. Nonetheless, by one device or another, he kept the wheels turning on their axles until the peace treaty was signed.

CHAPTER 46

THE GREAT TYPHUS EPIDEMIC

A major joint activity of many nations was to stop the sweep of typhus across Europe. It was moving eastward from the old trench lines along the Russian borders, from the Baltic to the Adriatic.

Now pestilence was for centuries regarded as one of the "Four Horsemen of the Apocalypse." [1]

[1] The "Four Horsemen" of St. John the Divine have been incorporated into every language of Christian peoples as the great symbol of war and its aftermaths. The popular identification of three of the Horsemen throughout nearly two thousand years is confirmed by the text of Revelation 6:2–8. Verse 2 states:

And I saw . . . a white horse: and he that sat on him had a bow . . . and he went forth conquering, and to conquer.

He was undoubtedly *War.*

Verse 8 states:

And I looked, and behold a pale horse: and his name that sat on him was Death, and Hell followed with him. And power was given . . . to kill with sword, and with hunger, and with death. . . .

We can accept him as *Death.* St. John himself names him *Death.*

Verses 5 and 6 say:

. . . And I beheld, and lo a black horse; and he that sat on him had a pair of balances in his hand.

And I heard a voice . . . say, A measure of wheat for a penny, and three measures of barley for a penny. . . .

We can accept the black horse as *Famine.* We might surmise also that his rider was either a profiteer or a food administrator, depending on whether he was raising prices or simply rationing what food there was with his balances and fixing prices in the usual shortage of war.

Verse 4 states:

And there went out another horse *that was* red: and power was given to him that

Whether St. John included *Pestilence* as his fourth Horseman or not, our organizations had to include it in huge dimensions.

On March 31, 1919, Lord Curzon of the British Cabinet sent the following telegram from Sir Horace Rumbold to the Big Four:

> Information has reached the Military Attache's Department . . . that spotted typhus . . . is pandemic all over the Ukraine and Serbia. It is stated that there are many cases of the disease also in Vienna where it has been brought by prisoners from Russia by means of lice and there is great danger of its being spread still further West. Count Max Thun is organizing committees in Vienna, Cracow and Buda Pesth and these include representatives of the Ukraine, Czecho-Slovakia, Roumania, Hungary, Servia, Austria and Jugo-Slavia. It is intended to appeal to the International Red Cross at Geneva to obtain the support of the great Powers. The plan of the organization is to form a barrier against the spread of the disease from Russia by a sanitary cordon and to deal according to a common plan with prisoners who return from Russia. It is stated that the Ukraine, Hungary and Poland cannot do this unassisted. There is great lack of linen and other materials. As the disease is a danger to all Europe the Committee are anxious that the matter should be taken up by the Interallied Conference.

Typhus is a disease transmitted by lice. In Europe its spread was aided by the scarcity of soap, since the people necessarily ate available fats instead of making them into soap. The disease was stimulated by lack of resistance, born of famine and filth, created by the destruction of homes and the consequent overcrowding of hovels in which people were forced to live.

We of the American governmental relief and reconstruction activities did not consider this problem our responsibility. But on April 4,

---

sat thereon to take peace from the earth . . . that they should kill one another: and there was given unto him a great sword.

It would appear from "kill one another" and "take peace from the earth" that the modern name of this rider might well be *Revolution.* This has support from the fact that St. John does not use the term "pestilence" anywhere in the Revelation, although he mentions every other form of punishment and weakness known to mankind. The Greek term for pestilence occurs frequently in the Old Testament and must, therefore, have been familiar to St. John. For a complete examination of this subject, see Herbert Hoover, with Marie Thérèse Nichols, "Myth of the Fourth Horseman," *Saturday Review* (September 20, 1958).

1919, the Supreme Council asked my advice. I said that this was a problem for the Red Cross societies and suggested that they be requested to assist the committees mentioned by Lord Curzon.

At the request of the Council we transmitted such information as we had to the American Red Cross headquarters in Paris. Robert A. Taft's letter of April 5 was as follows:

MY DEAR COLONEL OLDS:

I enclose herewith a copy of a telegram received by the British Section of the Relief Administration from Sir Horace Rumbold, the British Minister at Berne [to Lord Curzon]. It was agreed . . . that the Red Cross Societies should be asked to cooperate, taking such action as may be necessary to meet the above emergency.

I assume that you are already informed regarding the matter.

ROBERT A. TAFT

We received the following reply:

PARIS, 10 April 1919

DEAR MR. TAFT:

I acknowledge receipt of your letter of April 5th, inclosing a copy of the telegram from Sir Horace Rumbold to Lord Curzon. I have recently taken occasion to call this situation to the attention of the congress of Red Cross Societies now sitting at Cannes. The necessity for mobilizing surplus army supplies of all kinds to handle the relief work in Eastern Europe is becoming more and more pressing. The limited resources of both your organization and ours seem quite inadequate to meet the need.

ROBERT E. OLDS

I then suggested to the Supreme Council that the matter be placed directly in the hands of the newly created League of Red Cross Societies, with headquarters in Switzerland. The Council requested that I take it up with this organization. The League of Red Cross Societies took about three weeks to think it over. I transmitted its views to the Council on May 12:

The League of Red Cross Societies raised the question of the authority that would be given to them by the Governments of Eastern Europe.

They considered that it was necessary that they should have a practically complete police authority in order to make effectual the results of their effort. They also stated that they had no resources otherwise than for purposes of general organization, that while under the resources they possessed they could mobilize enterprises of this character, the entire expenditure would have to be met from governmental quarters. . . .

The Supreme Council as a body had no funds to meet such demands and was not prepared to take over domestic problems all over Europe. After more days had gone by, President Wilson, at the request of the Council, asked my organization to plan the attack on typhus. I pleaded total lack of experience, but Mr. Wilson stated that the Council thought we knew how to organize anything. Very unwillingly, we undertook the job—with an already overworked staff.

The worst of the scourge seemed to be in Poland. I telegraphed the Polish Minister of Health at Warsaw through our mission there and asked for information and recommendations. On May 29, he replied at great length. He declared that a cordon would have to be established from the Baltic to the Adriatic, thus isolating the infected areas, and that the people would have to be prevented from crossing the line. He said the following with regard to their present methods:

. . . The typhus-suspected . . . are detained, their hair is cut, they are bathed, while their . . . [clothes are] being disinfected and deloused and then clad in new suits when necessary; they must be fed during retention and placed when necessary for a period under observation, being finally released with a certificate of delousation. . . .

He then gave elaborate estimates of the new hospitals, equipment, supplies, and personnel that would be required.

I proceeded to seek information by telegraph from the Ministers of Health in all the countries petitioning Lord Curzon. Their reports indicated a possible total of one million cases, with about a hundred thousand deaths a week.

We were delayed getting into action by the search for staff who knew about such disease problems. Since I could find no available civilians, I turned again to General Pershing, who recommended Colonel H. L. Gilchrist of the Army Medical Corps.

Colonel Gilchrist and his staff were scheduled to go home and wanted to go. All this caused more delay. General Pershing was co-operative but needed official instructions from the President. I drafted the following letter to the General, which the President signed:

June 25, 1919

TO THE COMMANDER-IN-CHIEF OF
THE AMERICAN EXPEDITIONARY FORCES

You will issue orders directing Colonel Harry L. Gilchrist, Medical Corps, U.S. Army, and such additional personnel, commissioned and enlisted, as he may select, to report to the Minister of Public Health, Poland, for duty in connection with the extermination of the typhus fever epidemic now raging in that country.

WOODROW WILSON

To which the President added:

DEAR GENERAL:

I hope this can be done, but sign the order subject to your approval.

W.W.

General Pershing wanted a statement to send to the War Department. I wrote to him as follows:

June 27, 1919

MY DEAR GENERAL PERSHING:

Central Europe is now in the initial ravages of an epidemic of typhus that must be checked during this summer or it will lead to an appalling destruction of life next winter. . . .

After recounting the Red Cross refusals, I continued:

. . . The American Army has been freed of infestation by vermin through the activity of a special service organized for this work. At the present time this organization is about to be broken up and its members returned to the United States, where there is no need for this especial service. The officer who has been in charge of this work, Colonel H. L. Gilchrist, has completed his work in France. I know of no way in which our sympathy for the distressed peoples of Central Europe can be better expressed than in the transfer of American officers to this service for temporary duty. . . . I beg . . . that you authorize the transfer of Colonel Gilchrist and his trained personnel for temporary duty in Poland.

HERBERT HOOVER

General Pershing replied:

PARIS, June 30, 1919

DEAR MR. HOOVER,

I have your letter of June 27th regarding Colonel Gilchrist, and see no reason at all why you should not have him. In fact, orders have already been given for him to report to the Chief Surgeon to discuss the question of assistants, after which he will report to you. . . .

JOHN J. PERSHING

Colonel Gilchrist gave up the idea of going home and reported to our office in Paris. He selected the initial staff, including:

Lt. Col. H. H. Snively, M.C.; Lt. Col. L. R. Dunbar, M.C.; Major V. H. DeSomoskecy, M.C.; Major Willis E. Talbo, M.C.; Major Charles M. Bollman, M.C.; Major Francis M. Fitts, M.C.; Major Walter V. Von Zelinski, M.C.; and First Lt. F. B. Gryczka, M.C.

Colonel Gilchrist also interested the following non-medical staff officers:

Captain Fred Pumphrey, Captain J. G. Strobridge, Major A. W. Kipling, Major Crawford Blagden, Captain Clyde H. Morgan, Captain H. Y. Stebbins, Second Lt. Wm. A. Stack, and Second Lt. J. J. Skaggs.

There were some delays because of War Department red tape regarding the designation of line personnel, but in the end, we obtained about twelve hundred privates and two hundred efficient sergeants.

We secured the delousing equipment of the American, British, French, and German armies. As a gift, the first installment from the U.S. Army was 1,500,000 suits of underclothes, 3,000 beds, 10,000 hair clippers, 250 tons of soap, and 500 portable baths. With the President's approval I arranged for the United States Army Liquidation Commission to sell a huge amount of second-hand clothing and medicines to the Polish Government for a nominal sum.

Our American governmental relief operations ceased with the signing of the Peace in July, 1919. We arranged for our newly created voluntary American Relief Administration to carry on the work.

I continue the account of pestilence in Europe in Volume III of *An American Epic.*

APPENDICES

APPENDIX I

PERSONNEL OF THE FOOD ADMINISTRATION

The Food Administration embraced eight thousand persons, of whom only two thousand, mostly in clerical positions, were paid staff. To give all their names here is an impossible task, and I therefore list only our principal personnel. There were many shifts during the three years and four months of our official life, and several of our staff appear in more than one division.

FOOD ADMINISTRATION STAFF

HERBERT HOOVER, *United States Food Administrator*

PERSONAL STAFF

- GERTRUDE B. LANE
- MARK L. REQUA
- LAWRENCE RICHEY
- LEWIS L. STRAUSS
- FREDERIC C. WALCOTT

GENERAL STAFF

EDGAR RICKARD, *Director* (*later Assistant Food Administrator*)

ASSISTANTS

- MARGARET COONAN
- J. W. DUB. GOULD
- DUNCAN MCDUFFIE
- CYRIL MCNEAR
- MAJOR JAMES MILES
- SIDNEY A. MITCHELL
- RACHELLE H. OSBORNE
- CARL O. SPAMER
- CLINTON R. WHITNEY
- PHILLIPS WYMAN
- C. C. YOUNG

ASSISTANTS (*Cont.*)

C. Lewis, G. W. Bryan — *Accounting*
V. M. Hillyer, *Appointments*
L. A. Larsen, *Mail*
Lewis Barrington, *Files*
B. F. Durr, *Supplies*
Marion H. Jones, *Manager of Cafeteria*

LEGAL

Judge Curtis H. Lindley, *Chief Counsel*
Judge William A. Glasgow, Jr., *Successor*

ASSISTANTS

Harvey H. Bundy
Scott Hendricks
William C. Mullendore
Edmund W. Pugh
Edwin P. Shattuck
Robert A. Taft

Roland W. Boyden, *Director, Enforcement*

ASSISTANTS

W. A. Bratton
E. C. Brown
William D. Eaton
S. F. Evans
E. A. Foley
Alan Fox
James Garfield III
William E. Kellicott
William B. Owens
O. M. Wolff
Professor F. C. Woodward

STATE FOOD ADMINISTRATORS

John W. Hallowell, *Director*
John Richardson, *Successor*

ASSISTANTS

Ernest T. Attwell
Cecil Barnes
Kent S. Clow
W. A. Dupee
Franklin W. Fort
H. Alexander Smith
Frederic M. Stone
Herbert N. Straus
George A. Warrington

State	Name	Date of Oath
Alabama	RICHARD HOBBIE	August 30, 1917
Alaska	ROYAL A. GUNNISON	December 19, 1917 (died June 15, 1918)
	Successor, PHILIP R. BRADLEY	July 8, 1918
Arizona	TIMOTHY RIORDAN	August 22, 1917
Arkansas	HAMP WILLIAMS	August 22, 1917
California	RALPH P. MERRITT	August 29, 1917
Colorado	THOMAS B. STEARNS	September 27, 1917
Connecticut	ROBERT SCOVILLE	August 24, 1917
Delaware	EDMUND MITCHELL	January 21, 1918
District of Columbia	CLARENCE R. WILSON	November 1, 1917
Florida	BRAXTON BEACHAM	September 19, 1917
Georgia	DR. ANDREW SOULE	September 19, 1917
Hawaii	J. F. CHILD	January 12, 1918
Idaho	R. F. BICKNELL	September 19, 1917
Illinois	HARRY A. WHEELER	August 25, 1917
Indiana	DR. HARRY E. BARNARD	August 23, 1917
Iowa	J. F. DEEMS	August 29, 1917
Kansas	H. J. WATERS	August 31, 1917
	Successor, WALTER P. INNES	December 6, 1917
Kentucky	FREDERICK M. SACKETT	August 22, 1917
Louisiana	JOHN M. PARKER	August 22, 1917
Maine	DR. LEON S. MERRILL	August 22, 1917
Maryland	EDWIN G. BAETJER	August 22, 1917
	Successor, WILLIAM H. MALTBIE	October 16, 1918
Massachusetts	HENRY B. ENDICOTT	August 23, 1917
Michigan	GEORGE A. PRESCOTT	September 19, 1917
Minnesota	A. D. WILSON	September 19, 1917
Mississippi	P. M. HARDING	September 19, 1917
Missouri	F. B. MUMFORD	October 9, 1917
Montana	PROF. ALFRED ATKINSON	August 22, 1917
Nebraska	GURDON W. WATTLES	August 31, 1917
Nevada	HENRY M. HOYT	August 22, 1917
	Successor, H. A. LEMMON	March 8, 1918

State	Name	Date of oath
New Hampshire	Huntley N. Spaulding	August 29, 1917
New Jersey	James F. Fielder	September 19, 1917
	Successor, William S. Tyler	March 13, 1918
New Mexico	Ralph C. Ely	August 22, 1917
	Acting Admr. Henry G. Bush	September 20, 1918
	Successor, M. R. Johnston	September 26, 1918
New York City	John Mitchell Arthur Williams Jacob G. Schurman Charles Wieting	September 20, 1917 *
New York State	Charles E. Treman	December 6, 1917
North Carolina	Henry A. Page	August 22, 1917
North Dakota	Edwin F. Ladd	August 31, 1917
Ohio	Fred C. Croxton	September 19, 1917
Oklahoma	Dr. Stratton Brooks	August 25, 1917
	Successor, Charles B. Ames	April 5, 1918
Oregon	W. B. Ayer	August 27, 1917
	Acting Admr. W. K. Newell	December 7, 1918
Pennsylvania	Howard Heinz	August 25, 1917
Puerto Rico	Albert E. Lee	October 26, 1917
Rhode Island	Alfred M. Coates	August 24, 1917
South Carolina	David R. Coker	August 22, 1917
	Successor, William Elliott	January 7, 1918
South Dakota	C. M. Herreid	October 25, 1917
Tennessee	H. A. Morgan	August 24, 1917
Texas	E. A. Peden	September 20, 1917
Utah	W. W. Armstrong	September 17, 1917
Vermont	James Hartness	August 22, 1917
	Successor, Frank H. Brooks	May 15, 1918

* New York City was administered separately from the State.

State	Name	Date of oath
Virginia	Colonel E. B. White	August 20, 1917
	Successor, Hugh B. Sproul	May 8, 1918
Washington	Charles Hebberd	August 22, 1917
West Virginia	Earl W. Oglebay	August 11, 1917
Wisconsin	Magnus Swenson	August 22, 1917
Wyoming	Theodore C. Diers	August 22, 1917

REPRESENTATIVES IN EUROPE

James F. Bell
Joseph P. Cotton
E. Dana Durand
Edward M. Flesh
George S. Jackson
Dr. Vernon L. Kellogg
L. P. Sheldon
John L. Simpson
H. Alexander Smith
Dr. Alonzo E. Taylor
Frederic C. Walcott

ALLIED FOOD NEEDS

Dr. Alonzo E. Taylor
Dr. Vernon L. Kellogg

STATISTICS

Dr. Raymond Pearl, *Director*

ASSISTANTS

Dr. Frank M. Surface
J. B. Segall

INLAND TRANSPORTATION

Edward Chambers, *Director*
C. E. Spens, *Successor*

OVERSEAS TRANSPORTATION

Prentiss N. Cray, *Director*

ASSISTANT

J. D. Fletcher

REPRESENTATIVES ON OTHER GOVERNMENT AGENCIES

Dr. Alonzo E. Taylor, John Beaver White, W. Kingsland Macy — *War Trade Board*
Theodore F. Whitmarsh, *War Industries Board*
William F. Fisher, *Canadian Relations*
Dr. George McCarty, *Mexican Relations*

CO-ORDINATION OF ARMY, NAVY, AND ALLIED PURCHASES

Herbert L. Gutterson, *Director*
Frederic S. Snyder, *Successor*

ASSISTANTS

E. O. Heyl
Capt. John F. Lucey
William I. Nichols
M. V. S. Thorne

AGRICULTURAL ADVISORY COMMITTEE

Henry C. Stuart, Elk Garden, Va., *Chairman* (*Former Virginia Governor*)

MEMBERS

C. J. Barrett, Union City, Ga. (*President, Farmers Union*)

E. S. Brigham, St. Albans, Vt. (*Vermont Commissioner of Agriculture*)

W. L. Brown, Kingman, Kans. (*Member, Kansas State Board of Agriculture*)

Milo D. Campbell, Coldwater, Mich. (*President, National Milk Producers Federation*)

D. R. Coker, Hartsville, S.C. (*Chairman, State Council of Defense and its agricultural divisions*)

W. R. Dodson, Baton Rouge, La. (*Dean, Louisiana College of Agriculture*)

Eugene Funk, Bloomington, Ill. (*President, National Grain Association*)

N. H. Gentry, Sedalia, Mo. (*President, American Berkshire Association*)

W. C. GORDON, Humboldt, Tenn. (*Cotton Grower*)

JOHN GRATTAN, Broomfield, Colo. (*Editor, Agricultural Journal*)

J. N. HAGAN, Bismarck, N.D. (*Chairman, State Commission of Agriculture*)

F. J. HAGENBARTH, Spencer, Idaho (*President, American National Wool Growers Association*)

W. W. HARRAH, Pendleton, Ore. (*Member, Farmers Union and Farmers Cooperative Association*)

C. W. HUNT, Logan, Iowa (*Livestock Farmer*)

H. W. JEFFERS, Plainsboro, N.J. (*Member, New Jersey State Board of Agriculture*)

ISAAC LINCOLN, Aberdeen, S.D. (*Grower of Seed Grains*)

D. O. MAHONEY, Viroqua, Wis. (*President, American Tobacco Growers Society*)

D. M. MASSIE, Chillicothe, Ohio (*Farm Management Specialist*)

W. F. PRATT, Batavia, N.Y. (*Trustee, Cornell University*)

G. C. ROEDING, Fresno, Cal. (*President, California State Agricultural Society*)

MARTIN SAMSON, Ft. Worth, Texas (*Livestock Grower and Member, Board Federal Reserve Bank, Dallas*)

C. J. TYSON, Floradale, Pa. (*President, Pennsylvania State Horticultural Association*)

OLIVER WILSON, Peoria, Ill. (*Farmer*)

LABOR RELATIONS

Delegated by the American Federation of Labor
JAMES W. SULLIVAN, *Director*
M. B. HAMMOND, *Assistant*
WILLIAM N. DOAK, *Successor*

FOOD DISTRIBUTION

THEODORE F. WHITMARSH, *Director*
GEORGE A. ZABRISKIE, *Successor*
HENRY J. LAHEY, *Assistant to the Director*
HENRY T. LEGGETT, *Executive Secretary*

George E. Lichty, *Retail Stores*

ASSISTANTS

John Amerbach
Omar N. Cheer
Walter E. Coe
Louis T. Jaques
Dana F. Ward
Clement R. Winslow

Dana T. Ackerly, *Regulation of Wholesalers*

ASSISTANTS

Walter F. Blake
James W. Hunt
George W. Lawrence
Furman T. Nutt, Jr.
Richard R. Williams, Jr.

A. I. Esberg, *Director, Commercial Baking*
Duncan McDuffie, *Successor*

ASSISTANTS

Huntley M. Child
Benjamin R. Jacobs
Lester McCoy
Harry D. Tipton
Harry F. Vories

Bird W. Housum, *Merchandise Brokers*
Frank H. Millard, *Conservation by Wholesalers*
Charles Hatfield, *Sugar*
Frank A. Hoey, *Flour*

J. R. Leguenec, *Director, Rice*
Dana T. Ackerly, *Successor*

ASSISTANTS

Max A. Christopher
Albert N. Merritt
Irving H. Taylor
Frank S. Tracy
Richard J. Walsh

FOOD CONSERVATION

Dr. Ray Lyman Wilbur, *Director*
Sarah Field Splint, *Director, Home Conservation*
Martha Van Rensselaer, *Successor*

ASSISTANTS

Harriet Anderson
Ethel M. Bagg
Isabel Bevier
Katherine Blunt
John H. Cover
Abby L. Marlatt
Flora Rose
Florence Wardwell

John McE. Bowman, *Director, Hotels and Restaurants*

ASSISTANTS

P. B. Boden
Albert S. Crockett
Edward R. Grabow

Irwin S. Osborn, *Director, Garbage Utilization*

ASSISTANT

F. C. Bamman

Ben S. Allen, *Director, Public Education*
Frederick O'Brien, *Assistant Director*

ASSISTANTS

Tom Ellis
Russell M. MacLennan
Ida M. Tarbell
Roger S. Baldwin
Leonard Hatch
Charles Merz
Parmely W. Herrick
Everett W. Smith
Everett S. Brown
F. C. Woodward
R. C. Maxwell, *Outdoor Advertising*
Dr. Charles R. Van Hise, *Colleges*
Dean Olin Templin, *School Activities*
Charles W. Holman
John S. Pardee
Lloyd Allen
Mrs. Alice Allen
R. W. Madison
Edith Guerrier
A. S. Friend, *Moving Pictures*
A. U. Craig, *Negro Press*
Henry B. Quinan, *Posters*
Dr. Howard B. Grose, *Religious Press*
Mrs. Gertrude Mosshart, *Retail Stores*
James H. Collins, Trell W. Yocum } *Trade and Technical Press*

SPEAKERS BUREAU

A. E. Bestor, *Director*

ASSISTANTS

Sarah Louise Arnold
Everett Colby
John B. Lord
Edward F. Trefz

INFORMATION AND LIBRARY

Frances Moore, *Director*

ASSISTANTS

Suda L. Bane
Philena A. Dickey
Edith Guerrier

PERISHABLES

G. Harold Powell, *Director*

ASSISTANTS

H. J. Eustace
Daniel P. Boehm
Kenneth Fowler, *Fish*
W. F. Priebe, *Poultry and Eggs*
George E. Haskell, *Dairy Products*
William E. Lamb, *Milk*
Lou D. Sweet, *Potatoes*

COLLATERAL COMMODITIES

Charles W. Merrill, *Director*

ASSISTANTS

R. E. Cranston
Henry Wolfer, *Sisal and Jute*

CANNED GOODS

Charles H. Bentley, *Director*
John R. Munn, *Successor*

ASSISTANTS

Henry Burden, *Dairy Products*
S. J. Scudder, *Milk*
William T. Nardin, *Successor*

SUGAR AND THE SUGAR EQUALIZATION BOARD

George M. Rolph, *President*
George A. Zabriskie, *Successor*
Theodore F. Whitmarsh, *Vice President*
James F. Bell, *Treasurer*
Joshua Bernhardt, *Statistician*

DIRECTORS

William A. Glasgow, Jr.
Edgar Rickard
Edwin P. Shattuck
Robert A. Taft
Frank W. Taussig
Clarence M. Woolley

MEATS AND FATS

Joseph P. Cotton, *Director*
Frederic S. Snyder, *Successor*
B. E. Reuter, *Fats and Oils*
Dr. George H. Denny, *Director, Cottonseed Industry*

ASSISTANTS

S. J. Cassels
Hugh Humphreys
T. F. Justiss

WHEAT, FLOUR, COARSE GRAINS

The United States Food Administration Grain Corporation
Julius H. Barnes, *President*

FIRST VICE-PRESIDENTS

Edward M. Flesh
Frank G. Crowell

SECOND VICE-PRESIDENTS

E. G. Broenniman
Frank L. Carey
C. B. Fox
Percy H. Ginder
M. H. Houser
H. D. Irwin
George S. Jackson
Howard B. Jackson
Charles Kennedy
Bert H. Lang
R. A. Lewin
Fred J. Lingham
Charles T. Neal
E. F. Newing
D. F. Piazzek
W. A. Starr
John J. Stream

Edwin P. Shattuck, *General Counsel*
Gates W. McGarrah, *Treasurer*
Watson S. Moore, *Secretary*

William Beatty, *Comptroller*

ASSISTANTS

A. W. Frick
G. Roy Hall
George K. Hyslop
Howard M. Smith

PRESIDENT'S FAIR WHEAT PRICE COMMITTEE

Harry A. Garfield, *President, Williams College, Williamstown, Massachusetts* (*Chairman*)

C. J. BARRETT, *President, Farmers Union, Union City, Georgia*

WILLIAM N. DOAK, *Vice-President, Brotherhood of Railway Trainmen, Roanoke, Virginia*

EUGENE E. FUNK, *President, National Corn Association, Bloomington, Illinois*

EDWIN F. LADD, *President, North Dakota Agricultural College, Fargo, North Dakota*

R. GOODWIN RHETT, *President, Chamber of Commerce of the United States, Charleston, South Carolina*

J. W. SHORTHILL, *Secretary, National Council of Farmers Co-operative Association, York, Nebraska*

JAMES W. SULLIVAN, *American Federation of Labor, Brooklyn, New York*

L. J. TABOR, *Master, Ohio State Grange, Barnesville, Ohio*

FRANK W. TAUSSIG, *Chairman, United States Tariff Commission, Washington, D.C.*

THEODORE N. VAIL, *President, American Telephone and Telegraph Company, New York, N.Y.*

HENRY J. WATERS, *President, Kansas State Agricultural College, Manhattan, Kansas*

JOHN J. STREAM, *Director, Coarse Grains*

ASSISTANTS

GEORGE A. CHAPMAN

SCOTT F. EVANS

JAMES F. BELL, *Director, Milling*

ASSISTANTS

W. I. BEAM

FRED J. LINGHAM

FRED O. SEAVER

MISCELLANEOUS

FREDERIC C. WALCOTT, *Director*

ASSISTANTS

W. A. MILNE

MINA C. VAN WINKLE

DR. CHARLES M. MCCARTHY
WILDER H. HAINES } *Special Assignments*

APPENDIX II

AMERICAN PERSONNEL UNDER DIRECTOR GENERAL OF RELIEF AND RECONSTRUCTION AFTER THE ARMISTICE

PARIS HEADQUARTERS, A.R.A.

Herbert Hoover	*Director General*
Col. James A. Logan	*Executive Officer*
Lewis L. Strauss	*Secretary*
Robert A. Taft	*Counselor and Executive Assistant*
Dr. Alonzo E. Taylor	*Special Investigator, Conditions and Food Needs of Europe*
Dr. Vernon L. Kellogg	*Special Investigator, Conditions in Europe; liaison with German Government*
Lt. Col. A. J. Carlson	*Chief, Children's Division*
Col. Anson C. Goodyear	*Chief, Coal Mission*
Maj. Frank H. Fay	*Chief, Telegraph System (Communications)*
Col. William G. Atwood	*Chief, Railway Section*
Col. Harry L. Gilchrist	*Chief, Typhus Control*
Maj. F. H. McKnight	*Chief, Remittance Division*
Edwin Sherman	*Chief, German, Baltic and Finnish Division*
Hugh S. Gibson	*Duty with Director General*
Col. Alvin B. Barber	*Shipping and Programs*
E. Dana Durand	*Special Investigator*
Lincoln Hutchinson	*Special Investigator, Conditions in Europe*
Henry James, Jr.	*Representative, Allied Danube River Commission*

NEW YORK OFFICE, A.R.A.

Julius H. Barnes	*President, U.S. Food Administration Grain Corporation*
George M. Rolph	*President, Sugar Equalization Board*
George A. Zabriskie	*Successor to Rolph*

WASHINGTON OFFICE, A.R.A.

Edgar Rickard	*Assistant U.S. Food Administrator; A.R.A. Director*
Thomas E. Wilson	*Chairman, Chicago Packers Committee*

LONDON OFFICE, A.R.A.

Edward M. Flesh	*Chief, London Office; first Vice-President, U.S. Food Administration Grain Corporation*

OTHER OFFICES, A.R.A.

Hamburg
Lt. Col. W. B. Ryan, *Chief*
Rotterdam
Walter Lyman Brown, *Chief*
Trieste and Vienna
Capt. T. T. C. Gregory, *Director of Relief for Central Europe*

MISSIONS TO VARIOUS COUNTRIES

AUSTRIA AND HUNGARY

Gilchrist B. Stockton, *Chief of Mission*
Gardner Richardson, *Successor, Chief of Mission*
Dr. Raymond Herman Geist   Captain Clare M. Torrey
Captain F. Dorsey Stephens

BALTIC STATES

Colonel John C. Groome, *Chief of Mission*
Major George F. Felker   Lieutenant John Thors
Captain Evan H. Foreman

Estonia
Captain J. C. Miller, *Chief of Mission*
Latvia
Major W. DuB. Brookings, *Chief of Mission*
Lieutenant G. P. Harrington

Lithuania

Captain John B. Hollister, *Chief of Mission*
Major W. A. Burbank, *Successor, Chief of Mission*
Captain James T. Scott

CZECHOSLOVAKIA

Lincoln Hutchinson, *Chief of Mission*

DANZIG

Captain David C. Hanrahan
Major James W. Webb

FINLAND

Major Ferry K. Heath, *Chief of Mission*
Aarne Linko, *Chief, Children's Relief*

GERMANY

Edwin Sherman, *Chief of Mission*

POLAND

Colonel William R. Grove, *Chief of Mission*
W. Parmer Fuller, *Successor, Chief of Mission*
Captain Chauncey McCormick
Dr. Vernon Kellogg
(Lieutenant) Maurice Pate, *Chief, Children's Relief*
Major Frank K. Ross

RUMANIA

Captain Joseph C. Green, *Chief of Mission*
Colonel William N. Haskell, *Successor, Chief of Mission*
Colonel Lytton G. Ament
Captain Lyle S. Powell

TURKEY, BULGARIA AND THE NEAR EAST
(HEADQUARTERS: CONSTANTINOPLE)

Howard Heinz, *Chief of Mission*
Major David Arnold
Captain Abraham Tulin
Major Edward R. Stoever

YUGOSLAVIA

Colonel W. G. Atwood, *Chief of Mission*
John L. Simpson, *Successor, Chief of Mission*
Major David Klein, *Director, Children's Relief*

CHILDREN'S DIVISION, PARIS

Lt. Colonel A. J. Carlson, *Chief*

Walter L. Brown
Parmer Fuller
Maurice Pate
E. A. Peden (*formerly Chief*)
R. H. Simpson

COAL MISSION, EASTERN EUROPE

Colonel Anson C. Goodyear, *Chief*

1st Lieutenant F. E. d'Amour
Major L. A. Barton
Major W. S. Brand
Captain A. M. Butcher
Captain A. G. Fish
Major H. R. Gabriel
1st Lieutenant G. E. Greer
Sergeant H. J. Heiman
1st Lieutenant R. W. Howard
Captain A. P. King
Sergeant R. F. New
Lt. Colonel F. H. Newberry
Captain J. A. Stader
Captain M. C. Sturtevant
Captain F. B. Watterson
1st Lieutenant H. G. Wilson

COMMUNICATIONS, PARIS

Major Frank H. Fay, U.S. Army Signal Corps, *Chief of Telegraph System*
Captain Paul S. Clapp, U.S. Army Signal Corps, *Successor*

RAILWAY SECTION, PARIS

Colonel William G. Atwood, *Chief*
Colonel William B. Causey, *Chief, Southeastern Europe*
Colonel J. W. McIntosh, *Chief, Adriatic*
Colonel William B. Ryan, *Chief, Northeastern Europe*
Colonel T. R. Ryan, *Chief, Northern Europe*

TYPHUS CONTROL

Colonel Harry L. Gilchrist, *Chief*

Major Charles M. Billman
Major Crawford Blagden
Major V. H. DeSomoskecy
Lt. Colonel L. R. Dunbar
Major Francis M. Fitts
1st Lieutenant F. B. Gryczka
Major A. W. Kipling
Captain Clyde H. Morgan
Captain Fred Pumphrey
2nd Lieutenant J. J. Skaggs
Lt. Colonel H. H. Snively
2nd Lieutenant William A. Stack
Captain H. Y. Stebbins
Captain J. G. Strobridge
Major Willis E. Talbo
Major Walter F. Von Zelinski

C.R.B. PERSONNEL WHO SERVED DURING THE PERIOD FROM THE ARMISTICE TO THE PEACE

Fernand Baetens	December 1914–May 1919
Paul Beri	October 1917–August 1919
Carleton G. Bowden	December 1914–January 1916; June–October 1916; December 1918–May 1919
Walter Lyman Brown	December 1915–October 1923
Milton M. Brown	
	February 1916–April 1918; December 1918–June 1919
F. H. Chatfield	January–August 1916; December 1918–May 1919
Louis Chevrillon	January 1915–December 1922
Vice Adm. Thomas Craven	
Edward D. Curtis	Beginning to withdrawal; January–June 1919
Frederick Exton	February–August 1916; November 1916–to withdrawal; January–July 1919
Alfred C. B. Fletcher	February 1916–February 1920
Samuel A. Forter	December 1918–May 1919
Perrin C. Galpin	November 1914–May 1915; December 1918–August 1922
James A. Healy	November 1914–January 1920
Alexander J. Hemphill	November 1914–December 1920
Nathaniel Peter Hill	January–June 1919
George S. Jackson	November 1914–November 1915; February–July 1919
Robert A. Jackson	May 1915 to withdrawal; December 1918–August 1919
Vernon Kellogg	June–November 1915 July–August 1919
J. W. Krueger	December 1918–August 1919
Dr. Charles N. Leach	March 1916 to withdrawal; November 1918–July 1919
Dr. William P. Lucas	May–August 1916; February–March 1919

C.R.B. PERSONNEL WHO SERVED DURING
THE PERIOD FROM THE ARMISTICE TO THE PEACE (*Cont.*)

Dr. Alfred L. Malabre	January–April 1916; December 1918–July 1919
William B. Poland	September 1915–August 1925
Lewis Richards	January 1915–June 1919
Gardner Richardson	May 1915 to withdrawal; December 1918–July 1919
Edgar Rickard	October 1914–August 1925
Millard K. Shaler	October 1914–August 1922
Robert P. Skinner	October 1914–July 1, 1919
Robinson Smith	December 1914–October 1919
William H. Sperry	December 1914 to withdrawal; November 1918–August 1919
F. Dorsey Stephens	January 1915–April 1916; December 1918–May 1919
Lewis L. Strauss	September 1917–August 1922
William Hallam Tuck	September 1915–December 1916; December 1918–August 1922
L. C. Wellington	December 1914–May 1915; August 1915–September 1916; November 1918–June 1919
Francis C. Wickes	August 1915–June 1917; December 1918–October 1919
Randolph C. Wilson	September 1916–January 1920

SERVED IN LONDON

Ben S. Allen	October 1914–May 1919
George Inness Gay	July 1916–December 1929 (?)

SERVED IN NEW YORK

George Barr Baker	October 1915–August 1919
Julius H. Barnes	July 1918–September 1919
Edwin P. Shattuck	July 1917–August 1922

BIBLIOGRAPHY

BIBLIOGRAPHY

THE AMERICAN FRIENDS SERVICE COMMITTEE

Annual Reports, including financial statements, of the period from June 1, 1917, through May 31, 1934.

Brooks, Sydney. *America and Germany 1918–25.* New York, The Macmillan Company, 1925.

Comfort, William Wistar. *Quakers in the Modern World.* New York, The Macmillan Company, 1949.

Hinshaw, David. *Rufus Jones: Master Quaker.* New York, G. P. Putnam's Sons, 1951.

Jones, Lester M. *Quakers in Action.* New York, The Macmillan Company, 1929.

Jones, Mary Hoxie. *Swords into Ploughshares.* New York, The Macmillan Company, 1937.

Jones, Rufus M. *A Service of Love in War Time.* New York, The Macmillan Company, 1920.

Jorns, Auguste. *Quakers as Pioneers in Social Work.* New York, The Macmillan Company, 1931.

Pickett, Clarence E. Excerpts from an address, November 19, 1942. Reprinted in Russell Sage Foundation, *Administration of Relief Abroad,* No. 5.

Russell, Elbert. *The History of Quakerism.* New York, The Macmillan Company, 1942.

Surface, Frank M., and Raymond L. Bland. *American Food in the World War and Reconstruction Period.* Stanford University Press, 1931.

THE AMERICAN RED CROSS

Ames, Fisher, Jr. *American Red Cross Work among the French People.* New York, The Macmillan Company, 1921.

Annual Reports of the American Red Cross, 1914–1940.

Bakewell, Charles M. *The Story of the American Red Cross in Italy.* New York, The Macmillan Company, 1920.

Barton, Clara. *A Story of the Red Cross.* 1904.

Bicknell, Ernest P. *Pioneering with the Red Cross.* New York, The Macmillan Company, 1935.

———. *In War's Wake, 1914–1915: The Rockefeller Foundation and the American Red Cross Join in Civilian Relief.* Washington, American National Red Cross, 1936.

Davison, Henry P. *The American Red Cross in the Great War.* New York, The Macmillan Company, 1919.

Dulles, Foster Rhea. *The American Red Cross: A History.* New York, Harper & Brothers, 1950.

Financial Reports of the American Red Cross, 1914–1940.

Hurd, Charles. *The Compact History of the American Red Cross.* New York, Hawthorn Books, Inc., 1959.

Kernodle, Portia B. *The Red Cross Nurse in Action, 1882–1948.* New York, Harper & Brothers, 1949.

Surface, Frank M., and Raymond L. Bland. *American Food in the World War and Reconstruction Period.* Stanford University Press, 1931.

The Work of the American Red Cross: A Statement of Its War Time Activities Throughout the World. Washington, American Red Cross, December 1, 1918.

The Work of the American Red Cross: Financial Statement of Red Cross War Fund, March 1st, 1918.

The Work of the American Red Cross: Report by the War Council of Appropriations and Activities from Outbreak of War to November 1, 1917.

The Work of the American Red Cross During the War: A Statement of Finances and Accomplishments for the Period July 1, 1917 to February 28, 1919. Washington, American Red Cross, October, 1919.

THE CHRISTIAN SCIENTISTS

Christian Science War Time Activities. 1922.

THE CHURCH OF JESUS CHRIST OF LATTER-DAY SAINTS

General Board *Minutes,* October 15, 1914. Volume V.

General Board *Minutes,* October 1, 1915. Volume VI.

General Board *Minutes,* November 7, 1917. Volume VIII.

General Board *Minutes,* November 14, 1923. Volume XIII.

General Board *Minutes,* December 5, 1923. Volume XIII.

THE DAUGHTERS OF THE AMERICAN REVOLUTION

Report of the Publicity Director, War Relief Service Committee of the National Society of the Daughters of the American Revolution, to the 28th Continental Congress, Washington, D.C., 1919.

THE JEWISH JOINT DISTRIBUTION COMMITTEE

After Three Years: The Progress of the Jewish Farm Colonies in Russia. Reports of Dr. Joseph A. Rosen, Felix M. Warburg, and James H. Becker. October 22, 1927.

American Jewish Year Book, 1915–1940. Philadelphia, Jewish Publication Society of America.

Annual Reports, Jewish Joint Distribution Committee, 1915–1958.

Becker, James H. "The Joint Distribution Committee—A Bird's-eye View of Its Past Activities and Present and Future Problems." Milwaukee, June 20, 1921.

Engelman, Morris. *Four Years of Relief and War Work by the Jews of America, 1914–1918.* New York.

Fifteen Years of Effort on Behalf of World Jewry, October 1914–October 1929. New York.

Founding a New Life for Suffering Thousands. Report by Dr. Joseph A. Rosen. Philadelphia, September, 1925.

Golub, J. J. "The J.D.C. and Health Programs in Eastern Europe." Reprinted from *Jewish Social Studies,* Vol. V, No. 3 (1943).

Hyman, Joseph C. "25 Years of American Aid to Jews Overseas." American Jewish Committee. Reprinted from *American Jewish Year Book, 1939.*

Leavitt, Moses A. *The JDC Story 1914–1952.*

Marshall, Louis. *Report of the Special Commission to Investigate Conditions in Eastern European Countries.* April 8, 1922.

Morrissey, Evelyn. *Jewish Workers and Farmers in the Crimea and Ukraine.* New York, privately printed, 1937.

Proceedings of the Chicago Conference. American Jewish Relief Committee, September 24–25, 1921.

Report of Dr. Israel Kligler and Malaria Research Unit for the Year Ending August 31, 1923.

Report of Mr. Morris Wolf and Mr. M. J. Rosenau to the Special Commission. Vienna, August 22, 1922.

Report of the Palestine Orphan Committee of the American Joint Distribution Committee. Pamphlet, 1919–1924.

Report on Present-Day Conditions of the Jews in Europe. Submitted to the Joint Distribution Committee by David M. Bressler and Joseph C. Hyman and issued by the Allied Jewish Campaign in 1930.

Report on the Activities of the Joint Distribution Committee. Chicago, October 22–23, 1927.

Reports Received by the Joint Distribution Committee of Funds for Jewish War Sufferers. New York, 1916.

The Rescue of Stricken Jews in a World at War. Report on the work and plans of the American Jewish Joint Distribution Committee as contained in addresses delivered at its twenty-ninth annual meeting on December 4 and 5, 1943.

Rosen, Dr. Joseph A. "The Present Status of Russian Jewish Agricultural Colonization and the Outlook." October 9–10, 1926.

Rosenberg, James N. *On the Steppes: A Russian Diary.* New York, Alfred A. Knopf, 1927.

The Russian Famines 1921–22; 1922–23. Summary report by the Commission on Russian Relief of the National Information Bureau, Inc.

Schmidt, John W., and Cromwell Childe. *American Jews and the War.* 1917.

Statistical Abstract, 1946–1947. Issued by the Jewish Joint Distribution Committee.

Waldman, Morris D. "Conditions Up to Date in Poland." Chicago, October 22–23, 1927.

THE NEAR EAST RELIEF COMMITTEE

The American Committee for Relief in the Near East, Its History, Its Work and the Need for Support.

Annual Reports and *Minutes* of the various subcommittees of the Near East Relief Committee, 1915 to 1924.

Annual Reports to Congress of the Near East Relief Committee, 1921 to 1923.

Barton, James L. *The Story of Near East Relief.* New York, The Macmillan Company, 1930.

Ellis, Harry B. *Heritage of the Desert.* New York, The Ronald Press, 1956.

Hoskins, Halford L. *The Middle East: Problem Area in World Politics.* New York, The Macmillan Company, 1954.

Monroe, Paul, R. R. Reeder, and James I. Vance. *Reconstruction in the Near East.* New York, 1924.

Near East Foundation Carries On. Supplement to Dr. Barton's story of Near East relief. Prepared, upon the expiration of the Congressional charter on August 6, 1944, by a committee of trustees of the Near East Relief, William E. Doughty, Chairman.

Ross, Dr. Frank A., Dr. C. Luther Fry, and Elbridge Sibley. *The Near East and American Philanthropy.* Results of a survey commissioned by the Near East Relief Committee in 1925.

Surface, Frank M., and Raymond L. Bland. *American Food in the World War and Reconstruction Period.* Stanford University Press, 1931.

Vickrey, Charles V. *Cleveland H. Dodge: An Appreciation.* American Red Cross, December 1, 1918.

THE SALVATION ARMY

Annual Reports of the International Salvation Army, London, 1915–1919.

Booth, Evangeline, and Grace Livingston Hill. *The War Romance of the Salvation Army.* Philadelphia, J. B. Lippincott Company, 1919.

The War Cry. Salvation Army weekly newspaper. Issues from 1914 to 1923.

Wisbey, Herbert A., Jr. *Soldiers without Swords.* New York, The Macmillan Company, 1955.

INDEX

INDEX